1,000,000 Books

are available to read at

www.ForgottenBooks.com

Read online
Download PDF
Purchase in print

ISBN 978-0-266-12531-0
PIBN 10920520

This book is a reproduction of an important historical work. Forgotten Books uses state-of-the-art technology to digitally reconstruct the work, preserving the original format whilst repairing imperfections present in the aged copy. In rare cases, an imperfection in the original, such as a blemish or missing page, may be replicated in our edition. We do, however, repair the vast majority of imperfections successfully; any imperfections that remain are intentionally left to preserve the state of such historical works.

Forgotten Books is a registered trademark of FB &c Ltd.
Copyright © 2018 FB &c Ltd.
FB &c Ltd, Dalton House, 60 Windsor Avenue, London, SW19 2RR.
Company number 08720141. Registered in England and Wales.

For support please visit www.forgottenbooks.com

1 MONTH OF FREE READING

at

www.ForgottenBooks.com

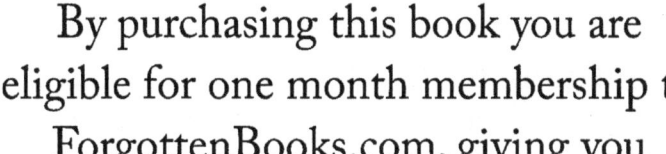

By purchasing this book you are eligible for one month membership to ForgottenBooks.com, giving you unlimited access to our entire collection of over 1,000,000 titles via our web site and mobile apps.

To claim your free month visit:
www.forgottenbooks.com/free920520

* Offer is valid for 45 days from date of purchase. Terms and conditions apply.

English
Français
Deutsche
Italiano
Español
Português

www.forgottenbooks.com

Mythology Photography **Fiction** Fishing Christianity **Art** Cooking Essays Buddhism Freemasonry Medicine **Biology** Music **Ancient Egypt** Evolution Carpentry Physics Dance Geology **Mathematics** Fitness Shakespeare **Folklore** Yoga Marketing **Confidence** Immortality Biographies Poetry **Psychology** Witchcraft Electronics Chemistry History **Law** Accounting **Philosophy** Anthropology Alchemy Drama Quantum Mechanics Atheism Sexual Health **Ancient History Entrepreneurship** Languages Sport Paleontology Needlework Islam **Metaphysics** Investment Archaeology Parenting Statistics Criminology **Motivational**

UNIVERSITY OF WISCONSIN

BULLETIN.

No. 35

General Series, No. 2.   APRIL 1900

CONTENTS.

COLLEGE OF LETTERS AND SCIENCE
COLLEGE OF AGRICULTURE
COLLEGE OF MECHANICS AND ENGINEERING
COLLEGE OF LAW.

    SCHOOL OF PHARMACY
    SCHOOL OF ECONOMICS, POLITICAL SCIENCE
        AND HISTORY
    SCHOOL OF MUSIC
    SCHOOL OF EDUCATION

        DEPARTMENT OF
        LIST OF TEACHERS

UNIVERSITY OF WISCONSIN
BULLETIN.

No. 35.

| General Series, No. 3. | APRIL, 1900. | Part IX. |

CONTENTS.

COLLEGE OF LETTERS AND SCIENCE.
COLLEGE OF AGRICULTURE.
COLLEGE OF MECHANICS AND ENGINEERING.
COLLEGE OF LAW.

    SCHOOL OF PHARMACY.
    SCHOOL OF ECONOMICS, POLITICAL SCIENCE, AND HISTORY.
    SCHOOL OF MUSIC.
    SCHOOL OF EDUCATION.

        DEPARTMENT OF GRADUATE STUDY.
        LIST OF TEACHERS AND STUDENTS.

Published bi-monthly by authority of law with the approval of the Regents
of the University and entered at the post office at
Madison as second-class matter.

MADISON, WISCONSIN.

SCHOOL OF COMMERCE.

AT a meeting held April 17, 1900, the Board of Regents established a School of Commerce in the College of Letters and Science of the University of Wisconsin. The purpose of this School is to supply facilities for the training of young men who desire to enter business careers, especially in such fields as domestic and foreign commerce and banking, or branches of the public service, like the consular, in which a knowledge of business is essential.

Students will be admitted to this School on the same conditions as those imposed for entrance to the Civic Historical, General Science, Modern Classical, or Engineering Courses of the College of Letters and Science.

Students who complete the prescribed course of study in this School will receive diplomas conferring upon them the degree of Bachelor of Commercial Science.

A circular has been prepared containing the course of study in detail and all other needed information regarding the School. This circular and any other desired information concerning this School will be furnished upon application to W. D. HIESTAND, Registrar, or to WILLIAM A. SCOTT, Director of the School.

CATALOGUE

OF THE

UNIVERSITY OF WISCONSIN

FOR

1899-1900.

MADISON, WIS.
PUBLISHED BY THE UNIVERSITY.
1900.

TABLE OF CONTENTS.

Calendar	5
Board of Visitors	6
Board of Regents	7
Officers of Instruction and Government	9- 19
Organization of the University	20- 49
Charges and Fees	38- 44
Department of Graduate Study	50- 56
College of Letters and Science	57-137
Admission	59- 72
Undergraduate Department	73- 80
Departments of Instruction	81-137
School of Economics, Political Science, and History	138-140
School of Education	141-143
University Extension Department	144-146
University Summer Session	148-168
College of Mechanics and Engineering	171-221
Courses of Study	186-194
Departments of Instruction	195-221
College of Agriculture	222-238
Instruction in Agriculture	233-235
Farmers' Institutes	235-238
College of Law	239-254
Admission	241-245
Courses of Study	246-249
School of Pharmacy	255-269
School of Music	270-277
Degrees Granted June, 1899	278-286
Students	287-357
Graduates	287-292
Undergraduates	292-346
College of Letters and Science	292-316
College of Mechanics and Engineering	316-324
College of Agriculture	324-334
College of Law	334-340
School of Pharmacy	340-341
School of Music	341-346
Summer Session	347-357
Summary of Students	358-360
Index	361-366

ALMANAC

1900 | 1901

JANUARY

S	M	T	W	T	F	S
..	1	2	3	4	5	6
7	8	9	10	11	12	13
14	15	16	17	18	19	20
21	22	23	24	25	26	27
28	29	30	31	..	..	..

JULY

S	M	T	W	T	F	S
1	2	3	4	5	6	7
8	9	10	11	12	13	14
15	16	17	18	19	20	21
22	23	24	25	26	27	28
29	30	31	..	..	..	..

JANUARY

S	M	T	W	T	F	S
..	..	1	2	3	4	5
6	7	8	9	10	11	12
13	14	15	16	17	18	19
20	21	22	23	24	25	26
27	28	29	30	31	..	..

FEBRUARY

S	M	T	W	T	F	S
..	..	..	..	1	2	3
4	5	6	7	8	9	10
11	12	13	14	15	16	17
18	19	20	21	22	23	24
25	26	27	28	..	..	..

AUGUST

S	M	T	W	T	F	S
..	..	..	1	2	3	4
5	6	7	8	9	10	11
12	13	14	15	16	17	18
19	20	21	22	23	24	25
26	27	28	29	30	31	..

FEBRUARY

S	M	T	W	T	F	S
..	..	..	..	..	1	2
3	4	5	6	7	8	9
10	11	12	13	14	15	16
17	18	19	20	21	22	23
24	25	26	27	28	..	..

MARCH

S	M	T	W	T	F	S
..	..	..	..	1	2	3
4	5	6	7	8	9	10
11	12	13	14	15	16	17
18	19	20	21	22	23	24
25	26	27	28	29	30	31

SEPTEMBER

S	M	T	W	T	F	S
..	..	..	..	..	..	1
2	3	4	5	6	7	8
9	10	11	12	13	14	15
16	17	18	19	20	21	22
23	24	25	26	27	28	29
30	..	..	..	..	..	..

MARCH

S	M	T	W	T	F	S
..	..	..	..	..	1	2
3	4	5	6	7	8	9
10	11	12	13	14	15	16
17	18	19	20	21	22	23
24	25	26	27	28	29	30
31	..	..	..	..	..	..

APRIL

S	M	T	W	T	F	S
1	2	3	4	5	6	7
8	9	10	11	12	13	14
15	16	17	18	19	20	21
22	23	24	25	26	27	28
29	30	..	..	..	..	..

OCTOBER

S	M	T	W	T	F	S
..	1	2	3	4	5	6
7	8	9	10	11	12	13
14	15	16	17	18	19	20
21	22	23	24	25	26	27
28	29	30	31	..	..	..

APRIL

S	M	T	W	T	F	S
..	1	2	3	4	5	6
7	8	9	10	11	12	13
14	15	16	17	18	19	20
21	22	23	24	25	26	27
28	29	30	..	..	..	..

MAY

S	M	T	W	T	F	S
..	..	1	2	3	4	5
6	7	8	9	10	11	12
13	14	15	16	17	18	19
20	21	22	23	24	25	26
27	28	29	30	31	..	..

NOVEMBER

S	M	T	W	T	F	S
..	..	..	..	1	2	3
4	5	6	7	8	9	10
11	12	13	14	15	16	17
18	19	20	21	22	23	24
25	26	27	28	29	30	..

MAY

S	M	T	W	T	F	S
..	..	..	1	2	3	4
5	6	7	8	9	10	11
12	13	14	15	16	17	18
19	20	21	22	23	24	25
26	27	28	29	30	31	..

JUNE

S	M	T	W	T	F	S
..	..	..	..	..	1	2
3	4	5	6	7	8	9
10	11	12	13	14	15	16
17	18	19	20	21	22	23
24	25	26	27	28	29	30

DECEMBER

S	M	T	W	T	F	S
..	..	..	..	..	..	1
2	3	4	5	6	7	8
9	10	11	12	13	14	15
16	17	18	19	20	21	22
23	24	25	26	27	28	29
30	31	..	..	..	..	..

JUNE

S	M	T	W	T	F	S
..	..	..	..	..	..	1
2	3	4	5	6	7	8
9	10	11	12	13	14	15
16	17	18	19	20	21	22
23	24	25	26	27	28	29
30	..	..	..	..	..	..

CALENDAR.

ACADEMIC YEAR, 1899-1900.

FIRST SEMESTER, September 27—February 10.
SECOND SEMESTER, February 12—June 21.
    Theses must be handed in, College of Letters and Science, College of Mechanics and Engineering, College of Law, School of Pharmacy, May 15.
    Legal Holiday, Wednesday, May 30.
    Examination of Candidates for Admission, Thursday and Friday, June 14, 15.
    Baccalaureate Address, Sunday, June 17.
    Class Day, Monday, June 18.
    Address to Law Class, Tuesday, June 19.
    Alumni Day, Wednesday, June 20.
COMMENCEMENT, Thursday, June 21, 9 A. M.
SUMMER VACATION, June 22—September 25.
SUMMER SESSION opens July 2, closes August 10, six weeks.

ACADEMIC YEAR, 1900-1901.

FIRST SEMESTER opens September 26, closes February 9.
    Examinations for Admission, Tuesday and Wednesday, September 25 and 26.
    Registration Days, September 24—26.
    First Recitations, Thursday morning, September 27.
    Legal Holiday, Thanksgiving, November 29.
    Christmas Recess, Saturday, December 22—Tuesday, January 1, inclusive.
    Examination Week, First Semester, February 4—8.
    First Semester closes, Saturday, February 9.
SECOND SEMESTER opens Monday, February 11, closes June 20.
    Registration Day, Second Semester, Monday, February 11.
    Examination Days for Second Semester, Thursday and Friday, February 7, 8.
    Legal Holiday, Friday, February 22.
    Easter Recess, Thursday, April 11—Monday, April 15, inclusive.
    Legal Holiday, Thursday, May 30.
    Examination Week, Second Semester, June 10—14.
    Commencement, Thursday, June 20.

OFFICIAL BOARD OF VISITORS, 1899-1900.

STATE-AT-LARGE—
: JOHN H. FRANK, Milwaukee.

STATE-AT-LARGE—
: MRS. S. L. GRAVES, Milwaukee.

STATE-AT-LARGE—
: JOHN G. McMYNN, Madison.

STATE-AT-LARGE—
: REV. AMOS A. KIEHLER, Milwaukee.

FIRST DISTRICT—
: JOHN H. HARRIS, Elkhorn.

SECOND DISTRICT—
: JOHN B. WINSLOW, *(Chairman)*, Madison.

THIRD DISTRICT—
: MISS ELLEN C. LLOYD-JONES, Hillside.

FOURTH DISTRICT—
: MRS. FANNIE WEST-WILLIAMS, Milwaukee.

FIFTH DISTRICT—
: JOHN R. DENNETT, Port Washington.

SIXTH DISTRICT—
: MRS. CARRIE E. EDWARDS, Oshkosh.

SEVENTH DISTRICT—
: CALEB M. HILLIARD, Durand.

EIGHTH DISTRICT—
: JAMES E. ELMORE, Green Bay.

NINTH DISTRICT—
: FRANK E. NOYES, Marinette.

TENTH DISTRICT—
: MRS. CARRIE B. OAKES, New Richmond.

BOARD OF REGENTS.

PRESIDENT OF THE UNIVERSITY, *ex-officio.*

STATE SUPERINTENDENT OF PUBLIC INSTRUCTION,
ex-officio.

		TERM EXPIRES.
STATE-AT-LARGE,	WILLIAM F. VILAS, Madison,	1901.
STATE-AT-LARGE,	GEORGE W. PECK, Milwaukee,	1903.
FIRST DISTRICT,	OGDEN H. FETHERS, Janesville,	1901.
SECOND DISTRICT,	B. J. STEVENS, Madison,	1902.
THIRD DISTRICT,	JOHN E. MORGAN, Spring Green,	1901.
FOURTH DISTRICT,	GEORGE H. NOYES, Milwaukee,	1902.
FIFTH DISTRICT,	JOHN R. RIESS, Sheboygan,	1902.
SIXTH DISTRICT,	C. A. GALLOWAY, Fond du Lac,	1901.
SEVENTH DISTRICT,	BYRON A. BUFFINGTON, Eau Claire,	1902.
EIGHTH DISTRICT,	ORLANDO E. CLARK, Appleton,	1901.
NINTH DISTRICT,	GEORGE F. MERRILL, Ashland,	1903.
TENTH DISTRICT,	J. H. STOUT, Menominee,	1903.

OFFICERS OF THE BOARD OF REGENTS.

GEORGE H. NOYES, *President.*

J. H. STOUT, *Vice-President.*

THE STATE TREASURER, *ex-officio Treasurer.*

E. F. RILEY, *Secretary.*

STANDING COMMITTEES OF THE BOARD OF REGENTS—

1899-1900.

[The President of the University is *ex-officio* a member of each Standing Committee.]

EXECUTIVE—

    B. J. STEVENS, WILLIAM F. VILAS, GEORGE W. PECK.

COLLEGE OF LETTERS AND SCIENCE—

    WILLIAM F. VILAS, L. D. HARVEY, GEORGE F. MERRILL, BYRON A. BUFFINGTON, C. A. GALLOWAY.

COLLEGE OF AGRICULTURE AND COLLEGE OF MECHANICS AND ENGINEERING—

    ORLANDO E. CLARK, J. H. STOUT, OGDEN H. FETHERS, JOHN R. RIESS, JOHN E. MORGAN.

COLLEGE OF LAW—

    OGDEN H. FETHERS, B. J. STEVENS, JOHN R. RIESS.

Officers of Instruction and Government.

FACULTY.

ADAMS, CHARLES KENDALL, LL. D., *President of the University.* Office, University Hall Room 10.   772 Langdon St.

PARKINSON, JOHN BARBER, A. M., *Vice-President, Professor of Constitutional and International Law.* Room 55, University Hall.   803 State St.

(Arranged in Alphabetical Order.)

AUSTIN, LOUIS WINSLOW, Ph. D., *Assistant Professor of Physics.* Room 17, Science Hall.   22 Mendota Court.

BABCOCK, STEPHEN MOULTON, Ph. D., *Professor of Agricultural Chemistry and Chief Chemist to the Experiment Station.* Room 12, Agricultural Hall.   432 Lake St.

BASHFORD, ROBERT McKEE, A. M., LL. B., *Professor of the Law of Private Corporations and Commercial Law.* Law Building.   423 N. Pinckney St.

BIRGE, EDWARD ASAHEL, Ph. D., Sc. D., *Dean of the College of Letters and Science.* Room 10, University Hall. *Professor of Zoology.* Room 44, Science Hall.   744 Langdon St.

BRUCE, ANDREW ALEXANDER, A. B., LL. B., *Assistant Professor of Law.* Law Building.   431 Lake St.

BRYANT, EDWIN EUSTACE, *Dean of the College of Law, Professor of Practice and Pleading, Equity and Railway Law, and the Law of Public Offices and Officers.* Law Building.   11 E. Gilman St.

BULL, STORM, M. E., *Professor of Steam Engineering.* Room 23, Science Hall.   141 W. Gorham St.

CARLYLE, WILLIAM LEVI, B. S. A., *Professor of Animal Husbandry.* Room 7, Agricultural Hall.   University Farm House.

CARPENTER, JAIRUS HARVLIN, LL. D., *Mortimer M. Jackson Professor of Contracts. Emeritus.* Law Building.   315 Wisconsin Ave.

CHENEY, LELLEN STERLING, M. S., *Assistant Professor of Pharmaceutical Botany.* Room 41, North Hall.   318 Bruen St.

CLEMENTS, JULIUS MORGAN, Ph. D., *Assistant Professor of Geology.* Room 26, Science Hall. 609 Lake St.

COFFIN, VICTOR, Ph. D., *Assistant Professor of European History.* Room 50, University Hall. 10 W. Gilman St.

COMSTOCK, GEORGE CARY, Ph. B., LL. B., *Professor of Astronomy and Director of Washburn Observatory.* Observatory Hill.

CURTIS, CHARLES ALBERT, A. B., Captain U. S. Army. *Professor of Military Science and Tactics.* Office, Room 1, Armory. 534 State St.

DANIELLS, WILLIAM WILLARD, M. S., Sc. D., *Professor of Chemistry.* Rooms 16 to 20, Chemical Laboratory. 515 N. Carroll St.

*DAVIES, JOHN EUGENE, A. M., M. D., LL. D., *Professor of Electricity and Magnetism and Mathematical Physics.* Room 16, Science Hall. 523 N. Carroll St.

DOWLING, LINNAEUS WAYLAND, Ph. D., *Assistant Professor of Mathematics.* Room 34, University Hall. University Heights.

ELSOM, JAMES CLAUDE, M. D., *Professor of Physical Culure and Director of the Gymnasium.* Room 2, Gymnasium. 515 Lake St.

ELY, RICHARD THEODORE, Ph. D., LL. D., *Director of the School of Economics, Political Science, and History, and Professor of Political Economy.* Law Building. University Heights.

EMERY, ANNIE CROSBY, Ph. D., *Dean of Women and Assistant Professor of Classical Philology.* Room 8, University Hall. 615 Lake St.

FARRINGTON, EDWARD HOLYOKE, M. S., *Associate Professor of Dairy Husbandry.* Office, Dairy Building. 315 Mills St.

FLINT, ALBERT STOWELL, A. M., *Assistant Astronomer.* Washburn Observatory. 420 Charter St.

FRANKENBURGER, DAVID BOWER, A. M., LL. B., *Professor of Rhetoric and Oratory.* Room 31, University Hall. 115 W. Gilman St.

**FREEMAN, JOHN CHARLES, LL. D., *Professor of English Literature.* 222 Langdon St.

---

*Died, January 22, 1900.
**On leave of absence in Europe for college year 1899-1900.

GIESE, WILLIAM FREDERIC, A. M., *Assistant Professor of Romance Languages.* Room 56, University Hall. 426 Bruen St.
GOFF, EMMETT STULL, *Professor of Horticulture.* Horticulture-Physics Building. 1113 University Ave.
GREGORY, CHARLES NOBLE, A. M., LL. B., *Professor of Law and Associate Dean of the College of Law.* Law Building. 145 W. Gilman St.
HARPER, ROBERT ALMER, PH. D., *Professor of Botany.* Room 39, Science Hall. 256 Langdon St.
HARRISON, CALEB NOTBOHM, B. C. E., PH. D., *Acting Professor of Machine Design.* Room 25, Science Hall. 422 N. Henry St.
HASKINS, CHARLES HOMER, PH. D., *Professor of Institutional History.* Room 51, University Hall. 629 Francis St.
HENRY, WILLIAM ARNOLD, AGR. B., *Dean of the College of Agriculture. Professor of Agriculture.* Room 5, Agricultural Hall. University Farm.
HILLYER, HOMER WINTHROP, PH. D., *Assistant Professor of Organic Chemistry.* Room 22, Chemical Laboratory. University Heights.
HOBBS, WILLIAM HERBERT, PH. D., *Professor of Mineralogy and Petrology.* Room 38, Science Hall. 223 N. Carroll St.
HUBBARD, FRANK GAYLORD, PH. D., *Professor of the English Language.* Room 66, University Hall. 227 Langdon St.
JACKSON, DUGALD CALEB, C. E., *Professor of Electrical Engineering.* Room 13, Science Hall. 616 Lake St.
JASTROW, JOSEPH, PH. D., *Professor of Experimental and Comparative Psychology.* Room 34, Science Hall. 227 Langdon St.
JOHNSON, JOHN BUTLER, C. E., *Dean of the College of Mechanics and Engineering. Professor of Engineering.* Room 21, Science Hall. 423 N. Carroll St.
JONES, BURR W., A. M., LL. B., *Professor of the Law of Evidence, Public Corporations, and Domestic Relations.* Law Building. 112 Langdon St.
KAHLENBERG, LOUIS, PH. D., *Assistant Professor of Physical Chemistry.* Chemical Laboratory. 306 Lake St.

KERR, ALEXANDER, A. M., *Professor of the Greek Language and Literature.* Room 40, University Hall. 140 Langdon St.

KING, CHARLES ISAAC, *Professor of Mechanical Practice.* Office, Machine Shop. 628 State St.

KING, FRANKLIN HIRAM, *Professor of Agricultural Physics.* Third floor, Horticulture-Physics Building. 1540 University Ave.

KNOWLTON, AMOS ARNOLD, A. M., *Assistant Professor of English.* Room 60, University Hall. 1717 Adams St.

KREMERS, EDWARD, Ph. G., Ph. D., *Professor of Pharmaceutical Chemistry and Director of the School of Pharmacy.* Room 11, North Hall. Wingra Park.

LAIRD, ARTHUR GORDON, Ph. D., *Assistant Professor of Ancient Languages.* Room 7, University Hall. 609 Lake St.

MACK, JOHN GIVAN DAVIS, B. S., M. E., *Assistant Professor of Machine Design.* Room 25, Science Hall. Wingra Park.

MARSHALL, WILLIAM STANLEY, Ph. D., *Assistant Professor of Zoology.* Room 50, Science Hall. 324 N. Carroll St.

MAURER, EDWARD ROSE, B. C. E., *Assistant Professor of Pure and Applied Mechanics.* Room 25, Science Hall. 215 Prospect Ave.

MAYHEW, ABBY SHAW, *Mistress of Ladies' Hall and Instructor in Physical Culture.* Office, Ladies' Hall.

McKERROW, GEORGE, *Superintendent of Agricultural Institutes.* Room 2, Agricultural Hall. 107 S. Butler St.

MEYER, BALTHASAR HENRY, Ph. D., *Assistant Professor of Sociology, Secretary of the Committee on Accredited Schools and of the Extension Department.* Room 30 A., University Hall. 311 Brooks St.

MILLER, WILLIAM SNOW, M. D., *Assistant Professor of Vertebrate Anatomy.* Room 43, Science Hall. 615 Lake St.

OLIN, JOHN MYERS, A. M., LL. B., *Professor of the Law of Real Property, Torts and Wills.* Law Building. 762 Langdon St.

OLSON, JULIUS EMIL, B. L., *Professor of the Scandinavian Languages and Literature.* Room A, University Hall. 1012 E. Gorham St.

OFFICERS OF INSTRUCTION AND GOVERNMENT. 13

O'SHEA, M. VINCENT, B. L., *Professor of the Science and Art of Education.* Room 30, University Hall. 140 Langdon St.

OWEN, EDWARD THOMAS, A. B., *Professor of the French Language and Literature.* Room 58, University Hall. 614 State St.

PARKER, FLETCHER ANDREW, *Professor of Music and Director of the School of Music.* 14 W. Gilman St.

PYRE, JAMES FRANCIS AUGUSTINE, PH. D., *Assistant Professor of English Literature.* Room 72, University Hall. 138 W. Gorham St.

REINSCH, PAUL SAMUEL, PH. D., LL. B., *Assistant Professor of Political Science.* Room 55, University Hall. 212 W. Gilman St.

RICHTER, ARTHUR WILLIAM, M. E., *Assistant Professor of Experimental Engineering.* Room 23, Science Hall. 426 Murray St.

ROSENSTENGEL, WILLIAM HENRY, A. M., *Professor of the German Language and Literature.* Room 1, North Hall. 640 Francis St.

RUSSELL, HARRY LUMAN, PH. D., *Professor of Bacteriology.* Room 14, Agricultural Hall. 1532 University Ave.

SCOTT, WILLIAM AMASA, PH. D., *Professor of Economic History and Theory.* Third floor, Law Building. 619 Langdon St.

SHARP, FRANK CHAPMAN, PH. D., *Assistant Professor of Philosophy.* Room 38, University Hall.
27 Mendota Court.

*SKINNER, ERNEST BROWN, A. B., *Assistant Professor of Mathematics.* 414 Charter St.

SLAUGHTER, MOSES STEPHEN, PH. D., *Professor of Latin.* Room 44, University Hall. 633 Francis St.

SLICHTER, CHARLES SUMNER, M. S., *Professor of Applied Mathematics.* Room 33, University Hall. 636 Francis St.

SMITH, CHARLES FORSTER, PH. D., *Professor of Greek and Classical Philology.* Room 6, University Hall. University Heights.

SMITH, LEONARD SEWELL, C. E., *Assistant Professor of Topographic and Geodetic Engineering.* Room 18, Science Hall. 939 University Ave.

---
*On leave of absence for college year 1899-1900.

SNOW, BENJAMIN WARNER, PH. D., *Professor of Physics.* Room 17, Science Hall. 518 Wisconsin Ave.

*SOBER, HIRAM ALLEN, A. B., *Assistant Professor of Latin.* 772 Langdon St.

STEARNS, JOHN WILLIAM, LL. D., *Director of School of Education. Professor of Philosophy and Pedagogy.* Room 30, University Hall. 512 Wisconsin Ave.

SWENSON, BERNARD VICTOR, B. S., *Assistant Professor of Electrical Engineering.* Room 13, Science Hall. 404 W. Mifflin St.

TURNEAURE, FREDERICK EUGENE, C. E., *Professor of Bridge and Sanitary Engineering.* Room 18, Science Hall. 929 University Ave.

TURNER, FREDERICK JACKSON, PH. D., *Professor of American History.* Room 50, University Hall. 629 Francis St.

VAN HISE, CHARLES RICHARD, PH. D., *Professor of Geology.* Room 32, Science Hall. 630 Francis St.

VAN VELZER, CHARLES AMBROSE, PH. D., *Professor of Mathematics.* Room 34, University Hall. 134 W. Gorham St.

VOSS, ERNST KARL JOHANN HEINRICH, PH. D., *Associate Professor of German Language and Literature.* Room 3, North Hall. 23 E. Johnson St.

WHITNEY, NELSON OLIVER, C. E., *Professor of Railway Engineering.* Room 18, Science Hall. 18 E. Gorham St.

WHITSON, ANDREW ROBINSON, B. S., *Assistant Professor of Agricultural Physics.* Office, Third Floor Horticulture-Physics Building.

WILLIAMS, WILLIAM HOLME, A. B., *Professor of Hebrew and Hellenistic Greek.* Room 5, North Hall. 407 Wisconsin Ave.

WOLL, FRITZ WILHELM, M. S., *Assistant Professor of Agricultural Chemistry.* Room 9, Agricultural Hall. 424 Charter St.

WOOD, ROBERT WILLIAMS, A. B., *Assistant Professor of Physics.* Room 17, Science Hall. 237 Langdon St.

INSTRUCTORS AND ASSISTANTS.

ALEXANDER, WALTER, M. E., *Instructor in Steam Engineering.* Room 23, Science Hall. 432 W. Gilman St.

*On leave of absence in Europe for college year 1899-1900.

ALLEN, KATHARINE, PH. D., *Assistant in Latin.*
Room 44, University Hall. 228 Langdon St.
ATHERTON, LEWIS OLIVER, M. S., *Assistant in
Vertebrate Anatomy.* Room 42, Science Hall. 813 State St.
BAER, ULYSSES S., *Instructor in Cheese Making.*
Dairy Building. Agricultural Hall.
BEATTY, ARTHUR, PH. D., *Instructor in English.*
Room 66, University Hall. 512 Lake St.
*BEEBE, MURRAY CHARLES, B. S., *Instructor in
Electrical Engineering.* Room 13, Science Hall. 609 Lake St.
BOYCE, SAMUEL ROBERT, PH. C., M. D.,*Instructor
in Pharmacognosy.* Room 14, North Hall. 302 State St.
BRAUER, HERMAN GUSTAV ADOLPH, M. A., *Instructor in French.* Room 70, University Hall. 424 Bruen St.
BURGESS, CHARLES FREDERICK, B. S., *Instructor in Electrical Engineering.* Room 13, Science
Hall. 609 Lake St.
BUTT, JENNIE HANNAH, *Student Assistant in
Elocution.* Room 25, University Hall. 222 Langdon St.
CAIRNS, WILLIAM B., PH. D., *Instructor in English.* Room 72, University Hall. 606 Madison St.
CASTLE, MILDRED ALICE, *Student Assistant in
French.* Room 50, University Hall. 606 Francis St.
COOK, ALFRED NEWTON, M. A., *Assistant in
Chemistry.* Chemical Laboratory. 917 W. Dayton St.
DAVIES, JOSEPH EDWARD, B. L., *Student Assistant in Gymnastics.* Gymnasium. 212 W. Gilman St.
DODGE, ROBERT ELKIN NEIL, M. A., *Instructor
in English.* Room 66, University Hall. 609 Lake St.
EATON, ABBIE FISKE, M. L., *Instructor in German.*
Room 9, North Hall. University Heights.
FERRIS, WILLIAM STEWART, B. S., *Assistant in
Pharmacognosy.* Room 12, North Hall. 793 State St.
FOWLER, ROY EDWARD, B. S., *Assistant in Chemistry.* Chemical Laboratory. 217 Murray St.
**FRANKENFIELD, BUDD, E. E., *Instructor in
Electrical Engineering.* Room 13, Science Hall. 609 Lake St.
FROST, WILLIAM DODGE, M. S., *Instructor in Bacteriology.* Room 18, Agricultural Hall. 311 Charter St.

---

*Resigned at end of first semester.
**Appointed February 12, 1900, to fill vacancy caused by the resignation of Mr. M. C. Beebe.

GAY, LUCY MARIE, B. L., *Instructor in French.*
Room 62, University Hall.   216 N. Pinckney St.
HARGRAVE, RUSSELL WILLIAM, B. S., *Instructor in Mechanical Practice.* Machine Shops.   212 N. Mills St.
HARRIS, SALLY PRIME, *Assistant in Physical Culture.* Ladies' Hall.   Ladies' Hall.
HASTINGS, EDWIN GEORGE, M. S., *Assistant Bacteriologist in College of Agriculture.* Room 16, Agricultural Hall.   707 State St.
HATHERELL, ROSALIA AMELIA, B. S., *Assistant in Biology.* Room 44, Science Hall.   1540 University Ave.
HERFURTH, SABENA MILDRED, M. L., *Assistant in German.* Room 6, North Hall.   703 E. Gorham St.
HOPKINS, ARTHUR GEORGE, B. AGR., D. V. M., V. S., *Assistant in Animal Husbandry, and Instructor in Veterinary Science.* Room 7, Agricultural Hall.   University Farm.
HUNT, MAY, M. L., *Instructor in English.* Room 2, University Hall.   212 W. Gorham St.
ISHIKAWA, GENSAMRO S., M. L., *Student Assistant in Gymnastics.* Gymnasium.   514 Lake St.
*JONES, EDWARD DAVID, PH. D., *Instructor in Economics and Statistics.* Seminary Room, Law Building.   209 W. Gilman St.
KELLOGG, LOUISE PHELPS, M. L., *Assistant in Ancient and Medieval History.* Room 51, University Hall.   228 Langdon St.
KELLY, FREDERICK THOMAS, B. S., *Instructor in Hebrew and Hellenistic Greek.* Room 5, North Hall.   311 Charter St.
LIBBY, ORIN GRANT, PH. D., *Instructor in History.* Room 7, University Hall.   426 Bruen St.
LOTTES, WILLIAM GEORGE, *Instructor in Forge Practice and Repairing.* Machine Shops.   315 Park St.
MEISNEST, FREDERICK WILLIAM, B. S., *Instructor in German.* Room 2, North Hall.   314 Murray St.
O'DEA, ANDREW M., *Instructor in Athletics and Assistant to the Director of the Gymnasium.* Gymnasium.   717 Langdon St.
PETERSON, FREDERICK BURNS, B. L., *Student Assistant in Gymnastics.* Gymnasium.   428 Lake St.

---
*On leave of absence for college year 1899-1900.

OFFICERS OF INSTRUCTION AND GOVERNMENT.

PYRE, WALTON HAWKINS, B. L., *Instructor in Elocution and Oratory.* Room 25, University Hall.
138 W. Gorham St.

REMINGTON, HARRIET TRAYNE, M. L., *Instructor in German.* Room 6, North Hall. 770 Langdon St.

RICHTMANN, WILLIAM OSCAR, Ph. G., B. S., *Instructor in Practical Pharmacy.* Room 4, North Hall. 1124 W. Johnson St.

RUNNING, THEODORE RUDOLPH, Ph. D., *Instructor in Applied Mathematics.* Room 27, University Hall. 407 E. Johnson St.

SCHREINER, OSWALD, Ph. G., M. S., *Assistant in Pharmaceutical Technique.* Room 12, North Hall.
1001 University Ave.

SHANNON, CHARLES HENRY, Ph. D., *Instructor in Latin.* Room 46, University Hall. 314 Mills St.

SHEDD, JOHN CUTLER, Ph. D., *Instructor in Physics.* Room 17, Science Hall. 823 W. Dayton St.

SHELDON, WILMON HENRY, Ph. D., *Assistant in Philosophy.* Room 26, University Hall. 919 University Ave.

SMITH, CHARLES MARQUIS, B. S., *Instructor in Physics.* Room 17, Science Hall. 412 Murray St.

SPARLING, SAMUEL EDWIN, Ph. D., *Assistant in Political Science.* Room 53, University Hall. 502 N. Henry St.

STANGEL, CHARLES GEORGE, B. S., *Assistant in Physics.* Room 4, Science Hall. 701 W. Dayton St.

STERLING, SUSAN ADELAIDE, M. L., *Instructor in German.* Room 8, North Hall. 811 State St.

TALLMAN, WILLIAM DUANE, B. S., *Instructor in Mathematics.* Room 1, University Hall. 916 W. Dayton St.

THURBER, EDWARD ALLEN, M. A., *Instructor in English.* Room 66, University Hall. 221 Langdon St.

TIMBERLAKE, HAMILTON GREENWOOD, M. S., *Instructor in Botany.* Room 49, Science Hall. 313 Mills St.

TINGLE, ALFRED, Ph. D., *Assistant in Chemistry.* Chemical Laboratory. 301 Lake St.

URDAHL, THOMAS KLINGENBERG, Ph. D., *Assistant in Economics and Statistics.* Room A, Law Building. 1037 Spaight St.

VIVIAN, ALFRED, Ph. G., *Assistant Chemist to Experiment Station.* Room 11, Agricultural Hall. 408 Charter St.

STAFF OF THE SCHOOL OF MUSIC.

PARKER, FLETCHER ANDREW, *Director, Organ, Theory and History.* Room 8, School of Music. 14 W. Gilman St.
SMITH, JAMES SARGENT, *Piano.* Room 10, School of Music. 125 E. Gilman St.
BIRD, ADA, *Piano.* Room 7, School of Music. 120 S. Fairchild St.
CARD, WINIFRED CORNELIA, *Piano.* Room 6, School of Music. 11 W. Gilman St.
FORESMAN, ADELAIDE, *Voice.* Room 10, School of Music. 120 W. Doty St.
ROBERTS, CHARLES EDWARD, *Voice.* Room 10, School of Music. 122 W. Washington Ave.
NITSCHKE, CHARLES, *Violin and other Orchestral Instruments.* Room 8, School of Music. 404 W. Washington Ave.
KEELEY, ELIZABETH MARY, *Harp.* Room 8, School of Music. 15 W. Doty St.
ANDERSON, HJALMAR O., *Mandolin.* Room 8, School of Music. 316 N. Carroll St.
BRAND, MRS. M. E., *Guitar.* Room 8, School of Music. Assembly P. O.
FOWLER, MYRON M., *Banjo.* Room 8, School of Music. 217 Murray St.
FOWLER, WILLIAM M., *Secretary.* Room 8, School of Music. 217 Murray St.

LIBRARY STAFF.

SMITH, WALTER McMYNN, A. B., *Librarian.* 218 Park St.
DUDLEY, WILLIAM HENRY, A. B., *Assistant Librarian.* 901 W. Johnson St.
CODDINGTON, HESTER, *Head Cataloguer.* 429 Park St.
MINER, SARAH HELEN, *Cataloguer.* 348 W. Washington Ave.
STUNTZ, STEPHEN CONRAD, B. S., *Library Assistant.* 314 Murray St.
PETERSON, CHARLES NELSON, *Student Assistant in Law Library.* 712 Langdon St.
MAXEY, JOHN, *Student Assistant in Law Library.* 709 University Ave.

OTHER OFFICERS.

RILEY, EDWARD F., *Secretary of the Board of Regents.* Law Building. 239 W. Gilman St.
HIESTAND, WILLIAM DIXON, *University Registrar and President's Secretary.* Room 10, University Hall. 16 W. Gorham St.
ADAMS, LESLIE H., *Farm Superintendent.* Farm House.
JENNINGS, JOHN THOMPSON WILSON, B. S., C. E., *Superintending Architect of Buildings and Grounds.* Law Building. 915 W. Johnson St.
MOORE, RANSOM ASA, *Assistant to the Dean of the College of Agriculture.* Room 6, Agricultural Hall. 207 Park St.

ORGANIZATION.

The University embraces:

  The Department of Graduate Study.
  The Undergraduate Departments.

Both Graduate and Undergraduate courses are included in the following colleges and schools of the University.

 I. The College of Letters and Science.
   The School of Economics, Political Science, and History.
   The School of Education.
   The Washburn Observatory.
   The Summer Session.
 II. The College of Mechanics and Engineering.
 III. The College of Agriculture.
 IV. The College of Law.
 V. The School of Pharmacy.
 VI. The School of Music.

The College of Letters and Science embraces:

   A. Graduate Courses.
   B. Undergraduate Courses.
 I. The Ancient Classical Course.
 II. The Modern Classical Course.
 III. The General Science Course.
 IV. The English Course.
 V. The Civic Historical Course. (School of Economics, Political Science, and History.)
 VI. The Special Science Course, antecedent to Medicine.
 VII. The Philosophical Course for Normal School Graduates.

The College of Mechanics and Engineering embraces:

   A. Graduate Courses in Engineering.
   B. Undergraduate Courses.
 1. The General Engineering Course.
 II. The Civil Engineering Course, including Railway, Bridge, Structural, Municipal and Highway Engineering.
 III. The Sanitary Engineering Course.
 IV. The Mechanical Engineering Course.
 V. The Electrical Engineering Course.
 VI. The Course in Applied Electro-Chemistry.

The College of Agriculture embraces:
   I. The Experiment Station.
   II. The Graduate Courses.
   III. The Long Agricultural Course.
   IV. The Short Agricultural Course.
   V. The Dairy Course.
   VI. The Farmers' Institutes.

The College of Law embraces:
   I. The Three Years' Course.

The School of Pharmacy embraces:
   I. The Graduate Courses.
   II. The Pharmacy Course.
   III. The Four Years' Pharmacy Course.

The School of Economics, Political Science, and History, embraces:
   I. The Graduate Courses.
   II. The Civic Historical Course.

The School of Education embraces:
   I. The Graduate Courses.
   II. The Course for Normal Graduates.
   III. Special Undergraduate Courses in Philosophy and Pedagogy.
   IV. The Department of University Extension.
   V. The Summer School.

The School of Music embraces:
   I. The Graduate Courses.
   II. The Collegiate Course.
   III. The Academic Course.

THE UNIVERSITY AND THE STATE.

The University of Wisconsin is a part of the free school system of the State. It was established by the constitution when the State was organized in 1848. The organic law establishing the University declares that its object shall be: "to provide the means of acquiring a thorough knowledge of the various branches of learning connected with scientific, industrial, and professional pursuits." In the educational policy of the State, the University sustains the same relation to the high schools that the high schools sustain to the primary and grammar schools. As those who have successfully completed the grammar grades may freely avail themselves of the advantages of the high schools, so those who have completed with credit any high school courses may advance to the opportunities offered by the University. If the courses of study in the high schools are denominated the 9th, 10th, 11th, and 12th grades, the four years' University course may with similar propriety be regarded as the 13th, 14th, 15th, and 16th grades. It is not expected that every pupil who completes the grammar grades will advance to the high school, and it is not practicable for every one who completes the high school to go forward to the University. Still, the school system of the State has been so arranged as to make the passage from one grade to another as easy and natural as possible, in order to afford every encouragement to the most complete and thorough education attainable. The State through the University undertakes to furnish thorough instruction in the various branches of a liberal education, as well as in the technical branches of agriculture, engineering, pharmacy, law, pedagogy, and music.

It is the general policy of the institution to foster the higher educational interests of the State, broadly and generously interpreted. It is its aim to make ample provision for the demands of advanced scholarship in as many lines as its means will permit. By prescribing a large portion of the studies of the regular courses in the earlier years, and by leaving a large number in the later portion to the selection of the student, it endeavors to give a wise measure of direction and at the same time leave sufficient room for choice to encourage individual adaptation and special development.

The University avoids all that is sectarian or partisan; but it endeavors to extend its sympathy and influence to whatever contributes to good citizenship and high character.

THE SUPPORT OF THE UNIVERSITY.

The University is supported partly by the income of federal grants, partly by taxation of the people of the State, and partly by private gifts. For such support there have been five federal grants, namely: The Two-Township Grant of 1848; The Supplementary Two-Township Grant of 1854; The Morrill Grant of 1862, for the support of studies pertaining to agricultural and mechanic arts; The Hatch Grant of 1887, for the support of agricultural experiment stations, and The Supplementary Morrill Grant of 1890.

Besides numerous appropriations for buildings and other specific purposes the State has made seven grants of a permanent nature, namely: the one-tenth mill tax of 1876, increased to one-eighth mill in 1883; the one-tenth mill tax of 1891; the appropriation for the support of the Observatory in 1887; the appropriation for the support of Farmers' Institutes of 1885, increased in 1887; the appropriation for the College of Engineering in 1889 of one per cent. of the railroad license tax; and the one-fifth mill grant of 1897. The legislature of 1899 consolidated the various mill taxes, specified above, and the grant of one per cent. of the railroad licenses, into a specific annual grant of $268,000. This sum is equal to the annual revenue from these various grants.

Of the private gifts that have come to the University that of Dane County for the purchase of lands for the University farm, that of the late Governor C. C. Washburn for the founding of the Washburn Observatory, and that of the late Judge Mortimer M. Jackson for the establishment of the Mortimer M. Jackson Professorship of Law, have been the most considerable and important.

HISTORY AND LOCATION.

In 1838 an act was passed by the territorial legislature establishing the University of the Territory of Wisconsin, and appointing a Board of Visitors for its government. No action toward establishing the University was taken under this law except the selection of two townships of land appropriated by Congress. In 1848 the constitution of the State of Wisconsin made provision for the establishment of a State University.

In 1849 the Board of Regents held its first meeting and began the work of organizing the University. The first building (now North Hall) was constructed in 1850. Four years from that time South Hall (Agricultural Hall) was completed, and in 1859 University Hall was occupied. Its interior arrangements have several times been changed; in 1895 the building was provided with additional stairways and halls, and in 1898-9 a wing was added to the south, nearly doubling the size of the building. In 1866 the University was reorganized by act of the legislature, which also provided for uniting with the University the College of Agriculture, endowed with the proceeds of the Agricultural College grant given by the United States in 1862. In 1867 the first appropriation, of about $7,000 a year, was made by the State. Since that date the State has made repeated and large appropriations of money for the construction of buildings and for providing apparatus, and also for meeting the ordinary expenses of the institution. The College of Law was established in 1868; the College of Engineering began its work in 1870; the School of Pharmacy in 1883, and the

School of Economics, Political Science, and History in 1892. The Summer School was organized in 1887, the School of Music in 1895, the School of Education in 1897, and the Summer Session of the University in 1899.

The University of Wisconsin is picturesquely situated at Madison, the capital of the State of Wisconsin. The University grounds comprise 300 acres, and extend for more than a mile along the south shore of Lake Mendota, a sheet of water about four miles in width and six miles in length. University hill occupies the eastern part of the grounds. It rises abruptly from the lake and has two summits, of which the eastern and higher reaches a height of about one hundred feet above the lake. Most of the college buildings are placed on the summit and eastern slope of this hill. The western part of the grounds is lower and more nearly level, and is occupied by the Experimental Farm, belonging to the College of Agriculture. East of the University hill lies a small tract known as the Lower Campus, used for athletic sports and as the drill ground. At the session of 1893 the legislature provided for the purchase of Camp Randall for an athletic field. This is a tract of ground including 42 acres, and joining the University grounds to the southwest. In 1898 160 acres were purchased for a special experimental farm for the College of Agriculture.

The buildings of the University which are used for instructional purposes are thirteen in number. The three oldest—University Hall, North Hall, and Agricultural Hall, stand on or near the eastern summit of University hill. Agricultural Hall is occupied by the offices, lecture rooms, and laboratories of the College of Agriculture; North Hall is used by the departments of German and Hebrew languages, and the School of Pharmacy; while University Hall contains the lecture rooms for most of the remaining departments of language and literature, and the offices of the President of the University, the Registrar and the Dean of the College of Letters and Science. These buildings were originally erected out of the money derived from sales of land granted by the national government. University Hall has been greatly enlarged during 1898-99 by the addition of a large wing on the south side. Across the east front of the campus, at the foot of University hill, is a row of buildings, all of them erected at the expense of the State of Wisconsin. At the south is Ladies' Hall, built in 1870, remodeled and enlarged in 1896, and used as a dormitory for young women; next stands the Library and Library Hall, completed in 1879. Still further north is Science Hall, the largest and most costly of the University buildings, completed in 1887, containing the lecture rooms, laboratories, and museums of most of the scientific departments of the University, and, at present, those of the College of Engineering. Next to Lake Mendota is the Chemical Laboratory, built in 1885, and behind this is the Machine Shop, erected in the same year and greatly enlarged in 1894. Near this building is the Central Heating Plant, built in 1885 and enlarged in 1894. Half way up the slope of University hill, on the south side, is the building for the Law School, which, in addition to the library and lecture rooms of the College of Law, contains the offices of the Board of Regents, and the rooms of the School of Economics, Political Science and History. Opposite the Law Building on the north side of the campus stands the new building of the College of Engineering for which the legislature of 1899 appropriated $100,000, and which will be occupied in the autumn of 1900. On the western summit of University hill is the Washburn Observatory, built in 1878 by the late Hon. C. C. Washburn, and presented to the University. Near it are the Students' Observatory and the astronomer's house. On the western slope of the hill is the building for the Dairy School, constructed in 1891, and near it are placed the buildings for the departments of horticulture and agricultural physics. Provision for an enlargement of the Dairy School and a Central Heating Plant was made by the legislature of 1899. The laboratories for horticulture were built in 1893, and the building was completed in 1896. Further west lie the barns and buildings of the Experimental Farm and the dwelling house for the Dean of the College of Agriculture. Between the lower campus and the lake is placed the Armory and Gymnasium, authorized by the legislature of 1891, and still nearer the lake is the University Boat House and the Rowing Tank. On the western part of the lower campus is the new Library for the State Historical Society and the University.

GOVERNMENT.

The government of the institution rests upon the inherent obligations of students to the University and to the State. The University is maintained at the public expense for the public good. Those who participate in its benefits are expected, as a matter of honor, not only to fulfill the obligations of loyal members of the institution, of the community, and of the commonwealth, but actively to aid in promoting the intellectual and moral interests. Every student owes to the public a full equivalent for its expenditure in his behalf, in the form of superior usefulness to it, both while in the instituton and afterwards. Students therefore cannot claim any exemption from the duties of good citizens and of loyal members of the community and of the University; on the contrary, they are under peculiar obligations loyally to fulfill every duty. As members of the institution, they are held responsible for regular attendance and the proper performance of their duties. The interests of faithful students and the well-being of the University demand that those who do not conform to these manifest obligations should withdraw from the institution or be excluded. As members of the community, students are amenable to the law; and, if guilty of its infraction, are liable to a termination of their relations with the University. The University recognizes its civic relations and rests its administration upon civic obligations.

CLASS OFFICERS.

The care of the students in their studies is placed in charge of class officers, chosen from the Faculty. Each division of the classes is under such an officer, who directs the work of the students, assigns to each his studies and reports his progress at the end of each semester to his parent or guardian. The class officers receive all reports from instructors, both those on work completed at the end of the semester and special reports of deficiency or failure on the part of invidual.

CONVOCATIONS.

A weekly assembly, or convocation, of the students is held on Friday at noon, which the members of the Freshman and Sophomore classes are required to attend, and which is open to the members of the other classes. At this meeting the President addresses the students on some matter of interest, either occupying the full time, or speaking more briefly; in which case a more formal address is given by another member of the Faculty, or by some person from abroad. Music is made a prominent feature of these convocations. Among the speakers from abroad during the current year have been Superintendent E. Benjamin Andrews of Chicago, Professors H. Morse Stephens and Hiram Corson of Cornell University, Professor Tomlins of Chicago, on the subject of music, Colonel H. G. Prout, Editor of the *Railway Gazette*, and Professor Graham Taylor of the Chicago Commons. The addresses usually concern some matter of University or student interest, questions of contemporary history or politics, or literary subjects. Through this convocation the students are enabled to meet as a body and to become acquainted with those members of the Faculty from whom they do not receive instruction, and also to listen to speakers who come from other universities or are distinguished in their respective professions.

LIBRARIES.

The libraries of the University are the General Library, the Law Library, the Agricultural Library, and the Woodman Astronomical Library. They contain in the aggregate over 60,000 volumes and 17,000 unbound pamphlets.

The General University Library, including the department libraries catalogued therewith, contains over 51,000 volumes and 15,000 unbound pamphlets. More than 500 periodicals are regularly received. The catalogue is the usual dictionary card catalogue of authors, subjects, and titles in one alphabetic arrangement. Subject to certain restrictions, books may be drawn by all members of the University. Students are required to make a guarantee deposit of $2.00 with the Secretary of the Board of Regents preliminary to borrowing books from the library. This amount is refunded on presenting to the Secretary the library deposit card properly endorsed by the librarian. For consultation the library is open twelve hours daily during the academic year except on Sundays and legal holidays.

Through the kindness of Professor Edward T. Owen, the General Library contains on deposit the Owen library of works on French language and literature, numbering 900 volumes. Special appropriations in recent years have rendered the library especially strong in the lines of economic and political science, and in classical philology.

During the past year liberal German-American citizens of Milwaukee have contributed a considerable sum of money ($3,200) for the purchase of a Germanic philology seminary library. This fund has been expended to supplement and develop the German department of the library, thus furnishing unexcelled facilities for the study of the German language and literature.

At the opening of the college year a course of lectures on the library and methods in library work is given to new students by the University librarian.

The College of Law has a special library of 4,000 volumes; and the Washburn Observatory is provided with the Woodman Astronomical Library, now containing 2,400 books and 2,200 pamphlets. Students also have free access to the State Law Library, comprising about 32,500 volumes, and by special arrangements are enabled to take out books from the free library of the City of Madison. This is a well-selected collection of over 16,000 volumes.

The library of the State Historical Society contains over 104,000 volumes and 100,000 pamphlets. It is exceptionally rich in manuscript and other material for the study of the history of the Mississippi valley. The collections of the late Dr. Lyman C. Draper are included in the library. Its files of newspapers and periodicals are among the most complete in the United States. There are over 5,000 volumes of bound newspapers published outside of Wisconsin, and the files cover, with but few breaks, the period from the middle of the seventeenth century to the present. There is an excellent collection of United States government documents, and the material for the study of American local history, Western travel, the Revolution, Slavery and the Civil War, is unusually abundant. In English history the library possesses the Calendars of State Papers, the Rolls Series, the publications of the Camden Society, the Records Commission, and the Historical Manuscripts Commission, the journals and debates of Parliament, and several important collections for the study of local history. The Tank collection (Dutch) offers facilities for the study of the Netherlands. The library of the Historical Society is accessible to all students of the University, and thus affords exceptional facilities for the prosecution of advanced historical work. The historical seminaries of the University have been generously granted special facilities in the rooms of the library. The Historical, State, University and City libraries afford duplicate copies of historical material most in use, and to a large extent supplement one another.

The State legislatures of 1895, 1897 and 1899, made provision for a fire-proof building for the libraries of the State Historical Society and the University. The erection of this building is in charge of a commission, selected by the Governor, the State Historical Society, and the Regents of the University. The building is placed on the western part of the lower campus of the University. The completion of the interior of the Library is in active progress and the building will be completed and occupied during the summer of 1900.

LABORATORIES.

Chemical Laboratories.—The Chemical Laboratories, six in number, are in a building devoted exclusively to Chemistry. Four of these are general laboratorities, viz.:

First. The Qualitative Laboratory, with accommodations for ninety-six students. *Second.* The Organic Laboratory, accommodating thirty-two students. *Third.* The Quantitative Laboratory, accommodating forty-eight students; and *Fourth.* The Laboratory of Physical Chemistry, accommodating twenty-five students.

These laboratories are large, well-lighted, conveniently arranged, and well supplied with the necessary apparatus and equipments.

Physical Laboratories.—The instruction in the department of physics is designed to meet the needs of all classes of students, from those just entering, with no knowledge of the subject, to those who have been well trained, and who are prepared to continue in the more advanced courses or to take up a line of original investigation.

The Physical Laboratories are located on the first floor and in the basement of the south wing of Science Hall, and are commodious and well lighted. Besides the lecture room and large apparatus room on the first floor, there are two laboratory rooms for purposes where great steadiness is not required. The lecture room has a seating capacity for 150 students, and is provided with all the appliances to facilitate a complete course of experimental lectures. In the basement are three large general laboratories for undergraduate work, all of which are liberally supplied with piers to insure the perfect stability of the instruments used. There are also in the basement a well-equipped photometric room and a number of laboratories devoted to special investigation. Besides current supplied from the numerous dynamos in the University shops, the various rooms of the physical laboratory are connected with the electric light and power circuits of the city.

The physical apparatus includes, in addition to the equipment for demonstration purposes, an excellent collection of instruments adapted to measurement and investigation. The laboratory offers special facilities for carrying out graduate study and research.

The Mineralogical Laboratory.—The laboratories for mineralogy are located on the second floor of Science Hall, and consist of a room fitted with desks and chemical reagents for courses in blowpipe analysis and determinative mineralogy, and a goniometer room which can be darkened for the study of crystals. In the mineralogical lecture room are the necessary models of crystals in glass and wood, and working collection of crystals and minerals.

The Petrographical Laboratory.—This laboratory is a large, well-lighted room supplied with numerous polarizing microscopes, other apparatus, and a very complete set of rocks and of rock and mineral sections, for complete courses in optical mineralogy and petrology. The general and special collections mentioned under Museums are available for all advanced students of petrology.

The lecture room for geology is provided with a full set of reference manuals, a set of Zittel's Palaeontologische Wandtafeln; a large relief map of the United States by E. E. Howell; a set of Shaler's models and photographs; a set of Davis' models showing the development of topographic features; numerous geological maps; a large collection of lantern slides; Newton's large electric projecting lantern, and other apparatus. The Newton lantern is adapted for projecting ordinary lantern slides, and has a front for microscopic slides, which projects directly on the screen thin sections of rocks both in ordinary and polarized light.

The Biological Laboratories.—The elementary laboratory for the departments of botany and zoology is arranged to accommodate seventy-two students, and is provided with compound microscopes, dissecting microscopes, and other apparatus necessary to an elementary course in botany and zoology. The departments have about ninety compound microscopes, chiefly by Leitz and by Bausch & Lomb, fitted for elementary and advanced work.

The laboratories for advanced work in botany are fitted up with the apparatus and reagents necessary to advanced courses in vegetable histology, physiology and cytology. All necessary reagents, ovens, paraffin baths, and microtomes are provided for histological and cytological work.

The laboratories for advanced work in zoology are two in number, one being devoted to histology, and the other to vertebrate anatomy and embryology. The histological laboratory is provided with a full equipment of reagents, microtomes of various patterns, and microscopes. The anatomical laboratory is furnished with a collection of vertebrate skeletons and of wax models illustrating the development of some of the more important vertebrates and invertebrates. For illustrating the lectures in botany and in zoology, there are Auzoux models, both of plants and animals, an electric projecting lantern and microscope, over 600 lantern slides, a large number of wall charts, microscope slides, etc.

The bacteriological laboratories are located in Agricultural Hall. The general laboratory occupies a part of the second floor; it accommodates twenty students, giving ample facilities for independent work. The laboratory is supplied with compound microscopes of late pattern, comprising the best American and German makes. The laboratory is well equipped with the usual supply of sterilizers and incubators, kept at different constant temperatures, as well as numerous pieces of apparatus of home manufacture intended for investigational and instructional purposes. A large and constantly increasing supply of pure cultures of bacteria is kept on hand.

A laboratory for advanced and graduate students is to be built this year. This will be especially equipped for work with the pathogenic bacteria. Special facilities will be offered in the way for private rooms for individual work.

The research laboratory of the Experiment Station occupies a part of the first floor, and is well equipped for original investigation. The green houses of the Experiment Station and the University Creamery afford facilities for the prosecution of work on plant diseases and dairy products. Nearly all of the general bacteriological journals are kept on file in the library for ready reference. A collection of lantern slides for lecture illustration is also in use.

The Psychological Laboratory.—The laboratory is designed to illustrate by practical experiments and demonstrations the courses in psychology; to give an opportunity to students of experimental psychology to study the methods, equipments and results of this science, and to provide for original research in many directions.

Original research has been carried on for several years and the more important results have been published in the *American Journal of Psychology*, the *Psychological Review*, and elsewhere.

In addition to four series of studies from the laboratory already published, the work done in the laboratory has been the basis of several articles that have appeared or are about to appear in various periodicals, as well as of theses submitted for degrees.

The engineering, assaying, pharmacy and agricultural laboratories are described under their respective departments.

UNIVERSITY MUSEUMS.

Officers.

CHARLES KENDALL ADAMS, LL. D., President of the University.

ROBERT A. HARPER, Ph. D., Professor of Botany, Curator for Botany.

WILLIAM S. MARSHALL, Ph. D., Assistant Professor of Zoology, Curator for Zoology.

WILLIAM S. MILLER, M. D., Assistant Professor of Vertebrate Anatomy, Curator for Vertebrate Anatomy.

WILLIAM H. HOBBS, Ph. D., Professor of Mineralogy and Petrology, Curator for Mineralogy and Petrology.

J. MORGAN CLEMENTS, Ph. D., Assistant Professor of Geology, Curator for Geology and Paleontology.

ROLLIN H. DENNISTON, B. S.,Curator for Pharmaceutical Collections.

The University Museums comprise the Geological and Mineralogical Museum, the Biological Museum, and the Herbarium, which occupy respectively the second and third floors of the south wing of

Science Hall. The collections in the College of Engineering and College of Agriculture are described in later pages.

The Geological and Mineralogical Museum has been built up for the most part with special reference to instructional work. It contains material for the thorough illustration of various lines of mineralogy and geology.

The Museum includes a large number of relief models to illustrate topographical and geological features, casts of gigantic fossil forms, and systematic collections of minerals, crystals, rocks, fossils, ores, etc. In the mineral collection is included the Henry collection, rich in minerals from southern Wisconsin, and in the paleontological collection is the Powers collection of Wisconsin Silurian fossils. The collection of the Wisconsin Academy of Sciences, in which are included the type fossils described in the volumes of the First Geological survey, is deposited in the museum. The rock collection includes Sturz's collection of typical European rocks, the Rohn collection of typical rocks from the Lake Superior region, and a number of other special sets.

A number of additional special collections are at present stored in the lecture rooms, laboratories, and offices, and are accessible to students interested. These include a collection of over 30,000 specimens, with about 15,000 thin sections, belonging to the Lake Superior Division of the United States Geological Survey, one of the largest of its kind in the world; a large collection of New England rocks belonging to the same survey; the collections of the Wisconsin Geological Survey; and the Hobbs collection, mainly of European rocks, supplied with over 1,000 thin sections. Of technical interest are the special collections of metallurgical, pharmaceutical, and engineering specimens, and the collection of Wisconsin building stones made by the Wisconsin Geological Survey.

The Zoological and Botanical Museum occupies the entire third story of the south wing of Science Hall, directly above the geological museum. Among the specimens at present placed in the cases may be named a good collection of vertebrate skeletons; a large number of Blaschka glass models of invertebrates; an alcoholic collection of invertebrates from the Naples Zoological Station; representative collections of echinoderms, corals, and mollusks. The botanical cases contain a collection of Auzoux models of flowers and a collection of specimens of wood. The Owen collection of Lepidoptera, comprising five thousand species, and over twenty thousand specimens, is deposited in Science Hall.

The Herbarium of the University (Room 41, Science Hall) includes the Lapham collection, chiefly of flowering plants, purchased by the State from the estate of I. A. Lapham, of Milwaukee. This contained about 8,000 species. These have been mounted and arranged, and are now accessible for consultation. The Wisconsin plants have been separated from the rest, and it is the intention to make them a basis of a complete representation of the Wisconsin flora. Large additions have been made to this herbarium by Professor L. S. Cheney and Professor H. L. Russell.

Mr. Lapham's collections also included a considerable number of algæ, lichens and mosses. The collection of mosses has been very greatly extended by gifts, purchases, exchanges, and collections, so that it now includes almost all of the species known in North America, and a large number of those of other countries. Many valuable types and sets of exsiccati are included.

When the museums are not open to the public, access may be gained by visitors at all reasonable hours by calling upon the janitor of the building, whose room is on the first floor of Science Hall.

THE PHARMACEUTICAL COLLECTIONS.

Economic Collection.—This collection includes an herbarium of medicinal plants of about 4,000 sheets, and many articles derived from plants, used for food, clothing, etc.; implements used in collecting or manufacturing plant products, and photographs illustrating plants of economic value. At present the economic collection is housed on the fourth floor of North Hall, in part with the drug collection, and in part in the herbarium room.

The Drug Collection.—At present this collection contains about 4,500 sample specimens of drugs for purely illustrative purposes. Each year large additions come to it as contributions from various sources. Among the larger contributors are Schimmel & Co., of Leipzig, Germany, Lehn & Fink, Parke, Davis & Co., and Gilpin, Langdon & Co. This collection is housed in a special room at the south end of the fourth floor of North Hall.

The Pharmacognostical Collection found on the fourth floor in a room especially devoted to it has been very largely increased by purchases made at the World's Fair; these acquisitions consisting chiefly of drugs of Asiatic origin. Notable among them are a collection of fifty Ceylon drugs and medicines and a collection of more than one hundred Malay medicines. Worthy of mention are also a collection of 122 handsome specimens of essential oils and allied synthetic products, liberally donated by Messrs. Schimmel & Co., of Leipzig, Germany; a collection of choice drugs from Messrs. Lehn & Fink, a materia medica cabinet from Parke, Davis & Co., a collection of official drugs from Schieffelin & Co., another from Gilpin, Langdon & Co., etc.

During the past year several hundred new entries have been made, so that at present the inventory comprises almost four thousand numbers. The collection has been relabeled and rearranged during the past year.

THE WASHBURN OBSERVATORY.

The Washburn Observatory is excellently equipped for astronomical work. Its principal instruments are: An equatorially-mounted telescope of 15½ inches aperture, constructed by Alvan Clark & Sons, and provided with graduated circles, driving clock, micrometers, a spectroscope, astro-photometer, and a very complete set of eye-pieces; a meridian circle, by A. Repsold & Sons, of Hamburg, with collimators, and the usual accessories of such an instrument.

A full account of the Washburn Observatory will be found on a later page, under the College of Letters and Science.

PHYSICAL TRAINING.

Military drill and gymnastic exercises are required of the young men of the Freshmen and Sophomore classes, and of special students of the first two years' attendance. Gymnastic exercise is also required of the young women, for whom a thoroughly equipped gymnasium has been provided. The University is situated on the shore of Lake Mendota, a beautiful sheet of water, which invites exercise and recreation in boating. The University Boat House Association has erected a boat house, and the University has built a Rowing Tank for the use of the University crew.

An Athletic Field of about ten acres has been enclosed in Camp Randall. The field has been graded, under-drained, provided with two tracks, one-third and one-fourth mile; and a grand stand has been built accommodating 1,500 spectators.

PUBLICATIONS OF THE UNIVERSITY.

The University issues four series of publications, known as the *Bulletins of the University of Wisconsin*, under the direction of a Committee of Publication, consisting of the President of the University and the following editors:

William H. Hobbs, Ph. D., (Chairman), Editor of the Science Series.

Charles Forster Smith, Ph. D., Editor of the Language and Literature Series.

Frederick J. Turner, Ph. D., Editor of the Economics, Political Science, and History Series.

Nelson O. Whitney, C. E., Editor of the Engineering Series.

The numbers which have been issued are the following:

Economics, Political Science, and History Series.
Volume 1.

No. 1. The Geographical Distribution of the Vote of the Thirteen States on the Federal Constitution, 1787-8, by Orin Grant Libby, A. M., with an introduction by Frederick J. Turner. Pp. 116, pls. 2.

No. 2. The Finances of the United States from 1775 to 1789, with Especial Reference to the Budget, by Charles J. Bullock, A. B. Pp. 157.

No. 3. The Province of Quebec and the Early American Revolution. A study in English-American Colonial History, by Victor Coffin, Ph. D. Pp. 307.

Volume 2.

No. 1. New Governments West of the Alleghanies since 1780, by George Henry Alden, Ph. D. Pp. 74.

No. 2. Municipal History and Organizations of the City of Chicago, by Samuel Edwin Sparling, Ph. D. Pp. 113.

No. 3. Congressional Grants of Land in Aid of Railways, by John B. Sanborn, M. L.

No. 4. English Common Law in the Early American Colonies, by Paul Samuel Reinsch, Ph. D. Pp. 64. (Completing volume 2.)

Science Series.
Volume 1.

No. 1. On the Speed of Liberation of Iodine in Solutions of Hydrochloric Acid, Potassium Chlorate and Potassium Iodide, by Herman Schlundt. Pp. 33.

No. 2. On the Quartz Keratophyre and Associated Rocks of the North Range of the Baraboo Bluffs, by Samuel Weidman. Pp. 21, pls. 3.

No. 3. Studies in Spherical and Practical Astronomy, by George C. Comstock. Pp. 50.

No. 4. A Contribution to the Mineralogy of Wisconsin, by William Herbert Hobbs. Pp. 48, pls. 5.

No. 5. Analytic Keys to the Genera and Species of North American Mosses, by Charles Reid Barnes and Fred DeForest Heald. Pp. 211.

Volume 2.

No. 1. On the Action of Dilute Electrolytes on the Sense of Taste, by Louis Kahlenberg, Ph. D. Pp. 31.

In preparation: Aspects of Mental Economy, by M. V. O'Shea.

Contributions from the Anatomical Laboratories of the University of Wisconsin, by W. S. Miller, M. D.

Language and Literature Series.

Volume 1.

No. 1. The Development of American Literature from 1815 to 1833, by William B. Cairns, Ph. D. Pp. 87.

No. 2. The Treatment of Nature in the Poetry of the Roman Republic, by Katharine Allen, M. A. Pp. 131.

In preparation: The Time Element in the *Oresteia*, by Jonathan Bailey Browder, Ph. D.

Engineering Series.

Volume 1.

No. 1. Track, by L. F. Loree, M. Am. Soc., C. E. Pp. 24.

No. 2. Some Practical Hints in Dynamo Design, by Gilbert Wilkes, M. Am. Inst. E. E. Pp. 16.

No. 3. The Steel Construction of Buildings, by C. T. Purdy, C. E. Pp. 27.

No. 4. The Evolution of a Switchboard, by A. V. Abbott, C. E. Pp. 32, pls. 4.

No. 5. An Experimental Study of Field Methods Which Will Insure to Stadia Measurements Greatly Increased Accuracy, by Leonard Sewell Smith, B. C. E. Pp. 45, pl. 1.

No. 6. Railway Signaling, by W. McC. Grafton, C. E. Pp. 38.

No. 7. Emergencies in Railroad Work, by L. F. Loree, M. Am. Soc. C. E. Pp. 42.

No. 8. Electrical Engineering in Modern Central Stations, by Louis A. Ferguson, A. B. Pp. 33.

No. 9. The Problem of Economical Heat, Light and Power Supply for Building Blocks, School Houses, Dwellings, etc., by G. Adolph Gerdtzen, B. S. Pp. 69.

No. 10. Topographical Surveys, Their Methods and Value, by J. L. Van Ornum, C. E. Pp. 39.

Volume 2.

No. 1. A Complete Test of Modern American Transformers of Moderate Capacity, by Arthur Hillyer Ford, B. S., with an introduction by Professor D. C. Jackson. Pp. 88.

No. 2. A Comparative Test of Steam Injectors, by George Henry Trautmann, B. S., with an introduction by Professor Storm Bull. Pp. 34.

No. 3. The Superintendent of Bridges and Buildings, by Onward Bates, C. E. Pp. 30.

No. 4. Some Unrecognized Functions of Our State Universities, by J. B. Johnson, C. E. Pp. 20.

The Washburn Observatory issues the *Publications of the Washburn Observatory*, edited by Professor George C. Comstock, now in its tenth volume.

From the College of Agriculture are issued the *Quarterly Bulletins*, of which thus far 80 have appeared; the *Annual Reports*, now numbering 16, and the *Bulletin of the Farmers' Institutes*, of which 13 numbers have appeared.

Besides the official publications of the University the following publications are edited at the University:

Bulletins of the Wisconsin Geological and Natural History Survey, edited by Professor E. A. Birge, Director.

Transactions of the Wisconsin Academy of Sciences, Arts, and Letters, edited by Professor Frank C. Sharp, Secretary.

The Pharmaceutical Review, edited by Professor Edward Kremers.

The Wisconsin Journal of Education, edited by Professor John W. Stearns.

GENERAL INFORMATION.

CHARGES AND FEES—GENERAL CHARGES.

All fees are required to be paid strictly in advance at the beginning of each semester, before cards are issued by the class officer entitling the student to admission to class; except those in the College of Law as indicated below. Graduate students, except honorary fellows, pay the same fees as undergraduates, whether they are in attendance at the University or *in absentia*.

Tuition is free for all students from the State of Wisconsin, except in the College of Law.

After ten days from the beginning of the semester, no fees are returned except by special vote of the Board of Regents.

Fees from Candidates for Higher Degrees.

From all candidates for advanced degrees, a diploma fee of $5 is required; such fee is required to be paid to the Secretary of the Board of Regents one month before commencement, and no diploma shall be made out until such fee has been paid. In case for any reason the degree is not conferred, the fee will be returned.

Each candidate for the degree of Ph. D. shall deposit in the library one hundred printed copies of his thesis. If the thesis is printed in some journal or as a bulletin of the University, reprints therefrom will be accepted by the library, but these must be provided with a special cover in proper thesis form. The candidate may receive his diploma before the thesis is printed, provided a written or typewritten copy of the thesis is deposited with the librarian, and the sum of fifty dollars with the Secretary. The money will be returned on presentation to the library of the required number of printed copies of the thesis.

College of Letters and Science, School of Economics, Political Science, and History, School of Education.

Tuition for non-resident students, per semester..........	$15.00
Incidental fee for all students, per semester..............	10.00
Additional fee for students electing studies in the College of Law, per year.....................................	25.00

College of Mechanics and Engineering, School of Pharmacy.

Resident, tuition...	FREE.
Non-resident, tuition per semester......................	$20.00
Incidental fee to all, per semester.......................	15.00

College of Agriculture.

Resident, tuition..	FREE.
Non-resident, long course, tuition, per semester...........	$15.00
Incidental fee, long course, to all, per semester............	10.00
Non-resident, short course, tuition, per term..............	15.00
Incidental fee to all, per term...........................	5.00
Non-resident, dairy course, tuition, per term.............	15.00
Incidental fee to all, per term...........................	5.00
Non-resident, dairy course, lecture fee...................	10.00

College of Law.

Tuition fee, first year...................................	$75.00
Tuition fee, second year.................................	50.00
Tuition fee, third year...................................	25.00
Tuition fee for students graduating in one year.............	100.00

The fees for students graduating in two years are the same as in the first two years of the three-year course.

The fees in the College of Law are to be paid for the year at the beginning of the first semester. There is no additional fee for non-resident students in this College.

Summer Session and Wisconsin Summer School.

General fee...	$15.00

Summer School of Library Science.

General fee for full course...............................	$15.00
Fee for special course in cataloguing.....................	10.00

School of Music.

Persons who are members of other colleges or schools of the University may take the general courses of music, without charge. Members of the School of Music and of other departments, who take special lessons, will pay fees as stated in the announcement of the School on a subsequent page of the catalogue.

Ladies' Hall.

Room rent, heat, and light, see page 43.

Board in Ladies' Hall, payable to the Matron, per week.... $3.50

These fees are subject to change at the opening of the college year.

LABORATORY FEES.

Biological Laboratories.—The laboratory fee for the elementary course in biology and for most of the advanced courses is $8.00 per year. The fee for vetebrate histology, for embryology, and for bacteriology, $8.00 per semester.

Chemical Laboratories.—In these laboratories the deposit for a year's course is twenty dollars. The amount refunded will depend on the chemicals used and the care exercised by the student. The ordinary cost of a year's course is from fifteen dollars to twenty dollars.

Geology and Mineralogy.—Blowpipe analysis, per semester, $5.00, blowpipe analysis, two-fifths study, $2.00; three-fifths study, $3.00; petrography, per semester, $5.00.

Physical Laboratories.—The laboratory fee in the physical laboratories is $2.00 for each unit-hour (two hours per week of actual work) per semester.

Psychological Laboratory.—The laboratory fee for the course in Experimental Psychology is $3.00; for other experimental work, $3.00 per semester, $5.00 per year.

College of Engineering.—The charge for laboratory work is $1.50 per unit-hour (two hours per week of actual work) per semester. There is also a charge of $1.50 per year for periodicals, supplied to the Engineering Reading Room.

School of Pharmacy.—For general laboratory privileges a charge is made of $1.00 per unit-hour and semester. A separate account will be kept with the accountant of the storage room for special apparatus and material. The student will purchase coupons from the Secretary of the Board of Regents ($5.00 at a time) and present them at the storage room. At the end of the year full credit will be given for such pieces of apparatus as are taken back, in accordance with the rules of the storage room.

College of Agriculture.—The following laboratory fees are required: Dairy School Laboratory, residents, $5.00; non-residents, $15.00; Advanced Dairy Course, $6.00; Pasteurizing Course, $1.00. Short Course Laboratory, non-residents, $10.00; Blacksmithing, $3.00; Carpenter Work, $3.00. Bacteriology: Long Course students, same as General Biology students.

Long Course students taking chemical work pay for gas and for apparatus at the same rate as in the General Chemical Laboratory.

GYMNASIUM AND MILITARY DRILL.

Young men in the College of Letters and Science, College of Mechanics and Engineering, and the four-year courses in Agriculture and Pharmacy, are required to take gymnastic exercises during the first two years of their course, and are also required to take military drill. Students required to drill must provide themselves with a uniform of color and pattern required by the Regents, which may be procured by special arrangement made with manufacturers.

Gymnasium fee... $2.00
Locker fee... 1.50

Young women are required to take gymnastic exercises during the first two years of their course. A gymnasium fee of $1.00 per year is required, and $1.00 additional from those who make use of a locker. They must also provide themselves with a suitable costume; directions for which will be furnished by the instructor in gymnastics on application.

Students entering the four-year academic courses of the University should expect to pay the fee for general expenses ($10), and if not residents of the State, the tuition fee ($15) mentioned above; the gymnasium fees ($2 or $3.50); and laboratory fees for such courses as begin in Freshman year. In the College of Engineering and School of Pharmacy the fee for general expenses is $15.00, and the non-resident tuition fee is $20.00. Young men must be prepared to defray the cost of a uniform, about $15, and young women must provide a gymnasium suit.

ROOMS AND BOARD.

Rooms, furnished and unfurnished, can be obained in the city at reasonable rates. The cost of board in clubs is from $2.00 to $2.50 per week; in private families from $2.50 to $4.00 per week. Washing costs from sixty to sixty-five cents per dozen. Many of the students support themselves in whole or in part. The places offering available work are eagerly sought for and cannot always be obtained at once. Those dependent on themselves should secure some means before coming here, and be ready to wait and learn how to help themselves.

LADIES' HALL.

Ladies' Hall was entirely rebuilt and greatly enlarged in 1896. The rooms are now arranged in suites of two, comprising a study and a chamber, and intended for two occupants, or in single rooms, intended for one student. The building will accommodate in this way eighty students.

The rooms are lighted by electricity and the heating apparatus is now connected with the central boiler plant, so that there is no fire for heating in the building. Freight and passenger elevators, operated by electricity, are provided.

An account of the Woman's Gymnasium will be found under the heading Physical Culture on a later page of the catalogue.

The rooms for the Department of Music, which are now entirely confined to the new addition, comprise offices, rooms for practicing, and a large lecture room.

Students' rooms are carpeted and furnished, but occupants are expected to provide washstand furniture, towels, napkins, napkin rings, sheets, pillow cases, counterpanes, and blankets. Young women occupying this building are under the immediate charge of the Mistress of Ladies' Hall, and are required to board in the Hall. They are expected cheerfully to conform to the requirements necessary for a family of students. No deduction is made for voluntary absence, and any commutation of charges for board in cases where students leave before the close of the semester, except in cases of necessity, is entirely voluntary with the matron in charge. The cost of board is $3.50 per week.

The prices of rooms at Ladies' Hall vary according to location. Persons occupying a room may retain the same for the succeeding year by application and making a deposit of $10 not later than May 1st. The deposit of $10 required from all students new as well as old, to secure room, will be credited on the rent of the room, if taken; but if the room is not taken, will be forfeited, unless notification is recived by the Secretary prior to September 1st. Application for rooms and the payment of fees for the same should be made in all cases to the Secretary of the Board of Regents, who will assign all rooms. The balance due for room rent must be paid to the Secretary, not later than the second week after the beginning of each semester. Rooms are rented to *bona fide* students of the University only. Application for rooms may be made at any time, but rooms will not be assigned to new students prior to May 1st. After that date they will be assigned in the order of application and the payment of the $10, and subject to the provision above made for former occupants.

If for any reason one of the occupants of a suite shall be obliged to give up her place in the suite, the remaining person must take a single room, if one is vacant, or pay the price for the full suite, during the time it is occupied by her alone.

A person entering the Hall for the second semester only, shall pay the price of the room charged for the second semester, with the additional sum of $10.

ROOMS AND BOARD.

LIST OF ROOMS IN LADIES' HALL WITH RENT OF EACH.
"A" is the first floor; "B" the second, etc.

Floor.	Room No.	Suits for Two or Single.	To Secure.	1st Semester.	2d Semester.	Total for Each Person.
A	1	Suite	$10	$20	$10	$40
A	2	"	10	25	15	50
A	3	"	10	25	15	50
A	4	"	10	25	15	50
A	5	"	10	25	15	50
A	6	"	10	20	10	40
B	1	Suite	10	20	10	40
B	2	"	10	25	15	50
B	3	"	10	25	15	50
B	4	"	10	25	15	50
B	5	"	10	25	15	50
B	6	"	10	20	10	40
B	7	"	10	20	10	40
B	8	"	10	25	15	50
B	10	Single	10	40	30	80
B	12	"	10	45	35	90
B	14	"	10	40	25	75
*B	16	"	10	50	35	95
B	20	"	10	40	30	80
B	22	"	10	40	30	80
B	24	"	10	45	35	90
B	26	"	10	40	30	80
B	28	"	10	45	30	85
B	30	"	10	30	20	60
B	11	"	10	20	10	40
B	13	"	10	20	15	45
*B	15	"	10	25	15	50
*B	17	"	10	25	15	50
C	1	Suite	10	20	10	40
C	2	"	10	25	15	50
C	3	"	10	25	15	50
C	4	"	10	25	15	50
C	5	"	10	25	15	50
C	6	"	10	20	10	40
C	7	"	10	20	10	40
C	10	Single	10	40	30	80
C	12	"	10	45	35	90
C	14	"	10	40	25	75
C	16	"	10	40	25	75
C	18	"	10	40	25	75
C	20	"	10	40	25	75
C	22	"	10	40	25	75
C	24	"	10	45	35	90
C	26	"	10	40	30	80

Floor.	Room No.	Suits for Two or Single.	To Secure.	1st Semester.	2d Semester.	Total for Each Person.
C	28	Single	$10	$40	$30	.$80
C	30	"	10	25	15	50
*C	Parlor	"	10	45	35	90
C	21	"	10	20	15	45
C	23	"	10	20	15	45
C	25	"	10	25	15	50
C	27	"	10	25	15	50
C	29	"	10	25	15	50
C	31	"	10	20	15	45
*D	8	Single	10	30	20	60
D	10	"	10	25	20	55
D	12	"	10	30	20	60
D	14	"	10	25	15	50
D	16	"	10	25	15	50
D	18	"	10	25	15	50
D	20	"	10	25	15	50
D	22	"	10	25	15	50
D	24	"	10	30	25	65
D	26	"	10	25	15	50
D	28	"	10	25	20	55
D	30	"	10	20	15	45
*B	16	If occupied by two.	10	25	15	50
*B	15		10	10	10	30
*B	17		10	10	10	30
*C	24		10	25	15	50
*C	Parlor		10	25	15	50
*D	8		10	15	10	35

THE COLLEGE YEAR.

The college year is divided into two semesters. The first semester opens on the last Wednesday in September. Registration and examinations for admission will be held on the preceding Tuesday, and on the opening day of the semester. The second semester will ordinarily begin on the second Monday in February. The studies of the University have been so arranged that students can begin their course with the second semester; but persons desiring to enter the University at this time should come to Madison during the week preceding the opening of the second semester, as the recitations will begin on Tuesday morning, and all arrangements for rooms, board, books, etc., as well as registration at the University, must be made before that time. Commencement occurs on the Thursday preceding the last Wednesday in June.

There are two recesses or vacations during the college year, one at Christmas and one at Easter. The Christmas recess begins with the morning of December 24th, and recitations are resumed on the morning of January 3rd. No regular class examinations occur at Christmas, and no new classes begin immediately after the Christmas recess, so that students cannot enter the University at this time. Those who cannot enter at the opening of the year must wait for the beginning of the second semester in February. There is no vacation between the first and second semesters.

The Easter recess occurs at Easter, beginning with the Thursday morning before Easter Sunday. Recitations will begin on the morning of Tuesday following Easter.

LITERARY AND SCIENTIFIC SOCIETIES, STUDENT PUBLICATIONS.

The literary societies, the Athenaean, Hesperian, and Philomathian, composed of gentlemen, and the Castalian, composed of ladies, are sustained with unusual interest and constitute an important means of intellectual training. Numerous public exhibitions are given by these societies, of which the annual Joint Debate between two of the gentlemen's literary societies is the most important literary event of the college year. This debate has now been maintained for more than twenty-five years. In oratory the main public events are the Junior Oratorical Exhibition, and the Annual Contest for the selection of a representative in the annual meeting of the Northwestern Oratorical League.

Besides these literary societies in the College of Letters and Science, three similar organizations are maintained in the College of Law, and two in the College of Agriculture. The College of Engineering maintains two engineering societies; and in the School of Pharmacy there is a Pharmaceutical Association. The most important scientific organization is the Science Club, including both officers of instruction and advanced students, which seeks to promote an interest in scientific study and research. It conducts public meetings for the untechnical discussion of scientific topics of current interest to which all members of the University are invited. A bronze medal, executed by T. Moring, London, will be annually awarded by the Club for the best thesis on a scientific subject. In several departments of the University there are held journal clubs or societies for furthering the distinct work of the departments. Among these are, the Bildungsverein; the Germanistische Gesellshaft; a Scandinavian society, the Nora Samlag; the Classical Club, the English Literature Journal Club, the Mathematical Club, the Physics Journal Club, the Biological Club, the Geological Club, and the Chemical Club. In other departments where no such organization has been effected similar results are reached by means of the various seminaries. The graduate students of the University have organized a Graduate Club, and the women have organized a Woman's Self Government Association. The religious organizations of the University include the Young Men's Christian Association with a membership of 225, and the Young Women's Christian Association with a membership of 78.

A monthly journal, the *Alumni Magazine*, is issued by the Alumni. The publications conducted by the students include the *Daily Cardinal;* a bi-weekly illustrated paper, the *Sphinx;* a monthly journal, the *Wisconsin Aegis;* and an annual, the *Badger*, issued by the Junior Class. The students of the College of Engineering issue a quarterly publication, the *University of Wisconsin Engineering Magazine.*

DEGREES.

FIRST DEGREES.

The baccalaureate degrees are conferred at graduation upon those who have successfully completed the regular courses leading to degrees, and who have conformed with all other requirements of the University. The degrees for the several courses are as follows:

Academic.

BACHELOR OF ARTS, for the Ancient Classical Course.
BACHELOR OF SCIENCE, for the General Science Course.
BACHELOR OF LETTERS, for the Modern Classical, the English, and the Civic Historical Courses.
BACHELOR OF PHILOSOPHY IN PEDAGOGY, for the Course for Normal Graduates.

Professional.

BACHELOR OF LAWS, for the Law Course.
GRADUATE IN PHARMACY, for the Pharmaceutical Course.
BACHELOR OF SCIENCE IN PHARMACY, for the Four Years' Pharmacy Course.

Technical.

BACHELOR OF SCIENCE IN AGRICULTURE, for the Agricultural Course.
BACHELOR OF SCIENCE IN ENGINEERING, for the courses in Civil Engineering, Mechanical Engineering, Sanitary Engineering, Electrical Engineering, and Applied Electro-Chemistry.

A graduate of any one of the courses may receive the baccalaureate degree of any other course by completing the additional studies required in that course, but two baccalaureate degrees cannot be taken in one year. For a second bachelor's degree in the College of Letters and Science there are required one year's additional study and a special thesis.

The conditions on which the bachelor's degrees are given will be found stated under the appropriate colleges and courses on subsequent pages.

HIGHER DEGREES.

The University confers the degrees of *Master of Arts, Master of Letters,* and *Master of Science* upon graduates who have previously taken the degrees of Bachelor of Arts, Bachelor of Letters, and Bachelor of Science in the College of Letters and Science. The degree of *Master of Philosophy* is conferred on those who have taken the degree of Bachelor of Philosophy in Pedagogy. The degree of *Doctor of Philosophy* is also granted. The conditions on which these degrees are given will be found stated under the Department of Graduate Study on pages 54, 55.

The higher degrees of *Civil Engineer, Mechanical Engineer,* and *Electrical Engineer* are conferred as second degrees in the College of Engineering. The degree of *Master of Pharmacy* is conferred as a second degree upon Graduates in Pharmacy and the degree of *Master of Science in Pharmacy* is given as a second degree to Bachelors of Science in Pharmacy.

The degree of *Master of Science in Agriculture* is conferred on Bachelors of Science in Agriculture.

The conditions on which these second degrees in the professional colleges are granted will be found stated under Department of Graduate Study and also under the head of the respective colleges.

HONORS.

HONORS IN SPECIAL STUDIES.

Honors are given at graduation for special work of high order of excellence done in any department. Such honors will be voted by the Faculty to those students whose graduation theses show exceptional excellence and who have completed with unusual success a long course of study in the department in which the thesis is presented. The thesis must show work additional to all requirements for graduation equal to two hours per week for one year. Students desiring to become candidates for special honors in any department must make application to the Faculty at the opening of the second semester through the professor in whose department the honors are sought.

UNDERGRADUATE SCHOLARSHIP.
The John A. Johnson Scholarships.

The University is indebted to the liberality of the Hon. John A. Johnson, of Madison, for ten scholarships of the annual value of about $35 each, established under the following conditions:

The sum received by one student in one year shall not exceed $50, nor the sum received during his college course exceed $200. These scholarships are at present limited to students speaking one of the Scandinavian languages (Norse, Swedish, Danish, or Icelandic). No student can receive aid from this fund unless he has attended a common school one year, or has attended the University one year. The recipient of aid will be expected to return the money received by him to the fund, if he shall at any time be able to do so. The income of the fund will be dispensed by a committee of the Faculty. This committee consists of the President of the University and Professors Olson and Bull.

The Amelia H. Doyon Scholarships.

By the will of Mrs. Amelia H. Doyon, late of Madison, the University has received a gift of five thousand dollars, to be known as The Amelia H. Doyon Fund. The income from this fund is to be divided into two equal parts, to be designated as The Amelia H. Doyon Scholarships, which are to be given to two young women in attendance at the University, to be selected by the Faculty. In making this selection the Faculty is to take into consideration the scholarship or standing of the persons selected and their need of financial help. Neither of these scholarships is to be bestowed on any young woman who has not been in attendance as a student at the University of Wisconsin for at least one year.

Hebrew Scholarship.

The Hebrew Lectureship and Scholarship Society will give a scholarship of $250 for special excellence in Hebrew studies. This is at present held by Mr. Louis B. Wolfenson.

The Biblical Alliance of Wisconsin offers a sum of money, at present amounting to fifteen hundred dollars, to provide scholarships for the encouragement of studies in the department of Hebrew and Hellenistic Greek. These may be held by graduates or undergraduates. Award is made on basis of excellence. Information regarding the scholarships will be given on application to Professor Williams.

An account of the Graduate Fellowships and Scholarships is given on later pages.

DEPARTMENT OF GRADUATE STUDY.

COMMITTEE ON GRADUATE STUDIES.

C. K. ADAMS, LL. D., President of the University.
C. F. SMITH, Ph. D., Professor of Greek and Classical Philology. *Chairman.*
E. A. BIRGE, Ph. D., Sc. D., Dean of the College of Letters and Science.
W. A. HENRY, Agr. B., Dean of the College of Agriculture.
J. B. JOHNSON, C. E., Dean of the College of Mechanics and Engineering.
R. T. ELY, Ph. D., LL. D., Director of the School of Economics, Political Science, and History.
J. C. FREEMAN, LL. D., Professor of English Literature.
EDWARD KREMERS, Ph. D., Professor of Pharmaceutical Chemistry.
W. H. ROSENSTENGEL, A. M., Professor of the German Language and Literature.
J. W. STEARNS, LL. D., Director of the School of Education.
F. J. TURNER, Ph. D., Professor of American History.
C. A. VAN VELZER, Ph. D., Professor of Mathematics.

ORGANIZATION.

The Graduate Department is organized for the encouragement of research at the University.

The University aims to afford adequate means for advanced study and research, and excellent facilities have already been provided along important lines. Personal assistance is rendered by professors to graduates according to individual needs. Classes for advanced students are organized and seminaries are conducted in which original research may be carried on.

The advanced studies of the various departments lead to graduate work. The preparation of theses by members of the senior class, and the courses of instruction leading to theses, are intended to foster the spirit of investigation, and to serve as an introduction to research work. Under the opportunities for elective studies the undergraduate student is enabled to concentrate work upon a leading line of study for several years, so that in his senior year he is enabled to do advanced work in certain classes designed for graduates and undergraduates.

Graduates from this University, and from other colleges and universities of recognized standing, and other advanced students suitably qualified, are permitted to become members of the graduate department.

The Regents of the University have established fellowships for the encouragement of graduate study; and in all of its departments the University furnishes abundant facilities for the publication of the results of original research. The laboratories and library facilities of the University, which are good in all lines, and are unexcelled in some directions, have been already described on preceding pages.

UNIVERSITY FELLOWSHIPS.

For the purpose of promoting higher scholarship and more extended original study than the academic courses afford, the Board of Regents has established ten University Fellowships of $400 each, of which two are specially devoted to Latin and Greek. The Alumni have established one Fellowship of $400.

The following are the regulations respecting these fellowships:

1. Any fellowship to which the present regulations apply may be held by any graduate of a college of recognized standing or by any one whose education is equivalent to that represented by a college degree. The Alumni Fellowship is open only to graduates of the University of Wisconsin, and no teaching is required of the holder. Those about to take such a degree are eligible as candidates, the regulations applying to the time of entrance upon the duties of the fellowship. Men and women are equally eligible.

2. Fellowships will be granted upon application only; such application, with accompanying evidence of merit, attainment, and ability, to be in the hands of the President before May 1st of the collegiate year preceding that during which the fellowship is held.

3. All fellowships will be filled each year. Fellows may be reelected for one additional year only.

4. Applications must be accompanied by evidence of scholarship, ability, and general worthiness; such as theses (whether prepared for this or other purposes), published writings, testimonials from instructors, outline of educational course pursued, special distinctions gained, and the like. Applications for reappointment should contain a full account of the work of the preceding year. Applications to receive attention must contain a definite statement of the special studies which the applicant intends to pursue.

5. The fellowships will be assigned to the several departments according to the studies which the fellows intend to pursue.

6. Each fellow shall pursue his studies under the direction of the professor or professors in charge of his special studies. Assignment of University services to the fellows shall be made by the President in consultation with the head of the department to which the fellow has been assigned, and the work assigned may be equivalent to one hour of teaching daily, or the supervison of laboratory work for two hours daily.

7. At a meeting of the Faculty in the month of May (which meeting shall be duly announced as the meeting of the election of fellows), the President shall call upon the several heads of the departments in which applications have been received, to make a statement of the merits of the candidates in their departments; after all such statements have been made, the members of the Faculty will cast their ballots for as many candidates as there are fellows to be elected, and those receiving the highest number of votes (provided that each receive a majority of the votes cast) shall be recommended to the Board of Regents for appointment to fellowships.

Vacancies in fellowships due to resignation or other cause may be filled, as they occur, at the option of the Faculty.

HONORARY FELLOWSHIPS.

The Regents have established honorary fellowships, equal in number to the regular fellowships, and filled in a similar way. No compensation is attached to these positions except the remission of University fees, and no teaching service is required from these fellows. Persons who have held fellowships in the University and who desire to continue graduate studies after the expiration of the term of the fellowship may be elected to honorary fellowships. Candidates for fellowships qualified in every respect to hold a regular fellowship, who desire to devote all of their time to study rather than perform the teaching service required of regular fellows, may be elected honorary fellows; but no person is eligible to an honorary fellowship unless he be a graduate of at least one year's standing.

PHARMACEUTICAL FELLOWSHIPS.

Through the generosity of friends of the School of Pharmacy, funds have been provided for the following fellowships in pharmacy:

The August Uihlein Fellowship.

Mr. August Uihlein, of Milwaukee, has generously established a pharmaceutical fellowship on a financial basis of $400 per annum for four years. During the present year the income from this fellowship is divided between Mr. I. W. Brandel, Ph. G. '99, and Mr. F. G. Ehlert, Ph. G. '99.

The Fred Vogel, Jr., Fellowship.

The sum of $500 generously contributed by Mr. Fred Vogel, Jr., of Milwaukee, for advanced work, was divided so as to make a graduate scholarship of $250 per annum for two years. The holder during the year 1899-1900 is F. C. Hitchcock, Ph. C., University of Michigan.

SCHOLARSHIPS FOR GRADUATES.

The Regents of the University have established two graduate scholarships of the value of $200 each; one in European history, held by Mr. J. P. Willard; the other in American history, by Mr. C. Macarthy.

Through the generosity of an alumnus two graduate scholarships of the value of $250 each are awarded annually in the literary department of the University. One of these, called the *William F. Allen Graduate Scholarship*, is held by Mr. E. T. Coleback, a graduate of the Ancient Classical Course; the other, called the *J. C. Freeman Graduate Scholarship*, is held by Mr. E. E. Calkins, a graduate of the English Course.

A friend of the University has founded a scholarship of the value of $200 annually, open to graduate students of Norwegian ancestry.

A Wisconsin friend of the University has given the Mendota Graduate Scholarship, amounting to $30 for the current year, (1899-1900).

A Chicago gentleman has given three graduate scholarships for the current year (1899-1900), each amounting to $30.

German-Americans of the City of Madison, wishing to awaken and encourage a deeper interest in the study of German from an historical and comparative point of view, have provided for a *University Graduate Scholarship in German Philology* of the annual value of $250 for each of the collegiate years ending June, 1899, 1900, and 1901. The scholarship is held by Mr. C. H. Handschin during the present year.

Applications for this scholarship ought to be made before May 1st, to the professor in charge of German philology in the University, Dr. Ernst Voss.

HIGHER DEGREES.

SECOND DEGREES.

The degrees of *Master of Arts, Master of Letters*, and *Master of Science* are conferred upon graduates who have previously taken the degrees of Bachelor of Arts, Bachelor of Letters, and Bachelor of Science, respectively, and who, after graduation, pursue an approved course of study equivalent to the work of one year of graduate studies in the University and who present a satisfactory thesis upon the leading subject pursued. Students who desire to do part of their work for the master's degree *in absentia*, may accomplish by this method not more than half of the work required for the degree. At least one semester must be spent in residence at the University.

The work must consist of one major and one minor subject, must be in the general line of advanced study implied by the degree sought, and must be approved by the Committee on Graduate Studies. Two-thirds of this study and must be devoted to the major subject and one-third to the minor. Study for a profession will not be accepted, but original investigation in connection with a profession, or special and scholarly study collateral to it, may be accepted, in the discretion of the Faculty. A thesis showing creditable original research must be presented at least one month before the close of the academic year, and if the thesis is satisfactory an examination will be conducted by a committee of the Faculty on the major and minor subjects.

Graduates of this or of similar institutions who pursue the course in law at the University, and who, by reason of their superior training, are able to take additional studies advantageously, may receive a second degree at graduation from the Law School on condition of having satisfactorily pursued graduate studies in the College of Letters and Science equivalent to five hours a week during two years of their course, and on conforming to the other required conditions.

The degrees of *Civil Engineer, Mechanical Engineer, Mining Engineer, Metallurgical Engineer*, and *Electrical Engineer* are conferred as second degrees upon Bachelors of Science in the Civil, Mechanical, Mining and Metallurgical, and Electrical Engineering courses respectively, (1) who pursue advanced professional study at the University for one year, and present a satisfactory project or thesis; or (2) who furnish suitable evidence of three years of professional work (of which one must be spent in a position of responsibility) and present a satisfactory thesis.

The degree of *Master of Pharmacy* will be conferred upon Graduates in Pharmacy who satisfactorily complete a course of one full year at the University in advanced pharmacy, or in some science or sciences specially allied to pharmacy, and who shall present a satisfactory thesis embodying the results of original investigation.

The degree of *Master of Science in Pharmacy* will be conferred upon Bachelors of Science in Pharmacy, under conditions similar to those required for second degrees in the College of Letters and Science.

THIRD DEGREES.

The degree of *Doctor of Philosophy* will be conferred upon successful candidates after three years of graduate study, of which the last year or the first two years must be pursued at this University. This degree will not, however, be conferred simply on the ground of the completion of study for the prescribed length of time. Special attainments are requisite; particularly the power of original thought and independent investigation. The candidate will be examined on three subjects, one major and two minors, which must be approved by the Committee on Graduate Studies not later than the beginning of the year in which the candidate expects to take the degree. A thesis must be presented which shall give evidence of original research and independent treatment. The applicant must announce himself as a candidate at least as early as the beginning of his last year of study, and his thesis must be placed in the hands of the Committee on Graduate Studies at least two months before the close of the academic year. The subject of the thesis must have the approval of the head of the department in which the major subject is carried on as early as November 1st of the collegiate year in which the candidate expects to take his degree.

In case the candidate is successful, he is required to put his thesis into print and deposit one hundred copies of the same in the Library of the University. If the thesis is printed in some journal, or as a Bulletin of the University, reprints therefrom will be accepted by the Librarian, but these must be provided with a special cover and title-page in proper thesis form. The diploma may be conferred before the thesis is printed, provided a written or typewritten copy is deposited with the Librarian, and the sum of fifty dollars with the Secretary of the Board of Regents. The money will be refunded on presentation of the printed copies.

All candidates for this degree must have a reading knowledge of French and German at least one year before the degree is conferred.

COURSES OF INSTRUCTION FOR GRADUATES.

In each of the departments of the University, graduate courses of instruction are offered, to which the courses offered for graduates and undergraduates of suitable attainments serve as an introduction. These courses are described on subsequent pages under the heading, Departments of Study, in the College of Letters and Science, College of Engineering, College of Agriculture, and School of Pharmacy.

In most departments the graduate courses change from year to year so that a consecutive course of graduate study can be elected, extending over two or three years.

EXPENSES.

The expenses for graduate students are the same as those for undergraduates. The tuition for students not residents of Wisconsin is $15.00 per semester. The general incidental fee is $10.00 per semester. A diploma fee of $5.00 is required. Students working in the laboratories are required to pay a fee to cover the cost of materials and instruments used by them. A list of these charges and deposits will be found under the head of Charges and Fees, on pages 38-40.

COLLEGE OF LETTERS AND SCIENCE.

STAFF OF INSTRUCTION.

C. K. ADAMS, LL. D., President of the University.
E. A. BIRGE, Ph. D., Sc. D., Dean, Professor of Zoology.
L. W. AUSTIN, Ph. D., Assistant Professor of Physics.
L. S. CHENEY, M. S., Assistant Professor of Pharmaceutical Botany.
J. M. CLEMENTS, Ph. D., Assistant Professor of Geology.
VICTOR COFFIN, Ph. D., Assistant Professor of European History.
G. C. COMSTOCK, Ph. B., LL. B., Professor of Astronomy.
C. A. CURTIS, A B., Professor of Military Science and Tactics.
W. W. DANIELLS, M. S., Sc. D., Professor of Chemistry.
*J. E. DAVIES, A. M., M. D., LL. D., Professor of Electricity and Magnetism and Mathematical Physics.
L. W. DOWLING, Ph. D., Assistant Professor of Mathematics.
J. C. ELSOM, M. D., Professor of Physical Culture.
R. T. ELY, Ph. D., LL. D., Professor of Political Economy.
ANNIE C. EMERY, Ph. D., Assistant Professor of Classical Philology.
D. B. FRANKENBURGER, A. M., Professor of Rhetoric and Oratory.
**J. C. FREEMAN, LL. D., Professor of English Literature.
W. F. GIESE, A. M., Assistant Professor of Romance Languages.
R. A. HARPER, Ph. D., Professor of Botany.
C. H. HASKINS, Ph. D., Professor of Institutional History.
H. W. HILLYER, Ph. D., Assistant Professor of Organic Chemistry.
W. H. HOBBS, Ph. D., Professor of Mineralogy and Petrology.
JOSEPH JASTROW, Ph. D., Professor of Experimental and Comparative Psychology.
F. G. HUBBARD, Ph. D., Professor of the English Language.
LOUIS KAHLENBERG, Ph. D., Assistant Professor of Physical Chemistry.
ALEXANDER KERR, A. M., Professor of the Greek Language and Literature
A. A. KNOWLTON, A. M., Assistant Professor of English.
A. G. LAIRD, Ph. D., Assistant Professor of Ancient Languages.
W. S. MARSHALL, Ph. D., Assistant Professor of Zoology.
ABBY S. MAYHEW, Mistress of Ladies' Hall, Director of Gymnastics for Women.

---
*Died January 22d, 1900.
**On leave of absence in Europe.

B. H. MEYER, Ph. D., Assistant Professor of Sociology.
W. S. MILLER, M. D., Assistant Professor of Vertebrate Anatomy.
J. E. OLSON, B. L., Professor of the Scandinavian Languages and Literature.
M. V. O'SHEA, B. L., Professor of the Science and Art of Education.
E. T. OWEN, A. B., Professor of the French Language and Literature.
F. A. PARKER, Professor of Music.
J. F. A. PYRE, Ph. D., Assistant Professor of English Literature.
J. B. PARKINSON, A. M., Professor of Constitutional and International Law.
P. S. REINSCH, Ph. D., LL. B., Assistant Professor of Political Science.
W. H. ROSENSTENGEL, A. M., Professor of the German Language and Literature.
H. L. RUSSELL, Ph. D., Professor of Bacteriology.
W. A. SCOTT, Ph. D., Professor of Economic History and Theory.
F. C. SHARP, Ph. D., Assistant Professor of Philosophy.
*E. B. SKINNER, A. B., Assistant Professor of Mathematics.
M. S. SLAUGHTER, Ph. D., Professor of Latin.
C. S. SLICHTER, M. S., Professor of Applied Mathematics.
C. F. SMITH, Ph. D., Professor of Greek and Classical Philology.
B. W. SNOW, Ph. D., Professor of Physics.
**H. A. SOBER, A. B., Assistant Professor of Latin.
J. W. STEARNS, LL. D., Professor of Philosophy and Pedagogy.
F. J. TURNER, Ph. D., Professor of American History.
C. R. VAN HISE, Ph. D., Professor of Geology.
C. A. VAN VELZER, Ph. D., Professor of Mathematics.
E. K. J. H. VOSS, Ph. D., Associate Professor of German Philology.
W. H. WILLIAMS, A. B., Professor of Hebrew and Hellenistic Greek.
R. W. WOOD, A. B., Assistant Professor of Physics.
KATHARINE ALLEN, Ph. D., Assistant in Latin.
L. O. ATHERTON, M. S., Assistant in Anatomy.
ARTHUR BEATTY, Ph. D., Instructor in English.
H. G. A. BRAUER, M. A., Instructor in French.
JENNIE H. BUTT, Student Assistant in Elocution.
W. B. CAIRNS, Ph. D., Instructor in English.
MILDRED A. CASTLE, Student Assistant in French.
A. N. COOK, M. A., Assistant in Chemistry.
J. E. DAVIES, B. L., Student Assistant in Gymnastics.
R. E. N. DODGE, M. A., Instructor in English.
ABBIE F. EATON, M. L., Instructor in German.

---

*On leave of absence.
**On leave of absence in Europe.

R. E. FOWLER, B. S., Assistant in Chemistry.
W. D. FROST, M. S., Instructor in Bacteriology.
LUCY M. GAY, B. L., Instructor in French.
SALLY B. HARRIS, Assistant in Physical Culture.
ROSALIA A. HATHERELL, B. S., Assistant in Biology.
SABENA M. HERFUTH, M. L., Assistant in German.
MAY HUNT, M. L., Instructor in English.
G. S. ISHIKAWA, Student Assistant in Gymnastics.
*E. D. JONES, Ph. D., Instructor in Statistics and Economics.
LOUISE P. KELLOGG, M. L., Assistant in Ancient and Medieval History.
F. T. KELLY, G. S., Instructor in Hebrew and Hellenistic Greek.
O. G. LIBBY, Ph. D., Instructor in History.
F. W. MEISNEST, B. S., Instructor in German.
A. M. O'DEA, Instructor in Athletics.
F. B. PETERSON, B. L., Student Assistant in Gymnastics.
W. H. PYRE, B. L., Instructor in Elocution and Oratory.
HARRIET T. REMINGTON, M. L., Instructor in German.
THEODORE RUNNING, Ph. D., Instructor in Mathematics.
C. H. SHANNON, Ph. D., Instructor in Latin.
J. C. SHEDD, Ph. D., Instructor in Physics.
W. H. SHELDON, Ph. D., Assistant in Philosophy.
C. H. SMITH, B. S., Instructor in Physics.
S. E. SPARLING, Ph. D., Assistant in Political Science.
C. G. STANGEL, B. S., Assistant in Physics.
SUSAN A. STERLING, M. L., Instructor in German.
W. D. TALLMAN, B. S., Instructor in Mathematics.
E. A. THURBER, M. A., Instructor in English.
H. G. TIMBERLAKE, M. S., Instructor in Botany.
ALFRED TINGLE, Ph. D., Assistant in Chemistry.
T. K. URDAHL, Ph. D., Assistant in Economics and Statistics.

ADMISSION TO THE UNIVERSITY.

I. EXAMINATIONS AT THE UNIVERSITY.

The regular examinations of the University are two in number; one in June and one in September. The earlier one is intended for those who wish to be examined while fresh from their preparatory studies and thus to set at rest all doubts as to their admission; and for those who wish to test their qualifications at an early date that they may have time to make up deficiencies if necessary. The September examination immediately precedes the opening of the fall term.

*On leave of absence.

For the current year the earlier examinations will be held on Thursday and Friday, June 14th and 15th, beginning at 9 o'clock A. M. The later examinations will be held on Tuesday and Wednesday, September 25th and 26th, beginning at 9 o'clock A. M. Students who are in any doubt as to their qualifications are urged to present themselves in June. All candidates are required to be present at 9 o'clock on the first day of the examinations.

Examinations will also be held on Thursday and Friday, February 7th and 8th, 1901.

The examinations will cover the following topics:

GROUP I. *Subjects required of all candidates:*

a. **Geography**, political and physical.
b. **History of the United States**: Channing, Thomas, Johnston, Montgomery (students), or an equivalent.
c. **Arithmetic.**
d. **Algebra**: Addition, substraction, multiplication, division, equations of the first degree with one unknown number, simultaneous equations of the first degree, factors, highest common factor, lowest common multiple, quadratic equations, simultaneous equations above the first degree, theory of indices (positive, negative, fractional, and zero), and radicals.

   Geometry: Plane and solid geometry. In solid geometry special attention should be given to the geometry of the sphere.
e. **English in General**: No pupil will be accepted in English whose written work is notably deficient in point of *spelling, punctuation, idiom, or division into paragraphs.*
f. **English Composition**: 1. The candidate will be required to write two essays of not less than two hundred words each, on subjects chosen by himself from a considerable number—perhaps ten or fifteen—set before him in the examination paper, and one of the topics chosen must be taken from the books assigned for general reading under English Literature.

   2. In place of the essay on the topic drawn from the books set for general reading, the candidate will be allowed to offer an exercise book containing the first draft of essays written during his preparatory course, on topics taken from the works prescribed for general reading. These essays must be written under the eye of the teacher without consulting the

books from which the subjects are taken, and without other assistance, must be kept in the care of the teacher, and sent by him to the examiner at least one week before the date of the entrance examination, with his certificate that they have been written in accordance with these requirements.

g. English Literature. The following lists include (1) a series of books for general reading, which may also be used as a basis for work in English Composition; (2) a limited number of masterpieces for thorough study. In addition to the essays called for under the head of *English Composition*, there will be required such further tests as seem suited to secure a careful reading of all the books prescribed in series (1). The written statement of the teacher will be sufficient, in general, for this purpose. In the case of the books set for more thorough study, the candidate will be examined on subject-matter, form, and substance, and the examination will be of such a character as to require a thorough study of each of the works named, in order to pass it successfully.

I. For General Reading and Composition work:

1900—Pope's Translation of the Iliad (Books I., VI., XXII., and XXIV.) The Sir Roger de Coverley Papers, Goldsmith's Vicar of Wakefield, Scott's Ivanhoe, De Quincey's Flight of a Tartar Tribe, Cooper's Last of the Mohicans, Tennyson's Princess, Lowell's Vision of Sir Launfal.

1901, 1902—George Eliot's Silas Marner, Pope's Translations of the Iliad (Books I., VI., XXII., and XXIV). The Sir Roger de Coverley Papers, Goldsmith's Vicar of Wakefield, Scott's Ivanhoe, Shakespeare's Merchant of Venice, Cooper's Last of the Mohicans, Tennyson's Princess, Coleridge's Rime of the Ancient Mariner.

1903, 1904, 1905—The Sir Roger de Coverly Papers, Goldsmith's Vicar of Wakefield, Scott's Ivanhoe, Shakespeare's The Merchant of Venice and Julius Cæsar, Coleridge's The Ancient Mariner, Carlyle's Essay on Burns, Tennyson's The Princess, Lowell's The Vision of Sir Launfal, George Eliot's Silas Marner.

2. For thorough study.

1900—Shakespeare's Macbeth, Milton's Paradise Lost (Books I. and II.), Burke on Conciliation with America, Macaulay's Essays on Milton and Addison.

1901—Shakespeare's Macbeth, Milton's L'Allegro, Il Penseroso,

Comus, and Lycidas, Burke on Conciliation with America, Macaulay's Essays on Milton and Addison.

1902—Shakespeare's Macbeth, Milton's L'Allegro, Il Penseroso, Comus, and Lycidas, Burke on Conciliation with America, Macaulay's Essays on Milton and Addison.

1903, 1904, 1905—Shakespeare's Macbeth, Milton's Lycidas, Comus, L'Allegro, and Il'Penseroso, Burke's Speech on Conciliation with America, Macaulay's Essays on Milton and Addison.

h. **English Grammar.** There is included in the requirement for entrance a knowledge of the leading facts of English Grammar, and tests of such knowledge will be made a part of the examination.

GROUP II. *Requirements for Admission to the Ancient Classical Course.*

a. The studies enumerated in Group I.

b. **Latin**: Grammar and Elementary Book (Collar and Daniell, Tuell and Fowler, Bennett, Scudder); Cæsar, four books or an equivalent amount of Nepos, Cæsar (at least two books) and selections; Cicero, seven orations (selections from the letters as given, for example, in Kelsey's edition, may be substituted for two orations); Virgil, six books; Composition (preferably in connection with Cæsar and Cicero, as for example in Daniell's Exercises in Latin Composition.)

c. **Greek**: Grammar; Lessons: Xenophon's Anabasis, four books; Homer's Iliad, three books or an equivalent amount of the Odyssey; Greek composition.

d. **Ancient History**: Myers' and Allen's Ancient History; Myers' Ancient History or a substantial equivalent.

e. **English History**: Gardiner's English History for Schools, or Montgomery's Leading Facts of English History.

Students prepared to enter the Modern Classical Course may be admitted as freshmen to the Ancient Classical Course and graduate with the degree of Bachelor of Arts on the following conditions: They shall take elementary Greek five times per week during the Freshman year; continue Greek four times a week during Sophomore and Junior years and complete all the other requirements of the Ancient Classical Course.

GROUP III. *Requirements for Admission to the Modern Classical Course.*

a. The studies enumerated in Group I.
b. **Latin** as stated in Group II., b.
c. **History** as stated in Group II., d., e.
d. **German:** Correct pronunciation; thorough drill in grammar and syntax, giving particular attention to translations from English into German; fifty (50) lessons of any standard reader including the memorizing of at least ten (10) poems; one term of prose readings. Practice in the oral and written use of German should be combined with the grammar and reading lessons. For prose readings, one or more of the following are recommended: Volkmann's Kleine Geschichten: Storm's Immensee; Heyse's L'Arrabbiata; Hillern's Hoeher als die Kirche; Wildenbruch's Der Lezte.

GROUP IV. *Requirements for Admission to the Civic Historical Course.*
a. The studies enumerated in Group I.
b. **Latin** as stated in Group II., b.
c. **History** as stated in Group II., d., e.
d. One of the following:
   1. German as stated in Group III., d., or
   2. Science as stated in Group V., c., d., e.; or
   3. English literature as stated in Group VI., c.; and physics as stated in Group V., c.

GROUP V. *Requirements for admission to the General Science Course, to all the Courses in Engineering, and to the Four Years' Pharmacy Course.*
a. The studies named in Group I.
b. **German** as stated in Group III., d., or an equivalent amount of French.
c. **Physics**: Carhart and Chute, Gage, or Avery, with laboratory work.
d. **Physiology**: Martin's The Human Body (briefer course), or an equivalent.
e. **Botany**: Two terms' study required, of which at least 60 hours shall be laboratory work devoted to the anatomy and physiology of plants. A knowledge of the main groups of cryptogams is required.
f. **Adaptive Work**, amounting to one daily recitation for two years.

This may consist of various subjects. The University advises:
   1. Two years' daily work in French or Latin; or,

2. One year's work in history, equivalent to that stated in Group II., d., e., and

One year's work in English literature, as stated in Group VI., c.

If these studies cannot be taken, a selection from the following studies may be offered:

3. Rhetoric, civil government, mental science, theory and art of teaching, zoology, astronomy, or other science. No subject can be offered which has been pursued in high school for a shorter time than twelve weeks, or which is less in amount than a standard high school text-book on the subject. The total amount offered must be equivalent to a daily recitation for two years. The two years' work may be made up of these studies in any combinations, under the conditions stated above.

GROUP VI. *Requirements for Admission to the English Course.*
a. **The studies named in Group I.**
b. **History** as prescribed in Group II., d., e.
c. **English Literature**: A brief outline of the History of the English Literature. Careful study of representative writers. For the outline history there may be substituted a study of Gayley's Classic Myths in English Literature. The whole to be equal to a daily recitation for one year.
d. **Science** as prescribed in Group V., c., d., e.
e. **Adaptive Work** as stated in Group V., f.

Students entering this course are advised to present either Latin, French, or German as their adaptive work. Candidates not presenting any foreign language are urged to make a thorough review of English grammar. Experience has shown that a not inconsiderable number of students fail in French and German at the University from deficient preparation in English grammar.

Real equivalents will be accepted for the requirements given above. Students desiring admission into any course must present those requirements which are essential to the work of the course.

Admission of Special Students.

Candidates under twenty-one years of age desiring to take special courses are required to present the same qualifications as candidates for one of the regular courses.

Persons twenty-one years of age, who are not candidates for a degree, and who wish to take special studies, are permitted to do so upon giving satisfactory evidence that they are prepared to take the desired studies advantageously. If they subsequently desire to become candidates for a degree, or to take a regular course, they must pass the required entrance examinations.

II. Admission Upon Certificate.

Accredited Schools.—Any high school or academy whose course of instruction covers the branches requisite for admission to one or more of the courses of the University may be admitted to its accredited list of preparatory schools after a satisfactory examination by a committee of the Faculty. Application for such an examination may be made by an officer of the school to the President of the University, on the basis of which a committee of the Faculty will examine the course of study and the methods of instruction in the school, and on their favorable recommendation and the concurrence of the Faculty it will be entered upon the accredited list of the University. No school will be placed upon the list whose course of study is not fully equal to the four-year course of high schools recommended by the State Superintendent. The *graduates* of such an approved school will be received by the University, on presentation of a proper certificate, into any of its courses for which they have been fitted. Students of an accredited school who are not graduates must expect to be examined on the same terms as other candidates.

The University desires to keep itself fully informed regarding the work of its accredited schools by means of annual reports and frequent inspections. Every accredited school is required to report each year concerning its teachers, course of study, methods of instruction, and material equipment. Blank forms are furnished by the University for this purpose. The University sends out inspectors at its own expense and at the convenience of the members of the staff. Especial attention is called to the necessity of promptly notifying the Secretary of the Committee on Accredited Schools of changes in the dates of examinations and vacations.

Principals of accredited schools are requested to note the statements regarding English, German, Latin, and adaptive work under Terms of Admission; and especial attention is called to the examination of freshmen in English as stated on p. 74.

ACCREDITED SCHOOLS.
For all Courses.

School.	Principal.
Austin (Ill.),	B. F. Buck.
Beaver Dam: Wayland Academy,	H. J. Vosburgh.
Beloit,	F. E. Converse.
Cedar Rapids, (Ia.)	Abbie S. Abbott.
Chicago High Schools:	
Calumet,	A. S. Hall.
Englewood,	J. E. Armstrong.
Hyde Park,	C. W. French.
Jefferson,	C. A. Cook.
Lake,	E. F. Stearns.
Lake View,	J. H. Norton.
Marshall,	L. J. Block.
Medill,	S. B. Sabin.
North Division,	O. S. Westcott.
North-West Division,	F. P. Fisk.
South Chicago,	C. I. Parker.
South Division,	E. R. Boyer.
West Division,	G. M. Clayberg.
Chicago: Harvard School,	J. J. Schobinger. / J. C. Grant.
Chicago: The Chi. Manual Training School,	H. H. Belfield.
Council Bluffs (Ia.),	W. N. Clifford.
Davenport (Ia.),	W. D. Wells.
Delafield: St. John's Military Academy,	Rev. S. T. Smythe.
Des Moines (Ia.); West,	W. O. Riddell.
Detroit (Mich.): School for Boys,	Mrs. Mary E. Whitton. / F. D. Green. / F. E. Searle.
Dubuque (Ia.),	F. H. Smart.
Evanston (Ill.): Evanston Township	H. L. Boltwood.
Evansville,	H. F. Kling.
Faribault (Minn.): Shattuck School,	James Dobbin.
Fond du Lac: Grafton Hall,	B. Talbot Rogers.
Hillside Home School,	Ellen C. Lloyd-Jones. / Jane Lloyd-Jones.
Janesville,	D. D. Mayne.
Kenosha,	E. C. Wiswall.
La Crosse,	W. R. Hemmenway.
La Grange (Ill.): Lyons Township,	E. G. Cooley.

ACCREDITED SCHOOLS.

School.	Principal.
Lake Forest (Ill.): Lake Forest Academy,	A. G. Welch.
Madison,	J. H. Hutchison.
Madison: Wisconsin Academy,	Charlt'e E. Richmond.
Menominee (Mich.),	B. S. Hopkins.
Milwaukee: East Division,	A. J. Rogers.
Milwaukee: South Division,	A. Burch.
Milwaukee: West Division,	C. E. McLenegan.
Milwaukee Academy,	Julius H. Pratt, Jr.
Milwaukee-Downer Col.: Seminary Dep't.,	Miss E. C. Sabin.
Monroe,	A. F. Rote.
Morgan Park (Ill.): Morgan Park Academy,	Wayland Chase.
Oak Park (Ill.),	J. C. Hanna.
Omaha (Nebr.),	A. H. Waterhouse.
Orchard Lake (Mich.): Mich. Mil. Academy,	F. Whitton.
Racine College,	H. D. Robinson.
Rockford (Ill.),	B. D. Parker.
Sheboygan,	J. S. Roessler.
Sioux City (Ia.),	W. H. Trumbull.
Waukesha: Carroll College,	W. L. Rankin.
Wauwatosa,	E. C. Cornelius.
Winona (Minn.),	W. A. Bartlett.

For Ancient Classical, Modern Classical, and Civic Historical Courses.

Rochester: Rochester Academy,	C. H. Farnum.

For Modern Classical, Civic Historical, General Science, English, Engineering, Four Years' Pharmacy, and Agricultural Courses.

Appleton: Ryan High School,	R. W. Pringle.
Ashland,	J. T. Hooper.
Aurora (Ill.): East,	W. C. Hazzard,
Aurora (Ill.): West,	Katharine Reynolds.
Baraboo,	H. A. Whipple.
Bayfield,	M. N. McIver.
Beaver Dam,	H. B. Hubbell.
Berlin,	F. A. Lowell.
Boscobel,	G. W. Gehrand.
Brodhead,	A. P. Hollis.
Burlington,	J. M. Turner.
Burlington (Ia.),	E. Poppe.
Chicago: Kenwood Institute,	Annice E. Butts.
Chippewa Falls,	S. B. Toby.

		PRINCIPAL.
.	. . . .	R. E. LOVELAND.
.	. . . .	M. H. JACKSON.
.	. . . .	J. M. STEVENS.
.	. . . .	E. A. PARKS.
.	. . . .	C. W. RITTENBURG.
.	. . . .	F. J. WELLS.
.	. . . .	A. W. BRETT.
.	. . . .	DE WITT ELWOOD.
.	. . . .	M. S. FRAWLEY.
.	. . . .	C. D. ROSA.
.	. . . .	C. D. KIPP.
.	. . . .	ELIZABETH WATERS.
.	. . . .	J. A. HAGEMANN.
.	. . . .	S. E. RAINES.
.	. . . .	G. T. BLYND.
.	. . . .	W. O. BROWN.
.	. . . .	A. W. BURTON.
.	. . . .	B. B. JACKSON.
. Train. H. School,		C. E. EMMERICH.
.	. . . .	A. H. TUTTLE.
.	. . . .	MISS A. F. OLCOTT.
.	. . . .	W. J. HAMMILL.
.	. . . .	J. S. BROWN.
.	. . . .	A. M. OLSON.
.	. . . .	J. N. FOSTER.
.	. . . .	L. L. CLARKE.
.	. . . .	W. H. LUEHR.
.	. . . .	H. J. EVANS.
.	. . . .	C. J. BARR.
.	. . . .	J. S. MCCOWAN.
.	. . . .	WM. KITTLE.
.	. . . .	J. E. HOYT.
.	. . . .	ANNA E. ANDERSON.
.	. . . .	A. R. JOLLEY.
.	. . . .	R. L. COOLEY.
.	. . . .	H. A. SIMONDS.
.	. . . .	OTTO GAFFRON.
.	. . . .	W. G. CLOUGH.
.	. . . .	J. A. PRATT.
.	. . . .	E. C. CROSBY.
.	. . . .	A. E. BRAINERD.

ACCREDITED SCHOOLS. 69

School.	Principal.
Ripon,	A. W. Tressler.
River Falls,	J. W. T. Ames.
Shullsburg,	E. L. Hancock.
Sinsinawa: St. Clara's Academy,	Dominican Sisters.
Sparta,	F. E. Doty.
Sterling (Ill.): Sterling Township,	O. L. Miller.
Stevens Point,	J. W. Simmons.
Stoughton,	A. H. Sholtz.
Superior: Blaine,	J. S. Griffin.
Superior: Nelson Dewey,	M. C. Potter.
Tomah,	C. H. Maxson.
Watertown,	C. F. Viebahn.
Waukesha,	H. L. Terry.
Waupaca,	C. R. Showalter.
Waupun: South Ward,	G. F. Loomis.
Wausau,	C. C. Parlin.
West Depere,	G. Guthormsen.
Whitewater,	H. C. Buell.

For Modern Classical, Civic Historical, General Science, Engineering, Four Years' Pharmacy, and Agricultural Courses.

Prescott, ... R. B. MacLean.

For Modern Classical, Civic Historical, English, and Agricultural Courses.

McGregor (Ia.), ... F. N. Williams.

For Civic Historical, General Science, English, Engineering, Four Years' Pharmacy and Agricultural Courses.

Mauston, ... A. H. Fletcher.

For Civic Historical, English and Agricultural Courses.

Dixon (Ill.), ... C. W. Groves.
Oregon (Ill.), ... W. J. Sutherland.
Sandwich (Ill.), ... W. W. Woodbury.

For General Science, English, Engineering, Four Years' Pharmacy and Agricultural Courses.

Antigo, ... F. F. Showers.
Appleton: Third Ward, ... W. F. Winsey.
Arcadia, ... G. O. Banting.

School.	Principal.
Augusta,	Albert Hedler.
Black River Falls,	J. H. Derse.
Centralia,	H. L. Van Dusen.
Charles City (Ia.),	G. S. Dick.
Clintonville,	W. H. Hickok.
Cumberland,	P. L. Pease.
De Forest: Windsor Township,	E. C. Meland.
East Troy,	D. R. Jones.
Fox Lake,	C. E. Lamb.
Kewaunee,	M. McMahon.
Lake Mills,	A. B. West.
Lodi,	J. Leidenberg.
Marshfield,	J. B. Borden.
Mason City (Ia.),	A. R. Sale.
Mayville,	L. S. Keeley.
Medford,	F. W. Thomas.
Mondovi,	J. W. Nesbit.
Milton Junction	J. T. Healy.
Neenah,	O. J. Schuster.
Neillsville,	L. W. Wood.
New Lisbon,	C. R. Thompson.
New London,	Taylor Frye.
New Richmond,	J. Callahan.
Oconomowoc,	M. M. Beddall.
Prairie du Sac,	J. F. Bergen.
Reedsburg,	W. P. Roseman.
Rhinelander,	F. S. Hyer.
Sauk City,	J. E. Phillips.
Seymour,	F. W. Axley.
Sharon,	E. T. Towne.
Spring Green,	G. F. Snyder.
Stoughton Academy,	K. A. Kasberg.
Sturgeon Bay,	E. E. Beckwith.
Two Rivers,	A. B. O'Niel.
West Bend,	D. T. Keeley.
West Salem,	C. E. Slothower.

For General Science, Engineering, Four Years' Pharmacy, and Agricultural Courses.

Rice Lake,	E. C. McClelland.
Shawano,	H. W. Rood.

For English and Agricultural Courses.

School.	Principal.
Algoma,	E. M. PHILLIPS.
Chippewa Falls: Notre Dame School,	SISTER M. F. XAVIER.
Durand,	D. E. KISER.
Elroy,	G. E. BUNSA.
Evansville Seminary,	A. H. STILWELL.
Glenwood,	A. L. THOMSEN.
Hartford,	C. L. GOTHAM.
Horicon,	P. J. ZIMMERS.
Juneau,	A. P. WEST.
Medford,	F. W. THOMAS.
Menasha,	G. H. LANDGRAF.
Omro,	E. E. SHELDON.
Onalaska,	B. F. OLTMAN.
Oregon,	FRANKLIN GOULD.
Poynette,	L. A. JONES.
Sheboygan Falls,	A. C. KINGSFORD.
Sun Prairie,	JAMES MELVILLE.

GRADUATES OF THE STATE NORMAL SCHOOLS.

The certified standing of any student in the regular courses of the Normal schools of this State will be accepted for entrance to the University in place of an examination in the subjects covered by the certificate.

The University offers a course designed especially for Normal graduates and leading to the degree of Bachelor of Philosophy in Pedagogy. This course includes advanced instruction in pedagogy and those studies in language and science, both required and elective, which will best fit the graduate of our Normal schools for the successful conduct of his chosen profession. To this course graduates of the Normal schools will be admitted with the rank of junior on the presentation of their diplomas. Graduates of the Normal schools who desire admission to the other courses of the University will be admitted to such courses with the provisional grade of junior. They will be required, however, to take two years of work of rank equivalent to that of juniors and seniors in the University and will be required to make good deficiencies in the work of the freshman and sophomore years. Full credit will be given for all work done in the Normal schools which is equivalent to that of the University courses.

STUDENTS FROM OTHER COLLEGES AND UNIVERSITIES.

Students from other institutions, who have pursued standard college courses equivalent to those of this University, will be admitted to a like standing upon the presentation of proper certificates of creditable standing and honorable dismission. Students of other colleges of good standing who have not taken such standard courses, but who have studied one year in the college proper, may be admitted to the University as special students without examination, or, upon such an examination as may be necessary to determine their attainments, they may be admitted to any course or to any class for which they are found fitted. Students coming from other institutions are required to present certificates of standing and honorable dismission, and the University reserves the right to test the value of class records by actual examination.

No person will be admitted to the University later than November 1st of the year in which he expects to graduate.

GRADUATE STUDENTS.

Graduates of this University and other colleges and universities of good standing are admitted to graduate courses without examination.

CHARGES AND FEES.

A list of charges and fees is given on pages 38-40.

THE GRADUATE DEPARTMENT.

For the full statement of the organization of the Graduate Department reference is made to the heading Department of Graduate Study, pages 50-56, and for the announcement of special courses for graduates see the statements made under the Department of Study on subsequent pages.

THE UNDERGRADUATE DEPARTMENTS.

REQUIREMENTS FOR GRADUATION.

The unit-hour is the standard for computing the amount of work required for graduation. This is equal to one hour of recitation or lecture per week per one semester. Two hours of laboratory work or two hours of regularly prescribed military drill or physical exercise in the gymnasium are credited as one unit-hour. Students are expected to take 15 hours per week in recitations, lectures, and laboratory work, making 30 unit-hours per year, and 120 for the course. In addition two hours per week (one unit-hour per semester) of gymnastics are required during the first two years, making a total of four unit-hours. The men are required to drill two hours per week during the first two years, giving a credit of four unit-hours. The total requirements for class-room work, military drill, and the gymnasium are, therefore, 128 unit-hours for the men and 124 for the women.

Students excused from drill or gymnastics are required either to make up the work before graduation, or if the excuse is based on permanent incapacity, to make good the requirement by work in other departments.

No student will be permitted to receive a credit toward graduation of more than eighteen unit-hours in one semester in regular studies except by permission of the Faculty obtained in advance.

GRADUATION IN LESS THAN FOUR YEARS—
SUMMER SESSION.

The attention of students is called to the announcement of the Summer Session of the University, as given on subsequent pages of the catalogue. Work in the Summer Session will be credited in the same way as work in the regular session of the University, and by attendance at one session a total amount of credit may be acquired not exceeding six unit-hours.

Students who desire to graduate in three years in one of the regular four-year courses may do so by taking 18 hours of recitations per week and by attending three Summer Sessions. Permission to take work to this amount will be given only to students whose standing in their studies is wholly satisfactory. No credit will be given for repetition in the Summer Session of studies taken in the regular session of the University, or for repeating in the University work done in the summer. Students will therefore need to select carefully their work for the summer with reference to the required and elective studies of the course in which they intend to graduate. The Summer Session offers exceptionally good opportunities for the preparation of senior thesis. Any student who expects to shorten his course by means of the Summer Session should consult his class officer in selecting his studies.

ADJUSTMENT OF UNDERGRADUATE AND LAW COURSES.

The courses of the College of Letters and Science and those of the College of Law have been so adjusted to each other that it is now possible for a student to graduate from both colleges of the University in six years. Students in the College of Letters and Science will be permitted to elect studies in the College of Law during the last two years of their course; the amount to be thus elected is not to exceed a total of six hours per week for one year. This privilege will not be extended to Normal graduates attempting to graduate in two years, nor to undergraduates of other colleges who enter this University with the rank of Seniors. Students who have completed this amount of work in the Law School will be admitted to the Middle Class of the College of Law on graduation from the College of Letters and Science, thus enabling them to complete the course for the degree of Bachelor of Law in two additional years. Members of the College of Law will also be permitted to elect studies in the College of Letters and Science which are related to the studies of their professional course, and may receive credit for this work in their law course, to an amount not exceeding four hours per week for one year.

ENGLISH FOR GRADUATION.

Course 1 in English, as described on page 112, is required of all freshmen. Early in the first semester the freshmen will be examined in English composition. This examination will be a practical one. The student will be required to write an essay, or more than one, on a familiar theme, planning his work by paragraphs and constructing both paragraphs and sentences in accordance with the simpler principles of composition. The stress will be laid on neatness of manuscript and the avoidance of errors in spelling, punctuation, and grammar. These are essentials. The examination is to ascertain the student's ability to put material with which he is familiar into clear, correct English, rather than his ability to recite rhetorical or grammatical rules. A students who fails in this examination will, for the present, be allowed to take English composition twice a week for one year as a preparatory study, and must take English 1 later in his course. Admission to course 1 is provisional. Students will be promptly dropped into the preparatory class if they are unable to carry the work.

On the completion of course 1, a provisional pass mark is given; if at any time, later in his course, a student is reported as deficient or careless in English composition he will be required to take additional work in that subject.

SENIOR THESIS.

All candidates for the baccalaureate degree are required to present a graduating thesis, the subject of which must be approved by the class officer and the professor at the head of the department under which the candidate is doing the work represented by the thesis. This approval, in writing, must be secured by the student and deposited with the registrar not later than the middle of October of his senior year. The thesis must represent some phase of the student's work during the later years of his course, and must have the character of a scholarly dissertation on the subject. The thesis must be typewritten on paper of good quality, 8x10 inches in size, and must be bound according to specifications furnished by the Librarian of the University.

Before the thesis is accepted, it must be approved by the instructor under whom the work has been done, and by the head of the department. If accepted, the thesis becomes the property of the University, and is deposited in the University Library. Thesis in the College of Letters and Science must be completed and deposited in the library by June 1st.

UNDERGRADUATE COURSES.

The University offers, in the College of Letters and Science, seven courses of study leading to the bachelor's degree: The *Ancient Classical Course*, leading to the degree of Bachelor of Arts; the *Modern Classical*, the *English*, and the *Civic Historical* courses, leading to the degree of Bachelor of Letters; the *General Science* and *Pre-medical* courses, leading to the degree of Bachelor of Science; the course for *Normal graduates*, leading to the degree of Bachelor of Philosophy in Pedagogy.

In the *Ancient Classical* and the *Modern Classical* courses, languages, ancient and modern, are the central studies. In the *General Science* and *Pre-medical* courses, science occupies the leading place; in the *English Course*, the English language and literature; in the *Civic Historical Course*, history, economics, and political science are the main lines.

The Pre-medical Course is intended to give a broad and solid foundation for the professional medical course, together with collegiate culture. Students desiring a similar course of scientific study introductory to the practice of pharmacy are referred to the account of the Four Years' Course in Pharmacy on a subsequent page.

The attention of students is directed to the opportunity offered in each course for election during Sophomore year. Through this privilege students can elect courses which are antecedent to the major study of junior and senior years. Since it is necessary for students to elect their major study at the opening of junior year, it will be wise for sophomores to consult with their class officers regarding this study.

Students who desire to specialize in a department which regularly offers no sophomore study in the course that they have entered may avail themselves of this means of securing the special instruction which they desire. This arrangement may be employed, for example, by students in the General Science Course, who desire to study the history, English, or languages offered in the sophomore year of other courses and to continue the studies of the selected department during junior and senior years. Similar combinations can be made by students in other courses.

GROUP STUDENTS.

Students who desire to extend the prosecution of a major study beyond the amount which would naturally come in the courses as described, may be accepted as group students in any department at the opening of the sophomore year. In this case they may substitute studies assigned by the head of the department to the amount of five hours in the place of studies required during sophomore year. In this manner, provision may be made for special study in those departments whose work does not ordinarily begin in sophomore year, such as philosophy, pedagogy, geology, astronomy, and bacteriology, and also for extending the courses in other departments.

Students who avail themselves of this privilege must complete before graduation at least 10 unit-hours of science and 24 unit-hours

REQUIREMENTS FOR DEGREES.

of language study in two languages besides English. The degree given will be that of the student's course with the name of the department in which the major study lies, but a student of the Ancient Classical Course will not receive the B. A. degree unless he completes the Latin and Greek of the sophomore year.

REQUIREMENTS FOR THE JUNIOR AND SENIOR YEARS.

In all courses the requirements for the two upper years are alike and are as follows:

Junior and Senior Years: The student must elect a major study from one department to the amount of five hours per week for two years. This amount, however, may include the senior thesis, for which a credit of two hours per week is given during senior year. All required studies which have been postponed from sophomore year must be completed and courses must be elected sufficient to complete 120 unit-hours of class and laboratory work, besides the required drill and gymnastics.

The major study may be elected by a student from any course or from any department which he is prepared to enter—in a language, or science, in philosophy, or history, etc. If the major is selected from the departments of ancient languages a smaller amount is permitted in consideration of the large amount of time devoted to these subjects in freshman and sophomore years. The total amount need be only five hours for one year, besides the thesis, in Greek and Latin or in both languages together.

REQUIREMENTS FOR THE DEGREE OF BACHELOR OF ARTS.

Ancient Classical Course.

Freshman Year: Greek 5*; Latin 4; mathematics 3; English 3; military drill 2; gymnastics 2; 34 unit-hours for the year, of which 30 are in class room.

Sophomore Year: Greek 3; Latin 3; modern language 4; science 5; history 2 or 3; elective 2-5; military drill 2; gymnastics 2; 34 unit-hours required for the year, of which 30 are in class room and laboratory.

During the Sophomore year the student must take military drill and gymnastics and must elect two of the three languages offered. From the remainder of the list he must choose enough to make a

---

*The figures denote the number of recitations per week.

total of 15 hours per week in regular class exercises, completing in junior and senior years studies postponed from sophomore year.

Junior and Senior Years: See p. 77.

REQUIREMENTS FOR THE DEGREE OF BACHELOR OF LETTERS.

1. Modern Classical Course.

Freshman Year: German 5*; Latin 4; mathematics 3; English 3; military drill 2; gymnastics 2; 34 unit-hours for the year, of which 30 are in class exercises.

Sophomore Year: German 3; Latin 3; French 4; science 5; history 2 or 3; elective 2-5; military drill 2; gymnastics 2; 34 unit-hours for the year, of which 30 are in class room and laboratory.

During the sophomore year a student must take military drill and gymnastics and must take two of the three languages offered. From the remainder of the list he must choose enough to make a total of 15 hours per week in regular class exercises, completing in junior and senior years studies postponed from sophomore year.

Junior and Senior Years: See p. 77.

2. Civic Historical Course (School of Economics, Political Science, and History.)

Freshman Year: Latin or German 4*; mathematics 3; history 5; English 3; military drill 2; gymnastics 2; 34 unit-hours for the year, of which 30 are in class exercises.

Sophomore Year: German 4 (if not taken in freshman year); French 4; history 3; economics and political science 3; science 5; elective 3-5; military drill 2; gymnastics 2; 34 unit-hours, of which 30 are in class room and laboratory.

During the sophomore year the student must take military drill and gymnastics, and from the remainder he must elect enough to make a total of 15 hours per week in regular class exercises, completing in junior and senior years studies postponed from sophomore year.

Junior and Senior Years: See p. 77.

3. English Course.

Freshman Year: German 4*; mathematics 3; history 5; English 3; military drill 2; gymnastics 2; 34 unit-hours for the year, of which 30 are in class exercises.

REQUIREMENTS FOR DEGREES.

Sophomore Year: Required study, German 4; Foreign language besides German 4; science 5; Anglo-Saxon 3; English literature 5; elective 3-5; military drill 2; gymnastics 2.

The student must take military drill and gymnastics and elect 11 hours from the work enumerated above, completing in junior and senior years studies postponed from sophomore year.

Junior and Senior Years: See p. 77.

REQUIREMENTS FOR THE DEGREE OF BACHELOR OF SCIENCE.

1. General Science Course.

Freshman Year: Biology 5*; German 4; mathematics 3; English 3; military drill 2; gymnastics 2; 34 unit-hours for the year, 30 of which are in class exercises.

Sophomore Year: German 3; French 4; physics 5; chemistry 5; elective 3-5; military drill 2; gymnastics 2; 34 unit-hours for the year, of which 30 are in class room and laboratory.

During the sophomore year the student must take military drill and gymnastics and elect 15 hours per week in regular class exercises, completing in junior and senior years studies postponed from sophomore year.

Junior and Senior Years: See p. 77.

2. Pre-Medical Course.

The required studies of the four years' Pre-Medical Course, leading to the degree of Bachelor of Science, are the same as those of the General Science Course. The students in the Pre-medical Course are required to turn their scientific work and their elections in the direction of those sciences which are preliminary to the study of medicine.

3. Pre-Engineering Course.

The required studies of the Pre-Engineering Course, leading to the degree of Bachelor of Science, are the same as those of the General Science Course. Students taking this course who expect to complete their work in Engineering in two subsequent years, are required to include among their electives, in the junior and senior years, those portions of the engineering course which they propose to take, and which they have not had, as are given in the freshman and sophomore years in the College of Engineering in that particular course.

---

*The figures denote the number of recitations per week.

4. Engineering and Agricultural Courses and Four-Years' Pharmacy Course.

For details of these courses, look under College of Engineering, College of Agriculture, and School of Pharmacy, on later pages.

REQUIREMENTS FOR THE DEGREE OF BACHELOR OF PHILOSOPHY IN PEDAGOGY.

Course for Normal Graduates.

Graduates of the advanced courses of the State Normal schools are admitted to advanced standing in the various courses of the University on conditions which may be found on page 71 of this catalogue. The following special course for normal graduates has been arranged, leading in two years to the degree of Bachelor of Philosophy in Pedagogy. The course contains a minimum required amount of advanced studies in philosophy and pedagogy, with opportunity for further elections in those subjects. It requires also a continuous study of foreign language during the two years of the course. In other directions the student may elect his studies. It is expected that the normal graduate will give especial attention to fitting himself for teaching in one or two of the main lines of instruction, and the requirements and electives have been so arranged as to permit him to attain this end. He may devote himself especially to science, to literature, to history, or to any practical combination of these studies. He will be required, however, to make one of these lines of study his major work, and will not be permitted to elect a large number of short, scattered courses of instruction, since it is the especial design of this course to enlarge and complete his knowledge in certain definite directions.

The attention of the student is called to the necessity of directing his work from the first to the preparation of a satisfactory graduation thesis. In most cases the thesis will probably be written on some topic suggested by pedagogy or philosophy. However, the student may arrange for his thesis in any other department, but in such case it will be necessary for him to plan his course from the beginning, so as to satisfy the requirements for a thesis.

Junior Year: Latin, French or German 4*; philosophy 3; advanced pedagogy 3; language, history, English, advanced mathematics, or science 5; electives 3 to 5; 18 hours per week required.

Senior Year: Continuation of Latin, French, or German 4; philosophy and advanced pedagogy 5; electives from language, science, history, economics, mathematics, or English 7; thesis 2; 18 hours per week required.

*The figures denote the number of recitations per week.

DEPARTMENTS OF INSTRUCTION.

Part of the courses of instruction described on the following pages are elementary courses for undergraduates, others are advanced courses for undergraduates and graduates, while still others in each department are designed especially for graduates.

PHILOSOPHY.

PROFESSOR STEARNS, PROFESSOR JASTROW, ASSISTANT PROFESSOR SHARP, DR. SHELDON.

Students who contemplate devoting special attention to philosophy may begin the subject in the sophomore or in the junior year. The courses best adapted to serve as introductory are: 1, 3, 15, 16, 17, 31, 32, and 35. Students may begin the work with any one of these.

Special seminaries will be formed to meet the needs of graduate students and of undergraduates who are specializing in philosophy.

1. General Psychology. James' Outlines of Psychology, lectures, and readings. *First semester; M., W., F., at 9 and 3.* Assistant Professor SHARP.
2. Advanced Analytic Psychology. *Second semester; twice a week.* Assistant Professor SHARP.
3. Introduction to Psychology. An elementary consideration of mental phenomena, with special reference to the functions of the senses and of the nervous system, and of the simpler psychological processes. James' Outlines of Psychology, and readings. *First semester; Tu., Th., at 9 and at 3.* Professor JASTROW.
4. Experimental Psychology. (a) Lectures and demonstrations covering in a fairly comprehensive and practical manner the field of experimental psychology. *Second semester; M., W., F., at 9.* (b) Laboratory practice course parallel with the lectures. The hours for laboratory work will be arranged on consultation. (a) and (b) together count as a full study. *Second semester; four hours weekly.* Professor JASTROW.
5. Research in Psychology. Special themes are experimentally treated and the appropriate literature critically reviewed under personal supervision. *Throughout the year; hours to be arranged on consultation.* Professor JASTROW.

6. Comparative Psychology. Lectures and assigned readings, covering the more important topics in animal psychology and in the development of the child. *Second semester; Tu., Th., at 10.* To be given in 1901-1902. Professor JASTROW.
7. Abnormal Psychology. Lectures upon illusions, dreams, hypnotism, insanity, idiocy, deaf-mutism, blindness, diseases of speech, of will, of the emotions, psychic epidemics, and allied topics. Given in 1900-1901. *Second semester; Tu., Th., at 9.* Professor JASTROW.
8. Anthropology. A brief survey of the more important problems of anthropology with special reference to the topics of psychological interest. Tylor's Anthropology. Lectures and readings. *First semester; M., W., at 3.* Professor JASTROW.
15. Deduction and Induction. *First semester; M., W., F., at 11.* Dr. SHELDON.
16. Applied Logic. Analyses of argumentative orations and of some scientific treatise, together with practice in constructing arguments. Course 21 is not required as a preliminary. *Second semester; M., W., F., at 11.* Dr. SHELDON.
17. History of Greek Philosophy. *First semester; M., W., F., at 10.* Professor STEARNS.
18. History of Modern Philosophy. *Second semester; M., W., F., at 10.* Dr. SHELDON.
19. Introduction to Modern Philosophy. *Second semester; three times a week at 8.* Dr. SHELDON.
20. The Philosophy of Modern Science. Discussion of some of the problems in the philosophy of nature. *First semester; Tu., Th., at 8.* Professor STEARNS.
21. Herbert Spencer's Doctrine of Evolution and some of its recent modifications. *Second semester; T., Th., at 8.* Dr. SHELDON.
22. The Theory of Cognition. An outline study of Descartes, Locke, and Berkeley. Hume's Treatise on Human Nature, Book I.; Kant's Critique of Pure Reason; Modern Theories. Course 17, 18, or 19, will be required preparatory to this course, except as special arrangements are made with the instructor. *Throughout the year; M., W., F., at 8.* Assistant Professor SHARP.
30. Systematic Ethics. Paulsen; System of Ethics. *Second semester; M., W., F., at 9.* Assistant Professor SHARP.
31. Problems in Applied Ethics. Course 30 is not required as a preliminary. *Second semester; Tu., Th., at 8.* Assistant Professor SHARP.

32. Advanced Systematic Ethics. Open only to students who have taken course 30. *First semester; Tu., Th., S., at 8.* Assistant Professor SHARP.
33. Aesthetics. (a) Philosophy of Art and Art Criticism. *First semester; Tu., Th., at 8.* (b) History of Art. *Second semester; Tu., Th., at 8.* Professor STEARNS.
35. General Introduction to the Study of Philosophy: being a survey of the problems and principles of philosophy, psychology, ethics, and education. This course is intended especially for students desirous of gaining a general view of the problems and methods in these subjects. *Second semester.* Professor STEARNS, Professor JASTROW, Assistant Professor SHARP, and Professor O'SHEA.

PEDAGOGY.

PROFESSOR STEARNS, PROFESSOR O'SHEA.

I. History and Philosophy of Education.

1. History of Educational Theories and Institutions, Greek, Roman and Modern, lectures, readings and essays. Special attention will be given to the development of modern educational thought. *First semester; M., W., F., at 9.* Professor STEARNS.
2. Modern Educational Systems. A comparative study of education in England, France and Germany, for graduate students. *First semester; twice a week at 8.* Professor STEARNS.
3. The Herbartian Pedagogy. Herbart's Science of Education; Rein's Pedagogics; Lange's Apperception. *Second semester; twice a week at 8.* Professor STEARNS.
4. School Supervision. The making and administration of courses of study; examination; promotions; inspections, etc. *First semester; Tu., Th., at 8.* Professor STEARNS.

Courses 3 and 4 are given in alternate years; course 3 will be given in 1900-1901.

5. The Philosophy of Education. Lectures, readings, and discussions on the nature, forms, and elements of education. *M. and W. at 9.* Professor STEARNS.
7. Seminary in Pedagogy, for the discussion of current educational problems. Open to those who have done one year's work in pedagogy. *Once a week throughout the year.* Professor STEARNS.

II. Science and Art of Education.

Mental Development. It will be the purpose in this course to consider in a theoretical and practical way the most important of the newer problems relating to the development of mind in the individual. Data will be gathered from the fields of neurology, biology, evolution, child-study, etc., and their detailed bearings upon education indicated. The hygiene and economy of mental growth and activity will have a prominent place throughout. The work will be suited to the needs of students, whether intending to teach or not. *First semester; M., W., F., at* 10. Professor O'SHEA.

Course 11 will be repeated. *Second semester; M., W., F., at* 9. Professor O'SHEA.

Teaching and Management in the High School. This course is designed as an especially practical one for those who desire to make preparation for teaching in the high school, or for supervision of grammar grade work. Opportunity will be given for observation of methods and management in the High and Grammar Schools of Madison, and this will be followed by critical discussion. *First semester; M., W., F., at* 9. Professor O'SHEA.

Course 13 will be repeated. *Second semester; M., W., F., at* 11. Professor O'SHEA.

Modern Educational Movements. The purpose of this course will be to acquaint the student with educational movements that are at present engaging the serious attention of educators. The conditions which gave rise to these movements, their aims, and the results thus far achieved will be considered; and the teachings of modern educational reformers will be critically examined. *First semester; Tu. and Th., at* 9. Professor O'SHEA.

Educational Classics. Readings from the works of great writers, ancient and modern, to ascertain their views upon education in respect alike of studies and methods. Readings will be made in Plato, Aristotle, Quintillian, Rosseau, Locke, Mill, Spencer, George Eliot. *Second semester; Tu., Th., at* 9.

Genetic Psychology. It will be the purpose in this work to study in a critical manner recent theories regarding the genesis of mental faculty in the individual and in the race. The views of Baldwin, Tarde, Hall, and others will be examined, and in addition a considerable body of original investigation bearing

upon the questions at issue will be submitted for consideration. The work is designed for students who have completed elementary studies in psychology, philosophy, and education. It will be offered in two courses: The genesis of the intellectual activities. *First semester; Tu., Th., at 10.* Professor O'SHEA.
18. Genetic Psychology. The genesis of feeling, with special reference to the ethical and social emotions. *Second semester; T., Th., at 10.* Professor O'SHEA.
19. Principles of Education. It will be the purpose in this course to consider the most fundamental laws upon which the training of the mind in all phases of educational work must depend, and to indicate in some detail their application to the making of a curriculum and method of teaching. *Second semester; M., W., F., at 10.* Professor O'SHEA.
20. Seminary for the discussion of questions affecting the professional life of the teacher. The teacher's relation to the community, to fellow teachers, to the University, and similar matters, will be discussed. The views of different members of the Faculty will be obtained. *First semester; one hour a week.* Professor O'SHEA.
21. Seminary. Work similar to course 20. *Second semester.* Professor O'SHEA.

ECONOMICS AND STATISTICS.

PROFESSOR ELY, PROFESSOR SCOTT, ASSISTANT PROFESSOR MEYER, DR. JONES, AND MR. HENRY.

Elementary Courses.

1. Economic History. A course in the economic history of England. Textbook: Gibbins' Industry in England.
Required of freshmen in the Civic Historical and English courses, and of all students who are beginning the subject of economics. *Repeated each semester, and given in connection with Course 2 in History. Tu., Th., at 8 and 9 first semester, and 2 and 3 second semester.* Professor SCOTT.
2. The Elements of Economic Science. Textbook: Ely's Outlines of Economics (college edition). This course must be taken before any one of the following courses may be elected. *Repeated each semester; Tu., Th., S., at 8 and 9.* Dr. JONES.
3. Money and Banking. Nicholson's Money and Monetary Problems, Laughlin's History of Bimetallism in the United States,

and Dunbar's History and Theory of Banking. *First semester; M., W., F., at* 8. Professor SCOTT.

4. Economic Problem. A study of socialism. Text-book: Ely's Socialism and Social Reform. Lectures and class reports on such topics as economic crises, co-operation, profit-sharing railroad problems, etc. *Second semester; M., W., F., at* 9. Dr. JONES.

5. The Economics of Agriculture. This course is designed primarily for the students of the College of Agriculture, though any student may be admitted. Lectures followed by class discussion. *Two hours per week from January 1st to April 1st.* Professor SCOTT.

6. Senior Seminary. The Seniors who write theses on economic topics meet in this Seminary for the presentation and discussion of reports on their respective topics. *Second semester; alternate weeks on Wednesday evenings at* 7. Professor SCOTT.

7. Economic Geography. Courses for graduates and undergraduates. The course will follow the outlines of the subject laid down by Ritter, and will include a discussion of the character of commercial relations, localization of industry, and such other peculiarities of the economic life of the chief European nations and the United States as can be traced to the influence of the physical environment. *First semester; Tu., Th., at* 10. Dr. JONES.

8. Statistics. The statistical method, considered as an aid in economic research. *Second semester; M., W., F., at* 10. Dr. JONES.

9. The Classical Economists. Adam Smith, Ricardo, and J. S. Mill. Study of characteristic parts of the works of these authors with lectures and class discussions. *Second semester; M., W., F., at* 8. Professor SCOTT.

10. Railway Transportation. This course is historical, economic, and legal. Lectures and assigned readings. *Second semester; M., W., at* 2. Assistant Professor MEYER.

11. Insurance. A series of lectures on the history, principles, and organization of insurance, supplemented by seminary work. *First semester; Tu., at* 5. Assistant Professor MEYER.

12. The Economic Functions of the State. This course consists of a series of lectures, historical and critical, on the state in its relation to industry, trade, and the professions, with special reference to pharmacy. *One lecture, weekly.* Assistant Professor MEYER.

13. History of Economic Thought. For undergraduates who have had courses 1 and 2, and for graduates who have not had a course in the history of economic thought. *Given in Summer Session; M., Tu., W., Th., at 3.* Professor ELY.

Graduate Courses.

14. The Distribution of Wealth. Part I. This course deals chiefly with the fundamental institutions in the existing social order and their relation to the present distribution of wealth. *Throughout the year; Tu., W., Th., at 3.* Open to graduate students and undergraduates who have had suitable preparation. Professor ELY.
15. Distribution of Wealth. Part II. A discussion of the separate factors in distribution, such as rent, interest and wages, and monopoly gains; the equilibrium of the factors in distribution; individual fortunes and differential gains; modifications in the distribution of wealth, actual and proposed, including a discussion of socialism; the distribution of wealth and social progress. *Throughout the year; Tu., W., Th., at 3.* May be taken by those who have not had Part I, Course 14. Professor ELY. (Not given in 1900-1901.)
16. Theories of Value. A critical study of value theories. Each student is expected to study carefully the writings of the theorists examined. *First semester; Tu., Th., at 12.* Professor SCOTT. (Not given in 1900-1901.)
17. Theories of Rent, Wages, Profits, and Interest. *Throughout the year; Tu., Th., at 12.* Professor SCOTT.
18. Theories of Production and Consumption. Theories of social prosperity, of population, and of capital, and the theories which concern the operation of physical forces, and the influence of the consumption of wealth on production and distribution. *Second semester; Tu., Th., at 12.* Professor SCOTT. (Not given in 1900-1901.)
19. Public Finance. A discussion of the revenues and expenditures of government. Open to graduates and advanced students. *Throughout the year; Tu., W., Th., at 4.* Professor ELY. (Not given in 1900-1901.)
20. American Public Finance. Part I. A critical and historical discussion of the finances of the Federal government. *First semester; Tu., W., Th., at 4.* Professor ELY.
21. American Public Finance. Part II. The finances of the American commonwealths, and local political units. Open to grad-

uates and advanced students. *Second semester; Tu., W., Th., at* 4. Professor ELY.

22. Economic Seminary. This is designed primarily for advanced students who wish to carry on special investigations under the guidance which the department affords. The subject for 1900-1901 is: The History of German Socialism. Special attention will be given to the materialistic conception of history.

A subordinate feature of the seminary work is the review of recent books and important articles published in the periodicals. *Tuesday evening throughout the year from* 8 *to* 10. Professor ELY, Professor SCOTT, Assistant Professor MEYER, and Dr. JONES.

SOCIOLOGY.

PROFESSOR ELY, ASSISTANT PROFESSOR MEYER, ASSISTANT PROFESSOR SHARP, AND DR. JONES.

1. The Elements of Sociology. A critical exposition of those elementary notions which various writers on Sociology have considered fundamental in their respective systems. Lectures and assigned readings. *First semester; M., Tu., W., at* 10. Assistant Professor MEYER.
2. Modern Sociological Thought. In these lectures an attempt is made to present and to discuss critically the leading characteristics of the works of sociological writers from Comte to the present time. *Second semester; M., Tu., W., at* 10. Assistant Professor MEYER.
3. The Psychological Sociologists. This course deals with that group of sociologists who approach the subject from a psychological point of view. Topics and lectures. *First semester.* Assistant Professor MEYER.
4. American Charities and Crime. Text-books: Warner's American Charities and Wines' Punishment and Reformation. An important feature of this course consists in the lectures given by men and women who have devoted special attention to some phase of charitable and correctional work. The class will also make excursions to the more easily accessible state and local institutions for the purpose of practical study. *First semester; M., W., F., at* 9. Dr. JONES.
5. Field Work. Students are encouraged to study charitable and correctional institutions in Madison and vicinity and opportunity is afforded for continuous practical work during the

DEPARTMENTS OF INSTRUCTION. 89

summer months. During past years students from the University of Wisconsin, some of whom have been aided by scholarships, have engaged in field work under the direction of Dr. P. W. Ayers, of New York, formerly of Chicago. Several of these students have taken up work of this kind as a career. Chicago, Cincinnati, and other cities offer opportunities for field work. It is believed that this method of continuous study, followed by continuous field work, yields the best results. It is the aim of this department to furnish secretaries of charity organization societies and other trained workers. At present the demand for such workers is larger than the supply.

6. Social Ethics. The connection between ethics and economics and the ethics of economic relations. *First semester; twice a week. M., W., at 3.* Professor ELY. (Not given in 1900-1901.)
7. Social Ethics. *Second semester; Tu., Th., at 9.* Assistant Professor SHARP.
8. Seminary in Sociology. Designed particularly for graduate students, and others of suitable preparation. Professors ELY and SCOTT and Dr. JONES participate in several of the discussions. *Second semester; once a week.* Assistant Professor MEYER.

POLITICAL SCIENCE.

PROFESSOR PARKINSON, ASSISTANT PROFESSOR REINSCH, AND DR. SPARLING.

Elementary Courses.

1. Elements of Political Science. (a) An introductory course to general political science. This course will be made as far as possible a Teachers' Course in Civics. *First semester; M., W., F., at 8. Second semester; M., W., Th., at 11.* Dr. SPARLING.
2. Elementary Law. The leading principles of law, and their application to every-day life. Special attention given to commercial law. *Throughout the year; M., W., at 12.* Assistant Professor REINSCH.
3. Elements of Administration. Introductory to the general field of administrative study. The theory of administration, and a survey of the administrative systems of the chief states of modern Europe, and of the South American republics. *First semester; Tu., Th., at 8.* Dr. SPARLING.

Advanced Courses.

8. Roman Law. History of the development of Roman Law from the Twelve Tables to the Corpus Juris of Justinian. Institutes of Roman Law. The work of each semester may be elected separately. *Second semester; Tu., Th., at 12.* Assistant Professor REINSCH.

9. Introduction to the History of European Law. Early Germanic law and its development in France and Germany. The reception of Roman law. The modern codes. Open to students of suitable preparation. *Second semester; Tu., Th., at 8.* Assistant Professor REINSCH. (Not given in 1900-1901.)

10. History of English and American Law. The development of legal institutions as an expression of social and political progress. *Second semester; Tu., Th., at 11.* Assistant Professor REINSCH.

11. Jurisprudence. Analysis of the main concepts of the science of law on the basis of the juristic classics, followed by a comparative study of some of the leading institutions and principles of the French, German, Spanish, English, and American law. Open to students who have had an elementary course in law. *Second semester; M., W., at 12.* Assistant Professor REINSCH. (Not given in 1900-1901.)

12. Constitutional Law. A short course of lectures on the English constitution, with emphasis upon its unwritten growth since the Revolution of 1688, to be followed by a study of the constitution of the United States, not simply as a document, but at work, and in the light of the highest judicial interpretation. *Throughout the year; M., W., F., at 9.* Professor PARKINSON.

13. Constitutional Law. Designed to follow, or at least to supplement, course 12, but may be taken independently by those of suitable preparation. Special attention will be given to the powers of Congress, the restrictions upon the states, the jurisdiction of the courts, and the meaning and scope of the amendments. The study of cases will be made prominent. Open to graduates and other advanced students. *Throughout the year; Tu., Th., at 9.* Professor PARKINSON.

14. Constitutional Law. A comparative study of the more striking features of the constitutions of England, France, Germany, Switzerland, and the United States. Lectures, co-operative work, and class discussions. Open to graduates and other ad-

vanced students. *Second semester;* M., W., at 10. Professor PARKINSON.

15. Municipal Government in Europe and the United States. *Second semester;* M., W., F., at 8. Dr. SPARLING.
16. State and Federal Administration. A course designed to outline the state and federal systems of administration, and the methods of conducting the business of government. May be elected separately, but should follow course 3, if possible. *Second semester;* Tu., Th., at 8. Dr. SPARLING.
17. Comparative Administrative Law. The scope of this course is essentially the same as covered in Vol. II., Goodnow's Comparative Administrative Law. This course has in view the needs of the legal profession. *First semester;* Tu., Th., at 9. Dr. SPARLING.
18. International Law. Lectures upon the nature, sources, sanctions and defects of international law; also upon its growth, improvement, and present status. *First semester;* M., W., F., at 10. Professor PARKINSON.
19. International Law. Designed to follow course 17, but may be taken independently. More attention will here be given to the subject of diplomacy, to the rights and obligations of neutrals, and to the methods of settling international disputes without resort to war. Open to graduates and other advanced students. *Second semester;* M., W., at 10. Professor PARKINSON. (Not given in 1900-1901.)
20. Contemporary Politics. A course of lectures on current international politics, the Chinese question, Russian politics and government, Indian and Egyptian government. *Throughout the year;* W., at 5. (A second hour for class discussion may be arranged for.) Assistant Professor REINSCH.
21. Colonial Politics. A study of the principal systems of colonial government, with special reference to their application to the dependencies of the United States. *First semester;* Tu., Th., at 12. Assistant Professor REINSCH.
22. Party Government. A study of the modern party system in its relation to legislation and administration. Special attention will be given to party organization and the methods of legislative bodies. Tu., Th., at 12. Dr. SPARLING.
23. Federal Consular and Customs Services. A study of the organization and functions of these branches of our public service. The course is intended to familiarize the student with

the duties of consuls and customs officers. *First semester; Tu., Th., at* 11. Dr. SPARLING.

24. Principles of Private Administration. A course of lectures dealing with the principles of organization, and the methods of business. Designed for those students intending to enter upon a business career. *Second semester; one hour per week. Hour to be announced.* Dr. SPARLING.

25. History of Political Thought and the Philosophy of the State. *First semester;* The development of political philosophy from the Greeks to the beginning of the present century, and its connection with political history. *Second semester;* Recent political thought in Europe and America, Philosophy of the state. Open to advanced students. *Throughout the year; M., W., F., at* 11. Assistant Professor REINSCH.

26. Seminary in Administration. The history of the central administration will be studied from the sources, supplemented with readings from secondary authorities. Open to graduates and seniors. *Both semesters, 2 hours. Hours and days to be determined later.* Dr. SPARLING.

27. Seminary in Political Philosophy. For 1900-1901, the political philosophy of the 18th century. The development of the rationalistic theory of the state in its principal exponents and critics in Europe and America. Open to graduate students. *Throughout the year; M.,* 4:30—6. Assistant Professor REINSCH.

28. Political Science Conference. A meeting of the graduate students in political science for the discussion of current literature in politics, and for the presentation of original investigations. Professor PARKINSON, Assistant Professor REINSCH, and Dr. SPARLING.

HISTORY.

PROFESSOR TURNER, PROFESSOR HASKINS, ASSISTANT PROFESSOR COFFIN, DR. LIBBY, MISS KELLOGG, MISS WATTS, AND MR. SCHAFER.

Introductory Courses.

1. Ancient History. A brief outline of Oriental history and a more particular study of the history of Greece and Rome. Professor HASKINS, Dr. LIBBY, and Miss KELLOGG.
    a. For freshmen in the Civic Historical Course. *First semester; M., Tu., W., Th., F., at* 9 *and* 10.

DEPARTMENTS OF INSTRUCTION. 93

b. For freshmen in the English Course. *Second semester; M., Tu., W., Th., F., at 8, 9, and 12.*
c. With special reference to the needs of classical students. *Throughout the year; M., W., F., at 11.* Classical sophomores may satisfy the requirement in history by taking either this course, course 2, or course 5.

2. English History. The work is in two divisions:
   a. Political History. *Repeated each semester; M., W., F., at 8 and 9.* Special attention is given to the formation and nature of the modern British Empire. Assistant Professor COFFIN, Miss WATTS, and Mr. SCHAFER.
   b. Economic History. See Course 1 in Economics for a description of this course. *Repeated each semester; Tu., Th., at 8 and 9.* Professor SCOTT.

   Both divisions of the course are required of freshmen in the English Course (first semester) and of freshmen in the Civic Historical Course (second semester); they are open to election either together or separately by other students.

3. Mediaeval History. A general survey of the history of continental Europe from the barbarian invasions to the close of the fifteenth century. *First semester; M., W., F., at 11.* Required of sophomores in the Civic Historical Course; open to all other students who have had course 1. Professor HASKINS.

4. Modern European History. A general survey extending from the close of the fifteenth century to the present day. *Second semester; M., W., F., at 11.* Required of sophomores in the Civic Historical Course. Assistant Professor COFFIN.

5. American History. A general survey with emphasis on political history. The course may be elected by separate semesters; by additional reading and topical reports it may be made to count as a three-hour course. The course is not open to freshmen or to first year specials.
   a. To the close of the War of 1812. *First semester; Tu., Th., at 11.*
   b. From the close of the War of 1812 to the present time. *Second semester; Tu., Th., at 11.* Professor TURNER.

Advanced Courses.

6. Europe during the later Middle Ages. Special study of the fourteenth and fifteenth centuries; in the second semester particular attention is given to the civilization of Italy in the period of the Renaissance. *Throughout the year; Tu., Th., at*

12. Open to all students who have had course 3. Alternates with course 7; (omitted in 1900-1901). Professor HASKINS and Miss KELLOGG.
7. Constitutional History of England. *Throughout the year; Tu., Th., at* 12. Open to juniors and seniors who have had course 2. Alternates with course 6; (given in 1900-1901). Professor HASKINS.
8. The French Revolutionary and Napoleonic Periods, 1789-1814. An advanced course, alternating with course 9, and open to those who have had course 4, or its equivalent. *Throughout the year; Tu., Th., at* 10; (given in 1899-1900). Assistant Professor COFFIN.
9. History of Europe in the Nineteenth Century, 1815-1900. Alternating with course 8. *Throughout the year; Tu., Th., at* 10; (given in 1900-1901). Assistant Professor COFFIN.
10. American Sectionalism. A study of the geographical distribution of political parties, with special reference to the economic factors in their rise and decline. The course may be elected by separate semesters and is open to juniors and seniors with suitable preparation.
    a. The Jacksonian Democracy, 1824-1840. *First semester; three times a week.*
    b. The Federal Party, 1775-1809. *Second semester; three times a week.* Dr. LIBBY.
11. History of the West. Particular attention is paid to the advance of settlement across the continent, and to the results of this movement. The course should be preceded by course 5, or its equivalent; (given in 1900-1901). *Throughout the year; M., W., F., at* 12. Professor TURNER.
12. Economic and Social History of the United States, to 1789. Must be preceded by course 5, or its equivalent; (not given in 1900-1901). *Throughout the year; M., W., F., at* 12. Professor TURNER.
13. Economic and Social History of the United States, 1789 to 1850. Must be preceded by course 5, or its equivalent; (not given in 1900-1901). *Throughout the year; M., W., F., at* 12. Professor TURNER.
14. Greek and Roman Institutions. *Tu., Th., at* 11. Open to graduate students and seniors of suitable preparation; (given in 1901-1902). Professor HASKINS.
15. Early Mediaeval Institutions. From the accession of Diocletian to the treaty of Verdun. *Tu., Th., at* 11. Open to graduate

students and seniors of suitable preparation. (Given in 1900-1901). Professor HASKINS.
16. History of French Institutions. From the ninth century to the close of the seventeenth century. *First semester;* $Tu.$, $Th.$, at 11, $F.$, at 10. Open to graduate students and seniors of suitable preparation; (omitted in 1900-1901). Professor HASKINS.
17. Methods of History Teaching, with special reference to the work of secondary schools. For juniors and seniors of suitable preparation; (given in 1900-1901). *Second semester;* $F.$, at 3. Professors TURNER and HASKINS.

Graduate Courses.

20. Methods of Research and Criticism. *First semester;* Historical bibliography. *Second semester;* Elements of historical criticism; (given in 1900-1901). $F.$, at 10. Professor HASKINS.
21. Palaeography and Diplomatics. (a) Elements of palaeography, with practical exercises in the reading of manuscript facsimiles; (b) elementary exercises in diplomatics. The first part of the course is identical with the first part of course 7b in Latin and is arranged for the benefit of advanced students of language as well as for students of history; (omitted in 1900-1901.) *Second semester;* $F.$, at 11 *to* 1. Professor HASKINS.
22. Seminary in Mediaeval History. During the present year the work consists mainly of the study of certain mediaeval formularies. In 1900-1901 the Germania of Tacitus will be interpreted during the first semester, and the second semester will be devoted to the critical examination of selected Frankish capitularies. $W.$, 2 *to* 4. Professor HASKINS.
23. Seminary in Modern European History. Intended for graduates and specially qualified seniors doing thesis work in this field. In 1899-1900 the work will be devoted to a careful examination of the *cahiers* of 1789. *Throughout the year;* $S.$, 11 *to* 1. Assistant Professor COFFIN.
24. Seminary in American History. The constitutional and political history of the United States is studied from the sources, combined with lectures and required reading in secondary authorities. For 1900-1901 the work will be in the colonial period. *Throughout the year;* $Tu.$, $Th.$ Professor TURNER.
25. Historical Conference. A fortnightly meeting of instructors and graduate students in the department for conference, consider-

ation of papers, and criticism of current historical literature. *Fortnightly throughout the year; F., 4 to 6.*

Special Lectures.

In the year 1899-1900 the following courses of special lectures are given in the department of history:

The Government of Colonies and Dependencies. Six lectures by Professor H. Morse Stephens, of Cornell University.

The History of Islam. Five lectures by Professor J. R. Jewett, of the University of Minnesota.

Arrangement of Courses.

The courses in the Department of History are divided into three groups. Courses 1 to 5 are planned so as to afford an introductory survey of the general field of history. They cannot be counted toward advanced degrees, and graduates are required to have completed them, or a substantial equivalent, before entering on their graduate studies. Courses 6 to 16 are designed to continue the studies begun in the preliminary courses in the direction of greater specialization in the fields of ancient, mediaeval, and modern European history, English history, and American history. They are open to undergraduates of sufficient advancement, and are also suited to the early years of graduate study. The remaining courses—except course 17, which is a special course for those intending to teach history in secondary schools—are designed to afford training in original research in representative fields of history; they are open to advanced students under conditions which vary in the different courses.

GREEK.

PROFESSOR SMITH, PROFESSOR KERR, ASSISTANT PROFESSOR LAIRD, ASSISTANT PROFESSOR EMERY, AND MISS SCRIBNER.

Elementary Courses.

a. *Elementary Greek.* White's Beginner's Greek Book, Xenophon's Anabasis, Homer's Odyssey I.—IV., Greek Composition. *Throughout the year; M., Tu., W., Th., at 12; S. at 11.* Miss SCRIBNER.

1. *First semester:* Lysias, Xenophon's Hellenics, Goodwin's Grammar. *M., Tu., W., Th., F., at 9.* Professor SMITH and Assistant Professor LAIRD.

    Second semester: Selections from Homer and Herodotus. *M., Tu., W., Th., F., at 10.* Professor SMITH and Professor KERR.

Greek Composition, *throughout the year;* Tu., at 9. Assistant Professor LAIRD. (Course 2 is required of Ancient Classical freshmen.)

2. *First semester:* The Philippics of Demosthenes, Euripides (the play Bacchae), Goodwin's Moods and Tenses. M., W., F., at 10. Professor KERR.

Second semester: Plato's Apology and Crito, Thucydides VII., Jebb's Primer of Greek Literature. M., W., F., at 10. Professor SMITH and Assistant Professor EMERY.

Greek Composition, *throughout the year;* W., at 10. Professor SMITH and Assistant Professor LAIRD. (Course 3 is required of Ancient Classical sophomores.)

Elective Courses.

2a. Herodotus, one book, Xenophon's Memorabilia, or selected dialogues of Lucian. *Throughout the year;* M., F., at 11. Assistant Professor LAIRD. (Course 2a is an elective for sophomores, but is open also to such freshmen as receive the permission of the instructor.)

5. *First semester:* Greek Lyric Poets, study of meters. M., W., F., *at 9, or hour to be agreed on.* Professor SMITH.

Second semester: Thucydides. M., W., F., *at 9, or hour to be agreed on.* Professor SMITH. Open to juniors and seniors. (Omitted in 1900-1901).

6. Greek Dramatic Poets. *First semester:* Aeschylus (two plays), Sophocles (two plays), study of meters.

Second semester: Aristophanes, Aristotle's Poetics, discussion of the Greek Drama. M., W., F., *at 9, or hour to be agreed on.* Professor SMITH. (Open to juniors and seniors).

7. Greek Orators. Tu., Th., at 9. Assistant Professor LAIRD. Open to juniors and seniors. (Omitted in 1900-1901).

8. Plato. The Republic. Books I., II., and X. This course is intended as an introduction to the study of Greek philosophy. *Throughout the year;* Tu., Th., at 9. Professor KERR. Open to juniors and seniors. (Omitted in 1899-1900).

12. Advanced Greek Composition. *First semester;* Tu., at 9. Professor SMITH and Assistant Professor LAIRD. Open to juniors, seniors, and graduates.

13. Modern Greek Language and Literature. A study of the changes in form and structure which the language has undergone since the classical period. Readings from contemporary Greek authors, and a comparison of their writings with the

prose and poetry of the Attic Greek. Papers and discussions upon topics connected with the course of reading. Elective for juniors and seniors. *Throughout the year; Tu., at 8.* Professor KERR.

14. Lectures on the life of the ancient Greeks, illustrated by means of lantern slides. Once a week *throughout the year; W., at 5.* Professor SMITH. A knowledge of Greek is not required for this course. (Omitted in 1899-1900).

Graduate Courses.

The object of the graduate courses in Greek is to secure, on the part of advanced students, graduates especially, wide reading in Greek authors, acquaintance with the latest results of philological investigation through constant reading of critical journals, the forming of habits and learning of methods of research. In pursuance of the last named purpose especially, the Greek Seminary meets to hear and to discuss carefully prepared papers, the members leading in turn. It is to be understood that the preparation for each lead will require the greater portion of a student's time for at least two weeks. The work will be occasionally varied and relieved by extempore exercises in reading and writing Greek. The work of the seminary will be supplemented by courses of lectures.

20. Thucydides, studied throughout the year, the whole of the author being read privately by the members of the class. Each member leads in turn, presenting a paper embodying a critical discussion of some passage of the text, or of some topic especially assigned. *Throughout the year, S., 9-11.* (Omitted in 1900-1901.) Professor SMITH.

21. Greek Drama. During the first semester several tragedies of Aeschylus or Euripides will be critically studied and interpreted, in the second semester certain comedies of Aristophanes, especial stress being laid upon the treatment of the dramas as literature. As supplementary to this course the Scenic antiquities will be studied, Haigh's Attic Theatre being used as a basis. Throughout the year, *S.*, 9-11. (Omitted in 1900-1901.) Professor SMITH.

22. Lyric Poetry. Especial attention is given to Pindar and to Bacchylides. Wide reading in the fragments of the other lyric poets will also be required of the class. *Throughout the year, S., 9-11.* Professor SMITH.

23. Greek Dialects. A study of dialect sounds and forms based on the inscriptions. Cauer's Delectus Inscriptionum Graecarum

will in the main be followed. The members of the class will lead in turn, and special problems for investigation will also be assigned. *Two hours a week for a portion of the year, as part of the regular seminary work.* Assistant Professor LAIRD.

24. Greek Antiquities, State and Private. One exercise a week, *throughout the year.* (Omitted in 1899-1900). Professor SMITH.
25. Journal Club. Reports on and discussions of current philological literature. *One hour a week throughout the year.* Professors SMITH, KERR, and SLAUGHTER, and Assistant Professors LAIRD, SOBER and EMERY.

   Courses 20-24 are conducted mainly on the seminary plan. Courses 20-25 are open to graduates, and, by special permission, to others who have had the junior 3 hour elective, or its equivalent.
26. Comparative Greek Grammar. (See Comparative Philology 3.)

Comparative Philology.

1. Lectures on the principles of the life and growth of language. *Second semester; F., 9.* Assistant Professor LAIRD. (Open to juniors and seniors. A knowledge of Greek and Latin is not required.)
2. Latin Grammar. History of the sounds and forms. *Second semester; Tu., Th., at 8.* Assistant Professor LAIRD. (Omitted in 1900-1901.
3. Greek Grammar. History of the sounds and forms. *Throughout the year; Tu., Th., at 8.* Assistant Professor LAIRD.
4. Elementary Sanskrit. Perry's Sanskrit Primer. Selections from Lanman's Reader. *Throughout the year; M., W., 10.* Assistant Professor LAIRD.
5. Advanced Sanskrit. Selections from the Rig-Veda. Wackernagel's Altindische Grammatik. *Throughout the year; W., 11.* Assistant Professor LAIRD.

(Courses 3 and 5 are intended primarily for graduates, but are open, by permission, to juniors and seniors.)

LATIN.

PROFESSOR SLAUGHTER, ASSISTANT PROFESSOR SOBER, ASSISTANT PROFESSOR EMERY, DR. SHANNON, DR. ALLEN, AND MISS PITMAN.

The attention of students preparing to teach Latin in secondary schools is called to the advanced courses, 7*a*, 8*a*, 10*b*, 11, 12 and 20.

These courses will be practically required of those who expect a recommendation to teach Latin.

Introductory Courses.

a. Cicero and Vergil. Cicero's Orations (3), Vergil's Aeneid (six books), Latin Grammar and Composition. This course is offered for the benefit of students whose preparation in Latin has for any reason been deficient. It can not be counted for the bachelor's degree. *Throughout the year; M., Tu., W., Th., F., at* 8. Miss PITMAN.

1. Cicero, Livy, Terence. Cicero de Senectute, Livy (two books), Terence (two plays), Latin Composition. Required of freshmen of Ancient Classical and Modern Classical courses and alternative with German for freshmen of the Civic Historical course. *Throughout the year; M., Tu., Th., F.* Four divisions: M. Cl. at 10, A. Cl. at 11, Civ. H. at 8. Assistant Professor EMERY, Dr. SHANNON, and Dr. ALLEN.

3. Horace. The Odes, Satires, and Epistles of Horace. Required of sophomores of Ancient Classical and Modern Classical courses. *Throughout the year; two divisions. M., Tu., Th., at* 9. Professor SLAUGHTER and Assistant Professor EMERY.

Advanced Courses.

5. (a) Cicero and Catullus. (b) Pliny and Martial. *Throughout the year; Tu., Th., at* 8. Assistant Professor SOBER.
6. Juvenal and Tacitus. *Throughout the year; Tu., Th., at* 8. Dr. ALLEN.

Courses 5 and 6 are given in alternate years and are open to all students who have had courses 1 and 2. Course 5 will be given in 1900-1901.

7. (a) Teachers' Course in Caesar. (b) Rapid reading course in easy prose authors. Open to juniors and seniors. *Throughout the year; Tu., Th., at* 9. A third hour will be arranged for students who desire it. Dr. SHANNON.

8. (a) Topography and Remains of Ancient Rome; lectures illustrated with lantern slides and photographs. (b) Reading of Latin Inscriptions and Manuscripts. (See Course 18, under History.) Open to seniors and graduates. *Throughout the year; Tu., Th., at* 9. Assistant Professor SOBER.

Courses 7 and 8 are given in alternate years. Course 8 will be given in 1900-1901.

9. (a) Plautus. (b) Lectures on Roman Literature. *Throughout the year; M., W., F., at 8.* Professor SLAUGHTER.
10. (a) Lucretius. (b) Vergil and the Roman Epic. *Throughout the year; M., W., F., at 8.* Professor SLAUGHTER.

Courses 9 and 10 are open to all students who have had courses 1 and 2, and are given in alternate years. Course 9 will be given in 1900-1901.

11. Exercises in writing Latin. Open to all students who have had course 1. *Weekly throughout the year; Th., at 3.* Dr. SHANNON.
12. Life of the Romans. Lectures, illustrated with lantern slides and photographs. Open to all students. A knowledge of Latin is not necessary for this course. *Weekly throughout the year; Th., at 4.* Professor SLAUGHTER.

Courses 11 and 12 are given in alternate years. Course 11 will be given in 1900-1901.

20. Latin Grammar. (See Comparative Philology, Course 2.)
21. Syntax. A course of lectures on Latin syntax is given in connection with the work of the Seminary, and is intended primarily for graduate students. The subjects are: (a) the simple sentence and course 20 (1899-1900); (b) the compound sentence; (c) the cases (1900-1901). *Twice weekly throughout the year; Tu., Th., at 9.* Assistant Professor EMERY.
22. Seminary. The Seminary is intended for graduate students, but will be open to others of suitable preparation with the consent of the director. To accommodate those who are studying for the doctor's degree, the work is arranged to cover three years: (a) The Roman Drama. The critical work of the Seminary will be based upon the Miles Gloriosus of Plautus. (Given in 1900-1901); (b) Lucretius, Bk. III. (Given in 1898-9); (c) Horace, critical and exegetical study of the Odes. (Given in 1899-1900.) *Throughout the year; W., F., at 9.* Professor SLAUGHTER.

HEBREW AND HELLENISTIC GREEK.

PROFESSOR WILLIAMS AND MR. KELLY.

Hebrew, Arabic and Assyrian.

1. The General Principles of the Hebrew Language. Reading of selections from Genesis. *Throughout the year. Four times a week.* Mr. KELLY.

2. This course is the same as course 1, but begins in the second semester of each year as a two-fifths study, and continues as a two-fifths study during the first semester of the following year. Mr. KELLY.
3. Historical Hebrew. The books of Samuel, with a review of the verb. *Twice a week; first semester.* Mr. KELLY.
4. Deuteronomy and a general review of Etymology. *Twice a week; second semester.* Mr. KELLY.
5. Minor Prophets. *Twice a week. Throughout the year.* Mr. KELLY.
6. Job, or Psalms (as students may elect). *Twice a week. Throughout the year.* Mr. KELLY.
Courses 5 and 6 will be given in alternate years.
7. Exercises in Writing Hebrew. *Once a week. Throughout the year.* Mr. KELLY.
8. Advanced Hebrew Grammar, with selected passages for reading. *Throughout the year. Twice a week.* Prof. WILLIAMS.
9. Hebrew Seminary: In alternate years, Isaiah I.—XXXIX. and XL.—LXVI., will form the center of the work. *Once a week (two hours).* Throughout the year. Professor WILLIAMS.
10. Arabic: *First Semester*: Easy reading and principles of the language. *Second semester*: Reading of selections, and some of the shorter suras of the Quran. *Twice a week.* Mr. KELLY.
11. Advanced Arabic: The Quran. *Once a week. Throughout the year.* Mr. KELLY.
12. Elementary Assyrian. *Once a week. Throughout the year.* Mr. KELLY.

Hellenistic Greek.

15. Selected chapters from the Gospels, and the general principles of Hellenistic Greek. For students who have not studied classical Greek. *Throughout the year. Four times a week.* Professor WILLIAMS.
16. This course is the same as Course 13, but begins as a two-fifths study in the second semester of each year and continues as a two-fifths study during the first semester of the following year. Professor WILLIAMS.
17. Matthew and Mark. *Throughout the year. Twice a week.* Professor WILLIAMS.
18. Luke and Acts. *Twice a week. Throughout the year.* Professor WILLIAMS.

19. John. Critical study and textual criticism. *Twice a week. Throughout the year.* Professor WILLIAMS.
20. Pauline Epistles. *Twice a week. Throughout the year.* Professor WILLIAMS.
21. Advanced Hellenistic Greek Grammar. *Twice a week Throughout the year.* Professor WILLIAMS.

FRENCH.

PROFESSOR OWEN, ASSISTANT PROFESSOR GIESE, MISS GAY, MR. BRAUER, AND MISS CASTLE.

Elementary.

1. General Elementary Course. Otto's French Conversation Grammar; Roman d'un Jeune Homme Pauvre and La Petite Fadette (the former read mainly and the latter altogether independently of the class-room); Le Cid, Le Misanthrope, Athalie. *Throughout the year; Tu., W., F., S., at* 10. Assistant Professor GIESE and Miss CASTLE.
2. Special Elementary Course for Classical Students. The same as course 1 with the addition of comment on the history of the French language, consideration of Latin etymologies, and treatment of the subject generally from the standpoint of the classics. Additional material for translation will be assigned if the progress of the class allows. *Throughout the year; Tu., W., Th., F., at* 8. Miss GAY.
3. Special Elementary Course for Engineers. A modification of course 1 in the interest of the College of Mechanics and Engineering. *Throughout the year; M., Tu., W., Th., F., at* 11. Mr. BRAUER.

   By subdivision of the above courses, six elementary classes are established, held in part at 8, at 12, or at both hours. As many students desire a reading knowledge only, the effort of the above elementary courses is concentrated upon reading. Students are expected at the end of an elementary course to read with sufficient ease and accuracy to make a practical use of French text-books in the prosecution of their other studies.

Reading.

5. Advanced Reading and Syntax. Reading in class of parts of Cinq-Mars, Ursule Mirouet; reading independently for examination of the Histoire de Charles XII. and other easy French to be assigned. *Throughout the year; M., W., F., at* 11. Professor OWEN.

6. Continuation of Course 5. Reading of Travailleurs de la Mer, etc. *Throughout the year, usually Tu., Th., at 12.* Professor OWEN.

Writing and Speaking.

10. Composition, etc. Written and oral translation into French from English, dictation, and original composition. *Throughout the year; Tu., Th., at 9.* Miss GAY.
11. Continuation of Course 10. *Throughout the year; two hours a week.* Miss GAY.
15. Conversation. This exercise is open only to students who have finished course 1, 2, or 3, or an equivalent. *Two hours a week throughout the year.* Assistant Professor GIESE.
16. Continuation of Course 15. *Throughout the year; two hours a week.* Assistant Professor GIESE.

Literature.

20. A general course of lectures on French literature, XVI.—XIX. centuries, with collateral reading. *Throughout the year; M., W., at 12.* Assistant Professor GIESE.

Philology.

25. Lectures on Thought and Language *weekly during the first semester.* At present embodied in course 5.
26. A philological course in the oldest French literature. *Throughout the year; two hours a week.* Alternates with course 27. Given in 1899-1900. Miss GAY.
27. A continuation of 26. *Throughout the year; two hours a week.* Miss GAY.

The method pursued in the above will approximate to that of the seminary. Special seminary courses will be furnished whenever this seems desirable.

Graduate.

30. The Principles of Language; especially the correspondence of thought and sentence, as illustrated in the Romance languages. *One hour weekly during first semester.* Professor OWEN.
31. History of French literature. XVI.—XIX. centuries. Lectures with collateral reading. *Three hours weekly; throughout the year.* Assistant Professor GIESE.
32. History of French literature, XIX. century. Lectures with collateral reading. This course will be conducted entirely in

French, and is open only to those who have had course 15 or its equivalent. *Three hours weekly throughout the year.* Assistant Professor GIESE.

33. "Les plus anciens Monuments de la langue Française," ed. Koschwitz; "La Vie de St. Alexis," ed. Gaston Paris; lectures on the phonetics and morphology of Old French. *Two hours weekly throughout the year.* Miss GAY.

34. "The Carlovingian Cycle," with readings from "La Chanson de Roland," ed. G. Paris, and "Le Voyage de Charlemagne," ed. Koschwitz. *Two hours weekly throughout the year.* Miss GAY.

35. "The Arthurian Cycle," with a special study of Chrestien de Troyes; Förster's edition of Chrestien's works is used. *Two hours weekly throughout the year.* Miss GAY.

36. The Picard and Norman dialects, with special reference to the history of the French element in English, "Aucassin et Nicolete," ed. Suchier; Les Voyages de St. Brandan, ed. Michel. *Two hours weekly throughout the year.* Miss GAY.

Courses 33 to 36 may be taken successively or two may be taken conjointly, with assigned readings sufficient to make a major for a second degree.

SPANISH.

ASSISTANT PROFESSOR GIESE AND PROFESSOR OWEN.

1. **Elementary.** Translations into English of the Spanish exercises in Sauer's Conversation Grammar, Knapp's Spanish Readings and Marsh's Doña Perfecta. *Throughout the year; three times a week.* Alternates with Italian. Given during the year 1899-1900. Professor OWEN.

2. **Advanced.** Reading of selections from Cervantes (Don Quixote), from Calderon (El Magico Prodigioso), and from modern poets. *Throughout the year; two hours weekly.* Given in 1900-1901. Assistant Professor GIESE.

ITALIAN.

ASSISTANT PROFESSOR GIESE AND PROFESSOR OWEN.

1. **Elementary.** Translation into English of the Italian Exercises in Sauer's Conversation Grammar, and of Manzoni's I Promessi Sposi. *Three hours a week throughout the year.* This course is in general like that in Spanish, with which it alternates. Given in 1898-99. Professor OWEN.

2. Advanced. Dante and other classics. *Throughout the year; two hours a week.* Given in 1899-1900. Miss GAY.

SCANDINAVIAN LANGUAGES.

PROFESSOR OLSON.

This department offers instruction in all of the Scandinavian languages (Norwegian, Danish, Swedish, and Old Norse.) From one year's instruction in Modern Norse the student is expected to be able to read both Norwegian and Danish authors, as Norway and Denmark have practically the same literary language. The principal courses are devoted mainly to Norwegian authors, but additional instruction in Danish and Swedish literature is offered to students desiring to pursue these branches beyond the limits of the prescribed courses.

1. a. Modern Norse. Olson's Norwegian Grammar and Reader, Bjornson's En glad Gut, and Gundersen's collection of Norske Digte. *Three times a week throughout the year.*
   b. Written and oral translation into Norse, and the reading of easy prose selections as a basis for work in composition and conversation. *Once a week throughout the year.* a. may be elected separately. a. and b. together may be taken as one of the language requirements in the English course.
2. Modern Norse. Selections from the Reader, Overland's Lærebog i Norges Historie, Kielland's Skipper Worse, Ibsen's Brand, or Peer Gynt, and selections from Norwegian and Danish poetry. A drama by Holberg and one by Oehlenschlæger are assigned for outside reading. *Three times a week throughout the year.*
3. History of Dano-Norwegian Literature. Seip and Broch's Dansknorsk Litteraturhistorie, with lectures, and papers presented by students on the authors under discussion. *Three times a week throughout the year.* Given in alternate years. 1900-1901.
4. Swedish Literature. Tegner's Frithiofs Saga, Runeberg's Fänrik Stals Sägner, Vinsnes and Aanrud's Svenske Digtere, and Warburg's Svensk Litteraturhistorie. *Twice a week throughout the year.* Given in alternate years. 1901-1902.
5. Old Norse. Vigfusson and Powell's Icelandic Prose Reader, or Kahle's Altisländisches Elementarbuch, and Nygaard's Udvalg af den norröne Literatur. *Twice a week throughout the year.*
6. a. Lectures on early Scandinavian literature and antiquities,

with illustrative readings in translation. *Once a week. First semester.*
  b. Lectures on modern Scandinavian authors and literary epochs, with illustrative readings in translation. *Once a week. Second semester.* Given in alternate years. 1900-1901.

A knowledge of the Scandinavian languages is not required for course 6a and 6b.

Advanced Courses.

7. Modern Norwegian Literature. The critical reading, with papers and discussions, of representative novels: Björnson's Synnöve Solbakken, Lie's Den Fremsynte, and Kielland's Skipper Worse. *Twice a week. One semester.*
8. Modern Norwegian Literature. The critical reading, with papers and discussion, of representative dramas: Björnson's Mellem Slagene, and Sigurd Slembe, and Ibsen's Kongsemnerne, Peer Gynt, and Et Dukkehjem. *Twice a week. One semester.*
9. Studies in Norwegian Poetry. Selections from Wergeland, Welhaven, Munch, Moe, Björnson and Ibsen, to illustrate the different epochs in the development of modern Norwegian literature. *Once a week. One semester.*
10. Norwegian Dialect Writers. Selections from Aasen, Vinje, Garborg, and Sivle, together with a study of the language-reform movement. *Once a week. One semester.*

GERMAN.

PROFESSOR ROSENSTENGEL, ASSOCIATE PROFESSOR VOSS, MISS STERLING, MISS REMINGTON, MR. MEISNEST, MRS. EATON, MISS HERFURTH, MISS VEERHUSEN.

Elementary and Required Courses.

English, Civic Historical, and Ancient Classical Courses—
1. Elementary German. Grammar and easy readings with practice in speaking and writing German.
   First semester: Thomas' German Grammar and Rosenstengel's Reader.
   Second semester: Continuation of grammar, Hillern's Hoeher als die Kirche, and Zschokke's Der zerbrochene Krug. *Four times a week.*

Section I. *M., Tu., Th., F.,* at 8. Miss REMINGTON.
Section II. *Tu., W., Th., F.,* at 10. Miss HERFURTH.
Section III. *Tu., W., Th., F.,* at 11. Miss HERFURTH.
Section IV. *Tu., W., Th., F.,* at 11. Miss VEERHUSEN.
Section V. *Tu., W., Th., F.,* at 9. ——— ———

2. Second-year German. For students who have had course 1, and also for those who have had two years of High School German or an equivalent: Modern prose, narrative and dramatic, and a drama of Lessing or Schiller. A rapid reading course with practice in speaking and writing German and review of grammar. *Four times a week.*

Sections I. and III. First semester: Baumbach's Die Nonna, and Freytag's Die Journalisten. Second semester: Lessing's Minna von Barnhelm and prose readings. Section I., Miss REMINGTON; *M., Tu., Th.,* at 9. Section III., Associate Professor VOSS; *Tu., W., Th.,* at 11.

Sections II. and IV. First semester: Riehl's Das Spielmann's Kind and Der Stumme Rathsherr, and Schiller's Der Neffe als Onkel. Second semester: Schiller's Jungfrau von Orleans, and prose readings. *Tu., W., Th.,* at 10. Miss REMINGTON, Section II. *Tu., W., Th.,* at 10. ——— ———, section IV.

Bernhardt's German Composition, Conversation and Grammar Review.
Section I. *F.,* at 9. Miss REMINGTON.
Section II. *F.,* at 10. Miss REMINGTON.
Section III. *F.,* at 11. Associate Professor VOSS.
Section IV. *F.,* at 10. ——— ———

Modern Classical Course—

3. Lessing's Minna von Barnhelm, and Schiller's Wilhelm Tell. Freshman; *daily,* at 8. Mrs. EATON.
4. Goethe's Hermann und Dorothea, and Schiller's Maria Stuart. Sophomore; *M., W., F.,* at 10. Mrs. EATON.

General Science Course—

5. Science reader. Freshman; *M., Tu., Th., F.,* at 10. Miss STERLING, Mr. MEISNEST.
6. Walther's Meereskunde (Sterling's), and scientific monographs. Sophomore; *M., W., F.,* at 9. Miss STERLING.

Engineering Course—

7. Science reader, and scientific monographs. Freshman (unless French is elected). *Four times a week.* Mr. MEISNEST.

8. Scientific Current Literature. Sophomore; *twice a week.* Mr. MEISNEST.

Elective Courses.

10. Lessing's Nathan der Weise, and Goethe's Iphigenie and Tasso. *M., W., F., at 9.* Professor ROSENSTENGEL.
11. Goethe's Goetz von Berlichingen (Goodrich's); first semester. Goethe's Egmont (Winkler's), second semester. Alternating with Schiller's Don Carlos and Lessing's Emilia Galotti. *Tu., Th., at 12.* Associate Professor VOSS.
12. Dramatic reading. *Once a week.* Associate Professor VOSS.
13. Schiller's Jungfrau von Orleans and Die Braut von Messina. *Twice a week. Hours and days on consultation.* Miss STERLING.
14. German lyrics and ballads. *Three times a week. Hours and days on consultation.* Miss STERLING.
15. First semester. Reading of selections from modern historians, with outlines of the literature of the corresponding periods. Second semester. Scheffel's Ekkehard or Hauff's Lichtenstein and Scheffel's Trompeter or Kleist's Prinz Friedrich von Homburg. *M., W., at 12.* Miss REMINGTON.
16. First semester. Readings illustrating the history of German civilization. Selections from Freytag's Bilder aus der Deutschen Vergangenheit and Meyer Das Deutsche Volkstum. Second semester. Maria Stuart or Hermann und Dorothea with outside readings. *Tu., Th., at 11.* Miss REMINGTON.
17. Modern German prose. Selections from the works of Freytag and Heyse. *Three times a week. Hours and days on consultation.* Mr. MEISNEST.
18. German comedies. *Twice a week. Hours and days on consultation.* Mr. MEISNEST.
19. Modern German. Selections from the works of Heine, Scheffel, and Riehl. *Three times a week. Hours and days on consultation.* Mrs. EATON.
20. Grillparzer's Sappho and Die Ahnfrau. (Given in 1900-1901). *First semester. Three times a week. Hours and days on consultation.* Mrs. EATON.
21. Goethe's Dichtung und Wahrheit. *Second semester. Three times a week. Hours and days on consultation.* Mrs. EATON.

For Undergraduates and Graduates.

25. Goethe's Faust. *First semester; M., W., F., at 11.* Professor ROSENSTENGEL.

26. A critical study of the Report of the Committee on Modern Languages with lectures and reports on methods of teaching modern foreign languages. *W., at 5. Second semester.* Associate Professor Voss.
27. Lessing's Laokoon. (Given in 1901). *First semester; three times a week. Hours and days on consultation.* Mrs. EATON.
28. General survey of the development of German language and literature. *Second semester; M., W., F., at 11.* Professor ROSENSTENGEL.
29. Lectures on the history of early German literature, with the reading of selections from authors of the periods considered (Old and Middle High German authors in modern German translations). *Three times a week. Hours and days on consultation.* Miss STERLING.
30. Lectures on the German literature of the eighteenth and nineteenth centuries, especially Schiller and Goethe. *First semester; twice a week. Hours and days on consultation.* Professor ROSENSTENGEL.
31. The German drama of the present. Lectures with readings from Sudermann and Hauptmann. *Second semester; three times a week. Hours and days on consultation.* Professor ROSENSTENGEL.
32. Lectures on the origin and history of fairy tales, sagas, fables, ballads, lyric poetry, and epic and dramatic poetry. *First semester; twice a week. Hours and days on consultation.* Professor ROSENSTENGEL.
33. The German romantic movement in its social and literary aspects. Lectures and assigned readings. *Twice a week. Hours and days on consultation.* Mrs. EATON.
34. Conversation, composition, and translation. *Three times a week. Hours and days on consultation.* Professor ROSENSTENGEL.
35. Advanced composition. *Twice a week. Hours and days on consultation.* Professor ROSENSTENGEL.
36. Teachers' class. Review of and lectures on German grammar, and systematic practice in teaching German. Open to students who have taken at least courses 3, 4, 10, 25, and 34. *Second semester; three times a week. Hours and days on consultation.* Professor ROSENSTENGEL.

GERMAN PHILOLOGY.

ASSOCIATE PROFESSOR VOSS.

Introductory Courses.

40. a. Introduction to Middle High German. Lectures and recitations with assigned readings. Paul's mhd. Grammatik and Bachmann's Mittelhochdeutsches Lesebuch. *First semester; Tu., Th., F., at 10.*

   b. The Middle High German Folk-epic, Nibelungenlied and Kudrun. Lectures and recitations. *Twice a week. Second semester; Tu., Th., at 10.*

41. Hempl, German Orthography and Phonology and studies in etymology. *Once a week, throughout the year. W., at 10.*

42. Early Modern High German. Meyer, Einfuehrung in das Aeltere Neuhochdeutsche. *First semester; Tu., Th., at 9.*

43. History and Grammar of the Modern High German Literary Language, based on Behaghel's Die Deutsche Sprache. *Second semester; Tu., Th., at 9.*

Advanced Courses.

44. Old High German. Braune's ahd. Grammatik, and readings from Braune's ahd. Lesebuch. *Twice a week. First semester.* In alternate years.

45. Gothic Grammar with readings from the Gospels. Braune-Balg, Gothic Grammar. *Two hours. Second semester.* In alternate years. (1901-1902).

46. a. Middle Low German from an historical point of view. Luebben's mnd. Grammatik nebst Chrestomathie. *Twice a week; first semester.*

   b. Old Saxon. Gallée-Behaghel, asaechs. Grammatik, and extracts from the Heliand, ed. Heyne. *Second semester. Two hours.* Given in alternate years. (1900-1901).

47. Studies in the language and literature of the XVI. century. Hans Sachs, Luther, Murner, Brant. Lectures and reading of selections from Braune's Neudrucke deutscher Litteraturwerke des XVI. und XVII. Jahrhunderts. *W., F., at 9, first semester; W., at 9, second semester.*

48. Philological Seminary: A proseminary, which meets once a week throughout the year, leads up to the work of the seminary. The programme of the proseminary will vary according to the needs of the students. The work of the seminary proper is distributed over three years. The chief aim is to

make the student acquainted with the scientific methods used by the foremost scholars and investigators in this line of work, and to teach him to work independently. In the seminary texts of the different stages of the language will be studied from an historical and comparative point of view. In addition to this, the members of the seminary are expected to furnish a paper on a self-chosen subject out of the realm of German philology or higher literary criticism. *Three hours a week, throughout the year; S., 9-12.*

In the seminary as well as in all the courses in Germon philology, German will be used as far as possible.

For the sake of promoting the interest in German philology in the broadest meaning of the word, the *Germanistiche Gesellschaft* has been organized to meet every fortnight throughout the year.

The attention of students who intend to teach German is called to courses 40, 41, 43, and 26.

ENGLISH.

PROFESSOR FREEMAN, PROFESSOR FRANKENBURGER, PROFESSOR HUBBARD, ASSISTANT PROFESSOR KNOWLTON, ASSISTANT PROFESSOR PYRE, DR. CAIRNS, DR. BEATTY, MR. DODGE, MR. THURBER, MISS HUNT, MR. W. H. PYRE, AND MISS BUTT.

1. English Prose Style. Composition. The elements of effective writing in prose, based upon direct study of selected authors, with training in composition, and in methods of investigation and of presenting results. *Three hours a week, throughout the year.* Eleven sections. For hours and rooms see time table of required studies. Required of freshmen in all courses. Professor HUBBARD, Assistant Professor KNOWLTON, Dr. CAIRNS, Dr. BEATTY, Mr. DODGE, Mr. THURBER, and Miss HUNT.

Rhetoric and Oratory.

2. Rhetoric and Composition. Elective for Sophomores who have finished the required English of Freshman year. *Tu., Th.* Dr. BEATTY.
3. Development of Oratorical Themes. *Tu., Th.*
4. Advanced Rhetoric. Open to those who have completed courses 1 or 2 above. Analysis of great essays, orations, and prose fiction, with higher rhetorical and literary criticism. Lectures with supplementary readings. *Throughout the year. M., W., F., at* 12 Elective. Professor FRANKENBURGER.

DEPARTMENTS OF INSTRUCTION.

5. Forensics. *M., W., F., at 11, throughout the year.* Elective. Professor FRANKENBURGHER..
6. Analytical study of masterpieces, ancient and modern. *Twice a week throughout the year; Tu., Th., at 11.* Elective. Assistant Professor KNOWLTON.
7. Advanced Composition. This course is supplementary to course 6. *Throughout the year; M., W., F., at 11.* Elective for juniors and seniors, and for sophomores who have done very good work on course 1. Assistant Professor KNOWLTON.
8. Rhetorical Seminary. Original composition; the philosophy of criticism with the deduction and application of literary canons. *Two hours a week in one session during the year.* Open to seniors and juniors. Professor FRANKENBURGER, Assistant Professor KNOWLTON and Dr. BEATTY.
9. Lectures on literary and rhetorical criticism. *Throughout the year; Tu., Th., at 9.* Dr. BEATTY.
10. Elocution and Dramatic Reading. Lectures; declamation with personal criticism; Macbeth and Othello, or Julius Cæsar and Hamlet. Open to those who have taken course 11 or its equivalent. *Throughout the year; Tu., Th., at 12.* Professor FRANKENBURGER.
12. Elocution. Lectures will be given upon vocal physiology, the proper use and care of the voice, reading, and gesture. *Throughout the year; M., W., F.* Mr. PYRE and Miss BUTT.
13. Oratorical Delivery. Open to those who have had sufficient previous preparation to be able to do the work. Declamations, readings and lectures. *First semester; M., W., F.* Mr. PYRE and Miss BUTT.
14. Elocution. Reading, declamation, and lectures. *Second semester; M., W.,.F., at 9.* Mr. PYRE and Miss BUTT.
15. Elocution and Oratory. (Elective in Law School.) Voice training for effective quality; special drill on methods of reading statutes and other documents before a court or a jury. Practice in declamation and reading from the great orators, and in extempore speaking. Lectures on vocal physiology, and on the use and care of the voice, and on principles of gesture. *Twice a week during the year.* Mr. PYRE and Miss BUTT.

Arrangements can be made for private lessons by consulting Mr. PYRE and Miss BUTT.

Language.

20. Anglo-Saxon and Middle English. *First semester*, Anglo-Saxon; *— second semester*, Middle English. *Throughout the year; M., W., F., at 8 and 9.* Required in the English course, junior year. The work of the first semester may be elected without the work of the second semester. Professor HUBBARD and Dr. BEATTY.
21. Anglo-Saxon Poetry. Study of selections, survey of Anglo-Saxon literature. *Second semester, M., W., F., at 8.* Open to students who have taken the Anglo-Saxon of course 1. Professor HUBBARD.
22. Beowulf. Introduction to the study of old Germanic life. *First semester; M., W., F., at 8.* Open to seniors. Professor HUBBARD.
23. Modern English Grammar. A course for teachers of English. *Second semester; Tu., Th., at 8.* Open to students who have taken course 1. Professor HUBBARD.
24. English Philology Seminary. Critical study of texts; historical Grammar; dialects. *Two hours a week throughout the year.* Open to graduates. Professor HUBBARD.

See also Comparative Philology, course 1; French, course 10.

Literature.

30. General Survey of English Literature. This course is pre-requisite to all other courses in English Literature. *Throughout the year; M., W., F., at 9, 10, and 11.* Required of sophomores in the English course. Assistant Professor PYRE and Dr. CAIRNS.
31. Chaucer. History of the literature of the XIV. and XV. centuries. *First semester; M., W., F., at 8.* Mr. THURBER.
32. The Literature of the Elizabethan period. *First semester; M., W., Th., F., at 10.* Given in alternate years; 1899-1900, 1901-1902. Assistant Professor PYRE.
33. The Eighteenth Century. *Throughout the year; M., W., F., at 10.* Mr. DODGE. Given in alternate years; 1899-1900, 1901-1902.
34. The English Romantic Movement. *First semester; M., W., at 10.* Professor FREEMAN. Given in alternate years; 1900-1901, 1902-1903.

35. The Victorian Era. *Second semester; M., W., F., at 10.* Assistant Professor PYRE. Given in alternate years; 1900-1901, 1902-1903.
36. The Drama. Shakespeare. *Throughout the year; M., W., F., at 11.* A part of the first semester is devoted to History of the English Drama, the remainder of the year to Shakespeare. Open to seniors. Professor FREEMAN.
37. The Epic. Milton, Spenser. *First semester; Tu., Th., at 10.* Professor FREEMAN. Given in alternate years; 1899-1900, 1901-1902.
38. English Lyric Poetry. *Second semester; Tu., Th., at 10.* Professor FREEMAN. Given in alternate years; 1899-1900, 1901-1902.
39. The Novel. *Second semester; M., W., at 11.* Professor FREEMAN. Given in alternate years; 1900-1901, 1902-1903.
40. American Literature. *Throughout the year; Tu., Th., at 9.* Dr. CAIRNS.
41. Spenser. The course aims to cover the bulk of Spenser's poetical work. It will deal as thoroughly as possible with his literary ideals and methods, and with his relations to the literature of his time. *First semester; M., W., F., at 9.* Mr. DODGE. Given in 1900-1901.
42. Poetics. The science of verse. The history of English verse-forms. *First semester; Tu., Th., at 12.* Assistant Professor PYRE.
43. The English Essayists. *Second semester; M., W., F., at 9.* Mr. DODGE.
44. English Literature Seminary. Subject for 1899-1900, Chaucer; 1900-1901, Milton. Two hours a week in one session, *throughout the year; Tu., 4-6.* Open to graduates and properly qualified seniors. Professor FREEMAN and Professor HUBBARD.

MATHEMATICS.

PROFESSOR VAN VELZER, PROFESSOR SLICHTER, ASSISTANT PROFESSOR SKINNER, ASSISTANT PROFESSOR DOWLING, DR. RUNNING, MR. TALLMAN, AND MISS PENGRA.

Elementary Courses.

1. Algebra. This course is required of students in all courses. Text-book: Van Velzer and Slichter's University Algebra. *First semester; three times a week.* Professor VAN VELZER, Professor SLICHTER, Assistant Professor SKINNER, Assistant

Professor Dowling, Dr. Running, Mr. Tallman, and Miss Pengra.

This course will be repeated in the second semester if a sufficient number of students desire it to form a class.

2. Trigonometry. This course is required of students in all courses. The ratio system is used exclusively and special stress is laid upon goniometry. *Second semester; three times a week;* same divisions as in course 1.
3. Algebra (continuation of course 1). This course is elective for all students who have taken course 1. *Second semester; twice a week.* Assistant Professor Skinner.
4. Analytic Geometry (elementary course). Straight line, conic sections, general equation of the second degree, transcendental curves, and an introduction to geometry of three dimensions. *Twice a week for one year.* Assistant Professor Dowling.
5. Calculus (elementary course). Differentiation and integration of functions of one variable with the usual geometric applications. *Three times a week for one year.* Assistant Professor Dowling.

Advanced and Graduate Courses.

10. Higher Trigonometry. This course must be preceded by course 5. *First semester; twice a week.* Assistant Professor Skinner.
11. Calculus (advanced course). Partial derivatives and multiple integrals with the usual geometric applications. *Twice a week for one year.* Assistant Professor Dowling.
12. Differential Equations. Ordinary and partial differential equations with a few geometric and mechanical applications. Murray's Differential Equations is used as a text. This course must be preceded by course 11 or taken along with it. *Three times a week for one year.* Professor Van Velzer.
13. Theoretical Mechanics. An elementary course in analytical mechanics. This course may be taken by those who have had analytic geometry and calculus. *Three times a week for one year.* Professor Slichter.
14. Analytic Geometry of Two Dimensions (advanced course). Modern methods in plane analytic geometry. This course must be preceded by course 4. *Three times a week for one year.* Professor Van Velzer.
15. Projective Geometry. Holgate's translation of Reye's Geometrie

DEPARTMENTS OF INSTRUCTION. 117

der Lage is used as a text. *Twice a week for one year.* Assistant Professor DOWLING.

16. Analytic Geometry of Three Dimensions. This course should be preceded by courses 11 and 14. *Twice a week for one year.* Professor VAN VELZER.

17. Quaternions. *Twice a week for one year* in alternate years. Assistant Professor SKINNER.

18. Theory of Probabilities. A course in this subject adapted to the needs of students of science and economics will be given occasionally. The mathematics of the freshman year is required for admission to the class. *Two hours a week for one semester.* Professor SLICHTER.

20. Elliptic Functions. This course must be preceded by course 12. *Twice a week for one year.* Assistant Professor DOWLING.

21. Theory of Functions. *Three times a week for one year* in alternate years. Assistant Professor DOWLING.

22. Newtonian Potential Function. Lectures and required readings on the theory of potential with an introduction to spherical harmonics. *Twice a week for one year.* Professor SLICHTER.

23. Partial Differential Equations of Mathematical Physics. Based on Riemann's Lectures, and Byerly's Spherical Harmonics. *Twice a week for one year* in alternate years. Professor SLICHTER.

30. Theoretical Hydrodynamics. Lectures on fluid motion. *Twice a week for one year* in alternate years. A course in the Theory of Elasticity may be substituted for this course. Professor SLICHTER.

32. Modern Algebra. Invariants, covariants, etc. This course must be preceded by courses 3 and 11. *Twice a week for one year in* alternate years. Professor VAN VELZER.

33. Theory of Substitution Groups. Lectures based on Weber's Lehrbuch der Algebra. *Three times a week for one year* in alternate years. Assistant Professor SKINNER.

34. Theory of Numbers. Congruences, quadratic residues, quadratic forms, etc. The work is based on Dirichlet's Zahlentheorie. *Twice a week for one year* in alternate years. Professor VAN VELZER.

35. Higher Plane Curves. The subject is presented from the point of view due to Clebsch as it has been perfected by Brill and Noether. *Twice a week for one year.* Assistant Professor DOWLING.

36. Mathematical Seminary. *Two-hour sessions once a week throughout the year.* Professor VAN VELZER, Professor SLICHTER, Assistant Professor SKINNER, and Assistant Professor DOWLING.

Mathematical Group.

Students who desire to take the degree of B. A., B. L., or B. S., in mathematics, will be admitted to the mathematical group at the beginning of the sophomore year. Such students may omit studies prescribed for the sophomore year of the course to an amount not exceeding six hours a week and substitute mathematics therefor. Students expecting to write theses in applied mathematics should take the course in mechanics in their junior year.

ASTRONOMY.

PROFESSOR COMSTOCK.

1. General Astronomy. Fundamental concepts of astronomy and the more important problems associated with them, so far as the latter admit of treatment by elementary methods. This course is essentially non-mathematical. *Three times a week during the first semester.*
2. Observatory Work and Methods. This course can be undertaken only by students who have completed course 1 in physics, the mathematics of freshman year, and course 1 in astronomy. The mathematics of the sophomore year must either precede or be taekn concurrently with the course. *First semester, twice a week; second semester, three times a week.*
3. Special Topics in Celestial Mechanics. Integration of the equations of motion. Computation of ephemerides for undisturbed motion. Double star orbits. Comet orbits. Special perturbations.
   This course presupposes in the student a working knowledge of the infinitesimal calculus and the elements of dynamics. *First semester, three times a week; second semester, twice a week.*
4. Astrophysics. An elementary course in astrophysics with special reference to spectroscopy and photometry is offered to students who have completed course 1 in astronomy. Especial attention will be given to the experimental side of the subject, including the use of the instruments both in the laboratory and when attached to the telescope. *Second semester, three times a week.*

5. Graduate Courses. Graduate students and others desiring to pursue advanced astronomical studies will be received in the Washburn Observatory as assistants and will take part in the regular series of observations with the equatorial telescopes or with the meridian instruments, at the same time continuing their theoretical studies. Facilities for independent original work will be afforded to such students, and such work, if of sufficient value, will be printed in the Publications of the Washburn Observatory. Ten volumes of these Publications, representing the work of the observatory prior to 1897, have already been issued.

For other courses of instruction consult the title Astronomy, in the announcement of the College of Mechanics and Engineering. See, also, the title Washburn Observatory.

PHYSICS.

GENERAL PHYSICS: PROFESSOR SNOW, ASSISTANT PROFESSOR AUSTIN, ASSISTANT PROFESSOR WOOD, DR. SHEDD, MR. SMITH, MR. STANGEL, AND MR. MAGNUSSON.

MATHEMATICAL PHYSICS: PROFESSOR DAVIES.*

Elementary Course.

1. General Lectures and Introductory Laboratory Practice. Given as a full study throughout the year. Required of students in the General Science and Engineering courses. Also elective for students in all other courses. A knowledge of plane trigonometry including the use of logarithms is required for registration. Lectures *M., Tu., W., Th., at* 12 o'clock. Professor SNOW. One recitation by the class in smaller sections at hours to be assigned. Professor SNOW, Dr. SHEDD, and Mr. SMITH. Laboratory practice twice a week at hours to be arranged. Assistant Professor AUSTIN, Dr. SHEDD, Mr. SMITH, Mr. STANGEL, and Mr. MAGNUSSON.

Advanced Courses.

2. Advanced Laboratory Practice. Presupposes the completion of course 1 or its equivalent. Required of juniors in the Physics Group and elective for all other courses. *Three times a week throughout the year.* Assistant Professor AUSTIN and Assistant Professor WOOD.

*Died January 22, 1900. Provision will be made for continuing the courses which Professor Davies gave.

3. Thesis Work. Required of seniors in the Physics Group. Full study throughout the year. Professor Snow, Assistant Professor Austin, and Assistant Professor Wood.

At the beginning of the first semester, the student is expected, with the advice of the instructors, to take up some special line of investigation, which is to be conducted, under the direction of those in charge of the department, throughout the year.

4. Precision of Electrical Measurements. A laboratory course in the exact determination of electrical quantities. *First semester; three times a week; hours to be assigned.* Required of juniors in Electrical Engineering. Dr. Shedd.

5. Theoretical Physics. Part I. Mathematical Introduction and Mechanics. Part II. Elementary Electricity and Magnetism. *Three hours per week throughout the year.* Required of juniors in the Physics Group. Assistant Professor Austin.

6 Theoretical Physics. Part III. Theory of Heat, including gas theory and elementary thermo-dyanmics. Part IV. Theory of Light, based on Preston's Light as a text, but with a more complete treatment of the dispersion theory and diffraction. *Three hours per week throughout the year.* Required of seniors in the Physics Group. Assistant Professor Wood.

Courses 5 and 6 are open to all students who desire a more thorough knowledge of physics than can be obtained in the general course. The small amount of the higher mathematics required is given in the introduction.

7. Introduction to the Study of Mathematical Physics. This course of lectures will treat of the fundamental equations of mathematical physics, and will be preparatory to the more advanced courses in mathematical physics. *Three times a week throughout the year.* Elective for juniors and seniors in the Physics Group. Professor Davies.

Courses Primarily for Graduates.

8. History of Mathematical Physics in the Nineteenth Century. This course is primarily intended for graduate students having a fair knowledge of the elements of mathematical physics, but is also open to such undergraduate students as can avail themselves of it. *Twice a week throughout the year.* Professor Davies.

9. Mathematical Theory of Sound. This course presupposes the equivalent of course 7. A knowledge of differential equations

will also be required. *Throughout the year; M., W., F., at 2.* Professor DAVIES.

10. Mathematical Theory of Electricity and Magnetism. This course follows the treatment of the subject as given in Gray's Treatise on Magnetism and Electricity, and Webster's Electricity and Magnetism. *Four lectures a week throughout the year.* Professor DAVIES.

11. Mathematical Physics. This course will supplement course 7. It will be mainly concerned with waves in elastic media, including electro-magnetic waves and light. The subject will be taught by lectures, reference being made to standard works on theoretical physics. *Three times a week throughout the year.* Professor DAVIES.

   This course can be continued as a graduate course by such students as desire to make a specialty of the subject.

12. Terrestrial Magnetism and Compass Deviations. Part I. General, and as far as possible without the aid of mathematics. Part II. Advanced course using all necessary mathematics. *Twice a week throughout the year.* Professor DAVIES.

13. Graduate Research. This course is designed for those who have completed the equivalent of the work represented by the undergraduate courses, and who now desire to devote some time to investigation in special lines. No feature of the department is emphasized more strongly than this. Persons desiring to enter upon such a course are advised, with the assistance of the instructors, to select some special line of research to which several months of time may be devoted. This work will be encouraged by reserving rooms in the laboratory which are devoted exclusively to research work, and by securing whatever special apparatus may be necessary to the successful carrying out of original investigation. Professor SNOW, Professor DAVIES, Assistant Professor AUSTIN, Assistant Professor WOOD.

14. Colloquium. A class, meeting one evening each week, for the critical reading and discussion of the current periodical literature. Professor SNOW, Professor DAVIES, Assistant Professor AUSTIN, Assistant Professor WOOD, Mr. SMITH, Dr. SHEDD, Mr. STANGEL and Mr. MAGNUSSON.

   Required of all students in the Physics Group.

CHEMISTRY.

PROFESSOR DANIELLS, ASSISTANT PROFESSOR HILLYER, ASSISTANT PROFESSOR KAHLENBERG, DR. TINGLE, MR. COOK, AND MR. FOWLER.

1. General Elementary Chemistry. A daily exercise throughout the year as follows: *First semester.* Descriptive Inorganic Chemistry; lectures and laboratory work. *Lectures at 2.* Professor DANIELLS, Assistant Professor HILLYER, Mr. COOK, and Mr. FOWLER. *Second semester.* Qualitative Analysis until the Easter recess; then Descriptive Organic Chemistry, lectures and laboratory work. Assistant Professor HILLYER, Mr. COOK, and Mr. FOWLER.
2. Advanced Inorganic Chemistry, second year, and Quantitative Analysis. *Daily throughout the year.* The amount of time devoted to this subject may be more or less than that of a full study, and will be arranged upon consultation with the instructors. Professor DANIELLS and Dr. TINGLE.
3. Advanced Inorganic Chemistry, third year. The amount of time and the character of the work will be arranged upon consultation with the instructors. Besides the work required for a graduation thesis, it may consist of advanced work in theoretical, physical, or analytical chemistry, or in research work. Professor DANIELLS and Assistant Professor KAHLENBERG. For graduates and undergraduates.
4. Toxicology. Urine Analysis, and Sanitary Water Analysis. *Second semester, daily.* Open only to those who have taken at least one semester of quantitative analysis. Professor DANIELLS.
5. Quantitative Analysis for students in Pharmacy, *daily during the first half of the first semester.* Professor DANIELLS and Dr. TINGLE.
6. Water Analysis for students in Engineering. *Daily during the second semester.* Professor DANIELLS.
10. Advanced Organic Chemistry. Lectures on the fatty series and on the aromatic series with laboratory work mainly in the preparation of aromatic compounds, accompanied by special work on assigned topics. *Full study; first semester.* Assistant Professor HILLYER.
11. Study of methods of preparation of organic compounds. Following this work either organic analysis may be taken up or the study of organic compounds of special interest to those pre-

paring for medicine or work in the biological sciences. For graduates or undergraduates. Assistant Professor HILLYER.

12. Investigations in Organic Chemistry. Students who desire some problem in organic chemistry as a subject for the senior thesis should make known their desire at the close of junior year so that the subject may be assigned and preliminary study may be done during the summer session or vacation. Graduates who intend to study organic chemistry should announce their intention at the earliest date, with a statement of their preparation, so that lines of study may be suggested to be pursued before the opening of the first semester of attendance. A knowledge of French and German is necessary. Assistant Professor HILLYER.

15. Physical Chemistry. General Course. *Full study throughout the year. Lectures and recitations, first semester; Tu., Th., at 8. Second semester; M., W., F., at 8.* The lectures and recitations are supplemented by laboratory exercises in physico-chemical measurements, thus making a full study. This course must be preceded by course 1 in chemistry. Assistant Professor KAHLENBERG.

16. Electrochemistry. Lectures and recitations twice a week. Laboratory work in electrochemical measurements and in electrolysis of various chemical compounds supplements the lectures and with them makes a full study. *Daily, throughout the year; hours to be arranged.* Assistant Professor KAHLENBERG.

17. Special Laboratory Course in Physical Chemistry. This course is for seniors in engineering who desire an acquaintance with the methods of physico-chemical measurement. *Daily, first semester; hours to be arranged.* Assistant Professor KAHLENBERG.

18. Research Work in Physical Chemistry. Students having sufficient training may take up research work in physical chemistry, to which special importance is attached and for which every facility is furnished. This course is especially designed for seniors who desire to prepare a thesis and for graduates seeking higher degrees. The character of the work will be determined largely by the preparation that the student has and by his individual inclinations. *Daily throughout the year; hours to be arranged.* Assistant Professor KAHLENBERG.

19. Seminary in Physical Chemistry. Advanced students meet for more detailed study of special subjects and of original researches in physical chemistry. The work will be conducted on the seminary plan. *Throughout the year, at least once a week; at hours to be arranged.* Assistant Professor KAHLENBERG.

Instructors and advanced students meet weekly during the year to report on articles in the current chemical journals and on assigned topics suggested by recent work in chemistry. Nearly all the more important chemical journals are accessible for use in this work, and the department library is steadily growing by accessions of the best books of reference.

GEOLOGY AND MINERALOGY.

PROFESSOR VAN HISE, PROFESSOR HOBBS, AND ASSISTANT PROFESSOR CLEMENTS.

For students who wish to take a general educational course in geology no definite prerequisites are specified. To pursue successfully a long course in mineralogy or geology, physics and chemistry are prerequisites. Further, all students who intend to take geology as a major study should, if possible, take mineralogy 2 during the first semester of the previous year, and a full year's work in this subject is a very advantageous preparatory study to advanced work in geology. It is advised that when possible the mineralogy be taken in the sophomore year. Under the group system the courses are arranged by the professor in charge. The special work may be geology, under Professor VAN HISE and Assistant Professor CLEMENTS, or mineralogy or petrology, under Professor HOBBS.

GEOLOGY.

PROFESSOR VAN HISE, AND PROFESSOR HOBBS, AND ASSISTANT PROFESSOR CLEMENTS.

1. Part I. General Geology. *Three times a week.* The geological forces now modifying the world; their past, present, and future work. *Twice a week:* The physiography of the United States, each province being treated in reference to its development, and in its relations to population. These courses are especially adapted to students who intend to teach physical geography, those making a specialty of history, and those wishing to obtain a general comprehension of the character of

the earth upon which we live. Numerous short excursions. First semester to holiday vacation. *M., Tu., W., Th., F.,* or *M., W., F.,* at 12. Professor VAN HISE.

Part II. Historical Geology. Special emphasis is given to the history of the North American continent, including both the development of the continent itself and of the forms of life which have inhabited it. Lecture room and laboratory work. First semester from holiday vacation. *M., Tu., W., Th., F.,* or *M., W., F.,* at 12. Assistant Professor CLEMENTS.

Required of seniors in civil engineering. This course is so arranged that it can be taken as a two-fifths, three-fifths or five-fifths study for the first semester.

2. Part I. Economic Geology. Treats of potable waters, structural materials, soils, mineral fertilizers, mineral fuels, iron, copper, lead, and zinc ores. Must be preceded by course 1. Required of seniors in civil engineering. First six weeks of second semester. *M., Tu., W., Th., F.,* at 12. Equivalent to two-fifths study for one semester. Assistant Professor CLEMENTS.

Part II. Field Geology. Study of selected areas adjacent to Madison. The particular line of work followed in any given year depends upon the size and character of the class. An excursion of several days' length is taken to study the districts including the quartzite ranges of Baraboo and the Dalles of the Wisconsin. Last 12 weeks of second semester. *F.,* 2-6, *Sat.,* 9-1, *and* 2-6. Equivalent to three-fifths study for the semester. This course may be taken by students having had course 1 as a three-fifths or five-fifths study, although the latter is recommended. Assistant Professor CLEMENTS, and Professor VAN HISE.

3. Systematic Paleontology. Students will have an opportunity of becoming familiar with the most characteristic fossils, by examination in the lecture room and more detailed study in the laboratory. *First semester; M., W., F. Hours to be determined on consultation.* Assistant Professor CLEMENTS.

4. Petrology. (a) General petrology and microscopic petrology. The characteristics of rocks and their geological classification. *Second semester; Tu., Th.,* at 9-11.

(b) Microscopic petrology. The study of rocks as mineral aggregates with the aid of the petrographical microscope. *Second semester; M., W., F.,* 9-11. Professor HOBBS.

5. Graduate Courses. The epigene and hypogene phenomena of

physical geology, as seen in the field and in the laboratory, are treated with reference to the laws of energy.

(a) General Physical Geology. Sedimentation by all agents. The deformation of rocks, including an analysis of folds, cleavage and fissility, faults, joints, and autoclastic rocks. Mountain-making. Stratigraphy, including a discussion of bedding, basal conglomerates, unconformity, structural work in nonfossiliferous rocks, and practical methods of field work. Lectures and seminary work. Professor VAN HISE.

(b) Principles of Metamorphism and the Metamorphic Rocks. Underground waters. The principles controlling the deposition of ores. The forces, agents, and general processes of metamorphism. Classification and description of the metamorphic sedimentary and metamorphic igneous rocks. Lectures and laboratory work. Professor VAN HISE.

(c) The Physical Geology of the United States. Each of the geological provinces is taken up separately, and considered in reference to its sediments, deformation, economic resources, and physiography. Lectures and seminary work. Professor VAN HISE.

All of these subjects are considered from the point of view of the investigator. In any one year only one of the courses (a), (b), and (c) is given. The course selected for any year depends upon the needs of the advanced students. Each of the courses runs through the year in such a manner as to be equivalent to a full study for one semester. Each of the courses is accompanied by seminary and laboratory work.

6. Research Work for Graduates. Research work adapted to the individual applicant is offered. Under the advice of the professors this work may be an investigation which has already been undertaken by the student, or, if desired, the work will be assigned by the instructors.

For this work, besides the ordinary Museum material, there is available the very large collection of rocks and slides from all parts of America, belonging to the United States Geological Survey, and smaller, but still large, collections of European rocks. (See statement under Geological Museum.) This material furnishes exceptional opportunities for research work in petrography and metamorphism. To advanced students are assigned sets of this material for study in connection with the general investigations being carried on by the officers of the departments.

A full or double study, as desired by the individual students. Professor VAN HISE and Professor HOBBS.

MINERALOGY.

PROFESSOR HOBBS.

1. General Course. Prerequisite, a general course in chemistry. Trigonometry should be taken if possible.
   Crystallography, physical mineralogy (except optical mineralogy), chemical mineralogy, study of the non-silicate minerals. *First semester; M., Tu., W., Th., F., at 11.*
   (a) Study of the silicate minerals. (b) Blowpipe analysis and determinative mineralogy. *Second semester; M., Tu., W., Th., F. (a) at 11. (b) at 11-1.*
2. Short Course. Especially adapted to the needs of Engineering students. The quick method of determining the common minerals, and especially those of economic importance. This course is required of Civil Engineers in their sophomore year. *Last half of first semester; M., W., 9-11, and S., 9-1.*
3. Optical Mineralogy. Lectures, quizzes, and laboratory work with the polarizing microscope. A prerequisite to petrology. *First semester; M., W., F., 9-11.*
4. Crystallography. A course in the goniometrical and optical determination of crystals, especially adapted to students of chemistry and pharmacy. This course is given only when a sufficient number of students desire it. *First semester; Tu., Th., at 9.*
5. Graduate Course in Advanced Crystallography. The measurement and calculation of crystals. Individual work arranged with the instructor.

BIOLOGY.

PROEFSSOR BIRGE, PROFESSOR HARPER, PROFESSOR RUSSELL, ASSISTANT PROFESSOR MILLER, ASSISTANT PROFESSOR MARSHALL, ASSISTANT PROFESSOR CHENEY, MR. TIMBERLAKE, MR. FROST, MR. ATHERTON, AND MISS HATHERELL.

1. General Biology. Introductory to both botany and zoology, and required as preliminary to all advanced work in either department. Two recitations or lectures and eight hours' laboratory work a week, using as handbooks Arthur, Barnes & Coulter's Plant dissection and Marshall's The Frog.

Lectures, M., W., at 3. Professor HARPER and Profesor BIRGE. For laboratory work the class is divided into two or three sections, each meeting for two hours daily. Assistant Professor MARSHALL, Mr. TIMBERLAKE, and Miss HATHERELL. Quiz divisions are also required to meet once each week. Required of freshmen in General Science course, elective in other courses.

The first semester is devoted to a study of the general principles of biology as illustrated by plants. The second semester is given to zoology. Students can enter the course in either semester.

Zoology.

2. Vertebrate Anatomy. Laboratory work and lectures. First semester, the skeleton, muscles, and the viscera; second semester, the nervous and vascular systems. *Throughout the year;* 11-1. Assistant Professor MILLER and Mr. ATHERTON.

3. Invertebrate Zoology. A general course in the morphology and classification of Invertebrates. *Throughout the year;* 2-4. Professor BIRGE.

4. Human Physiology. A. Nutrition, respiration, excretion. *Firse semester; M., W., F., at* 8. B. Motion, nervous system, and sense organs. *Second semester; Tu., Th.,* 8. Text-book, Martin's The Human Body. Professor BIRGE.

5. Vertebrate Histology. Laboratory work and lectures. This course should be preceded by course 2. *Full study; first semester,* 9-11. Assistant Professor MILLER.

6. Vertebrate Embryology. This course follows course 5. The development of the chick during the first four days is studied. Laboratory work and lectures. *Full study; second semester,* 9-11. Assistant Professor MILLER.

7. Advanced work in Histology and Embryology. This course is open to graduate students and such undergraduate students as may wish to carry on their work along special lines. Courses 2, 6, and 7 are prerequisite. Modern methods of research and reconstruction methods will receive special attention. Assistant Professor MILLER.

8. Thesis work in Vertebrate Anatomy, Histology, or Embryology. Students who make the course in vertebrate anatomy their major study will take course 2 in their sophomore year, and courses 5 and 6 in their junior year, leaving the senior year free for thesis work. The subject of the thesis should be se-

lected during the junior year, and the preliminary work begun. Assistant Professor MILLER.

9. Entomology. A general course in the anatomy, embryology, and classification of insects, with special attention to forms of economic importance. *First semester; full study.* Assistant Professor MARSHALL.

10. Invertebrate Embryology. The segmentation of the egg, and the formation of gastrula in various groups of invertebrates, and the leading types of metamorphosis of invertebrates. *Second semester; full study.* Assistant Professor MARSHALL.

11. Research Courses in the Study of Plankton and Invertebrate Zoology. For senior theses, and graduates. Group students in zoology may take their major subject in invertebrate zoology, following courses 1 and 3 by 10. Professor BIRGE and Assistant Professor MARSHALL.

Students can take a major line of study in either invertebrate or vertebrate zoology. Persons intending to teach zoology in high schools should take at least course 3 in addition to course 1.

12. Summer Courses in Zoology. See announcement of summer session on later pages.

Botany.

15. Plant Morphology. The course presupposes course 1. Lectures and laboratory work. *Daily,* 2-4. Lectures, *Tu., Th., at* 3. Professor HARPER.

16. Vegetable Histology. Systematic study of the tissues of phanerogams and ferns. Use of reagents and stains, modes of imbedding, section cutting, and mounting. Laboratory guide: Strasburger's Practical Botany. *Daily, first semester; hours on consultation.* Assistant Professor CHENEY.

17. Reproduction and embryology of the flowering plants. A study of the life history of a few types of flowering plants, including the phenomena of pollination, fertilization, development of organs and tissues, and discussions of morphological homologies and allied developmental problems. *Second semester; three hours a week.* Mr. TIMBERLAKE.

18. Cytology. General physiology of organisms. Lectures and experimental work on the reproduction, irritability, and nutrition of the cell. Must be preceded by courses 15 or 16 and an ability to read German is desired. *Daily. Hours on consultation.* Professor HARPER.

19. Mycology. Special work on the morphology and classification of the fungi or in plant pathology is offered to advanced or graduate students. *Hours on consultation.* Professor HARPER.
20. Botanical Methods. Methods of preparing plant tissues and of growing various algae and fungi for use in the class room; practice in simple demonstrations in Physiology. *Three times a week, second semester. Hours on consultation.* Professor HARPER and Mr. TIMBERLAKE.
21. Research work. Students whose preparation is adequate may on consultation be assigned special subjects of investigation. Professor HARPER.
22. General Morphology of Plants. An elementary course designed primarily for pharmacy students, but open to others who desire to begin the study of botany. *First semester*, the morphology of fungi, algae, lichens, mosses, and ferns. *Second semester*, the form and structure of the organs of seed plants, the identification of selected flowering plants and the preparation of an herbarium. The course will be supplemented by botanical excursions. *Daily*, 8-10. Excursions on Saturdays. Assistant Professor CHENEY.
23. Trees and their Characteristics. A course designed for those who desire to acquaint themselves with forest trees. Lectures and laboratory work with occasional excursions. The course presupposes the equivalent of one semester's work in general botany. *Twice a week through the year.* May be taken either semester or both. *Hours to be arranged on consultation.* Assistant Professor CHENEY.
24. Advanced Work in Anatomy. Special subjects for original investigation will be assigned to such students as are properly qualified, and who desire to do advanced work. Assistant Professor CHENEY.
27. Summer Courses in Botany. See announcement of the summer session on later pages.

Bacteriology.

30. General Bacteriology. This course considers the bacteria in their general biological aspect.
    This course is fundamental and should be regarded as a basis on which further specialization along lines of applied science can take place, as in medical, sanitary, and dairy bacteriology.

Lectures or equivalent, M., W., F., at 11. First semester. Full study. Professor RUSSELL and Mr. FROST.

31. Medical Bacteriology. This course is especially designed for pre-medical students. Course 30 is a pre-requisite. *Lectures twice a week, M., F., at 11. Full study, second semester.* Mr. FROST.

32. Thesis Work in Bacteriology. Students who desire to select their theses in this department must take course 30 in their junior year or before, and select the subject for their thesis before the close of the junior year. Professor RUSSELL and Mr. FROST.

33. Advanced Work in Bacteriology. Students who have had sufficient preliminary work (courses 30 and 31 or their equivalent) will be assigned special topics for study. Laboratory work and conferences. Professor RUSSELL and Mr. FROST.

34. Research Work in Bacteriology. Opportunity is offered for work in original investigation which may be arranged for on consultation. A reading knowledge of French and German is necessary. Professor RUSSELL and Mr. FROST.

35. Communicable Diseases: Their Cause and Prevention. Weekly lectures of a non-technical character, intended primarily for students in other than the General Science Course. No previous work in science is required. *Second semester, one-fifth study.* Mr. FROST.

36. Biology of Water Supplies. This course is adapted to the needs of students in Sanitary Engineering. *First semester, full study, lectures and laboratory work.* Required of juniors in Sanitary Engineering. Mr. FROST.

For Courses in Dairy and Agricultural Bacteriology see announcement under College of Agriculture.

The Bacteriological Journal Club meets bi-monthly on Thursdays for the review of Current Bacteriological literature.

MUSIC.

PROFESSOR PARKER.

The courses in music are open as electives to students in any department of the University who show sufficient musical ability to pursue them with profit.

For admission to course 1, no previous knowledge of music is required.

Those desiring to take course 2 must be able to read and play simple four-part music. Course 1 will be found useful in strengthening preparation for the courses in Harmony and Counterpoint. Courses 1 and 2, or their equivalent, are required as a preparation for course 6. Students may take the lectures of the second semester of course 7, without having taken those of the first semester.

Students may be admitted to advanced courses on examination.

Special students may substitute private lessons in piano playing or singing for one or more studies on recommendation of the Professor of Music. See the statement of the School of Music on subsequent pages.

Classes meet in Room 12, Ladies' Hall.

1. Musical Theory and Choral Practice. *Two hours a week. Throughout the year; M., W., at 5.*
2. Elementary Harmony. *Two hours a week. Throughout the year; Tu., Th., at 4.*
3. Advanced Harmony. *Three hours a week. First semester; M., W., F., at 11.*
4. Counterpoint. *Three hours a week. Second semester; M., W., F., at 11.*
5. Double Counterpoint and Fugue. *Three hours a week. Throughout the year; M., W., F., at 10, subject to change.*
6. Musical Composition. *Two hours a week. Throughout the year;* hours to be arranged.
7. History of Music. Lectures. *Two hours a week. Throughout the year; Tu., Th., at 3.*
8. Advanced Piano Playing. Senior and junior years only. Hours and credit to be arranged with the instructor and director of the School of Music, but not to exceed a total of 5-5 for one year.

Students who are competent may join the University Orchestra, receiving a credit of 1-5 for the work. One rehearsal each week. *Throughout the year; Sat., 11 to 1.* Mr. NITSCHKE.

Students who desire to become connected with the University Military Band should confer with Mr. Nitschke.

MILITARY SCIENCE AND TACTICS.

CAPTAIN CURTIS, U. S. A.

This department of the University is maintained in accordance with the statutes of the United States and the State. By the regulations of the University, all the able-bodied male students of the freshman and sophomore classes, and of special courses, for the first two years of such courses, are required to take military drill.

The work of the department embraces a course in drill regulations, a course of lectures on military subjects and practical instruction in the school of the soldier, company, and battalion, target practice, artillery drill and signal drill. The class in drill regulations is organized each year, and may be elected by both classes. All commissioned officers, the sergeant-majors, quartermaster-sergeants and sergeants are required to take the course, which continues through the winter. The study value of drill regulations and the lecture course is that of a two-fifths and one-fifth study respectively.

Freshmen who, prior to their entering the University, have received the equivalent of one year's instruction in the University battalion, may, at the discretion of the commandant, be required to drill one year only; *provided*, that they furnish certificates from the principals of military schools they have attended, or the commanding officers of military companies in which they have served, setting forth in detail the military duty performed; and that they take the full course in drill regulations, maintaining a good class standing. Freshmen or sophomores who, prior to their connection with the University, have served in the army or navy of the U. S. and been honorably discharged, may receive full credit for drill at the University, without further military instruction.

Drills will begin at the opening of the first semester and be held twice each week throughout the year.

The standing in military drill will be marked on a scale of 100. One unexcused absence will remove 5. Two unexcused absences will remove 10. Three unexcused absences will remove 15. Four unexcused absences will be reported as a condition. Ten unexcused absences will be reported as a failure. Three unexcused lates of over five minutes and less than ten will be marked as an absence. Any article of apparel out of uniform will be marked as an absence. Soiled gloves or untidy clothing will be marked as an absence.

Students of the freshman or sophomore classes or first and second year specials, who enter, as candidates, the crews and athletic teams recognized by the athletic council, will not be excused from drill until they are regularly elected to membership of such organizations.

When a member of a crew or an athletic team shall be discharged from such crew or team he will report to the commandant for drill at the next drill succeeding his discharge.

All appointments to office in the companies shall originate in the sophomore class, but officers may be promoted and continued in office during their junior and senior years.

Students excused from drill will be required to take, before graduation, an additional one-fifth study in the academic course for each semester in which they were excused from drill.

The uniform of the regiment is similar to the fatigue or undress uniform of the army, and can be obtained in Madison at a cost of $9.50 to $15.00.

ORGANIZATION.

The organization is that of a regiment consisting of two battalions of four companies each, with a full quota of officers, a brass band of over twenty-four pieces, a bugle corps, and a signal squad. Students are at liberty to enter any organization except the signal squad. The latter consists of those selected by the Commandant.

Upon graduation specially qualified students receive from the Governor of Wisconsin State commissions of honorary second lieutenants.

Roster for 1899-1900.

Commandant.

Captain Charles A. Curtis, U. S. Army.

Student Officers.

FIELD AND STAFF.

Colonel Bernard M. Palmer.
Lieutenant-Colonel John M. Dreyer.
Major Enoch W. Underwood, Adjutant.
Major John C. Taylor, Quartermaster.
Sergeant-Major Frederick A. DeLay.

FIRST BATTALION.

Major Henry H. Taylor.
Captain Eric W. Allen, Adjutant.
Captain Allan S. Nielson, Quartermaster.
Sergt.-Major Walter S. Hopkins.

SECOND BATTALION.

Major James H. McNeel.
Captain William F. Dickinson, Adjutant.
First Lieut. Stephen C. Phipps, Quartermaster.
Sergt.-Major Gustave W. R. Ehreke.

DEPARTMENTS OF INSTRUCTION.

COMPANY OFFICERS.

A—Captain William C. Burdick.
  1st Lieut. James E. Smith.
  2d Lieut. Wm. L. Thorkelson.
  1st Sergt. John W. Nevins.
  2d Sergt. Ernst C. Meyer.

C—Captain Paul Stover.
  1st Lieut. Ashbel V. Smith.
  2d Lieut. Henry O. Winkler.
  1st Sergt. Samuel G. Higgins,
  2d Sergt. John V. Brennan.

E—Captain Burton S. Bridge.
  1st Lieut. Hawley D. Lennon.
  2d Lieut. George F. Markham.
  1st Sergt. Fred H. Carpenter.
  2d Sergt. George B. Vinson.

G—Captain Gustav A. Fritsche.
  1st Lieut. Arthur B. Grindell,
  2d Lieut. Percy E. Schroeder,
  1st Sergt. Fred A. Vogel.
  2d Sergt. Arthur P. H. Inbusch,

COMPANY OFFICERS.

B—Captain Hugo W. Rohde.
  1st Lieut. Archy B. Carter.
  2d Lieut. Bertram F. Adams.
  1st Sergt. Harry G. Kemp.
  2d Sergt. George L. Gust.

D—Captain Harry E. Bradley.
  1st Lieut. Fred L. Hook.
  2d Lieut. Harvey P. Clawson.
  1st Sergt. Paul C. Foster.
  2d Sergt. Harry T. McNiell.

F—Captain Frederick D. Taylor.
  1st Lieut. William L. Dale.
  2d Lieut. John R. Kimball.
  1st Sergt. Charles E. Long.
  2d Sergt. Cecil L. Clifford.

H—Captain Lynn H. Tracy.
  1st Lieut. John R. Henry.
  2d Lieut. Myron R. Johnson.
  1st Sergt. William D. Eaton.
  2d Sergt. J. Barton Patrick.

SIGNAL DETACHMENT.

Captain Nathaniel C. Hurd, Instructor and Officer in Charge.

PHYSICAL EDUCATION.

DR. ELSOM, MISS MAYHEW, MISS HARRIS, AND STUDENT ASSISTANTS DAVIES, PETERSON AND ISHIKAWA.

Gymnastics for Men.

The Armory and Gymnasium is 200 feet in length, 100 feet in width, and three stories in height. On the ground floor are ample accommodations for bathing, such as shower and spray baths, tubs, and a natatorium 80 feet long by 20 feet wide. Lecture room, offices, and locker rooms are found also on this floor, the latter fitted up with 600 lockers for the use of students. Four bowling alleys, thoroughly equipped, have been placed in an attractive portion of the ground floor. On the main floor, besides the necessary offices, there is an unobstructed hall 165x95 feet in dimension, for the purpose of military drill and gymnastic practice. This room is thoroughly fitted with the most improved and latest scientific developing apparatus. The gymnasium in its equipment is not surpassed by any in the West, and in size it is absolutely the largest in the United States. On the third floor is the padded running track, twelve laps to the mile; a base-ball cage, 160 feet in length; two rifle ranges, hand-ball, and tennis courts, etc., besides space for general indoor athletic practice.

Each student on entering the department undergoes a thorough physical examination, in order that his physical condition may be known, and suitable exercise prescribed. Various strength tests, and measurements are given; the heart, lungs, and eyes are examined, and the utmost caution used in the advice regarding individual exercise. One examination during each semester is required, the latter demonstrating any improvement or change in the student's physical condition. Anthropometric cards and charts are platted for students when desired.

Systematic class work in gymnastics is required on two days of the week, of all freshmen, sophomores, and special students ranking with these classes. This work consists of vigorous drill with dumb-bells, clubs, bar-bells, etc., besides progressive graded work on the various pieces of gymnastic apparatus, always under the careful direction of competent instructors.

In the scheme of gymnastics, such exercises as are promotive of health, grace, and self-control, are sought for rather than heavy and dangerous athletic performances.

Every facility is provided for track-athletics, base-ball, foot-ball, tennis, aquatics, etc. The Lower Campus, directly in front of the gymnasium, furnishes a large, level area for the practice of all athletic sports. In addition, the University owns the large tract known as Camp Randall, which is fitted up with a large grand stand, a one-fourth mile track, and other necessary features.

The University is situated on the shores of Lake Mendota, a beautiful sheet of water, which invites exercise and recreation in boating. The University Boat House Association has erected a boat house at a cost of over $4,000.

During the second semester, a course of lectures on personal hygiene, health culture, etc., is given to the freshman class, illustrated by various physical charts and other apparatus. Attendance at these lectures is required of all freshmen.

Gymnastics for Women.

Ladies' Hall contains a finely equipped gymnasium for the use of the young women attending the University. This room is two stories high, has a floor space of 71x40 feet, and is provided with 27 dressing rooms, and 128 lockers. The dressing rooms connect with shower baths supplied with hot and cold water, furnishing ample bathing facilities for those who take gymnastics.

The apparatus is complete and varied, consisting of chest weights, dumb-bells, wands, bar-bells, etc., besides a complete outfit of Swedish apparatus, and other forms of appliance for development and physical improvement. Music is used in all class drills. The first object of the training for women is of maintaining and conserving the health, and incidentally there are derived benefits of a very valuable character, such as the acquirement of grace, muscular control, self-reliance, and strength.

Each student will undergo a careful physical examination on entering the department, in order that the physical condition may be known, and suitable exercise prescribed for individual cases. A second examination is given during the second semester, in order that the improvements and benefits of the course of exercise may be shown.

The work is required of all freshman and sophomore students, and all special students ranking with them. Excuse may be granted from the required work on account of physical disability.

The Tennis and Cycling Clubs afford ample opportunity for outdoor exercise and recreation, when the season and weather permit. Games, such as basketball, newcombe, basquette, etc., are practiced indoors during the winter season, and several teams organized for work in these games.

Course in Teacher's Gymnastics.

A class in theory of Physical Training and in practice of teaching gymnastics meets once a week throughout the year. *One-fifth credit each semester.*

SCHOOL OF ECONOMICS, POLITICAL SCIENCE AND HISTORY.

STAFF OF INSTRUCTION.

C. K. ADAMS, LL. D., President of the University.
R. T. ELY, Ph. D., LL. D., Director, and Professor of Political Economy.
C. H. HASKINS, Ph. D., Professor of Institutional History.
J. B. PARKINSON, A. M., Professor of Constitutional and International Law.
W. A. SCOTT, Ph. D., Professor of Economic History and Theory.
F. J. TURNER, Ph. D., Professor of American History.
VICTOR COFFIN, Ph. D., Assistant Professor of European History.
F. C. SHARP, Ph. D., Assistant Professor of Philosophy.
B. H. MEYER, Ph. D., Assistant Professor of Sociology.
P. S. REINSCH, Ph. D., Assistant Professor in Political Science.
O. G. LIBBY, Ph. D., Instructor in History.
S. E. SPARLING, Ph. D., Assistant in Public Administration.
E. D. JONES, Ph. D., Instructor in Economics and Statistics.
T. K. URDAHL, Ph. D., Assistant in Economics.
W. P. TRENT, Ph. D. (University of the South), Special Lecturer on History.
H. M. STEPHENS, M. A. (Cornell University), Special Lecturer on History.
J. R. JEWETT, Ph. D. (University of Minnesota), Special Lecturer on History.
A. E. HENRY, M. A., Fellow in Economics.
JOSEPH SCHAEFER, M. L., Fellow in History.
*JENNY C. WATTS, M. A., Fellow in History.

GENERAL STATEMENT.

The purpose of the school is to afford superior means for systematic and thorough study in economics, political and social science, and history. The courses are graded and arranged so as to meet the wants of students in the various stages of their progress, beginning with elementary and proceeding to the most advanced work. They are also designed to meet the needs of different classes of students;

*Resigned.

as, for instance, those who wish to enter the public service, the professions of law, journalism, the ministry or teaching, and those who wish to supplement their legal, theological, or other professional studies with courses in economics, social science, or history. Capable students are encouraged to undertake original investigations, and assistance is given them in the prosecution of such work through seminaries and the personal guidance of instructors. A means for the publication of the results of investigations of merit and importance is provided in the University Bulletins, p. 34.

Courses in other departments may be advantageously combined with those offered in the school. Especial attention is called to the large number of related courses in philosophy and ethics.

The work of the School consists of the following departments:

1. Graduate Seminaries and Classes. These are open to graduates of colleges of good standing who have had the necessary preliminary studies. Graduate students whose training has been defective will be required to make up deficiencies by work in the prerequisite undergraduate courses.

2. The Civic Historical Course. This is designed to afford a liberal course of undergraduate training with emphasis upon the studies especially adapted to the promotion of good citizenship. It is parallel to the other four-year undergraduate courses of the University and leads to the degree of Bachelor of Letters. Students are admitted by examination or after graduation from an accredited school; the requirements for entrance are stated on page 63. The requirements for graduation in the course are stated on page 78.

3. Courses in economics, political science, and history offered to students in other departments. The various classes in the School are open to all properly qualified students of the University. In the College of Letters and Science students in the Ancient Classical and Modern Classical courses are required to take course 1 in history during the freshman year, and courses 1 and 2 are required of freshmen in the English course; the other studies of the School are elective, and count toward graduation on the same basis as the work of other departments. Course 5 in economics is part of the required work in the Short Course in Agriculture. Several courses in the school are peculiarly suited to the needs of students in the College of Law, and may be taken to advantage in connection with their professional studies.

Candidates for the degree of Doctor of Philosophy in this School are required to present in their principal subject the equivalent of at least two full graduate courses during two years, in their first subordinate the equivalent of at least one such course during two years, and in their second subordinate the equivalent of at least one such course during one year.

Candidates for the master's degree must present in their principal subject the equivalent of at least two full graduate courses during one year, and in their subordinate subject the equivalent of at least one such course.

The other requirements for the master's and doctor's degree may be found on pages 54, 55.

The courses of study offered in this school are described under the head of Economics and Statistics (page 85), Sociology (page 88), Political Science (page 89), and History (page 92).

THE SCHOOL OF EDUCATION.

The School of Education at present embraces three separate organizations:
    I. The School of Education proper, composed of the departpartments of Pedagogy and Philosophy.
    II. The University Extension Department.
    III. The Wisconsin Summer School and the Summer School of Library Science.

I. THE SCHOOL OF EDUCATION.

Staff of Instruction.

C. K. ADAMS, LL. D., President of the University.
J. W. STEARNS, LL. D., Director and Professor of Philosophy and Pedagogy.
M. V. O'SHEA, B. L., Professor of the Science and Art of Education.
JOSEPH JASTROW, Ph. D., Professor of Experimental and Comparative Psychology.
F. C. SHARP, Ph. D., Assistant Professor of Philosophy.
B. H. MEYER, Ph. D., Assistant Professor of Sociology, and University Extension Lecturer in Economics.
W. H. SHELDON, Ph. D., Assistant in Psychology.
JOHN W. BAIRD, A. M., Fellow in Philosophy.

GENERAL STATEMENT.

This School aims to afford practical and helpful instruction to students who wish to prepare themselves for teaching in public schools and colleges; to those who wish to become school principals and school superintendents; and to those who desire to pursue studies and investigations in the science of education. Persons looking forward to the professions of journalism, law, or the ministry, will find in some of the courses instruction adapted to their needs; while the history and general principles of education form a valuable addition to the courses for general culture. The four main lines of instruction in pedagogy are the history, the philosophy, the science, and the practice of education, all of which present extensive fields for investigation. The history of education very properly occupies a place in courses for general culture, as an important and practical branch of the history of civilization, and it also affords the best introduction to the problems of pedagogy. The science of education is closely connected with philosophy, and especially with psychology in its modern physiological and comparative forms. Beyond the courses which are outlined below, ample opportunity will be given for the study of special problems in the laboratory and in the school room. The seminaries will afford opportunities for critical discussion of teaching work, and of educational problems, and will acquaint the student with the most important current literature of education.

The work of the School naturally falls into the following divisions:

I. Classes for undergraduate students of the university as part of general culture courses. For this purpose courses 1, 5, 10, and 11, in pedagogy, are specially suited.

II. Courses for undergraduate students who wish to prepare themselves for teaching in the public schools. Those in regular courses of the University who fulfill the following conditions will be entitled to receive a University Teacher's Certificate: (1) That they have completed at least ten-fifths for one semester of study in psychology and pedagogy in the School of Education; (2) that they have made special scholarly preparation for teaching in at least one department of work represented in the high schools, which preparation shall be stated in the Certificate; (3) that they shall have taken the course for teachers offered in the department in which they have made special preparation.

III. Courses for students specializing in education. Those who expect to take their first degree in the educational group are required (1) to pursue work in the department to the extent of one full study for two years; (2) to prepare a thesis in this department. The courses adapted to serve as introductory to the study of education are: In philosophy, courses 1, 2, 3, and 31; in pedagogy, courses 1, 5, 13, and 18.

IV. For Normal School graduates the Philosophical Course of two years, looking to a more advanced and extended study of the theory and practice of education, has been outlined as follows:

Junior year: Latin, French, or German 4; philosophy 3; advanced pedagogy 3; language, history, English, advanced mathematics, or science 5; electives 3 to 5; 18 *hours per week required.*

Senior year: Continuation of Latin, French, or German 4; philosophy and advanced pedagogy 5; electives from language, science, history, economics, mathematics, or English 7; and thesis; 18 *hours per week.*

V. Graduate students, and those looking to the supervision of large schools or school systems, and to the detailed study of educational problems, will find work suited to their needs in the seminaries and advanced courses of the school.

An account of the courses offered in Philosophy and Pedagogy will be found on pages 81-83. Teachers' courses are offered in other departments, and are described under the appropriate heads. Among these courses are Latin 7, p. 100; German 36, p. 110; botany 20, p. 130; history 17, p. 95; English grammar 23, p. 114. See also the courses announced for teachers in the Summer Session of the University on subsequent pages.

UNIVERSITY EXTENSION DEPARTMENT.

Staff.

CHARLES KENDALL ADAMS, LL. D., President of the University.
J. W. STEARNS, LL. D., Director and Professor of Philosophy and Pedagogy.
B. H. MEYER, Ph. D., Secretary, Lecturer on Economics, and Assistant Professor of Sociology.
A. A. BRUCE, A. B., LL. D., Assistant Professor of Law.
E. R. BUCKLEY, Ph. D., Geologist, Geological and Natural History Survey.
G. C. COMSTOCK, Ph. B., LL. B., Professor of Astronomy.
J. C. FREEMAN, LL. D., Professor of English Literature.
W. F. GIESE, A. M., Assistant Professor of Romance Languages.
LOUIS KAHLENBERG, Ph. D., Assistant Professor of Physical Chemistry.
M. V. O'SHEA, B. L., Professor of the Science and Art of Education.
J. F. A. PYRE, Ph. D., Assistant Professor of English Literature.
P. S. REINSCH, Ph. D., Assistant Professor of History and Political Science.
H. L. RUSSELL, Ph. D., Professor of Bacteriology, and Bacteriologist to the Experiment Station.
E. D. JONES, Ph. D., Instructor in Statistics and Economics.
F. C. SHARP, Ph. D., Assistant Professor of Philosophy.
C. F. SMITH, Ph. D., Professor of Greek and Classical Philology.
S. E. SPARLING, Ph. D., Assistant in Political Science.

GENERAL INFORMATION.

The University Extension Department of the University of Wisconsin, as at present organized, carries on its work of giving instruction at a distance from the University by courses of lectures delivered in person by University instructors.

I. UNIVERSITY EXTENSION LECTURES.

University Extension lectures are lectures delivered by university professors and instructors on subjects which they treat in their regular classes.

Under the system adopted by the University of Wisconsin, the University Extension lectures are delivered only in courses of six lectures. The purpose of delivering the lectures in courses is to concentrate attention upon one subject.

A printed syllabus, free to each student, will give an epitome of the subject considered, an analysis of each lecture, references to the best books on the subject, and other helpful suggestions.

The class, which is held before or after each lecture, furnishes the student an opportunity to question the lecturer and to have special difficulties explained. In the class, the lecturer will take the opportunity to elaborate his subject or to emphasize its salient features.

The lecturer will hold at the end of the course a written examination which may be taken only by those who have attended the lectures and classes, read the required books and sent in the required papers. To such as comply with these requirements and pass the examination the University of Wisconsin will award a certificate, having a recognized value on the University records and credited accordingly, should the holder ever study at the University.

EXPENSES.

The expenses of a course consist of local expenses and the charges of the University. Under the former head are included hall rent, printing, advertising, etc., which are managed by the local center, and which vary, of course, in different towns and circumstances. Often a church or school hall may be obtained for the lectures without expense.

The charges of the University consist of:

1. A fee of $100 for a course of six lectures.
2. The lecturer's traveling expenses, including sleeping-car and meals, when necessary. In the case of a circuit, the lecturer's traveling expenses are divided equally between the centers forming the circuit.
3. The lecturer's hotel bill. Where the lecturer is entertained by members of the local center, the item disappears.
4. If lantern illustrations are given, the actual cost will be paid by the local center.

COURSES OF LECTURES.

The following is the program of courses for 1899-1900:

Professor M. V. O'SHEA: Applied Psychology and Child-Study.

Assistant Professor FRANK C. SHARP: Problems of Moral Progress.

Assistant Professor B. H. MEYER: An introduction to Economic Problems; Some Leading Economists.
Assistant Professor ANDREW A. BRUCE: Society and the Law-Maker.
Dr. EDWARD D. JONES: Charity and Crime.
Dr. SAMUEL E. SPARLING: The Modern City and Its Problems; American Political Parties and Their Relation to Government.
Assistant Professor PAUL S. REINSCH: The Constitution and the Founding of the Federal Government; The Statesmen of the Civil War; Contemporary World Politics; Historic Towns and Sites in Italy.
Professor JOHN C. FREEMAN: English Life and Literature; Studies in Shakespeare; Great Epics of the World.
Assistant Professor JAMES F. A. PYRE: American Writers and American Culture; Typical English Poems.
Assistant Professor WM. F. GIESE: The French Classic Poets; The Skeptical Movement in French Literature from the Renaissance to the 19th Century.
Professor CHARLES F. SMITH: Greek Life; Greek Literature.
Professor GEORGE C. COMSTOCK: Astronomy.
Dr. ERNEST R. BUCKLEY: Geographic Geology; Economic Geology with Special Reference to Wisconsin.
Professor HARRY L. RUSSELL: Microbes and Their Work.
Assistant Professor LOUIS KAHLENBERG: Chemistry.

WISCONSIN SUMMER SCHOOL.

SESSION OF 1900.

J. W. STEARNS, LL. D., Director of School.

The thirteenth annual session of the Summer School will extend from July 2, to Aug. 10, 1900.

The work of the Summer School is consolidated with that of the University. The courses of study formerly given in the Summer School are included in the summer session and will be found announced under the appropriate departments of study on preceding pages. The terms of admission to the School remain as heretofore and the fee is the same as that for the summer session of the University, as stated on page 000. The Summer School courses will be found adapted, as heretofore, to recent high school graduates who intend to enter the University; to University and college students who expect to teach and desire to review the studies which they will be called upon to teach; to teachers who wish to study the principles of teaching and still further prepare themselves in the branches in which they are giving instruction; to principals and superintendents who desire to aid to the better understanding of the theory and practice of their work. Persons who intend to take the state examinations for teachers will also find means of completing their preparation.

THE SUMMER SESSION.

STAFF OF INSTRUCTION.

C. K. ADAMS, LL. D., President of the University.
J. B. PARKINSON, A. M., Vice-President, Professor of Constitutional and International Law.
E. A. BIRGE, Ph. D., Sc. D., Dean of the College of Letters and Science; Director of the Summer Session; Professor of Zoology.
L. W. AUSTIN, Ph. D., Assistant Professor of Physics.
J. B. CARTER, Ph. D., Assistant Professor of Latin.
VICTOR COFFIN, Ph. D., Assistant Professor of European History.
W. W. DANIELLS, M. S., Sc. D., Professor of Chemistry.
L. W. DOWLING, Ph. D., Assistant Professor of Mathematics.
J. C. ELSOM, M. D., Professor of Physical Culture and Director of the Gymnasium.
R. T. ELY, Ph. D., LL. D., Director of the School of Economics, Political Science, and History, and Professor of Political Economy.
N. M. FENNEMAN, A. B., Professor of Physical Geography.
D. B. FRANKENBURGER, A. M., LL. B., Professor of Rhetoric and Oratory.
R. A. HARPER, Ph. D., Professor of Botany.
H. W. HILLYER, Ph. D., Assistant Professor of Organic Chemistry.
F. G. HUBBARD, Ph. D., Professor of the English Language.
JOSEPH JASTROW, Ph. D., Professor of Experimental and Comparative Psychology.
A. A. KNOWLTON, A. M., Assistant Professor of English.
A. G. LAIRD, Ph. D., Assistant Professor of Ancient Languages.
W. S. MARSHALL, Ph. D., Assistant Professor of Zoology.
ABBY S. MAYHEW, Mistress of Ladies' Hall and Instructor in Physical Culture.
B. H. MEYER, Ph. D., Assistant Professor of Sociology.
W. S. MILLER, M. D., Assistant Professor of Vertebrate Anatomy.
J. E. OLSON, B. L., Professor of the Scandinavian Languages and Literature.
M. V. O'SHEA, B. L., Professor of the Science and Art of Education.
E. T. OWEN, A. B., Professor of the French Language and Literature.
W. A. SCOTT, Ph. D., Professor of Economic History and Theory.
M. S. SLAUGHTER, Ph. D., Professor of Latin.

C. S. SLICHTER, M. S., Professor of Applied Mathematics.
W. M. SMITH, A. B., Librarian.
B. W. SNOW, Ph. D., Professor of Physics.
J. W. STEARNS, LL. D., Director of the School of Education. Professor of Philosophy and Pedagogy.
MARY E. TANNER, Professor of Drawing.
F. J. TURNER, Ph. D., Professor of American History.
E. K. J. H. VOSS, Ph. D., Associate Professor of German Language and Literature.
W. H. WILLIAMS, A. B., Professor of Hebrew and Hellenistic Greek.
H. G. A. BRAUER, M. A., Instructor in French.
W. B. CAIRNS, Ph. D., Instructor in English.
ABBIE F. EATON, M. L., Instructor in German.
SALLY P. HARRIS, Assistant in Physical Culture.
O. G. LIBBY, Ph. D., Instructor in History.
W. H. PYRE, B. L., Instructor in Elocution and Oratory.
ANNIE N. SCRIBNER, A. B., Fellow in Greek.
J. C. SHEDD, Ph. D., Instructor in Physics.
C. M. SMITH, B. S., Instructor in Physics.
S. E. SPARLING, Ph. D., Assistant in Political Science.
SUSAN A. STERLING, M. L., Instructor in German.
W. D. TALLMAN, B. S., Instructor in Mathematics.
H. G. TIMBERLAKE, M. S., Instructor in Botany.
F. M. TISDEL, M. A., Instructor in English Literature.

SPECIAL LECTURERS.

KUNO FRANCKE, Ph. D., Professor of German Literature, Harvard University.
F. H. GIDDINGS, Ph. D., Professor of Sociology, Columbia University.
JESSE MACY, LL. D., Professor of Political Science, Iowa College.
W. M. PAYNE, Editor of *The Dial*, Lecturer on English Literature.
H. M. STEVENS, M. A., Professor of Modern European History, Cornell University.
M. C. TYLER, A. M., L. H. D., Professor of American History, Cornell University.

GENERAL STATEMENT.

The University of Wisconsin will hold in 1900, its second summer session. This session will continue for six weeks, beginning Monday, July 2, and closing Friday, Aug. 10. While the summer session of the University includes the Summer School for Teachers, which has been in operation for some years, it is not an enlargement of that school, but has a different purpose. This additional term of the University will provide elementary, advanced, and graduate instruction throughout the range of subjects ordinarily covered by the Faculty of Letters and Science.

Terms of Admission.

The requirements for admission are the same for the summer session as for the other sessions of the University (See pp. 60-66). Graduates of the University of Wisconsin or other colleges and universities of good standing are admitted to graduate courses without examination.

Persons twenty-one years of age who are not candidates for a degree and wish to take special studies are permitted to enter as adult special students upon giving satisfactory evidence that they are prepared to profit by the courses desired.

For the summer session permission to take particular courses is also extended to teachers who convince the professors in charge that they are able to take the courses to advantage.

Students will be admitted to the elementary courses of the Summer School without special examination. They will also be admitted to University courses for which they are qualified, but University credit will be given only to students who have satisfied the regular entrance requirements of the University.

Fees.

The fees for the summer session of the University and the Summer School are the same. A general fee of fifteen dollars will be charged.

Special Lectures.

Several courses of lectures will be given by members of the regular faculty of the summer session. In addition, courses will be offered of especial interest from lecturers belonging to other universities. Professor Moses Coit Tyler, of Cornell University, will lecture on American history; Professor Kuno Francke, of Harvard University, will lecture on the development of German literature and on Flemish and German religious painting of the 15th and 16th centuries; Professor Giddings, of Columbia University, will offer elementary and advanced courses in sociology; Professor H. Morse Stephens, of Cornell University, will give a course on the enlightened despotism of the eighteenth century; Professor Jesse Macy of Iowa College will deliver a course on the political parties in the United States during the reconstruction period. Mr. W. M. Payne, of Chicago, editor of *The Dial*, will lecture on the greater English poets of the nineteenth century; Assistant Professor Carter, of Princeton University, will offer a course on the Roman religion.

These lectures will be given at hours which will conflict as little as possible with the regular recitation and laboratory courses of the summer session.

DEPARTMENTS OF STUDY.

The statement of courses below gives in detail the work offered in the various departments for the summer of 1900 together with the credit to which students are entitled on the completion of each course. Credits are stated in fractions of a "full study," by which is meant a study consisting of five class exercises a week for one semester. *The total amount of credit which a student may receive for the six weeks' work cannot exceed six-fifths for one semester.* Candidates for the Bachelor's degree are required to have completed twenty-four full studies. The Master's and Doctor's degrees are conferred upon the basis of scholarly attainment, rather than upon the completion of any prescribed number of credits; but a minimum of one year's graduate study is required for the Master's degree and a minimum of three years' graduate study for the Doctor's degree, and work done in the summer session will be accepted toward these degrees on the same basis as work done at any other time of year.

PHILOSOPHY AND PEDAGOGY.

PROFESSOR STEARNS, PROFESSOR O'SHEA, AND PROFESSOR JASTROW.

1. General Psychology. The course will have especially in view the theory of teaching, and will therefore be directed to those topics which bear most closely upon pedagogy. *Five hours a week at 8.* Professor STEARNS. Two-fifths credit.
2. Introduction to Experimental Psychology. The course is intended to give an insight into the problems and methods of modern psychology, and may be expected to interest those engaged in teaching and general students of philosophy and of other cognate studies. *Five hours of lectures weekly and five hours of laboratory demonstration.* Professor JASTROW and Assistant. Three-fifths credit.
3. Practical Course in Experimental Psychology. This course is intended for those desirous of gaining familiarity with psycho-

logical apparatus, methods, and manipulations. *One hour daily.* One-fifth credit. Professor JASTROW and Assistant.

4. Logic as Applied to Science. *Three times weekly.* Professor JASTROW. One-fifth credit. With additional reading, two-fifths credit.

5. History of Educational Theories. The course will follow as a guide Quick's Essays on Educational Reformers. *Five hours a week at 9.* Professor STEARNS. Two-fifths credit.

6 Mental Development. It will be the purpose in this course to consider in a theoretical and practical way the most important of the newer problems relating to the development of human beings from birth to maturity. *M. to F., at 10.* Professor O'SHEA. Three-fifths credit.

7. Theory and Art of Teaching. It will be the purpose in this course to review from the standpoint of the teacher the laws upon which the training of the mind must depend, and to indicate in some detail their application to the making of a curriculum and methods of teaching and management. *M. to F., at 10.* Professor O'SHEA. Three-fifths credit.

ECONOMICS AND SOCIOLOGY.

PROFESSOR ELY, PROFESSOR GIDDINGS, PROFESSOR SCOTT, AND ASSISTANT PROFESSOR MEYER.

1. Elements of Economic Science. A study of the nature and leading principles of the science. Text: Ely's Outlines of Economics (college edition). *Six hours a week; M. to S., at 8.* Assistant Professor MEYER. Three-fifths credit.

2. Railway Transportation. Lectures and assigned readings covering historical, economic and legal phases of the study of the railway as an institution. *Tu., W., Th., F., at 11.* Assistant Professor MEYER. Two-fifths credit.

3. Money and Banking. The theory and principles of monetary science, with a discussion of current monetary and banking problems. Dunbar's History and Theory of Banking. Laughlin's History of Bimetallism in the United States. Conant's Modern Banks of Issue. *M., Tu., at 12, F., S., at 8.* Professor SCOTT. Two-fifths credit.

4. Economic Thought since John Stuart Mill. Lectures and assigned reading. *M., Tu., W., Th., at 8.* Professor SCOTT. Two-fifths credit.

5. Public Finance. Text-book: H. C. Adam's Finance. Reference Books: Ely's Taxation in American States and Cities, and Seligman's Essays on Taxation. *M., Tu., W., Th., at* 9. Professor ELY. Two-fifths credit.
6. Monopolies and Trusts. This course will be based on Ely's Monopolies and Trusts, and will consist of lectures and discussions supplementary to that work. Reference books: Gunton's Trusts, Hobson's Economics of Distribution, and the Proceedings of the Chicago Conference on Trusts. *M., W., Th., F., S., at* 10. Professor ELY. Two-fifths credit.

SOCIOLOGY.

PROFESSOR GIDDINGS.

1. Elementary Course. This course will present an analysis of the phenomena studied in descriptive sociology. The lectures will be accompanied by class exercises, the preparation of brief papers, and practice in the interpretation of material contained in official reports, periodical discussions, and current news. *F. and S., at* 9.
2. Advanced Course. The advanced course will deal with methods of investigation in sociology, and their application in a sociological study of the American people. The lectures will be accompanied by exercises in induction, criticism of evidence, chart making and map making. *M. and T., at* 10.

POLITICAL SCIENCE.

PROFESSOR PARKINSON, PROFESSOR MACY, AND DR. SPARLING.

1. Constitutional Law. A course of lectures upon the English constitution, with emphasis upon its unwritten growth since the Revolution of 1688. *Tu., Th., at* 10. Professor PARKINSON. One-fifth credit.
2. Constitutional Law. A study of the constitution of the United States, giving special attention to the relation between the commonwealths and the nation, to the powers of congress and of the courts, and to the meaning and force of the amendments as a "bill of rights." *Daily except Saturday at* 9. Professor PARKINSON. Two-fifths credit.
3. International Law. This course is intended to cover in outline the entire field of the subject as completely as can well be done in the time allotted. *M., W., F., at* 10. Professor PARKINSON. One-fifth credit.

4. Elements of Political Science. A study of the nature and leading principles of political life. *M., T., W., Th., F., S., at* 8. Dr. SPARLING. Three-fifths credit.
5. Municipal Government. A study of the modern city. A comparative study of the organization and functions of the cities of Europe and United States. Text, readings and discussions. *M., T., Th., F., at* 9. Dr. SPARLING. Two-fifths credit.
6. American Political Parties. A course of lectures upon political parties in the United States during the reconstruction period. Opportunity will be offered for investigative work. *Three hours weekly.* Professor MACY. Two-fifths credit.

HISTORY.

PROFESSOR TURNER, PROFESSOR TYLER, PROFESSOR STEPHENS, ASSISTANT PROFESSOR COFFIN, AND DR. LIBBY.

1. Greek History. A general survey, with special reference to the needs of teachers of ancient history in secondary schools. *M., T., W., Th., F., at* 10. Open to all students, but designed especially for those in the Summer School. Dr. LIBBY. Two-fifths credit.
2. Political History of England. An elementary course which may be substituted for the Course 2a, required of Civic-Historical and English students. *M., T., W., Th., F.; at* 11. Assistant Professor COFFIN. Two-fifths credit.
3. Modern European History. An introductory course; from the Reformation to the French Revolution. *M., T., W., Th., F., at* 11. Open to all students. Assistant Professor COFFIN. Two-fifths credit.
4. American History, 1750-1830. An elementary survey, open to all students. *M., T., W., Th., F., at* 11. Dr. LIBBY. Two fifths credit.
5. History of the West. An advanced course designed to exhibit the main aspects of the westward movement in the United States, with the economic, social, and political effects upon the nation. *M., T., W., Th., at* 8. Professor TURNER. Two-fifths credit.
6. Seminary in the Foreign Relations of the Administrations of Washington and Adams. A course designed to furnish training in original research. *M., W., F., at* 11. Professor TURNER. Two-fifths credit.

7. The Enlightened Despotism of the Eighteenth Century. An advanced course on the important European conditions antecedent to the French Revolution. *S. and M.* Professor STEPHENS. One-fifth credit.
8. Great Leaders and Great Issues in American Politics since 1783. *M. to F.* Professor TYLER. Two-fifths credit. This course will begin July 9.
9. The Teaching of History. A brief course of lectures designed to acquaint the teacher with the most recent ideas and literature on this subject. *Weekly.* Professor TURNER.
10. Historical Conference. One hour weekly will be devoted to an informal conference with graduate students at which reports will be made upon individual investigations and current historical literature will be discussed. Professor TURNER.

GREEK.

ASSISTANT PROFESSOR LAIRD AND MISS SCRIBNER.

1. Elementary Greek. The essentials of the grammar: Xenophon's Anabasis, Book I. *Twelve hours a week.* Assistant Professor LAIRD and Miss SCRIBNER. Four-fifths credit.
2. Homer's Odyssey. The instruction presupposes such knowledge of Greek as is required for entrance to the Freshman class. Especial attention will be given to the reading of the verse and to the literary treatment of the author. *Daily at 9.* Miss SCRIBNER. Two-fifths credit.
3. Plato. Apology and Crito. Intended for students of the grade of Sophomore. *M., T., W., Th., F., at 12.* Miss SCRIBNER. Two-fifths credit.
4. Thucydides VI. and VII. or (should the class prefer it) the *Oedipus Tyrannus* of Sophocles and the *Frogs* of Aristophanes. Equivalent to a Junior or Senior elective; open also to graduates. *M., T., W., Th., F., at 11.* Assistant Professor LAIRD. Two-fifths credit.
5. Greek Seminary. Attic Inscriptions. Attention will be directed mainly to the linguistic side, to points that will prove useful to the teacher of Greek in high schools. As the course is intended to give preliminary training in seminary methods, a knowledge of historical Greek grammar will not be demanded as a prerequisite. *F., 9 to 11.* Assistant Professor LAIRD. One-fifth credit.

LATIN.

PROFESSOR SLAUGHTER AND ASSISTANT PROFESSOR CARTER.

1. Cæsar and Prose Composition. This course is intended for teachers and will deal with the methods of Latin instruction in secondary schools. Attention will be paid to questions of syntax, the Roman pronunciation, reading at sight, and other features of Latin teaching. Some time will be given to reading and writing Latin. *Daily, except Saturday, at 8.* Professor SLAUGHTER. Two-fifths credit.
2. Catullus and Horace. Selected poems of Catullus and Horace will be read. This course is open to students who have had the equivalent of one year's work in Latin in the University, and is also intended for students who want to reread favorite poems of Catullus and Horace. *Daily, except Saturday, at 10.* Assistant Professor CARTER. Two-fifths credit.
3. Vergil. This course is intended for graduates, advanced undergraduates and teachers of Vergil. The entire Aeneid will be assigned for outside reading and reports will be expected from members of the class. The course will be conducted mainly by lectures. Selected passages will be read and translated by the instructor. *Daily, except Saturday, at 9.* Professor SLAUGHTER. Two-fifths credit.
4. Roman Religion. A course of six public lectures on the religion of the ancient Romans. Assistant Professor CARTER.

HEBREW AND HELLENISTIC GREEK.

PROFESSOR WILLIAMS.

1. Hebrew for Beginners. Instruction will be given in the principles of the language, using the first chapters of Genesis as the basis of the work. *T., W., Th., and F., at 10.* Two-fifths credit.
2. Samuel. This course is intended as a review of Hebrew etymology and syntax and as a critical study of the First Book of Samuel. *T. and Th., at 11.* One-fifth credit.
3. Hellenistic Greek for Beginners. The general principles of the language will be studied and the first chapters of the Fourth Gospel. *T., W., Th., and F., at 9.* Two-fifths credit.
4. The Fourth Gospel. It is intended to make this course a review of the principles of Hellenistic Greek Grammar and also a critical, non-theological study of the book. *W. and F., at 11.* One-fifth credit.

FRENCH.
PROFESSOR OWEN AND MR. BRAUER.

1. Grammar (mainly). Otto's French Conversation Grammar; Roman d' un Jeune Homme Pauvre. *Daily at 8 and 9.* Mr. BRAUER. Four-fifths credit.
2. Translation. La Petite Fadette; Le Cid. *M., W., F., at 10 and 11.* Professor OWEN. For credit see below.
3. Readings. Britannicus; L'Avare. *T., Th., F., at 10.* Mr. BRAUER. Courses 2 and 3 taken together entitle to a four-fifths credit.
4. Lectures on Thought and Language topics. *M., at 12.* Professor OWEN. A useful introduction to the field more fully examined in the first semester.

SCANDINAVIAN LANGUAGES.
PROFESSOR OLSON.

1. Modern Norse. Elementary. Olson's Norwegian Grammar and Reader. *M., T., W., Th., F.* Two-fifths credit.
2. Modern Norse. Advanced. Selections from the Reader, Ibsen's Brand, and Gundersens' Norske Digte. *M., T., W., Th., F.* Two-fifths credit.
3. History of Danish and Norwegian Literature. Seip and Broch's Literaturhistorie, with assigned reading. *Three times a week.* One-fifth credit.
4. General Lectures on Scandinavian Literature. No previous knowledge of the Scandinavian languages required. *Twice a week.* One-fifth credit.

GERMAN.
ASSOCIATE PROFESSOR VOSS, PROFESSOR FRANCKE, MISS STERLING, AND MRS. EATON.

1. Grammar and Reader. For beginners, *ten hours weekly at 10.* Miss STERLING, Mrs. EATON. Credit according to amount accomplished, with maximum of five-fifths.
2. Scientific German. Dippold's Science Reader. *Five hours of class work weekly, at 9, and assigned private reading;* if a sufficient amount of work is satisfactorily completed, a credit of four-fifths will be given, corresponding to the first semester of the general science and engineering courses. Miss STERLING.
3. Conversation and composition, based on modern prose texts. *Five hours a week, at 9.* Mrs. EATON. Two-fifths credit.

4. Schiller's and Goethe's Dramas. Interpretation and critical study of the most important dramas. Lectures in German. The students will read the dramas and leading criticisms privately and report to the class on assigned topics. *Five hours a week.* Mrs. EATON. Two-fifths credit.
5. German Literature. Lectures on the history of early German literature, with reading of selections from writers of the periods considered. This course may be taken as a three-fifths, or, with assigned private reading, as a five-fifths. Miss STERLING. One-fifth or two-fifths credit.
6. German Composition, Conversation, and Grammar Review. For students who have had two years of high school German, or an equivalent. *Four hours a week, at 10.* Associate Professor VOSS. Two-fifths credit.
7. Narrative and Dramatic Prose. A rapid reading course. *Four hours a week at 9.* Associate Professor VOSS. Two-fifths credit.
8. A Critical Study of the Report of the Committee on Modern Languages, with lectures and reports on methods of teaching modern foreign languages. *Two hours a week.* Associate Professor VOSS. One-fifth credit.

Courses 6, 7, and 8 especially for teachers of German in high schools.

9. A Drama of Schiller or Lessing, with outside reading. *Three hours a week, at 9.* Associate Professor VOSS. Two-fifths credit.
10. Middle High German. Introductory Course. *Two hours a week.* Associate Professor VOSS. One-fifth credit.
11. Gothic. Introductory Course. *Two hours a week.* Associate Professor VOSS. One-fifth credit.
12. Epochs of German Literature, with special study of selected masterpieces. Eighteen lectures and outside reading. Professor FRANCKE. Two-fifths credit.
13. Some Phases of Flemish and German Religious Painting of the 15th and 16th Centuries. Six lectures, illustrated by the stereopticon. Professor FRANCKE.

In addition to these courses, Professor Francke will assist advanced students in research work in German literature. *One conference a week.*

ENGLISH.

PROFESSOR HUBBARD, MR. PAYNE, ASSISTANT PROFESSOR KNOWLTON, DR. CAIRNS, AND MR. TISDEL.

1. Study of Prose Style. Composition. Exercises, themes, conferences with individual students for criticism of written work. *Ten hours a week, at* 8. Assistant Professor KNOWLTON. This course is equivalent to the second semester's work of English, course 1, College of Letters and Science. Three-fifths credit.

English Language.

2. Anglo-Saxon. This course aims to enable the student to read ordinary Anglo-Saxon prose with ease, and thus give a foundation for thorough work in English language and English literature. *Ten hours a week, at* 8. Professor HUBBARD. Three-fifths credit. This course corresponds to the work of the first semester in course 20, College of Letters and Science.

English Literature.

4. General Survey of English Literature. The lectures will cover the period from the earliest times to 1600, and will be supplemented by assigned collateral reading. *Ten hours a week, at* 8. Dr. CAIRNS. Three-fifths credit. This course corresponds to the work of the first semester in course 30, College of Letters and Science.
5. American Literature. A brief preliminary outline of the general development of American literature, 1620-1860, and especial study of the "New England group" of authors. *Three times a week.* Dr. CAIRNS. One-fifth credit.
6. Shakespeare. Othello, Twelfth-Night, and Macbeth. *Five times a week.* Mr. TISDEL. Three-fifths credit.
7. The Drama before 1600. From the Miracle Plays to the Masterpieces of Shakespeare. *Three times a week,* with assigned readings. Mr. TISDEL. Two-fifths credit.
8. The Romantic Movement in English Poetry. The principal authors studied are Wordsworth, Coleridge, Keats, Shelley, Byron, and Scott. *Five times a week.* Mr. TISDEL. Three-fifths credit.
9. The Greater English Poets of the Nineteenth Century. *Twice a week.* Mr. PAYNE. One-fifth credit.

Summer School courses without University credit.

10. Rhetoric and composition, with direct reference to the teaching of these subjects in high schools. The method and the economy of the criticism and correction of written work will be presented by lectures, discussions, and written exercises. *M., W., Th., F., at* 11. Assistant Professor KNOWLTON.
11. A study of English classics with direct reference to teaching. The following are likely to be taken up: Milton's Paradise Lost (Books I. and II.), Burke on Conciliation with America, Macaulay's Essays on Milton and Addison. *M., W., F., at* 10. Professor HUBBARD.

ELOCUTION AND ORATORY.

PROFESSOR FRANKENBURGER AND MR. PYRE.

1. Dramatic Reading, with talks on gesture; declamation with personal criticism. The reading of Macbeth and Othello or Hamlet and the Merchant of Venice. *Daily.* Professor FRANKENBURGER. Three-fifths credit.
2. Forensics. The study of the construction and delivery of orations. *Daily.* Professor FRANKENBURGER. Three-fifths credit.
3. Elocution. An elementary course, especially adapted to the needs of teachers in the secondary schools. *Daily, at hours to be fixed on consultation.* Mr. PYRE. Three-fifths credit.

MATHEMATICS.

PROFESSOR SLICHTER, ASSISTANT PROFESSOR DOWLING, AND MR. TALLMAN.

1. Algebra. A review of the important parts of algebra. The course in algebra is planned with reference to the special needs of high school instructors and those who are preparing for examination. *Five times a week, at* 10. Professor SLICHTER. Three-fifths credit. The equivalent of the algebra of the freshman year, College of Letters and Science, may be obtained by making up some additional work.
2. Geometry. A review of the important theorems in plane geometry, and a study of solid geometry. No previous knowledge of solid geometry will be required. *Five times a week, at* 11. Completion of this course satisfies the entrance requirement of geometry to the University. Professor DOWLING.
3. Plane Trigonometry and Logarithms. No previous knowledge of the subject will be assumed, but plane geometry and algebra

through quadratics are prerequisites to the course. *Five times a week*, at 8. Mr. TALLMAN. Two-fifths credit.

4. Analytic Geometry. A fairly complete treatment of the different forms of equations representing straight lines and a brief treatment of the equations of conic sections. *Five times a week*, at 2. Mr. TALLMAN. Two-fifths credit.
5. Calculus. Differentiation and integration of functions of one variable with geometric applications. *Five times a week*, at 3. Mr. TALLMAN. Two-fifths credit.
6. Theory of Potential. A course of lectures for students who have had the calculus. *Five times a week*, at 11. Professor SLICHTER. Two-fifths credit.
7. Rigid Dynamics. A course of reading on the motion of the rigid body. The conferences will be held two or three times a week and credit will be given on the basis of the work accomplished. Professor SLICHTER.
8. Theory of Functions. This course will be given by lectures based upon Burkhardt. *Five times a week*, at 9. Assistant Professor DOWLING. Two-fifths credit.
9. Seminary for Teachers. Topics in the history of elementary mathematics that are of greatest importance to teachers will be taken up and discussed. A session of two hours will be held each week. *Th.*, 4-6. Conducted by Professor SLICHTER, assisted by the department. One-fifth credit will be given to those who do the requisite amount of reading.
10. Seminary for Advanced Students. Some advanced topic will be chosen for discussion, presumably invariants and covariants of binary quantics. Two hour sessions each week, *Tu.*, 4-6. Conducted by Assistant Assistant Professor DOWLING, assisted by the department. Credit will depend work accomplished.

PHYSICS.

PROFESSOR SNOW, ASSISTANT PROFESSOR AUSTIN, AND DR. SHEDD.

1. General Lectures. *Daily except Saturday, at 5.* Dr. SHEDD. One recitation by the class in smaller sections at hours to be arranged. Dr. SHEDD.

   In the summer sessions it is designed to complete in three years the year's work of course 1 in physics, taking mechanics and heat during the summer of 1899, electricity and magnetism in 1900, and acoustics and optics in 1901. A knowledge of plane trigonometry is required for registration. Two-fifths credit.

2. Theoretical Physics. These lectures will vary from year to year, completing in four years the ground covered by courses 5 and 6 in the general catalogue. In 1900 electricity and magnetism will be given. *Five hours per week.* Assistant Professor AUSTIN. Two-fifths credit.
3. Introductory Laboratory Practice. This is the equivalent of the regular sophomore laboratory given during the rest of the year, and is designed to accompany course 1. *Twenty hours per week;* a smaller number of hours may be taken if desired. Assistant Professor AUSTIN and Dr. SHEDD. One-fifth credit for each thirty hours of work performed.
4. Advanced Laboratory Practice. This course is the same as course 2 of the general catalogue, and presupposes the completion of courses 1 and 3 mentioned above, or their equivalents. One-fifth credit for each thirty hours of work performed. *Twenty or thirty hours per week during the session.* Assistant Professor AUSTIN.
5. Thesis Work. The laboratory will be open during the summer to receive all who wish to complete a part or the whole of their theses. Course 3 of the general catalogue. *Fifty hours per week during the session will be necessary to complete the course.*
6. Graduate Research. Every facility is offered for carrying on original investigation, special apparatus will be secured as required, and special rooms in the laboratory are set aside for this purpose. Professor SNOW and Assistant Professor AUSTIN.

Summer School courses without University credit:

7. Lectures. A course of lectures will be given daily except Saturday at 12 upon the subjects of mechanics and heat, electricity and magnetism, acoustics, and optics. Professor SNOW. Carhart & Chute's Physics will be used as a text.
7a. Elementary Laboratory Practice. In connection with these lectures there will be offered a course of laboratory practice in which especial attention will be given to acquainting the teacher with such methods and experiments as will aid him in conducting his own classes in physics. The completion of the above two courses will be accepted as the requirement in physics for entrance to the University.

CHEMISTRY.

PROFESSOR DANIELLS AND ASSISTANT PROFESSOR HILLYER.

1. Inorganic Chemistry. A course of lectures and experiments with a discussion of chemical theories and the facts of observation upon which these theories are based. Laboratory work supplements the lectures. *M. to F., at 2.* Professor DANIELLS.
2. Qualitative Analysis. This course consists of a careful study of the reactions used in the detection and separation of inorganic bases and acids. Professor DANIELLS AND ASSISTANTS. Courses 1 and 2 taken together give a three-fifths credit.
3. Quantitative Chemistry. (a) Work in determining the equivalence of elements, the synthesis and analysis of gaseous substances, etc. (b) Quantitative Analysis. This course includes both gravimetric and volumetric methods. Professor DANIELLS. Credit according to amount of work done.
4. Organic Chemistry. This course includes the study of the more important hydrocarbons and their simpler derivatives. *Lectures daily except Saturday.* Laboratory work two hours per day. Assistant Professor HILLYER. Four-fifths credit for lectures and laboratory work.

Students who have had course (4) or its equivalent may take up any of the following courses:

5. Detailed study of the aromatic group of compounds. *Lectures daily except Saturday. Laboratory work two hours daily.* Assistant Professor HILLYER. Four-fifths credit for lectures and laboratory work.
6. Ultimate Analysis of Organic Compounds, determination of carbon, nitrogen, the halogens, and sulphur. Credit according to the amount of work done. Assistant Professor HILLYER.
7. Special Chapters in Organic Chemistry, study of chemical literature by assigned topics; lectures on classical researches and important generalization of organic chemistry. *Two lectures and three meetings for reports on topics per week.* Assistant Professor HILLYER. Three-fifths credit.
8. Research Work in Organic Chemistry. This course may be taken by those who have had course (5) or its equivalent, and should be accompanied by course (6) if its equivalent has not been taken. Two hours laboratory work daily credited as two-fifths for one semester. Assistant Professor HILLYER.

GEOLOGY.

PROFESSOR FENNEMAN.

1. Physical Geography. The subject will therefore be treated from the dynamic point of view, the purpose being to develop the principles of the subject in such a way that a teacher may apply them to local features. *Lectures five times a week with excursions two or three times a week.* Three-fifths credit.
2. General Geology. The geological forces, both epigene and hypogene, now modifying the world. *Lectures five times a week, with excursions two or three times a week.* Three-fifths credit.

ZOOLOGY.

ASSISTANT PROFESSOR MARSHALL, PROFESSOR BIRGE.

1. General Course. The student should be already familiar with the elements of classification or should prepare them from a text book during the term. The lectures will deal with general topics not sufficiently developed in most text books. *Lectures daily, at 8.* Assistant Professor MARSHALL.
1a. Laboratory Work. A course of at least two hours of laboratory work daily, accompanying the lectures. Assistant Professor MARSHALL and ASSISTANT. Three-fifths credit.
2. Entomology. A course in structural and systematic entomology, consisting of two hours of laboratory work daily, and at least two hours each week devoted to field work and the arrangement and classification of specimens. Assistant Professor MARSHALL. Two-fifths credit.
3. Investigations of Lake Biology. An elementary course on lake life, including the determination of the main general of microscopic plants and animals found in the littoral and limnetic regions. Professor BIRGE. Three-fifths credit.

HISTOLOGY AND ANATOMY.

ASSISTANT PROFESSOR MILLER.

1. Vertebrate Histology. Instruction in this course will consist of daily lectures, at 9, supplemented by work in the laboratory. Three-fifths credit.
2. Mammalian Anatomy. This course is a laboratory course in dissection. It is of special value to teachers of physiology who have not had opportunity for such work and to students who wish to enter the regular classes in histology and embry-

ology the following semester. Students must have passed their first year's biology. *Daily, at* 11.

BOTANY.

PROFESSOR HARPER AND MR. TIMBERLAKE.

1. General Botany. The course includes a study of the structure and life histories of types of the principal groups of plants, including bacteria, algæ, fungi, liverworts, mosses, ferns, horsetails and flowering plants. *Lectures M., W., Th., at 9, and laboratory work daily, M. to F.,* 10-12. Professor HARPER and Mr. TIMBERLAKE.
2. Fungi. A general view of the morphology of the fungi will be given in the lectures. Especial attention will be given in the laboratory to the study of forms having economic significance as causes of plant diseases. *Three times a week, M. to W. a. m.* Professor HARPER and ASSISTANT.
3. Plant Life of Lakes and Streams. Especial attention will be given to the algæ. Problems of zonal distribution, the plankton, etc., will be discussed in the lectures and the morphology of types of the main groups of the algæ will be studied in the laboratory. *Three times a week, W. to F., a. m.* May be taken in connection with course 2 or with course 3 in zoology, the two together giving a three-fifths credit. Professor HARPER and ASSISTANT.
4. Morphology of the Flowering Plants. A study of the life history of several types of flowering plants representing the larger groups. The phenomena of pollination, fertilization and development of organs and tissues in the seed will be especially considered. *Daily laboratory work and two lectures a week.* Mr. TIMBERLAKE.
5. Plant Life of the Ocean. Supplementary to course 3. *One lecture a week.* Professor HARPER.
6. Cytology. Advanced and graduate students will be given opportunity to begin or continue research work on problems connected with the structure and physiology of the cell. Modern apparatus and facilities for such work are provided in the botanical laboratory. *Daily, M. to F.* Professor HARPER and Mr. TIMBERLAKE.

DRAWING.

MISS TANNER.

The drawing courses will be of practical value to those who desire art instruction and yet do not wish to take a regular course in an art school. Teachers who feel themselves incompetent to teach this subject and yet are obliged by their course of study to make some effort to do so will receive great benefit from work in this department.

1. Daily lecture on free-hand perspective. Practical application of lecture in object drawing—interiors and exteriors of buildings—streets. Sketching from still life and nature. Blackboard drawing.
2. Light and Shade Sketching from still life and nature. Figure drawing from life in pencil and ink wash. Out-door sketching in pencil and charcoal.
3. The work in this course will be water-color study of still-life, nature and out-door sketching. A special Saturday out-door sketching class will be arranged for students taking this course.

PHYSICAL CULTURE.

DR. ELSOM, MR. G. S. ISHIKAWA, MR. W. G. WILLIAMS.

During the summer session, all students of the University will be allowed the use of the Gymnasium without charge. A small fee for lockers only will be required.

Regular courses will be offered, and four classes a week will be given on all the forms of gymnastic apparatus, as follows:

Light Gymnastics. Instruction and practice in various gymnastic drills, in free movements, and with dumb-bells, wands, and Indian clubs; methods of conducting classes, setting-up exercises, and the lighter gymnastics.

Heavy Gymnastics. Horizontal and vaulting bars; horses, bucks, parallel bars, flying and traveling rings, trapeze; tumbling, simple and advanced; jumping, etc.

For regular attendance at these classes, a credit of one-fifth (or for one semester's work) will be given to those who desire to make up this work in the summer. The classes are open, also, to any who desire to improve their own physical condition by means of systematic exercise.

Physical examinations, strength tests, etc., are given by the Director in all cases, and appropriate corrective exercises prescribed whenever needed.

Normal Course.

In addition to the above, a Normal Course in Gymnastics is offered those who propose to fit themselves as teachers of physical training in schools, normal schools, colleges, etc.

A fee of $5.00 will be charged for this course.

Further information may be had by addressing the Director of the Gymnasium.

PHYSICAL TRAINING FOR WOMEN.

MISS MAYHEW AND MISS HARRIS.

A general course, one hour's class work a day, includes exercises for poise, breathing, free hand drills, Americanized Delsarte gymnastics, Swedish exercises, wand, dumb-bell and club drills, and marching calisthenics. This course may be credited as one semester's work in gymnastics.

A special course designed for those wishing to fit themselves as teachers will be given similar to the one outlined by Dr. Elson. Those entering this course will also take the general course. This course may be credited for one semester's work in gymnastics.

Those who expect to take this course should provide themselves with suitable gymnastic costume. Directions for making can be secured from Miss Mayhew, Ladies' Hall.

For a circular giving a detailed account of the summer session of the University apply to W. D. Hiestand, Registrar, Madison, Wis.

SUMMER SCHOOL OF LIBRARY SCIENCE.

The sixth annual session of the Summer School of Library Science will be held at the University of Wisconsin, beginning July 9 and closing August 31, 1900. Students are requested to register on July 7, as the lectures begin promptly at 9 o'clock on July 9.

Three courses will be given:

1. The Wisconsin Course, which is planned for librarians of small libraries.
2. The Regular Course, which, in addition to the Wisconsin Course, includes lectures in reference work, bibliography, and a larger amount of technical work.
3. The Teachers' Course, which includes six special lectures on the care of school libraries and requires two hours each week of class work.

4. Course in Children's Literature. A special course of fifteen lectures on children's literature and children's work in libraries.

The tuition for the full course in any department is $15. Teachers who are attending the Summer Session of the University will be admitted, without extra tuition, to the Teachers' Course and the lectures on children's literature. For a full circular of information regarding the Library School address the Wisconsin Free Library Commission, Madison, Wisconsin.

WASHBURN OBSERVATORY.

STAFF.

C. K. ADAMS, LL. D., President of the University.
G. C. COMSTOCK, Ph. B., LL. B., Director and Professor of Astronomy.
A. S. FLINT, M. A., Assistant Astronomer.
W. A. HOYT, Student Clerk.
F. H. REHBERG, Student Assistant, Meteorology.
JOHN DOESCHER, Janitor.

The Washburn Observatory was established in the year 1878 through the munificence of the late Gov. C. C. Washburn. Although its obligations and opportunities as a branch of a teaching university have not been ignored, the energies of its staff from the beginning have been directed mainly to astronimical research. Among the lines of research which have been cultivated may be specified the measurement of the positions and motions of the heavenly bodies, the discovery and measurement of double stars, the investigation of variable stars, the study of changes of latitude and of the amount and character of the atmospheric refraction, the determination of the amount of the aberration of light, problems of stellar color and a systematic investigation of the parallaxes of all accessible stars which have large proper motions. The Observatory also maintains a tri-daily meteorological service.

The principal instruments of the Observatory are:

An equatorially mounted telescope of 15½ inches aperature, constructed by Alvan Clark & Sons, and provided with graduated circles, driving clock, a filar micrometer, double image micrometer by Steinheil, a spectroscope, astro-photometer, and a very complete set of eye-pieces; a meridian circle, by A. Repsold & Sons, of Hamburg, with collimators, transit micrometer, and the usual accessories of such an instrument. This instrument is figured in the last edition of the Encyclopaedia Britannica as the type of its class. The objective of the instrument was made by the Clarks, and has an aperature of 4.8 inches and a focal length of 58 inches. The circle is graduated to 2 minutes of arc. For the past four years this instrument has been employed for an extensive series of determination of stellar parallax. A floating mirror has been added to it as an auxiliary for the determination of its horizontal points and flexures. There are also a sidereal clock by Hohwü, of Amsterdam, two mean-time clocks by Howard, of Boston, all excellent time-pieces, and a chronograph, by Fauth & Co., of Washington.

In the Student's Observatory are mounted a six-inch equatorial telescope, by Alvan Clark & Sons, a transit instrument of the broken telescope type, by Bamberg. These instruments, while primarily intended for instruction, are well adapted to and are employed for certain classes of original work. In particular, the equatorial telescope has been provided with reflecting prisms (Loewy), and employed as one of the principal instruments of the Observatory in an investigation of the refraction and the constant of aberration, and the Bamberg instrument is used for latitude determinations by the Talcott method and for the time service of the Observatory. The Observatory also possesses a considerable number of subsidiary instruments, such as portable telescopes, spectroscopes, photometers, chronometers, sextants, an engineer's transit, an altazimuth, a universal instrument of the German type, a spherometer caliper, seismoscopes, and a complete set of meteorological instruments.

The Woodman Astronomical Library, established in connection with the Observatory, and supported from the income of a fund given by the late Cyrus Woodman, Esq., possesses a large and valuable collection of works upon astronomy and kindred subjects.

By provisions of law the results of important investigations conducted at the Washburn Observatory are published by the State, and under this provision ten volumes, representing the more important work done at the Observatory, have been issued.

Students of sufficient technical attainments are admitted to the Observatory and take part in the investigations in progress. Meritorious original work of such students may be included in the Publications of the Observatory, or in the Bulletins of the University. The courses of instruction in astronomy are stated upon pages 117 and 118.

COLLEGE OF MECHANICS AND ENGINEERING.

STAFF OF INSTRUCTION.

C. K. ADAMS, LL. D., President of the University.
J. B. JOHNSON, C. E., DEAN, and Professor of Engineering.
STORM BULL, M. E., Professor of Steam Engineering.
D. C. JACKSON, C. E., Professor of Electrical Engineering.
C. N. HARRISON, C. E., Acting Professor of Machine Design.
C. I. KING, Professor of Mechanical Practice.
J. G. D. MACK, M. E., Assistant Professor of Machine Design.
E. R. MAURER, B. C. E., Assistant Professor of Pure and Applied Mechanics.
A. W. RICHTER, M. E., Assistant Professor of Experimental Engineering.
L. S. SMITH, C. E., Assistant Professor of Topographic and Geodetic Engineering.
B. V. SWENSON, B. S., Assistant Professor of Electrical Engineering.
F. E. TURNEAURE, C. E., Professor of Bridge and Sanitary Engineering.
N. O. WHITNEY, C. E., Professor of Railway Engineering.
WALTER ALEXANDER, M. E., Instructor in Steam Engineering.
C. F. BURGESS, E. E., Instructor in Electrical Engineering.
R. W. HARGRAVE, B. S., Instructor in Mechanical Practice.
BUDD FRANKENFIELD, E. E., Instructor in Electrical Engineering.
MICHAEL BONN, Foreman of Foundry.
WILLIAM LOTTES, Foreman of Blacksmith Shop.
IRVING MUTCHLER, Assistant in Wood Shop.
W. J. FENNELL, Student Assistant in Machine Shop.

Members of the Faculty of the College of Letters and Science who give instruction to students in the College of Mechanics and Engineering. Arranged alphabetically.

L. W. AUSTIN, Ph. D., Assistant Professor of Physics.
J. M. CLEMENTS, Ph. D., Assistant Professor of Geology.
G. C. COMSTOCK, Ph. B., LL. B., Professor of Astronomy.
C. A. CURTIS, A. B., Professor of Military Science and Tactics.
W. W. DANIELLS, M. S., Sc. D., Professor of Chemistry.
D. B. FRANKENBURGER, A. M., Professor of Rhetoric.
W. F. GIESE, A. M., Assistant Professor of Romance Languages.
LOUIS KAHLENBERG, Ph. D., Assistant Professor of Physical Chemistry.

H. W. HILLYER, Ph. D., Assistant Professor of Organic Chemistry.
W. H. HOBBS, Ph. D., Professor of Mineralogy and Petrology.
E. T. OWEN, A. B., Professor of French.
W. H. ROSENSTENGEL, A. M., Professor of German.
E. B. SKINNER, A. B., Assistant Professor of Mathematics.
C. S. SLICHTER, M. S., Professor of Applied Mathematics.
B. F. SNOW, Ph. D., Professor of Physics.
C. R. VAN HISE, Ph. D., Professor of Geology.
ARTHUR BEATTY, Ph. D., Instructor in Rhetoric.
H. G. A. BRAUER, M. A., Instructor in French.
W. B. CAIRNS, Ph. D., Instructor in Rhetoric.
W. D. FROST, M. S., Instructor in Bacteriology.
LUCY M. GAY, B. L., Instructor in French.
F. W. MEISNEST, B. S., Instructor in German.
H. W. PYRE, B. L., Instructor in Elocution and Oratory.
THEODORE RUNNING, M. S., Instructor in Mathematics.
J. C. SHEDD, Ph. D., Instructor in Physics.
C. M. SMITH, B. S., Instructor in Physics.
C. G. STANGEL, B. S., Assistant in Physics.
SUSAN A. STERLING, M. L., Instructor in German.
ALFRED TINGLE, Ph. D., Assistant in Chemistry.

SPECIAL LECTURERS.

C. B. STEWART, C. E., U. S. Assistant Engineer, "The Hydraulics of the Great Lakes."

B. A. BEHREND, E. E., "Engineering Schools and Industrial Progress in Germany."

COL. H. G. PROUT, C. E., Editor R. R. Gazette, "Railway Management."

R. C. CARPENTER, M. M. E., Professor of Experimental Engineering, Cornell University, "The Manufacture of Portland Cement."

MAGNUS SWENSON, M. S., Manufacturer, "The Chemical Engineer."

W. J. KARNER, Assistant to Chief Engineer Illinois Central Ry., "Engineering in Mexico."

W. B. SNOW, M. E., "Mechanical Ventilation and Heating."

D. W. MEAD, C. E., Consulting Engineer, "The Water Supply of Rockford, Ill."

A. O. POWELL, C. E., U. S. Assistant Engineer, "The Government Work in the St. Paul District."

W. B. POTTER, E. E., Engineer Ry. Dept. General Electric Co., "Three-Phase Railway Work."

GEO. B. LEIGHTON, President Los Angeles Terminal Railway, "Some Recent Economic Events."

ORGANIZATION OF THE COLLEGE.

The College of Engineering is organized in the belief that a thorough-going fundamental training is the first essential to a successful engineer, but that this fundamental training may be best secured in connection with a certain amount of study of the practical applications of the principles involved and not solely by theoretical study. It is further a leading thought that after the fundamental principles have been mastered, a certain measure of specialization in the main lines of engineering is advisable, because of the great development of engineering in recent years, and the various phases which it is rapidly assuming. It is the endeavor of this institution to combine a prudent amount of specialization in the closing years with a thorough grounding in the fundamentals in the earlier portion of its courses; and in carrying out this plan, it endeavors to make the mathematical and theoretical courses strong in the earlier years, and the applied courses strong in the later years, while the draughting and shop courses continue progressively from the beginning to the end. It also introduces sufficient foreign language to enable its graduates to read the professional German or French literature, and aims to give so much of the mastery of the English language as to enable its graduates to present professional subjects with ease, clearness, and effectiveness.

The General Engineering Course.

There is coming to be a great demand in our expanding industrial and commercial business for technically educated men who cannot be classified as engineers, properly speaking. Superintendents and managers, presidents and secretaries, owners and members of boards of directors, of all large manufacturing and commercial enterprises, as well as of all transportation, lighting, and power companies, should be acquainted with the fundamental principles and practices of some of the ordinary applications of science to modern industry. For the practical education of such men a General Engineering Course has been established, with only the fundamental engineering sciences required, together with some modern languages, economics, and history. This leaves about one-third of the entire time to be filled by such elective studies in the College of Engineering or in other departments as the student may find best suited to his particular needs. It may well be, also, that some students who expect to practice engineering will prefer to elect a considerable portion of their course in place of taking any one of the fixed engineering courses. This course is very elastic, and leads to the degree of Bachelor of Science in Engineering.

The Pre-Engineering Collegiate Course.

Especial encouragement is given to those who can afford the time to graduate in a collegiate course before entering the course in engineering. By electing the mathematics and some other subjects required of engineers, during the collegiate course, the degree in engineering can be obtained in two additional years. Greater satisfaction and profit is gained from the study of engineering when the student has already acquired a broad and thorough general training. Engineers are often called upon to fill the highest positions in the community, demanding breadth of view and wide general training. The opportunities for acquiring this breadth of education, such as is given by a complete collegiate course, are few, after the student has begun the active practice of his profession.

The College of Mechanics and Engineering offers seven systematic courses, as follows:

A Course in CIVIL ENGINEERING.
A Course in SANITARY ENGINEERING.
A Course in MECHANICAL ENGINEERING.
A Course in ELECTRICAL ENGINEERING.
A Course in APPLIED ELECTRO-CHEMISTRY.
A Pre-Metallurgical Course in ENGINEERING.
A General Course in ENGINEERING.

REQUIREMENTS FOR ADMISSION.

There are two methods of admission to the University.
I. By examination at the University.
II. By certificates from accredited schools.

I. Examinations at the University.

The regular examinations of the University are two in number, one in June and one in September. For the current year the earlier examination will be held on Thursday and Friday, June 14 and 15, beginning at 9 A. M. The latter examination will be held on Tuesday and Wednesday, September 25 and 26, beginning at 9 A. M. Examinations will also be held on the opening day of the second semester. Candidates must be present at the first examination of the first day. The examinations for admission to the freshman class in any of the engineering courses will cover the following subjects.

GEOGRAPHY, political and physical.

HISTORY OF THE UNITED STATES: Montgomery's or Johnson's History of the United States.

ARITHMETIC.

ALGEBRA: Addition, subtraction, multiplication, division, equations of the first degree, with one unknown quantity, simultaneous equations of the first degree, factors, highest common factor, lowest common multiple, quadratic equations, simultaneous equations above the first degree, theory of indices (positive, negative, fractional, and zero), and radicals.

GEOMETRY: Plane and solid geometry. In solid geometry, special attention should be given to the geometry of the sphere.

ENGLISH: 1. An analysis of short extracts from prose and poetry, as to forms and meaning of words, structure of sentences, paragraphing, and figures of speech.

2. Each candidate will be required to write a short essay on a subject to be announced at the time of the examination. The essay will be taken as a test of a candidate's knowledge of spelling, punctuation, use of capital letters, grammar, structure of sentences, and paragraphs.

GERMAN: Correct pronunciation; thorough drill in grammar and syntax, giving particular attention to translations from English into German; fifty (50) lessons of any standard reader including the memorizing of at least ten (10) poems; one term of prose readings. Practice in the oral and written use of German should be combined with the grammar and reading lessons. For prose readings, one or more of the following are recommended: Volkmann's Kleine Geschichten; Storm's Immensee; Heyse's L'Arrabbiata; Hillern's Hoeher als die Kirche; Wilderbruch's Der Letzte.

FRENCH: Instead of German, an equivalent amount of French may be offered.

PHYSICS: Carhart and Chute, Gage, or Avery, with laboratory work.

PHYSIOLOGY: Martin's the Human Body (briefer course).

BOTANY: Two terms' study required, of which at least 60 hours shall be laboratory work devoted to the anatomy and physiology of plants. It is urged that part of this time be given to a study of cryptogams. For entrance in 1898-99 and thereafter a knowledge of the main groups of cryptogams will be required.

ADAPTIVE WORK; amounting to one daily recitation for two years.

This may consist of various subjects. The University advises:

1. Two years' daily work in French or Latin; or

2. One year's work in history and one year's work in English literature.

If these studies cannot be taken, a selection from the following studies may be offered:

3. Rhetoric, civil government, mental science, theory and art of teaching, zoology, astronomy, or other science. No subject can be offered which has been pursued in high school for a shorter time than twelve weeks or which is less in amount than a standard high school text-book on the subject. The total amount offered must be equivalent of a daily recitation for two years. The two years' work may be made up of these studies in any combination, under the conditions stated above.

Real equivalents will be accepted for the requirements given above. Students desiring admission into any course must present those requirements which are essential to the work of the course.

Conditions in entrance examinations will be limited to those cases in which the Board of Examiners think that the maturity and strength of the student will allow him to carry the regular work of his course and make up the conditions.

Admission of Special Students.

Candidates under twenty-one years of age desiring to take special courses will be required to present the same qualifications as candidates for one of the regular courses of the University.

Persons twenty-one years of age, who are not candidates for a degree, and who wish to take special studies, will be permitted to do so upon giving satisfactory evidence that they are prepared to take the desired studies advantageously. If they subsequently desire to become candidates for a degree, or to take a regular course, they must pass the required entrance examination.

II. Admission Upon Certificates.

Graduates of schools which have been accredited to the University for the General Science and Engineering courses will be admitted to any one of the Engineering courses upon presentation of a certificate from the principal of the school.

Preparation in Algebra for the Engineering Courses.

Thorough preparation in mathematics is of the greatest importance to students entering the engineering courses of the University; and it is therefore advised that such students carefully review algebra either during the last term of their high school course or during the summer preceding their entrance into the University. The University faculty consider it advisable that the review be made, wherever practicable, during the last term of the high school course.

DEGREES.

The University confers upon the graduates in the Engineering courses the degrees of Bachelor of Science in Civil, Sanitary, Mechanical, Electrical Engineering, or Applied Electro-Chemistry, and for the general course Bachelor of Science in Engineering.

The degrees of Civil Engineer, Mechanical Engineer and Electrical Engineer are conferred as second degrees upon Bachelors of Science in the Civil, Mechanical, and Electrical Engineering courses respectively, (1) who pursue advanced professional study at the University for one year, and present a satisfactory project or thesis; or (2) who present suitable evidence of three years of professional work, of which one must be in a position of responsibility, and a satisfactory thesis.

University Fellowships.

For the purpose of promoting higher scholarship and more extended original study than the academic courses afford the Board of Regents has established ten University Fellowships of $400 each, conditioned upon proper qualifications and upon a prescribed amount of instruction rendered in the University.

BUILDINGS.

Through the generosity of the Legislature of 1899, the College of Mechanics and Engineering will hereafter occupy its own building, which will be completed, ready for occupany, when college opens in September, 1900. This is probably the most beautiful and best arranged engineering building in America. It faces the upper campus opposite the Law Building, and is designed so as to be extended northward towards Lake Mendota in two wings. All the professional work of the College of Engineering is given in this building and in its accompanying laboratories, except some of the electrical laboratory work and the shop instruction, which are given in the commodious shop buildings near by. For chemistry the engineering students go to the Chemical Building, for physics and other natural sciences to Science Hall, and for language, mathematics, and other similar work, to the literary halls of the University. In this way the students of

Engineering come into daily contact with the students in the other University courses, to the great advantage of all classes.

LIBRARIES.

The library facilities of the University are very great. Besides the University library, containing more than 54,000 volumes, of which a good share of the books pertain to the engineering profession, there are the library of the State Historical Society (150,000 volumes) and the City free library. (15,000 volumes) to which the students have free access. The College of Mechanics and Engineering subscribes for eighty-five technical periodicals, and also purchases duplicate copies of standard engineering works of reference, one set of which, together with the engineering periodicals, are kept in the engineering reading room, on the first floor of the Engineering Building, in order to facilitate the frequent use of them by the engineering students. The files of technical periodicals in the library are unusually complete, and additions are made every year.

Laboratories and Apparatus.

The engineering laboratories are well equipped for purposes of instruction and investigation.

The Testing Laboratory occupies the high sub-basement under the assembly room of the Engineering Building. It is supplied with a recently purchased one-hundred-thousand-pound Riehlé automatic and autographic testing machine, permitting the testing of materials of the larger sizes used in practice. In addition to this there are also other Riehlé machines, also Olsen and Thurston machines for making tests in tension, compression, bending, ond torsion. These machines are supplied with extensometers, clamps, devices for autographic records, and other special devices.

The Cement Laboratory contains a full supply of necessary apparatus for making tests according to the American Society of Civil Engineers' standard; baths, self-recording thermometer, Boehme hammer complete, 1,000-lb. Riehlé testing machine, a new electro-power stone saw, and grinding and polishing wheels. The machines in the Testing Laboratory are also used for testing brick, stone, and cement. The foundry rattler is available for paving brick tests.

The Hydraulic Laboratory contains high and low level tanks fitted for experimenting upon the flow of water through orifices. nozzles, pipes, and over weirs. In the laboratory are several water motors, water meters, current meters, lines of pipe, etc., all available for experimental work. There is also a convenient supply of gauges and other apparatus required in accurate hydraulic experiments.

The Steam Laboratory is located in the new Engineering Building. The main laboratory, which is 74 feet by 50 feet, is a one-story addition to the building, in the rear of the same, and is so placed that the wings, which ultimately will be added to the building, will leave this laboratory in the court thus created. The floor of this laboratory will be on the same level as the main basement of the building; but a gallery arranged especially for visitors runs around the whole laboratory, to which gallery one gains entrance from the first floor, being on the same level with it. A part of this wide gallery is partitioned off to serve as a computing room for the students working in the laboratory. The room is very light and airy, being more than 20 feet high. It is lighted by numerous large skylights and by windows in the rear wall. It is believed that very few colleges in the country, if indeed any, possess such a fine room for the experimental work in Steam Engineering. The tunnel from the Boiler House, through which all steam pipes for the heating of the building and for power purposes are run, terminates at the rear of the laboratory, and all the steam pipes for the various engines, etc., are placed in trenches below the floor, with heavy iron covers. The floor of the room is granolithic, with ample facilites for cleaning and draining it.

On the same level in the eastern wing of the new building are the separate laboratories for gas and coal analysis; these rooms are both large and well lighted, and will furnish splendid opportunity for extended researches for these very important branches of steam engineering. Next to these rooms will be found a large apparatus and store room, as well as a general office for the instructors in the laboratory.

The general steam laboratory is well equipped with a variety of steam engines, specially arranged for experimental work. The most important of these is a fifty-horse-power cross compound engine, so arranged that either cylinder can be supplied with live steam from the boilers and run as a single cylinder engine. The surface condensor and air pump can also be disconnected so that the engine may be run as a non-condensing one. Both cylinders and receiver are provided with steam jackets, which may be used at will. By means of a Proell governor the number of revolutions may be varied from 50 to 125. The cut-off of the steam is automatically controlled by the governor, and may vary between zero and ninety-five per cent. of the stroke. A fifty-horse-power Root boiler, belonging to the department, but installed in the boiler house of the University, is connected in such a manner that it can furnish the steam for this engine alone.

In addition to seven steam engines contained in the laboratory there are one hot-air engine, one three-horse-power Otto gas engine, one ten-horse-power gasoline engine and a five-ton ammonia refrigerating plant especially arranged for experimental purposes. This plant, which is a recent addition to the equipment, is deemed very valuable, as it was especially designed for experimental purposes. The ammonia compressor is a triple one and of the single-acting type, and is arranged in such a manner that the clearance may be varied very readily.

The laboratory is supplied with friction brakes, transmitting dynometers of various kinds and capacities, mercury column, and other means for testing steam and vacuum gauges and indicators, and various devices for special tests. There are also the necessary tanks, weighing apparatus, pyrometers, thermometers, calorimeters, some twenty-five indicators, revolution counters, tachometers, recording gauges, reducing motions, water meters, etc., for making complete tests of the economy and capacity of boilers and engines. The laboratory is also supplied with a very large number and variety of injectors, and with special facilities for making tests of the same.

The boiler house of the University, which furnishes steam for nearly all of the buildings of the institution, both for heating and for power purposes, is also equipped in such a manner that experimental work with reference to the economy of boilers under various conditions may easily be carried out.

The laboratories for gas and coal analysis are thoroughly equipped with all the necessary apparatus and facilities for thorough investigations, in these subjects, and in connection with the boiler house of the University, which contains boilers of about 1,200-horse-power capacity, there is ample opportunity for a thorough study of these subjects. This boiler house, as well as the heating system of all the buildings connected with it, being in charge of the head of the department, furnish unusual opportunities for advanced students to investigate the subject of central heating plants, as well as the efficiency of various kinds of heating plans for buildings.

The Electrical Laboratories are well supplied with exact scientific and commercial instruments, and are arranged for instruction and investigation. With the space and apparatus which is allowed through the generosity of past legislatures, the equipment has been made unusually complete in the lines of continuous current, and single and polyphase alternating current, generation and distribution, and commercial electro-chemistry and electro-metallurgy.

The dynamo collection consists of a large number of continuous-current and alternating-current generators and motors of various types (including four types of arc-light machines), which are specially installed for the purposes of instruction and experiment. These are arranged in a large laboratory room and are arranged to be driven by an engine specially provided for the purpose. For use in testing dynamos all necessary apparatus is supplied, including large lamp banks, transformer banks, and water rheostats for loading generators, special prony brakes, etc., for loading motors, cradle dynamometer, and accurate electrical instruments of all useful types. A transformer bank for use in instruction and testing, which represents nearly all American and some foreign products, and an equally complete bank of recording electric meters, are also located in this room.

Another large room is occupied by the appliances and apparatus required for instruction and experiments relating to electric batteries, electrolysis, electroplating, and electrometallurgy. The equipment for this laboratory consists of dynamos and tanks for depositing metals and for other electrolytic processes; apparatus for cleaning, polishing, and burnishing; various electric furnaces for electrometallurgical processes requiring the intense heat of the electric arc; and proper measuring instruments. The equipment is one of the first and most complete of its kind.

Other rooms are dedicated to work in electrical testing, measuring illumination, and various other branches of laboratory instruction and investigation.

A great number of amperemeters, voltmeters, wattmeters, wheatstone bridges, variable self-inductance and mutual-inductance boxes, condensers, galvanometers, electrodynamometers, electric balances, 100,000 ohm and megohm resistances, Clark cells, Burgess electrometer testing sets, and other apparatus are supplied for general use, while standard apparatus for determining the adjustments of the general instruments is at hand. Special means are provided for the important functions of insulation testing, testing the magnetic qualities of metals (including a Ewing hysteresis tester, a Ewing magnetic bridge, and an improved bridge designed at the University), for photometry of arc and incandescent lamps, and for measuring the distribution of illumination (in which the equipment is very full), etc. Apparatus is also provided for class-room demonstration, such as apparatus for demonstrating the phenomena of polyphase current transformation and polyphase motors, a fine set of models and charts (made at the University) illustrating the different forms of armature windings, etc.

A Thomson electric welder, located in the dynamo room, gives opportunity for instruction upon the electrical working of metals, and a transformer of twenty kilowatts capacity furnishes alternating current at 50,000 volts pressure for instruction in high pressure testing and the phenomena of high pressure electric power transmission. Alternating and polyphase (2-phase and 3-phase) currents of the ordinary frequencies are on tap, at the switchboards, and other frequencies may be generated at will by means of rotary transformers, one of which has a capacity of 30 kilowatts. Continuous currents of any desired value up to 400 amperes and pressures up to 1,000 volts can be had at will.

All electrical elaboratory instruction is made to conform with, and illustrate, the class room instruction. Of the total number of hours given to instruction in the electrical engineering courses, about one-half is devoted to work in the laboratories.

The Bridge Engineering Department has recently purchased a set of Fraenkel's autographic apparatus for the testing of bridges under moving train loads. This includes two extensometers for measuring strains in members and a deflectometer for measuring vertical and lateral deflections. The department also possesses several large size models of bridge joints and a large collection of drawings and photographs to which additions are constantly being made.

The Assay Laboratory, situated in the south part of the basement of the Chemical laboratory, is one of the largest and best equipped laboratories of its kind in the country. It has separate rooms for furnaces, tables, wet assaying, and balances. The furnace room is supplied with eleven crucible and three muffle furnaces, as well as a small gas plant. It has steam power, a Sturtevant blower, bullion rolls, a Blake ore crusher, and other pulverizers. The table room has space for twenty-four students, and is well supplied with ordinary balances. In the balance room are first-class quantitative balances by Becker, and an Oertling gold balance.

The Surveying Laboratory. By an agreement with the director of Washburn Observatory, the surveying laboratory shares in the free use of the extensive apparatus belonging to that observatory, and including, in addition to the large equatorial telescope, and meridian circle, collimators, transit micrometers, chronograph, sidereal and meantime clocks, zenith telescopes, a transit instrument of the broken type, chronometers, an altazmuth, a universal instrument of the German type, spherometer calipers, and complete set of meteorological instruments.

In addition to this equipment the surveying laboratory contains all the portable, astronomical, and field instruments needed for an extensive triangulation and topographic and hydrographic surveys, including one 8-inch direction theodolite by Fauth, reading to single seconds, three theodolites by Buff and Berger, Fauth, and Bambey, reading to ten seconds, an altazimuth by Hyde, reading to six seconds, a tidal gauge, six heliotropes, a complete precise level outfit by Kern, a sounding apparatus, a base line apparatus, one direction current meter by Ritchie-Haskell, and one current meter by Buff and Berger, fifteen engineer's transits of various designs, one complete mining transit with auxiliary side and top telescope and lamp targets by Buff and Berger, four solar transits and compasses, an ample number of wye, dumpy, and architects' levels, plane-tables, telemeters, level rods, surveyors' compasses, and such special instruments as planimeters, pantographs, trignometers, sextants, computing machines, aneroid barometers, odometers, pedometers, clinometers, binocular telescopes, telescopic hand levels, etc., etc.

The Machine Shop affords excellent facilities for mechanical practice. It embraces a main machine room properly equipped; a carpenter shop supplied with wood-working machines; a forge room, provided with forges and their equipment, with blast and exhaust fan; a foundry room whose equipment consists of a cupola, brass furnace, and core oven, with the necessary small tools; a wood-work room supplied with benches, carpenter tools, and wood-turning lathes; and a pattern room furnished with the requisite tools. The shop is supplied with convenient lockers, closets, and washroom with hot and cold water. The space and equipment of the shop has lately been increased nearly three-fold to provide for the rapid increase in the number of students entering the classes of the College of Engineering. New lathes, forges, drills, and benches have been added with the increase of space until 150 students may be instructed in the different branches of the work at one time.

The Engineering Museum contains a complete set of Schroeder's models for descriptive geometry, including shades, shadows, and perspective; also a small collection of Schroeder's kinematic models, besides a number of smaller models, made by students, illustrating problems in kinematics. An excellent industrial collection is in process of development.

The draughting rooms contain a large and varied collection of general working and detail drawings illustrating a great variety of engineering structures and machines.

The standards of weights and measures belonging to the State are kept in the Civil Engineering Department, and all official comparisons are made here.

INSPECTION TOURS.

An inspection tour by the members of the junior class is provided for just previous to the Easter recess. In this tour visits are made to great manufacturing establishments and to other important private and public engineering work in Chicago, Milwaukee, and elsewhere. Similar tours by sections of the senior class are provided for in the fall or just before commencement. These tours are made under the guidance of the professors and are deemed an important part of the student's work.

EXPENSES.

Tuition for residents of the State of Wisconsin	FREE.
Tuition for non-resident students—per semester	$20.00
General fee—first semester	15.00
General fee—second semester	15.00
Engineering and periodical fee for the year	1.50

A laboratory fee of $1.50 per semester, for each two hours' work per week, is charged in all engineering laboratories.

Students working in any of the other laboratories of the University are also required to pay a fee or to make a deposit to cover the cost of the materials and repairs of instruments used by them. For a list of these fees, see p. 39.

Rooms, furnished and unfurnished, can be obtained in the city at reasonable rates. The cost of board in clubs is from $2.25 to $3.00 per week; in private families from $2.50 to $3.50 per week.

COURSES OF STUDY.

The Pre-Engineering Collegiate Course.

The attention of students who propose to pursue an engineering course is specially called to the opportunity which is presented for them to complete a general University course, and by taking advantage of the elections as described on p. 174, to complete the technical course in two additional years. All students who can afford the time are strongly advised to pursue this plan.

A FIVE-YEAR SCHEME IN THE COLLEGE OF ENGINEERING.

The amount of work required in the College of Engineering throughout the entire four years, is just one-fourth more than that required in the other courses in the College of Letters and Science. It is necessary to make the work very heavy in order to cover the ground requisite to the granting of the Engineering degrees. Many students find it difficult to perform this work satisfactorily, and they would prefer to devote to it an additional year; this would either lighten the work or it would enable them to elect some additional studies. To satisfy this demand the class officers in the College of Engineering are authorized to arrange the work with the students who desire to extend the length of their course in this manner, so as to make it cover five years, in place of four. It has not been thought wise to formally arrange the work in the several courses to cover a five-year period, since different students would prefer to take it in different ways. The Faculty in the College of Engineering recommend that students devote this additional year to the work, whenever they feel that they can afford the time and the expense. Students who elect to do this should not, therefore, feel that it is any reflection upon their abilities or upon their industry. It would rather indicate a disposition to obtain a more thorough preparation for their life work.

Requirements in the Modern Languages for all Courses in the College of Mechanics and Engineering.

1. When German is offered for entrance: There is required a 4-5 course in German throughout the freshman year and a 2-5 course in technical German throughout the sophomore year. Also for those taking the course in five years an elective of a 4-5 course in French throughout the sophomore year and a 2-5 course in technical French throughout the junior year.

2. When French is offered for entrance: There is required a 4-5 course in German throughout the freshman year and a 2-5 course in technical French throughout the sophomore year. Also for those taking the course in five years there is offered as an elective a 4-5 course in German throughout the sophomore year and a 2-5 course in technical German throughout the junior year.

3. When four years of Latin is offered for entrance: There is required a 4-5 course throughout the freshman year and a 2-5 course of technical reading throughout the sophomore year, in either French or German. Also for those taking the course in five years the alternative language can be obtained as above in the sophomore and junior years.

4. When neither a modern language nor Latin is offered for entrance: Students who are well prepared in all their other work

will be received without a preparation in modern language but subject to a condition in the same. In this case there will be required a 4-5 course in either German or French throughout the freshman year, this being in lieu of the modern language requirements for entrance. If German be taken in the freshman year there will be required a 4-5 course in German throughout the sophomore year, and a 2-5 course in technical German throughout the junior year. If French be taken in the freshman year there will be required a 2-5 course in technical French throughout the sophomore year, and a 4-5 course in German throughout the junior year.

The modern language requirements as given in the detailed statements below must be interpreted by, and made consistent with, the general requirements as stated above.

FRESHMAN YEAR.
For all Courses in the College of Engineering.
First Semester.

	Hrs.
German 5 or French 3.....................................	4
English 2, Rhetoric and Composition......................	3
Mathematics 1, Algebra...................................	5
Descriptive Geometry.....................................	5
Chemistry 1..	4

Second Semester.

German 5 or French 3.....................................	4
English 2, Rhetoric and Composition......................	3
Mathematics 2 and 3, Trigonometry and Analytical Geometry.	5
Descriptive Geometry.....................................	2
Chemistry 1..	3
Topographical Engineering 2, Elementary Surveying........	2
Shop-work 1, and 2, Wood-work and Foundry...............	2

CIVIL ENGINEERING COURSE.
SOPHOMORE YEAR.—First Semester.

Mathematics 3, and 4, Analytical Geometry and Calculus....	5
Physics 1 and 2..	5
Mineralogy 2...	2
Topographical Engineering 3, Elementary Surveying........	3½
Shop-work 5, 6, and 7, Machine-work and Forging...........	2
German or French, Technical Reading......................	2
Topographical Engineering 1, Elementary Drawing..........	1½

Second Semester.

	Hrs.
Mathematics 4, Calculus	3½
Physics 1 and 2	4
Mechanics 1 and 2, Analytical Mechanics and Graphical Statics	8
Topographical Engineering 4, Advanced Surveying	3½
German or French, Technical Reading	2
Topographical Engineering 6, Trigonometric Survey	2 weeks

Junior Year, First Semester.

Mechanics 3, Strength of Materials	5
Hydraulics 1, and 3	3
Steam Engineering 7, 9, Steam Engine	3
Structural Engineering 1, Structural Details	2
Railway Engineering 1, 2, Location	5
Materials of Construction 1	3

Second Semester.

Railway Engineering 3, Maintenance of Way	2
Topographical Engineering 5, Geodesy	2
Structural Engineering 2, 3, 4a, Masonry, Arches and Dams	5½
Structural Engineering 5a, Bridge Stresses; 7a, Roof Trusses and Girders	6
Materials of Construction 2, Testing Laboratory	1½
Astronomy or Electrical Engineering	4
Topographical Engineering 6, Trigonometric Survey	2 weeks

Senior Year, First Semester.

Structural Engineering 4b, Dams and Sterotomy	3
Structural Engineering 5b, 7b, Bridge Stresses	6
Railway Engineering 5, Railway Economics	2
Geology 1, General Geology	3
Municipal Engineering 1, Water Supply	3
Elective	4

Second Semester.

Railway Engineering 7, Tunnels and Substructures	2
Rivers and Canals 1	1½
Municipal Engineering 2, Sanitary Engineering	3
Municipal Engineering 4, Roads and Pavements	1½
Geology 5	2
Contracts and Specifications	1
Thesis and Elective	10

Graduate Courses.

For graduate students and students desiring to specialize, opportunity is afforded in the elective courses and in courses arranged on consultation with the instructors, for advanced study in railway, structural, municipal, topographic or geodetic engineering, and for special laboratory investigations.

SANITARY ENGINEERING COURSE.

Freshman Year.

See page 186.

Sophomore Year.

Same as Civil Engineering Course.

Junior Year, First Semester.

	HRS.
Mechanics 3, Strength of Materials	5
Hydraulics 1 and 3	3
Railway Engineering 1, 2, Location	5
Materials of Construction 1	3
Biology of Water Supplies	5

Second Semester.

Railway Engineering 3, Maintenance of Way	2
Topographic Engineering 5, Geodesy	2
Structural Engineering 2, 3, 4a, Masonry Arches, and Dams	5½
Structural Engineering 5a, 7a, Bridge Stresses, Roof and Bridge Design	5
Chemistry 2, Water Analysis	5
Materials of Construction 2, Testing Laboratory	1½
Topographical Engineering 6, Trigonometric Survey	2 weeks

Senior Year, First Semester.

Steam Engineering 7, 9, Steam Engine	3
Structural Engineering 4b, Dams and Stereotomy	3
Structural Engineering 6, 7b, Bridge Design	4
Municipal Engineering, 1, 3, Water Supply	5
Geology 1	3
Steam Engineering 12, Heating and Ventilation	2

Second Semester.

Railway Engineering 7, Tunnels and Substructures	2
Municipal Engineering 2, 3, Sewerage and Drainage	5

COLLEGE OF MECHANICS AND ENGINEERING. 189

	Hrs.
Municipal Engineering 4, Roads and Pavements	1½
Geology 5	2
Electrical Installations 11	4
Contracts and Specifications	1
Thesis and Elective	5½

MECHANICAL ENGINEERING COURSE.

Freshman Year.

See page 186.

Sophomore Year, First Semester.

Mathematics 3, 4, Analytical Geometry, Calculus	5
Physics 1, 2	5
Machine Design 1, Kinematics	6
Shop-work 2, 3, 4, Foundry, Chipping Iron	3
German or French, Technical Reading	2

Second Semester.

Mathematics 4, 6, Calculus, Differential Equations	5
Physics 1, 2	4
Mechanics 1, Analytic	5
Machine Design 2, Drawing and Blue Printing	2
Shop-work 5, 6, 7, Machine Work and Forging	3
German or French, Technical Reading	2

Junior Year, First Semester.

Mechanics 3, Strength of Materials	5
Steam Engineering 1, 2, 8, Thermodynamics, Heat Engines	5
Machine Design 3, Elementary Design	6
Shop-work 8, 9, and 10, Machine Work and Tool Making	5

Second Semester.

Materials of Construction 1	3
Hydraulics 1, 2, 3	5
Steam Engineering 2, 3, 8, Steam Engine, Laboratory	6
Machine Design 4, Crane Design and Graphic Statics	5
Shop-work 11, Machine Construction	2

Senior Year, First Semester.

Machine Designs, Machine Elements and Power Transmission	5
Steam Engineering 5, 8, Steam Engine Design, Laboratory	6½

	HRS.
Materials of Construction 2, Testing, Laboratory..........	1½
Applied Electro-Magnetics 3, Electrical Machinery, Laboratory	5
Shop-work 12, Construction and Pattern Work.............	3

Second Semester.

Machine Design 5, Machine Elements, Power Transmission....	5
Steam Engineering 5, Steam Engine Design................	5
Contracts and Specifications.............................	1
Thesis and Elective.....................................	10

ELECTRICAL ENGINEERING COURSE.

Freshman Year.
See page 186.

Sophomore Year.
Same as Mechanical Engineering Course.

Junior Year, First Semester.

Mechanics 3, Strength of Materials......................	5
Physics 5, Precision of Measurements...................	2
Applied Electro-Magnetism 1, 2, Electro Magnets and Dynamos	5
Machine Design 3, Elementary Design...................	5
Shop-work 8, 9, 10, Machine Work and Tool Making..........	4

Second Semester.

Hydraulics 1, 2, 3.......................................	
Steam Engineering 6, 11, Thermodynamics and Laboratory..	
Applied Electro Magnetism 1, 2, Electro Magnets and Dynamos	
Electrical Installations 2, Electrical Testing...............	
Materials of Construction...............................	5
Elective in Civil and Mechanical Engineering..............	3

Senior Year, First Semester.

Alternating Currents 1, 2...............................	5
Steam Engineering 6, 11, Thermodynamics and Laboratory..	4
From Electrical Installations 3, 5, 7, 8, 10, and Applied Electro-Chemistry 1, 2.....................................	7
*Thesis and Elective.....................................	5

Second Semester.

Alternating Currents 1, 2...............................	2
From Electrical Installations 3, 4, 5, 6, 8, and Alternating Currents 3, 4..	10

	HRS.
Contracts and Specifications	1
Materials of Construction 2, Testing Laboratory	1½
*Thesis and Elective	6

*Note.—The thesis should consume at least five hours for one semester. The work should begin in first semester and should usually continue through the year.

APPLIED ELECTRO-CHEMISTRY COURSE.

Freshman and Sophomore Years.

Same as Electrical Engineering Course.

Junior Year, First Semester.

Mechanics 3, Strength of Materials	5
Physics 5, Precision of Measurements	3
Applied Electro Magnetism 1, 2, Electro Magnets and Dynamos	5
Chemistry 2, Inorganic	3
Chemistry 9, Electro Chemistry	5

Second Semester.

Applied Electro-Magnetism 1, 2, Electro-Magnets and Dynamos	5
Materials of Construction	3
Chemistry 2, Advanced Inorganic	3
Chemistry 10, Electro Chemistry	5
Elective	5

Senior Year, First Semester.

Applied Electro-Chemistry 2, Electrolysis	5
Alternating Currents 1, 2	5
Chemistry 9, Physical Chemistry	4
Steam Engineering 7, 12	3
Materials of Construction 2, Testing Laboratory	1½
*Thesis and Elective Mineralogy, Structures, etc.	3

Second Semester.

Alternating Currents 1, 2	2
Electrical Installations 4, Electric Lighting and Power	3
Applied Electro-Chemistry 3	5
To Be Elected from Electrical Installations 6, 8, 10, and Alternating Currents 3, 4	6

	Hrs.
Contracts and Specifications	1
*Thesis and Elective	4

*Note.—The thesis should consume at least five hours for one semester. The work should begin in first semester and should usually continue through the year.

Graduate Courses.

Graduates and advanced students are offered instruction in advanced design and experimental investigations relating to electrical engineering as is more fully explained in later pages under Departments of Instruction, and also in earlier pages under Department of Graduate Study.

GENERAL COURSE LEADING TO THE DEGREE OF BACHELOR OF SCIENCE IN ENGINEERING.

REQUIRED STUDIES.

Freshman Year.

All the studies of this year are required, and are the same as in the specialized engineering courses.

Sophomore Year, First Semester.

Mathematics 3 and 4, (Analytical Geometry and Calculus)	5
Physics 1 and 2	5
History 2a (Political History of England)	3
History 2b (Economic History)	2
Elective	3 to 5

Second Semester.

Mathematics 4 (Calculus)	5
Physics 1 and 2	4
Elements of Economic Science	3
Mechanics	5
Elective	2 to 4

Junior Year, First Semester.

Mechanics 3 (Strength of Materials)	5
Applied Electro Magnetism 2 and 3	5
Materials of Construction	3
Elective	5 to 8

Second Semester.

	Hrs.
Mechanics 5 (Testing Materials)	1½
Steam Engineering 6	3
Machinery and Mechanical Transmission	3
Mechanics (Hydraulics 4a)	2
Elective	8 to 11

Senior Year, First Semester.

Geology 1	3
Sanitary Engineering (Special Course)	2
Steam Engineering 6	2
Elective	10 to 13

Second Semester.

Geology (Economic Geology)	2
Engineering Contracts and Specifications	1
Elective and Thesis	15 to 18

Suggested Electives for the General Engineering Course.

English 4 (Advanced Rhetoric, 1 semester)	2
French, German, or Spanish (1 to 3 semesters)	3
Chemistry (1 to 4 semesters)	3
Biology of Water Supplies (first semester)	5
Mineralogy 2 (1 semester)	2
Mathematics 9 (Differential Equations, 2 semesters)	3
Astronomy (Descriptive and Practical, 1 or 2 semesters)	3
History 4 and 5 (Mod. European and Amer., 1 to 2 semesters)	3
Economics 3 and 10 (Finance and Transportation, 1 or 2 semesters)	3
Mechanics 2 (Graph. Statics, 1 semester)	3
Topographical Engineering (1 to 3 semesters)	3
Structural Engineering (1 to 3 semesters)	3
Railway Engineering (1 to 3 semesters)	3
Steam Engineering (1 to 4 semesters)	3
Machine Design (1 to 4 semesters)	3
Alternating Currents (1 to 2 semesters)	5
Electrical Installations (1 or 2 semesters)	3
Illumination and Photometry (1 semester)	2
Applied Electro Chemistry (1 to 4 semesters)	5
Mineralogy (1 or 2 semesters)	5
Advanced Geology (1 or 2 semesters)	5

	HRS.
Petrogrophy and Ore Deposits (1 or 2 semesters)	2
Metallurgy (1 to 4 semesters)	3
Heating and Ventilation (1 semester)	2
Shop-Work (1 to 4 semesters)	3
Commercial Law (1 semester)	3
Economics 19, 20, and 21, (Public Finance for Advance Students)	3
Municipal Government (Political Science, 2nd semester)	3

Pre-Mining and Pre-Metallurgical Engineering Courses.

Students who take the General Engineering Course may group their electives in chemistry, mineralogy and geology in such a way as to prepare them for specialization in mining or metallurgical engineering studies. Students who thus group their studies will be able to obtain their degree in metallurgy or in mining engineering at a mining school in one or two years, depending upon the electives taken and the ability of the man.

The electives in the College of Letters and Science will be as follows:

    Sophomore year: Mineralogy I., five hours.
    Junior year: Chemistry II., five hours.
                 Geology I. and II., five hours.
    Senior year: Chemistry III., five hours.
                 Geology IV. and V., five hours.

It is believed that students who take the general engineering course, with the electives here specified, and afterwards complete a course at some mining school, will be better trained in mining and metallurgy than they would be had they entered a mining school at the outset and completed their course in four years.

For those who begin the General Engineering Course as freshmen in 1900 the electives given below are adapted. Those who began as freshmen in 1899 and enter the General Engineering Course as sophomores will be obliged to take mineralogy in the junior year and geology in the senior year.

ELECTIONS FOR STUDENTS IN GENERAL UNIVERSITY COURSES.

Students who plan to graduate in engineering, after taking a degree in any other college of the University, should aim to make the following elections during their undergraduate course, in order that the engineering course may be completed in two additional years:

Freshman Year.

Mathematics, all courses; Topographical Engineering, 1 and 2a, or Machine Design, 1.

Sophomore Year.

Mathematics, all courses; Physics, 1 and 2; Topographical Engineering, 2 and 4, or Machine Design, 1, 2, and 3; Pure and Applied Mechanics, 1.

Graduates in any of the Engineering courses may graduate in any other Engineering course after one year of additional study. Students who contemplate doing this should, however, make their elections, especially in the senior year, with this end in view.

DEPARTMENTS OF INSTRUCTION.

The number of hours given is the actual number of hours of instruction. Class-room work and lectures require outside preparation, draughting room and laboratory work do not.

FRENCH.

PROFESSOR OWEN, ASSISTANT PROFESSOR GIESE, MISS GAY, AND MR. BRAUER.

3. Special Elementary Course for Engineers, essentially as follows: Roman d'un Jeune Homme Pauvre, La Petite Fadette (the former read mainly and the latter altogether independently of the classroom), Le Cid, Le Misanthrope. *Throughout the year;* M., Tu., W., Th., F., at 11. Mr. BRAUER.
4. Composition, etc. Written translation into French of the English exercises in Otto's Grammar, oral translation into French of Howard's Aids to French Composition. *Throughout the year; two hours a week.* Miss GAY.
5. Continuation of Course 4. *Throughout the year; two hours a week.* Assistant Professor GIESE.
20. A general course of lectures on French Literature, XVI.—XIX. centuries, with collateral reading. *Throughout the year;* M., W., at 12. Assistant Professor GIESE.

GERMAN.

PROFESSOR ROSENSTENGEL, MISS STERLING, AND MR. MEISNEST.

5. Science Reader, and Scientific Monographs required of Freshmen, unless French is elected. *Daily, at* 11. Miss STERLING and Mr. MEISNEST.

The aim of this course is to impart a reading knowledge of scientific German, thus enabling students to read German scientific works in connection with their special line of study.

ENGLISH.

DR. BEATTY, MR. PYRE, AND MISS BUTT.

1. Freshman English. English Prose Style. Composition. The elements of effective writing in prose, based upon direct study of selected authors, with training in composition, and in methods of investigation and of presenting results. *Three hours a week, throughout the year.* For hours and rooms see time table of required studies. Required of freshmen in all courses.
14. Elocution. Voice training and plain reading and speaking. *First semester; three times a week.*
Elective for Engineers.

PHYSICS.

PROFESSOR SNOW, ASSISTANT PROFESSOR AUSTIN, DR. SHEDD, MR. SMITH, AND MR. STANGEL.

1. General Lectures and Introductory Laboratory Practice. Lectures daily at 12 o'clock. Professor SNOW. One recitation by the class in smaller sections at hours to be assigned. Professor SNOW, Dr. SHEDD, and Mr. SMITH. Laboratory practice twice a week. *First semester; Tu., Th., 9-1. Second semester; W., F., 2-4.* Assistant Professor AUSTIN, Dr. SHEDD, Mr. SMITH, and Mr. STANGEL.

    The Introductory Physical Laboratory is open daily. Students may therefore make other arrangements as to time, if necessary.
    Required of sophomores in Engineering.
4. Precision of Measurements. An advanced laboratory course in Electrical and Magnetic Measurements. Testing and calibration of electrical instruments, and determination of constants. *Three times a week for first semester; M., W., 2-5.* Dr. SHEDD.
Required of juniors in Electrical Engineering.

CHEMISTRY.

PROFESSOR DANIELLS, ASSISTANT PROFESSOR HILLYER, ASSISTANT PROFESSOR KAHLENBERG, DR. TINGLE, MR. COOK, AND MR. FOWLER.

1. Descriptive Inorganic Chemistry and Qualitative Analysis. Lectures and laboratory work. *First semester; M., Tu., W., Th., F., 2-4.*

Second semester: C. E., first twelve weeks, one lecture and six hours laboratory; E. E. and M. E., one lecture and six hours laboratory work per week for the semester.

2. Advanced Inorganic Chemistry, second year, and Quantitative Analysis. *Daily throughout the year.* The amount of time devoted to this subject may be more or less than that of a full study, and will be arranged upon consultation with the instructors. Professor DANIELLS and Assistants.

15. Physical Chemistry. General Course. *Full study throughout the year. Lectures and recitations, first semester; Tu., Th., at 8. Second semester; M., W., F., at 8.* The lectures and recitations are supplemented by laboratory exercises in physico-chemical measurements, thus making a full study. This course must be preceded by course 1 in chemistry. Assistant Professor KAHLENBERG.

16. Electrochemistry. Lectures and recitations twice a week. Laboratory work in electro-chemical measurements and in electrolysis of various chemical compounds supplements the lectures and with them makes a full study. *Throughout the year at hours to be arranged.* Assistant Professor KAHLENBERG.

MINERALOGY.

PROFESSOR HOBBS.

2. Mineralogy. A short course adapted to the needs of Engineering students, taken mainly in the laboratory, when with the use of the blow-pipe and study of the physical characters the student is taught to identify minerals. The minerals of economic importance and the common rock builders are the ones given particular attention. *First semester; M., W., 9.*
Required of sophomores in Civil Engineering.

GEOLOGY.

PROFESSOR VAN HISE AND ASSISTANT PROFESSOR CLEMENTS.

1. Part I. General Geology. The geological forces and the work they accomplish; the physiography of North America; rocks and their original and secondary structures. Numerous short excursions. First semester to holiday recess. *M., Tu., W., Th., F., or M., W., F., at 12.* Professor VAN HISE.

   Part II. Historical Geology. Special emphasis is given to the history of the North American Continent, including both its physical and life development. Lecture room and laboratory

work. First semester from holiday recess. *M., Tu., W., Th., F., or M., W., F., at* 12. Assistant Professor CLEMENTS.
Required of seniors in Civil Engineering. This course is so arranged that it can be taken as a three-fifths or five-fifths study for the first semester.

2. Applied Geology. Treats of potable waters, structural materials, soils, mineral fertilizers, mineral fuels, and iron ores. Must be preceded by course 1. Required of seniors in civil engineering. First six weeks of second semester. *M., Tu., W., Th., F., at* 12. Assistant Professor CLEMENTS.

MATHEMATICS.

PROFESSOR SLICHTER, ASSISTANT PROFESSORS SKINNER, MACK, SMITH, AND MESSRS. RUNNING AND ALEXANDER.

1. Algebra. This course includes progressions, arrangements, and groups, binominal theorem, the theory of limits, undetermined coefficients, logarithms, imaginaries, and rational integral functions of one variable. Text-book: Van Velzer and Slichter's University Algebra. *First semester; M., Tu., W., Th., F., at* 10 (*90 hours in class room*). Professor SLICHTER, Assistant Professor SKINNER, and Mr. RUNNING.
Required of freshmen in Engineering.

2. Plane Trigonometry. *Part of second semester; M., Tu., W., Th., F., at* 10 (*36 hours in class room*). Professor SLICHTER and Assistant Professor SKINNER.
Required of freshmen in Engineering.

4. Analytic Geometry. Straight line, conic sections, and introduction to geometry of three dimensions (74 hours in classroom). *Part of second semester; M., Tu., W., T., F., at* 10. Required of freshmen in Engineering. *Part of first semester; M., Tu., W., Th., F., at* 8 *and* 9. Required of sophomores in Engineering. Professor SLICHTER and Assistant Professor SKINNER.

5. Calculus. *Part of first semester, and second semester; M., Tu., W., Th., F., two sections, at* 8 *and* 9 (*136 hours in class room.*) Professor SLICHTER, Assistant Professor SKINNER, and Mr. RUNNING.
Required of sophomores in Engineering.

6. Differential Equations. *Part of second semester; M., Tu., W., Th., F., at* 8 *and* 9 (*24 hours in class room.*) Professor SLICHTER, Assistant Professor SKINNER, and Mr. RUNNING.

Required of sophomores in Mechanical and Electrical Engineering.

ASTRONOMY.

PROFESSOR COMSTOCK.

6. Astronomical Practice. This course gives training in the theory and use of instruments of precision, and teaches the more important practical applications of astronomy, such as the determination of time, latitude, longitude, and the direction of the meridian. Attention is paid to methods of computation and the numerical treatment of observed data.
7. Method of Least Squares. The subject is treated from the empirical side, and stress is laid upon the application of principles rather than upon the purely mathematical problems which accompany them. *Second semester; M., Tu., W., F., 2-4.*
Elective for juniors in Civil and Sanitary Engineering.

BIOLOGY OF WATER SUPPLIES.

MR. FROST.

36. Biology of Water Supplies. This course is adapted to the needs of students in Sanitary Engineering. It includes a study of the microscopical plants and animals usually found in water supplies; the isolation and cultivation of water bacteria and their relation to disease; the testing of filters and other methods for the purification of waters; and the disposition of sewage by means of sand filtration. *First semester. Full study.* Lectures and Laboratory work. Mr. FROST.
Required of seniors in Sanitary Engineering.

APPLIED MECHANICS.

ASSISTANT PROFESSOR MAURER AND ACTING PROFESSOR HARRISON.

1. Analytic Mechanics. Shaped with special reference to the practical requirements of engineers. Principles rather than formulas are emphasized. Deals with statics, kinematics, kinetics, energetics, center of gravity, moment of inertia, friction, and units and dimensions of mechanical quantities. *Second semester; M., Tu., W., Th., F., at 8 or 9.* Assistant Professor MAURER, and Acting Professor HARRISON.
Required of sophomores in Engineering.
2. Graphic Statics. Co-ordinated with analytical statics. Appli-

cations are mainly the determination of stresses in framed structures under fixed loads, of shear and bending moment in simple beams under fixed and moving loads, and of the centroid and moment of inertia of plane figures. The work consists mainly of draughting. *Second semester; M., W., F., 10-12.* Assistant Professor MAURER, and Acting Professor HARRISON.
Required of sophomores in Civil and Sanitary Engineering.

3. Strength of Materials. The elastic properties of the most important materials of construction from a theoretic standpoint. Applications of theory to practical problems in beams, columns, shafts, riveting, springs, etc. *First semester; M., Tu., W., Th., F., at 10 or 11.* Assistant Professor MAURER.
Required of juniors in Engineering.

4. Graphics. The application of graphic methods of analysis in various departments of mechanics. *First semester, twice a week;* hours to be assigned. Assistant Professor MAURER. Open to students who have completed 1, 2, 3, or the equivalent.

5. Advanced Mechanics of Materials. An elaboration of course 3, embracing discussions of the inertia circle, inertia ellipse, kern, beam of unsymmetric cross section under any load; applications of the principle of least work; stress ellipse, etc. *Second semester.* Assistant Professor MAURER. Open to students who have completed 1 and 3 or the equivalent.

THE MATERIALS OF CONSTRUCTION.

PROFESSOR JOHNSON, AND ASSISTANT PROFESSOR RICHTER.

1. A review of the principles and mechanics applicable to the strength of materials at rupture; the methods of manufacture, the methods of testing, and the physical properties of all the materials of engineering construction. *Three hours per week; repeated each semester.* Required of all Juniors in the College of Engineering. Professor JOHNSON.

2. Testing of Materials of Construction. Each student is required to make a definite series of tests of wrought iron, cast iron, steel, and wood in tension, compression, bending, and torsion. (*54 hours in laboratory*), *first semester; Tu., Th., 2-5.* Required of seniors in Mechanical Engineering. *Second semester; Tu., Th., 8-10; M., 2-5.* Required or juniors in Civil Engineering and of seniors in Electrical Engineering. Assistant Professor RICHTER.

3. **Testing Materials.** An advanced course will be offered, the special line of work to be agreed upon after consultation with the professor in charge. *M., W.,* hours to be assigned. Assistant Professor RICHTER. Open to graduate students and to those students who have completed course 5.

DESCRIPTIVE GEOMETRY.

The study of this subject consists of text-book work in the class room supplemented by the solution of problems in the drafting room.

Throughout the work in the drafting room special attention is devoted to free-hand lettering and the last four weeks of the second semester to the application of the principles of descriptive geometry to mechanical drawing.

First semester 5 hours per week; second semester 2 hours per week.

Required of all freshmen in Engineering.

TOPOGRAPHIC AND GEODETIC ENGINEERING.

ASSISTANT PROFESSOR SMITH.

1. **Elementary Drawing.** Consists of lectures on the care and use of drafting instruments, followed by practical instruction in the free hand lettering of working drawings. Use is made of selected titles from drawings prepared in several of the larger bridge and railroad offices. Smith's Free-hand Lettering. *First semester; M., Tu., W., Th.,* 2-4, *for four weeks.* Required of freshmen. *M., W., Fr.,* 2-4, *for last nine weeks.* Required of sophomores in Civil and Sanitary Engineering.

2. **Elementary Surveying.** Includes the study of the construction and adjustment of the common surveying instruments and their use in simple surveying problems. Text: Johnson's Surveying and Smith's Field Manual. *First and second semesters. Recitations M. and W., at* 8 *or* 9. Field work Saturdays, 8-12. First 9 weeks of first semester or last half second semester. Required of freshmen for one semester.

3. **Elementary Surveying.** This course is a continuation of course (2) and includes the Field and Office work of a variety of practical problems in the use of the engineer's transit and level. Text: Johnson's Surveying. Instruction given in the lecture room, drawing room, and field. *First semester; recitations Tu., Th., at* 9. *Field work, first nine weeks;* (54 *hours*).

Section I., *M., W., Th.,* 10-12. Section II., *Tu.,* 10-12; and *Sat.,* 8-12.

Required of sophomores in Civil and Sanitary Engineering.

4. Advanced Surveying. This course is a continuation of course 3, and includes a study of the higher instruments of precision, and their use in topographic, hydrographic, city, and mining surveying. *Second semester; Tu., Th., at* 10. *First ten weeks. Field work* (50 *hours*). Section I., *M.,* 2-4, *W.,* 2-6. Section II., *Sat.,* 8-1, *T.,* 2-4. *Last eight weeks.*

Required of sophomores in Civil and Sanitary Engineering.

5. Elementary Geodesy. A general treatment of the subject by texts and assigned readings, including the figure of the earth, the apparatus and methods used in measuring base lines; the construction of stations; the method of measuring angles and adjusting triangulation; the principles of projecting maps and a study of the instruments and methods used in spirit and trigonometrical leveling. Text: Johnson's Surveying. *Second semester; first* 11 *weeks; M., W., at* 10, *and Th., at* 12.

Required of juniors in Civil and Sanitary Engineering.

6. Trigonometrical Survey. This course furnishes the necessary field work for illustrating course 5. Each year a portion of the neighboring lake region will be covered by an accurate triangulation, and also by a topographic and hydrographic survey. Survey begins the Monday of examination week and continues for two weeks (120 hours). Professors SMITH, WHITNEY, and TURNEAURE.

Requires of sophomores and juniors in Civil and Sanitary Engineering.

7. Advanced Geodesy. A general study of the economics of geodesy, also a study of the computations and adjustments of some of the important triangles of the United States Coast and Geodetic Survey. Taught partly by lectures, assigned readings, and in the field. Text-book. Wright's Adjustment of Observations. *First semester. Two hours per week.*

Elective for seniors in Civil Engineering and for graduates who have taken courses 2, 3, 4, and 5, or their equivalents.

8. Advanced Geodesy. An elaboration of courses 5 and 6. Formulæ for computing geographical positions, the theory of the figure of the earth, station error, measurements of gravity, the results of precise leveling considered in connection with warped equipotential surfaces, etc., are studied in detail. Taught by

lectures, assigned readings, and in the field. *Second semester. Two hours per week.*

Elective for seniors in Civil Engineering and for graduates who have had courses 2, 3, 4, and 5, or their equivalents.

9. Rapid Topography. This course is designed for training topographers for the U. S. Geological Survey, and for any others who may wish to familiarize themselves with approximate methods of taking topography for small scale maps.

Elective for seniors in Civil Engineering and for others who have had course 2.

10. Mining Surveys. This course will consist of the necessary field and office work of an underground survey of the various University tunnels, aggregating over 3,000 feet in length, including the preparation of a complete map and profile of same. It is believed that the conditions and obstacles to be met and overcome on such a survey will furnish a good substitute for an actual mine survey. *Second semester.* (60 *field hours,*)

Elective for students who have had Topographic Engineering 2 and 3.

RAILWAY ENGINEERING.

PROFESSOR WHITNEY.

1. Railway Surveying. A preliminary line about three miles in length is laid out, topography taken adjacent thereto, and platted. Each member of the class, given certain limits as to grades and curves, makes an independent projection for final location. Approximate estimates of the cost are made, and the best line is located on the ground. All necessary field and office work required to survey and construct such a line is performed. *First semester; F., 2-6; S., 8-12; 144 hours in field and office.*

Required of juniors in Civil and Sanitary Engineering.

2. Preliminary and Location Surveys; Construction. Class-room work to accompany course 1. A good field book is studied part of the time. Lectures and recitations on construction, including rock-work, explosives, tunneling, dredging, and docking. *First semester; Th., at 8; 18 hours in the class room.*

Required of juniors in Civil and Sanitary Engineering.

3. Maintenance of Way. Lectures and recitations on track work in general, including street railways; freight and passenger yard construction; and standard structures. The various sig-

nal and interlocking systems are studied. *Second semester; Tu., Th., at 11; 32 hours in the class room.*
Required of juniors in Civil and Sanitary Engineering.

4. A short course in the above subjects, especially adapted to city and interurban railways, and including masonry constructions and foundations, is offered as an elective to those who have had course 2 T. E. Given partly in the class room, draughting room, and in the field. *First semester; 18 hours in class room and 36 hours in the field and office.*

5. Railway Economics. A study of the sources of income; operating expenses; relative values of distance, gradient, and curvature, and their influence upon net receipts; classification of locomotives, and their relative power; rolling-stock, and train resistance. Text-book: Wellington's Economic Theory of Railway Location. *First semester; Tu., Th., at 11; 36 hours in the class room.*
Required of seniors in Civil Engineering.

6. Railway Standards. Continuation of courses 3 and 5. It is intended to give the student some degree of familiarity with designing various railway standards. The work is carried on in the draughting room, aided by careful study of numerous blue prints of the standards of the best railways. *First semester.*
Elective for seniors in Civil Engineering, and for graduates.

7. Tunneling and Substructures. The various methods of tunneling, shaft-sinking, ordinary and deep-foundation work are studied, principally from reports of the engineers in charge as contained in the transactions of engineering societies and technical journals. The best of such reports are selected for the students to study and report upon. References: Drinker's Tunneling and Patton's Foundations. *Second semester; M., W., at 9; 32 hours in the class room.*
Required of seniors in Civil Engineering.

8. Municipal Railways. A course of lectures and assigned readings on the location, construction, maintenance, operation, and traffic of elevated, surface, and underground lines of railway. *Second semester.*
Elective for seniors in Civil Engineering and for graduates.

For course in railway transportation, course 10 in Economics, see p. 88.

This course on the historical, economic, and legal aspects of the subject is offered as an elective to seniors and graduates in Civil Engineering.

RIVERS AND CANALS.

PROFESSOR WHITNEY.

1. River and Harbor Improvement and Canal Construction. Lectures and assigned readings on the early history of transportation in the United States; on the artificial improvements of rivers and harbors for navigation and protection; and on the construction, operation, and traffic of canals in the United States and abroad. *Second semester; M., W., and F., at 11, for the last half of the semester; 24 hours in the class room.* Required of seniors in Civil Engineering.

HYDRAULIC ENGINEERING.

PROFESSOR BULL, ASSISTANT PROFESSORS RICHTER AND MAURER.

1. Hydraulics. Hydrostatic pressure, theory of fluid motion, hydro-dynamic pressure; theoretical and experimental formulas for flow through orifices and pipes, over weirs, and in conduits, canals, and streams. Assistant Professor MAURER. Required of juniors in Engineering. Civils, *first semester; Tu., Th., at 9*; Mechanicals and Electricals, *second semester; first six weeks; M., Tu., W., Th., F., at 10.*
2. Hydraulic Motors and Pumping Machinery. The theory of the various kinds of turbines is first given, followed by rules for their design, based upon both theory and practice. The course concludes with a short study of pumping machinery. *Second semester.* Required of juniors in Mechanical and Electrical Engineering. *Daily, at 8. Eight weeks during second semester; (36 hours in class room.)* Professor BULL.
3. Hydraulic Laboratory. Special attention is given to the determination of the coefficients of the flow of water through pipes, orifices, and over weirs; and to the testing of turbine wheels, hydraulic rams and other hydraulic machinery; *(30 hours in laboratory).* Assistant Professor RICHTER. Required of juniors in Engineering. Civils, *first semester;* Mechanicals and Electricals, *second semester.*

STEAM ENGINEERING.

PROFESSOR BULL, ASSISTANT PROFESSOR RICHTER, AND MR. ALEXANDER.

1. Thermodynamics. This course covers those principles of the mechanical theory of heat which are preliminary to the study of the various kinds of heat engines. The course is intended to be very thorough, especially with reference to steam. Text-book: Peabody's Thermodynamics of the Steam Engine. *First semester; first twelve weeks; M., Tu., W., Th., F., at 12 (60 hours in class room).* Professor BULL.
Required of juniors in Mechanical Engineering.

2. Theory of Heat Engines. In this study the various kinds of heat engines, especially the steam engine, are studied thoroughly. The compound and triple expansion engines receive their share of attention, and the influence of clearance, jacketing, cylinder condensation, wet and superheated steam are considered. The subject of injectors is also studied, and at the end of the course the subjects of compressed air and refrigerating machinery are taken up. The study is partly given by lectures; for a large part of the work Peabody's Thermodynamics is used as a text-book. *First semester, last six weeks; M., W., F., at 12. Second semester, first eight weeks; T., W., Th., F., at 9, (50 hours in class room).* Professor BULL.
Required of juniors in Mechanical Engineering.

3. Steam Boilers. The general subject of combustion and its application to steam boilers is studied, the theoretical and practical efficiency of those is developed, and rules for the design of boilers, chimneys, etc., are given. Text-book: Peabody's and Miller's Steam Boilers, but the study is partly taught by lectures. *Second semester; M., W., F., at 2, (54 hours in class room).* Professor BULL.
Elective; open to all who have had either course 1 or 6.

4. Valve Gears of Steam Engines. All the various types of valves are studied principally by means of the Zeuner Valve Diagram. The text-book used is Peabody's Valve Gears for Steam Engines. The work in the class room is supplemented by the work in the draughting room. *Second semester, last ten weeks; Tu., W., Th., F., at 9, (40 hours in class room).* Professor BULL.
Required of juniors in Mechanical Engineering.

5. Design of the Steam Engine. In this course the diameter stroke, and number of revolutions of the engine are assumed to be

known, as well as the steam pressure, cut-off, compression, etc., and from these data the other dimensions are either computed or deduced according to practice. Special attention is given to the fly-wheel, governor, and reciprocating parts, and their relation to each other. The study is taught by lectures. The work in the class room is supplemented by the work in the draughting room, where each student is required to work out a complete problem. Class work: *First semester, M., W., at 10; second semester, Tu., F., at 11,* (72 *hours in class room*). Draughting: *First semester, Tu., Th.,* 8-11; *second semester, M., W., F.,* 11-1, (198 *hours in draughting room*). Professor BULL.

Required of seniors in Mechanical Engineering.

6. Short Course in Thermodynamics, the Steam Engine and the Steam Boiler. Only the fundamental principles of thermodynamics can be touched upon in this course, but to a sufficient degree to enable the student to study the steam engine and boiler intelligently. The theory of the steam engine is given to the exclusion of all other heat engines. The subjects of valve gears, fly-wheels, and governors are treated briefly, and the course concludes with a practical study of the boiler. *Second semester, M., W., F., at* 8; *first semester, Tu., Th., at* 8, (90 *hours in class room*). Assistant Professor RICHTER.

Required of juniors in Electrical Engineering.

7. Course in Steam Engineering for Civil Engineers. In this course the stress will be laid on the steam engine and boiler, and but very little time will be spent on thermodynamics. It will be the aim of the course to impart sufficient knowledge to the students that they may understand the working of the steam engine thoroughly, and also be able to make a good selection of an engine and boiler for specified purposes. *First semester; first 12 weeks, M., W., F., at* 11; 36 *hours.* Mr. ALEXANDER.

Required of juniors in Civil Engineering, and of seniors in Sanitary Engineering and in the course of Applied Electro-Chemistry.

8. Heating and Ventilation. R. C. Carpenter's book on this subject will serve as the groundwork in this study. But assigned readings of the literature in this branch of engineering, as well as lectures on special topics, will supplement the instruction. *First semester; Tu., Th., at* 11; 36 *hours.* Professor BULL.

9. Gas and Gasoline Engines. These important motors will be treated both from a theoretical and an experimental point of view. The subject will be taught partly by lectures and partly by assigned readings of the current literature. *Second semester; M., W., at 9; 36 hours.* Professor BULL.
10. Advanced Course in Steam Engineering. Thurston's Handbooks on the Steam Engine and on the Steam Boiler will be used in this course; but the study will be prosecuted principally by means of lectures and assigned readings of the various works on steam engineering. *First and second semester; M., W., F.,* the hours to be assigned after consultation. Professor BULL. Open to graduate students and to those students who have completed the courses 1, 2, 3, 4, and 5 in Steam Engineering.
11. Long Laboratory Course. For this study the compound experimental engine of the laboratory and the fifty-horse-power Root boiler, besides the various other smaller engines and the gas and hot air engines owned by the department, are used with all the necessary appliances for making complete tests of engines and boilers. At the end of the course, the class makes a complete twenty-four hour test of a large power plant not connected with the University. The department also owns a large number of injectors, pumps, and other boiler appliances of which accurate tests are made. The methods are explained in connection with the class work of thermodynamics. *Four hours per week.* Assistant Professor RICHTER.
12. Short Laboratory Course. This course is intended for civil engineering students, and is more elementary than the long course in boiler and engine testing. The student will, however, learn enough to conduct an ordinary commercial test of a pumping engine. *Six hours per week during the last six weeks of the first semester; M., W., F., 11-1.* Mr. ALEXANDER. Required of juniors in Civil Engineering, of seniors in Sanitary Engineering and in the course of Applied Electro-Chemistry.
13. Advanced Course in Laboratory Work. An advanced course will be offered in any of the different lines of experimental work, to conform with the special line of work the student wishes to follow. Stress will be laid on original research and investigation. *Tu., Th.;* the hours to be assigned. Assistant Professor RICHTER.
    Open to graduate students and to those students who have completed the required courses in the line they wish to follow.

MACHINE DESIGN.

ASSISTANT PROFESSOR MACK, AND MR. ALEXANDER.

1. Kinematics of Mechanisms. This is a study of the relative motions of machine parts, including belting, toothed gears, cams and linkages.
   Text-book: Machine Design, Part I., by Forrest R. Jones.
   First semester; (two hours of lectures and recitations, and eight hours drafting per week).
   Required of sophomores in Mechanical and Electrical Engineering, and for the first semester of year 1900-1901 of juniors in these courses. Assistant Professor MACK and Mr. ALEXANDER.

2. Mechanical Drawing. The work of this course is a continuation of the mechanical drawing begun in the latter part of the freshman year. Drawings are made from machines, models, and plates, the object being to give the student a general idea of the forms of machine parts, and the methods of putting them together. Line shading, tracing, blue printing, perspective and isometric projection are taught in this course. A trade catalogue of machinery and tools is used as a text-book to give a knowledge of names and uses of machines and tools.
   Second semester; one hour class and two hours drafting per week.
   Required of sophomores in Mechanical and Electrical Engineering. Mr. ALEXANDER.

3. Machine Design. Continuation of course 2. Design of machine parts involving but a small amount of calculation and the making of shop drawings. Special attention is given to the figuring of costs of production of machinery of the class under consideration. *First semester.*
   Required of juniors in Mechanical and Electrical Engineering. Assistant Professor MACK.
   [Note.—Course 3 will not be given during year 1900-1901.]

4. Crane Design and Graphic Statics of Mechanism. A simple form of crane is selected to design for the reason that the stresses in its parts can be determined with more accuracy and certainty than in any other machine in common use. The parts are studied in detail in the class room, and the complete crane is designed in the drafting room.
   This is followed by a study of machine parts which involve calculation in design, as gearing, bearings, rope transmission, pulleys, etc.

Second semester; two hours class work and ten hours drafting per week.

Required of juniors in Mechanical Engineering. Assistant Professor MACK.

5. Machine Elements and Power Transmission Devices. The form, strength, and proportions of the frames and moving parts of machines are studied in connection with the stresses due to the load supported, the moving parts, and the work done by the machine. The design of the frames of punching, shearing, and riveting machines, which are subjected to heavy stresses, is given special attention, and a complete machine of this class is designed. A study is made of the design of machine tools, special and automatic machinery, and the production of interchangeable parts.

Throughout the year. Three hours class and four hours drafting per week.

Required of seniors in Mechanical Engineering. Assistant Professor MACK.

6. Patent Office Drawing. A course giving practice in the preparation of drawings as required by the U. S. Patent Office. Open to all who have had course 2. Amount and time arranged upon consultation. Professor MACK.

7. Special and Automatic Machinery. The design of machinery of the above classes is too diversified in character to be included at length in any regular course. A study is made of various types of special and automatic machinery. A piece of work is selected, which would not be formed with ordinary machines and tools, except at comparatively great cost, and a special machine designed for the purpose of making it according to commercial requirements.

Elective for seniors in Mechanical Engineering. Four hours drafting per week. Assistant Professor MACK.

8. Locomotives. A study of the design, construction, maintenance and operation of the different types of modern locomotives. Lectures and class work twice a week during the second semester.

Elective for seniors in Mechanical and Electrical Engineering. Mr. ALEXANDER.

9. Locomotive Design. Calculation and complete designing of all parts of the locomotive. Three or five times a week in drafting room during the second semester.

Elective for seniors who are taking Locomotives. Mr. ALEXANDER.

10. Mechanical Engineering Seminary. The seminary gives an opporunity for the study and discussion of general and special features and problems which are not included in regular courses, but which are of great importance. The current engineering literature relating to Mechanical Engineering is regularly reviewed, and new inventions and discoveries in this field discussed.

Elective for seniors in Mechanical and Electrical Engineering. Throughout the year. Two hours per week. Professor BULL and Assistant Professor MACK.

APPLIED ELECTRO-MAGNETISM AND THE CONSTRUCTION OF DYNAMOS.

ASSISTANT PROFESSOR SWENSON AND MR. FRANKENFIELD.

1. Electromagnets and Dynamos. A discussion of the simple forms of electromagnets; the development of the laws of magnetization by electric currents; the laws of simple magnetic circuits and the windings of electromagnets; the practical design, construction, and testing of dynamos. *Three times a week throughout the year.* (*108 hours in class room and 36 hours in draughting room.*) Assistant Professor SWENSON.

Required of juniors in Electrical Engineering and Applied Electro-Chemistry.

2. Testing Direct Current Dynamos and Motors. The testing and operation in the laboratory of direct current generators, motors, and accessory apparatus. *Twice a week throughout the year.* (*144 hours in the laboratory.*) Mr. FRANKENFIELD.

Required of juniors in Electrical Engineering and Applied Electro-Chemistry.

Required of seniors in Mechanical Engineering during first semester.

3. Electrical Machinery and Appliances. A short course in the theory, construction, and testing of generators, motors, transformers, etc. *Three times a week during first semester and twice a week during second semester.* (*90 hours in the class room.*) Assistant Professor SWENSON.

Required of seniors in Mechanical Engineering during first semester and elective during second semester.

4. Advanced Design and Construction of Large Direct-Current Dy-

namos. By seminary method, following the treatment of the subject outlined by Fischer-Hinnen and E. Arnold. This course includes the working out of complete designs and may be elected either as three or five-hour course through the year. Assistant Professor SWENSON.

Open to graduates and others who have had the equivalent of courses 1 (or 3) and 2.

ALTERNATING CURRENTS AND ALTERNATING CURRENT MACHINERY.

PROFESSOR JACKSON AND MR. FRANKENFIELD.

1. Theory and Application of Single-Phase Alternating Currents. The theory of the generation and utilization of alternating electric currents; the design, construction and operation of single-phase alternating current dynamos and transformers; and methods for testing alternating current machinery. *Three times a week during first semester and twice a week during second semester.* (*90 hours in the class and draughting room.*) Professor JACKSON.

    Required of seniors in Electrical Engineering and Applied Electro-Chemistry. Elective for graduates.

2. Testing Alternating Current Machinery and Appliances. The testing and operation in the laboratory of single-phase alternating current generators, motors, transformers, meters, and other appliances. *Twice a week throughout first semester.* (*72 hours in the laboratory.*) Mr. FRANKENFIELD.

    Required of seniors in Electrical Engineering and Applied Electro-Chemistry. Elective for graduates.

3. Elementary Polyphase Currents. Following the treatment in Jackson's Alternating Currents and Alternating Current Machinery. *Twice a week throughout second semester.* (*36 hours in class room.*) Professor JACKSON.

    Open to students who have had the equivalent of courses 1 and 2.

4. Testing Polyphase Machinery and Appliances. *Twice a week throughout second semester.* (*72 hours in the laboratory.*) Mr. FRANKENFIELD.

    Open to students who are pursuing or have completed course 3.

5. Elementary Theory of Alternating Currents. Open to advanced students in applied mathematics and physics who desire to obtain a reasonably brief vector treatment of alternating currents and the properties of alternating current circuits. Omit-

ted in 1900-1901. *Twice a week throughout the year.* Professor JACKSON.

Open to seniors and graduates.

6. Advanced Alternating Currents (including Polyphase Currents and Machinery). A study, by seminary method, of the treatments of Rodet, Kraemers, Steinmetz, Kapp, and Loppé et Bouquet, with lectures which treat in detail the properties of alternating current circuits and machinery. *Three times a week throughout the year.* Two hours of laboratory work may be elected in addition. Professor JACKSON.

Open to graduates and others with requisite preparation.

APPLIED ELECTRO-CHEMISTRY AND ELECTRO-METALLURGY.

MR. BURGESS.

1. Primary and Secondary Batteries. Batteries as a source of electricity; theory, construction, and working of primary and secondary battries and their commercial use.
2. Electrolysis and Electrometallurgy. The theory and application of electrolysis and electrometallurgy. Industrial electro-chemistry, the treatment of ores, electrolytic separation and refining of metals, electrotyping, and electroplating.

    Must be preceded by courses in chemistry.

    Five times a week through first semester; (54 hours in class room and 72 hours in laboratory). Mr. BURGESS.

    Open to seniors and graduates.

    Required of seniors in Applied Electro-Chemistry.
3. Applied Electro-Chemistry. One lecture per week on special applications of electricity in chemical and metallurgical operations. Sufficient laboratory work of an independent nature will be taken up to fulfill the requirements of a 3-5 or 5-5 study, as desired. *Three or five times a week throughout second semester.* Mr. BURGESS.

    Open to graduates and others who have completed courses 1 and 2.

    Required of seniors in Applied Electro-Chemistry.
4. Electricity as Applied to the Treatment of Metal Surfaces. Electrolytic principles applied to corrosion of metals, and methods for preventing corrosion, including electroplating and galvanizing; also electricity applied to cleaning metals. *Once a week throughout first semester.* Elective for students in Civil and Mechanical Engineering. Mr. BURGESS.

ELECTRICAL INSTALLATIONS.

PROFESSOR JACKSON, ASSISTANT PROFESSOR SWENSON, AND MR. BURGESS.

2. Electrical Testing. The construction, testing, maintenance, and operation of lines and appliances, used in telephony, telegraphy, and electric signalling. *Three times a week throughout second semester.* (18 hours in class room and 54 hours in laboratory.) Mr. BURGESS.
Required of juniors in Electrical Engineering.
3. Testing Wires and Cables. Laboratory practice in insulation and breakdown tests, location of faults, testing insulators, etc. Study of the phenomena produced by high pressures on electric circuits. *Twice a week throughout either semester.* Mr. BURGESS.
Open to seniors and graduates.
4. Electric Lighting and Transmission of Power. The location, erection, and cost of transmission and distribution lines; the application of electric motors to the general purpose of power distribution, and the problems of long distance transmission of power by electricity. *Three times a week throughout second semester.* Mr. BURGESS.
Open to seniors and graduates. Required of seniors in Applied Electro-Chemistry.
5. Graduate Conference. A conference or seminary for the detailed study of engineering problems.
Open to seniors and graduates.
6. Electric Railways. The road-bed, rolling-stock, electric circuits, and power plants for city, town, and suburban railways; the location and construction of street railways in cities and towns; track foundation and types of rail; selection of cars and motors to be used under different conditions; methods of conveying the electric current from the generator to the motors; and the best methods for meeting the severe conditions imposed on electric railway power plants. *Three times a week throughout second semester.* Assistant Professor SWENSON.
Open to seniors and graduates.
7. Electricity in Mining and Quarrying. The practice in mining and quarrying where electricity can be satisfactorily applied and the advantages and limiting conditions of long-distance transmission of power by electricity from water power to

mines. *Once a week throughout first semester.* Professor JACKSON.

Open to seniors and graduates.

8. Central Station Design, Management, and Estimates. The selection and arrangement of machinery for generating plants; effect on operating expenses of the arrangement of power and generating plants and circuits, and the use of meters; estimating costs of power and generating plants, and the cost of lines and weights of copper. *Twice a week during first semester, and three times a week during second semester.* Professor JACKSON.

Open to seniors and graduates.

9. Inspection Tours. An inspection tour is made at the Easter recess and another at the end of the second semester. Each student is expected to accompany two of the parties during the last two years of his course if possible. The tours comprise visits to Chicago, Milwaukee, and other manufacturing centers, for the purpose of inspecting manufacturing plants and great engineering works under operation or construction.

10. Illumination and Photometry. A study of light sources; the manufacture and use of incandescent and arc lamps; the selection, arrangement, and relative economy of light sources under various conditions; the practical testing of the luminous intensity and efficiency of light sources, and the illumination of streets and interiors. *First semester; twice a week.* (18 *hours in class room and 36 hours in laboratory.*) Assistant Professor SWENSON.

Open to seniors and graduates.

11. Elements of Electric Lighting and Power Distribution. A short general course particularly designed for students in civil engineering, treating of the theory, testing, and use of electrical machinery and appliances; the various methods of power distribution; the construction of distributing lines; and the application of electric motors to hoisting machinery and other purposes. A special short laboratory course in testing electrical machinery and appliances is given in conjunction with this course. *Four times a week second semester; two times a week first semester.* Assistant Professor SWENSON.

Open to juniors and seniors.

STRUCTURAL ENGINEERING.

PROFESSOR TURNEAURE AND PROFESSOR WHITNEY.

1. Structural Details. The designing of simple forms of members and of joints in wood and iron, and of wooden roof and bridge trusses. *First semester; Tu., Th.,* 11-1. Professor TURNEAURE.
   Required of juniors in Civil Engineering.
2. Masonry Construction and Testing of Materials.
   (a) Theory governing the design of masonry structures, as dams, retaining walls, piers, and abutments; foundations. *Second semester; Tu., Th., at 10; 36 hours in class room.* Professor WHITNEY.
   Required of juniors in Civil and Sanitary Engineering.
   (b) Testing of hydraulic cements, paving bricks, and stone. *Second semester; Th., 2-5; 48 hours in the laboratory.* Professor WHITNEY.
   Required of juniors in Civil and Sanitary Engineering.
3. Engineering Architecture. Treats of those principles of artistic design applicable to engineering structures, especially those of masonry. *Second semester; four lectures in connection with course* 4.
4. Masonry, Arches, Dams, and Stereotomy.
   (a) Arches. A discussion of the theory of the stability of masonry arches, both right and oblique, is followed by the complete design of an arch. Specifications and estimates of cost are furnished. Most of the time is spent in the draughting room. *Second semester; F.,* 8-10, 2-4.
   Required of juniors in Civil and Sanitary Engineering.
   (b) Dams; Stereotomy. A design for a high masonry dam is made, followed by several problems in stereotomy. Reference is made to the works of Krantz, Rankin, Wegmann, and Warren. *First semester; M., W., F.,* 10-12, *principally in the draughting room.* Professor WHITNEY.
   Required of juniors in Civil and Sanitary Engineering.
5. Bridge Stresses. The instruction in this subject is given by text-book, together with the working of numerous problems. Text-book: Johnson, Bryan, and Turneaure's Modern Framed Structures.
   (a) Simple Bridge Trusses. Determination of stresses by both graphical and analytical methods in the modern types of trusses, for uniform, and for concentrated moving loads. Sec-

ond semester; M., W., F., at 11. 48 *hours in class room.* Professor TURNEAURE.

Required of juniors in Civil and Sanitary Engineering.

(b) Suspension, Swing, Cantilever, and Arch Bridges; deflection formulæ and stresses in redundant members. *First semester; M., W.,* 9; 36 *hours in class room.* Professor TURNEAURE.

Required of seniors in Civil Engineering.

6. Bridge Design. Location and economic length of span, formulæ for working stresses, design of individual truss members, combined and secondary stresses, and questions relating to the designing of details. *First semester; F., at* 9; 18 *hours in class room.* Professor TURNEAURE.

Required of seniors in Civil and Sanitary Engineering.

7. Designs and Estimates. In this course each student makes a complete design of one structure of each class mentioned below in accordance with some standard specifications, prepares detail drawings and makes an estimate of the quantity of material and cost; complete working drawings are made of at least one structure. Stiffness as well as strength is aimed at, and special attention is given to the proper distribution of stress into members at joints and to questions relating to economy of manufacture. Constant use is made of the large collection of drawings belonging to the department.

(a) Roof Trusses and Plate Girders. *Second semester; M., Tu., Th.,* 8-10; 96 *hours in draughting room.* Professor TURNEAURE.

Required of juniors in Civil and Sanitary Engineering.

(b) Riveted and Pin-Connected Trusses. *First semester; Tu., Th.,* 8-11; 96 *hours in draughting room.* Professor TURNEAURE.

Required of seniors in Civil and Sanitary Engineering.

(c) Swing Bridges. Design of truss and turn-table with specifications for material and manufacture and for the operating machinery. *First semester;* 72 *hours in the draughting room.* Professor TURNEAURE.

Elective for seniors and graduates in Civil Engineering.

8. Bridge Specifications, Construction, and Testing. The first part of this course is devoted to a critical study of specifications for bridge structures, results and methods of testing of material and of full-sized bridge members and complete structures. A brief study is then made of bridge construction, including mill-work, shop-work, inspection and erection. The last four weeks of the course are spent in making actual

tests on bridges under moving train loads by means of the Fraenkel apparatus. The members of the class are assigned various parts of the bridge and the results of the experiments are worked up and the observed stresses compared with the computed. *Second semester; Tu., Th., at 10; two-fifths study.* Professor TURNEAURE.

Elective for seniors and graduates in Civil Engineering.

9. Structural Design. Short general course in the designing of roofs and buildings. *Second semester; 96 hours in the draughting room.* Professor TURNEAURE.

Elective for students in Electrical and Mechanical Engineering who have had Mechanics 3.

10. Secondary Stresses. Advanced theory and experimental work. *Two hours per week throughout the year.* Professor TURNEAURE.

Open to graduates.

MUNICIPAL AND SANITARY ENGINEERING.

PROFESSOR TURNEAURE AND PROFESSOR WHITNEY.

1. Water Supply Engineering. Sources of supply, collection, and storage of water; interpretation of chemical and biological analyses; purification and distribution of water, including the study and design of filtering plants, reservoirs, standpipes, pumping stations, and distributing systems. Lectures, problems, and assigned reading. *First semester; M., W., F., at 8; 54 hours in class room.* Professor TURNEAURE.

Required of seniors in Civil and Sanitary Engineering.

2. Sanitary Engineering. Design and construction of sewerage and drainage systems; house drainage; street cleaning; sewage and garbage disposal, and the design of disposal works. Lectures, recitations, and designs. *Second semester; M., W., F., at 10; 48 hours in class room.* Professor TURNEAURE.

Required of seniors in Civil and Sanitary Engineering.

3. Designs of Water Supply and Sewerage Systems. Complete designs and estimates of water supply and sewerage systems, and purification plants. *First and second semesters; W., 2-6.* Professor TURNEAURE.

Required of seniors in Sanitary Engineering; elective for others.

4. Roads and Pavements. Lectures and assigned readings on the location, construction, and maintenance of country roads and city pavements. *Second semester; M., W., F., at 11; 27 hours*

in the class room for first half of the semester. Professor WHITNEY.

Required of seniors in Civil and Sanitary Engineering.

5. Sanitary Engineering. Brief comprehensive course treating of the problems pertaining to the water supplies of cities, the construction and management of public water-works and works for the disposal of city wastes. *Twice a week, first semester.* Professor TURNEAURE.

Required of seniors in the General Engineering Course.

For course in Biology of Water Supplies see page 216; and for course in Municipal Railways see page 223.

These courses are elective for seniors and graduates in Civil Engineering.

ENGINEERING CONTRACTS AND SPECIFICATIONS.

PROFESSOR JOHNSON.

The law of contracts as applied to engineering work, together with typical forms of specifications governing both the commercial and the technical features of engineering construction, and of all the related documents pertaining to engineering contracts. *One hour a week. Second semester.*

Required of all seniors.

SHOP WORK.

PROFESSOR KING, MR. HARGRAVE MR. MUTCHLER, MR. LOTTES, AND MR. BONN.

1. Bench and Machine Work in Wood.

    (a) A systematic course in the use of the plane, saw, gouge, bit, and kindred tools. This covers the principles of joining and joint work involved in building construction. Lectures each day precede new operations. Exercises in free-hand sketching are required three times a week.

    (b) Systematic training at the lathe in the use of the gouge and chisel in plain and ornamental turning in hard and soft wood. Lectures and sketching as before. *First semester.* Professor KING and Mr. MUTCHLER.

    Required of sophomores in Mechanical and Electrical Engineering. 72 *hours.*

    Second semester.

    Required of sophomores in Civil Engineering, 36 *hours.*

2. Foundry Work. Practice in pattern making and moulding. The patterns chosen are those giving the best illustration of the principles involved in their construction and in the methods of moulding. Lectures on these subjects and on the methods of core making and core work are given with this course. Free-hand sketching is required. *First semester;* 18 *hours.* Professor KING and Mr. BONN.
Required of sophomores in Mechanical and Electrical Engineering.
Second semester.
Required of sophomores in Civil Engineering, 18 *hours.*

3. Bench Work in Iron. Embraces practice in wrought and cast iron with the hammer, chisel, and file at the vise. *First semester;* (36 *hours.*) Professor KING and Mr. HARGRAVE.
Required of sophomores in Mechanical and Electrical Engineering.

4. Production of Flat Surfaces and Straight Edges. Training in the use of file and scraper on surfaces of large area. *First semester;* (18 *hours*). Professor KING and Mr. HARGRAVE.
Required of sophomores in Mechanical and Electrical Engineering.

5. Machine Work in Iron. Practice on the engine lathe, in connection with which are taught the elementary features of boring, turning, and screw cutting. Lectures on these subjects at the beginning of the semester. *Second semester;* (36 *hours*). Professor KING and Mr. HARGRAVE.
Required of sophomores in Mechanical, Electrical, and Civil Engineering.

6. Practice on the Planing and Milling Machines. Gives some knowledge of the variety of work which may be done on these machines and a comparison of the time required for the same work on the two machines. *Second semester;* (18 *hours*), Required of sophomores in Mechanical, Electrical and Civil Engineering. Professor KING and Mr. HARGRAVE.

7. Forge Work. Training in the fundamental features of forge practice, such as drawing, upsetting, bending, welding, tool making, and tempering. *Second semester;* (36 *hours*). Required of sophomores in Mechanical, Electrical and Civil Engineering. Professor KING and Mr. LOTTES.

8. Practice at the Lathe and Milling Machine. This includes instruction in the methods of determining the diameter of blanks for spur, bevel, spiral, and tangent wheels on the

lathe, and in cutting the teeth with the milling machine. *Second semester;* (54 *hours*). Required of sophomores in Mechanical and Electrical Engineering. Professor KING and Mr. HARGRAVE.

9. Tool Making. The methods of making taps, dies, reamers, and milling cutters are the prominent features. Some instruction in brass work is also given. *First semester;* (90 *hours*). Required of juniors in Mechanical Engineering. Professor KING and Mr. HARGRAVE.

10. Machine Construction. Attention is given to the cost of production. *First semester;* (90 *hours*). Required of juniors in Mechanical Engineering. (72 *hours*). Required of juniors in Electrical Engineering. Professor KING and Mr. HARGRAVE.

11. Machine Construction. Continuation of course 10. *Second semester;* (72 *hours*). Lectures on Mechanical Practice in the development of the Locomotive. Required of juniors in Mechanical Engineering. Professor KING and Mr. HARGRAVE.

12. Construction and Pattern Work. Practice in pattern work, and fitting together machine parts. This will require also some moulding and forge work, including tool dressing and tempering. *First semester;* (108 *hours*). Lectures on Mechanical Practice in the development of the Locomotive. Professor KING, Mr. HARGRAVE, and Mr. LOTTES.
Required of seniors in Mechanical Engineering.

13. This course is similar to course 10, but to it will be added practice in the erection of line shafting and machinery. Lectures on Shop Design, Erection, and Management will be given. *second semester;* (36 to 180 *hours*). Professor KING and Mr. HARGRAVE.
Elective for seniors in Mechanical and Electrical Engineering.

COLLEGE OF AGRICULTURE.

STAFF OF INSTRUCTION AND RESEARCH.

C. K. ADAMS, LL. D., President of the University.
W. A. HENRY, B. AGR., DEAN, Professor of Agriculture.
S. M. BABCOCK, Ph. D., Professor of Agricultural Chemistry.
W. L. CARLYLE, B. S. A., Professor of Animal Husbandry.
E. S. GOFF, Professor of Horticulture and Economic Entomology.
F. H. KING, Professor of Agricultural Physics.
F. W. WOLL, M. S., Assistant Professor of Agricultural Chemistry.
H. L. RUSSELL, Ph. D., Professor of Bacteriology.
E. H. FARRINGTON, M. S., Associate Professor of Dairy Husbandry.
A. R. WHITSON, B. S., Assistant Professor of Agricultural Physics.
GEORGE MCKERROW, Superintendent of Farmers' Institutes.
R. A. MOORE, Assistant to Dean, in Charge of Short Course.
A. G. HOPKINS, D. V. M., B. AGR., Instructor in Veterinary Science.
ALFRED VIVIAN, Ph. G., Assistant in Agricultural Chemistry.
U. S. BAER, Instructor in Cheese Making.
E. G. HASTINGS, M. S., Assistant in Bacteriology.
R. A. HARPER, Ph. D., Professor of Botany.
E. A. BIRGE, Ph. D., Sc. D., Professor of Zoology.
J. C. W. BROOKS, Professor of Military Science and Tactics.
W. W. DANIELLS, M. S., Professor of Chemistry.
W. D. FROST, M. S., Instructor in Bacteriology.
D. B. FRANKENBURGER, A. M., Professor of Rhetoric.
H. W. HILLYER, Ph. D., Assistant Professor of Organic Chemistry.
C. I. KING, Professor of Practical Mechanics.
A. W. RICHTER, M. E., Assistant Professor of Experimental Engineering.
W. H. ROSENSTENGEL, A. M., Professor of German.
W. A. SCOTT, Ph. D., Professor of Economic History and Theory.
B. W. SNOW, Ph. D., Professor of Physics.
C. R. VAN HISE, Ph. D., Professor of Geology.
C. A. VAN VELZER, Ph. D., Professor of Mathematics.
FRANK DEWHIRST, Instructor in Farm Dairying.
JULIUS BERG, Instructor in Cheese Making.
WM. WATERSTREET, Instructor in Cheese Making.
DEWITT GOODRICH, Instructor at Butter Worker.

Roy L. Smith, Instructor in Pasteurizing.
J. R. Robison, Instructor at Separators.
Thomas Corneliussen, Instructor at Separators.
John McCready, Instructor in Milk Testing.
Peter A. Dukleth, Assistant Instructor in Farm Dairying.

Officers of the Experiment Station.

C. K. Adams, President of the University.
W. A. Henry, Director.
S. M. Babcock, Chief Chemist.
F. H. King, Agricultural Physicist.
E. S. Goff, Horticulturist.
W. L. Carlyle, Animal Husbandry.
F. W. Woll, Chemist.
H. L. Russell, Bacteriologist.
E. H. Farrington, Dairy Husbandry.
A. R. Whitson, Assistant Agricultural Physicist.
Arthur G. Hopkins, Veterinarian.
R. A. Moore, Assistant to Director.
Alfred Vivian, Assistant Chemist.
Frederic Cranefield, Assistant in Horticulture.
E. G. Hastings, Assistant Bacteriologist.
Leslie H. Adams, Farm Superintendent.
Miss Ida Herfurth, Clerk.
Miss E. M. Close, Librarian and Stenographer.

Staff of Farmers' Institutes.

Geo. McKerrow, Superintendent.
Miss Harriet V. Stout, Clerk and Stenographer.

Institute Conductors.

Corps No. 1.—Thos. Convey, Ridgeway.
Corps No. 2.—Alex. A. Arnold, Galesville.
Corps No. 3.—Chas. Thorp, Burnett.
Corps No. 4.—W. C. Bradley, Hudson.
Corps No. 5.—L. E. Scott, Neenah.

Regular Assistants.

R. J. Coe, Ft. Atkinson.
F. H. Scribner, Rosendale.
H. M. Culbertson, Medina.

DAVID IMRIE, Misha Mokwa.
GEO. WYLIE, Leeds.
C. E. MATTESON, Pewaukee.

Occasional Assistants.

N. E. FRANCE, Platteville.
W. J. FLICK, Dunnville.
W. F. STILES, Lake Mills.
H. A. BRIGGS, Elkhorn.
H. C. TAYLOR, Orfordville.
C. P. GOODRICH, Ft. Atkinson.
CHAS. LINSE, LaCrosse.
MRS. HELEN ARMSTRONG, (Cooking School Teacher), Chicago.
PROFESSOR W. A. HENRY, Madison.
PROFESSOR H. L. RUSSELL, Madison.
PROFESSOR F. H. KING, Madison.

GENERAL INFORMATION.

Three of the University buildings are devoted to agricultural instruction and investigation. Agricultural Hall is a stone building 120 feet in length by 42 feet in width, four stories in height. It contains two large lecture rooms, offices for the several instructors and investigators, library rooms, chemical and bacteriological laboratories.

Hiram Smith Hall is devoted to dairying. This structure of brick and stone has a frontage of 95 feet by 48 feet in depth, and is three stories in height. It contains an office, lecture room, reading room, dairy laboratory, and rooms devoted to creamery practice, cheese making, farm dairying, pasteurizing, cheese curing, etc.

The Horticulture-Physics building has a frontage of 78 feet by 60 feet in depth, three stories in height; at the rear are glass houses covering a space of 88x75 feet. The right wing of the building with its greenhouses is devoted to plant life and horticulture. The left wing with its large glass house is devoted to instruction and investigation in the physics and mechanics of agriculture.

At the college farm are the fields, barns and live stock. Here, as elsewhere, all arrangements have in view investigation and instruction in agriculture.

By its association with the various University laboratories of science and the practical arts, open to agricultural students, with departments in which are taught all the foreign languages that contain much agricultural literature, with an active experiment station equipped with special laboratories and library, and with a farm where practical tests are carried on, the College of Agriculture affords exceptional opportunities to those who desire to become agricultural experts.

LIBRARIES.

The Agricultural Library contains 4,500 bound volumes and several hundred pamphlets relating to agriculture, all of which are available for the use of students. They have access also to the various other libraries of the University and the city. See page 27.

SOCIETIES.

The Short Course and Dairy students maintain literary societies. These organizations afford opportunities for drill in parliamentary practice, for training in declamation, debate and essay-writing, as well as for discussions of the many professional and practical questions relating to agriculture and dairying.

FEES AND EXPENSES.

I. Graduate Course and Long Course.

Tuition for residents of the State of Wisconsin............. FREE.
Tuition for non-resident students, per semester............ $15.00
Incidental fee, payable by all students, per semester........ 10.00

II. Short Course in Agriculture.

Tuition for residents of the State of Wisconsin............. FREE.
Incidental fee for resident students, per term................ $5.00
Incidental, tuition, and laboratory fees for non-residents, per term 30.00

III. Dairy Course.

Tuition for residents of the State of Wisconsin............. FREE.
Incidental and laboratory fees for resident students, per term..$10.00
Incidental, tuition, and laboratory fees for non-resident students, per term..................................... 45.00

The expenses of resident students in the Graduate and Long Courses are practically the same as for those pursuing regular University courses.

Expenses of the resident students pursuing the Short Course in Agriculture will vary from $55.00 to $65.00 for the term for room, board, washing, and necessary books.

The expenses of the resident Dairy students will vary from $60.00 to $70.00 for the term.

PLAN OF AGRICULTURAL EDUCATION.

The University system of agricultural education has three aims:

First, to develop agricultural science through investigation and experiment, and to disseminate the same through bulletins and reports;

Second, to give instruction in agriculture at the University;

Third, to disseminate agricultural knowledge among the farmers of the state by means of institutes and popular publications.

THE AGRICULTURAL EXPERIMENT STATION.

The purpose of the Experiment Station is the promotion of agricultural science by investigation and experimentation. In the choice of subjects it endeavors to select those which possess the greatest importance to the farmers of Wisconsin, so far as the facilities at hand permit. The endeavor at all times is to give the investigations a fundamental character in order that the results may be real contributions to agricultural science. The Station is also a means of disseminating general and miscellaneous information on agricultural topics, and its staff cheerfully devotes the necessary time to private and public correspondence and to personal interviews.

By direction of the general government, which supplies a large portion of the funds for maintaining the Experiment Station, there are issued an annual report and frequent bulletins. Sixteen reports and eighty-two bulletins have been issued to date. Fifteen thousand copies of the report are printed annually, and the edition of the bulletins generally comprises about twelve thousand copies. These bulletins and reports are free to all residents of the state upon application. The Station mailing list now embraces twelve thousand names of farmers and others to whom the reports and bulletins are regularly sent.

INSTRUCTION AT THE UNIVERSITY.

Systematic courses in agriculture have been arranged to meet the wants of students having different purposes in view.

The *Graduate Course* offers to advanced students opportunities for professional training and original investigation, made possible through an active Experiment Station, associated with numerous scientific laboratories. The special lines of study will be left largely to the selection of the students, subject to the approval of the Agricultural Faculty. It will be practicable to a large extent for such students to participate in experiments in progress and, after suitable experience, to conduct independent investigations. When contributions to knowledge of permanent value are made they will be published through the bulletins of the Experiment Station under the name of the contributor.

The *Long Course* offers scientific training in agricultural chemistry, agricultural physics, horticulture, animal husbandry, and dairying. Besides the strictly professional branches it embraces general training in chemistry, physics, botany, zoology, geology, bacteriology, and similar branches which have an agricultural bearing. The field is so broad, however, that it is impossible for the student in four years to pursue all the courses offered, in addition to acquiring the necessary fundamental studies, and hence a large liberty of selection is allowed.

The *Short Course* is provided for those who can devote only a limited time to study, and who wish to return at once to the active operations of the farm, and therefore desire the greatest amount of directly useful knowledge that can be acquired in the brief time allowed.

The *Dairy Course* is designed for those who intend to operate creameries and cheese factories.

TERMS OF ADMISSION.

Graduate Course in Agriculture. Graduates of this University and of other colleges and universities in good standing are admitted to this course without examination.

Long Course in Agriculture. The requirements for admission to this course are the same as those for the General Science Course given on pp. 63 and 64.

Short Course in Agriculture. Students in this course must be at least sixteen years of age, and have a good common-school education. No entrance examinations are required, but those who come poorly prepared cannot expect the full benefits of the course.

Dairy Course. The terms of admission to this course are the same as for the Short Course, excepting that the candidate must have had not less than four months' experience in a creamery or cheese factory before entering the course.

Special Students in Agriculture. As many of the youth of the farming communities are not within reach of schools giving instruction in all the branches required for admission to the Long Course, limited concessions will be made to young men of exceptional strength and maturity by which they will be permitted to enter the University as special students in agriculture.

DEGREES.

The degree of Bachelor of Science in Agriculture is conferred on students who successfully complete the Long Course in Agriculture. The degree of Master of Science in Agriculture is conferred on Bachelors of Science in Agriculture who complete one year of advanced study at the University and present an acceptable thesis on a topic approved by the Faculty.

LONG COURSE IN AGRICULTURE.

Freshman Year: Biology 5*; German 4; mathematics 3; English 3; military drill 2; gymnastics 2; 34 unit-hours for the year, of which 30 are in class exercise.

Sophomore Year: German 3; French 4; physics 5; chemistry 5; electives 3-5; military drill 2; gymnastics 2; 34 unit-hours for the year, of which 30 are in class room and laboratory.

Junior and Senior Years: Two years in one of the following subjects: agricultural chemistry, agricultural physics, animal husbandry, bacteriology, or horticulture, as a major study; one year in one of the above subjects to be assigned as a minor study by the professor in charge of the major subject.

Elective studies enough to complete 120 unit-hours of class and laboratory work besides the required drill and gymnastics.

SHORT COURSE IN AGRICULTURE.

This course covers two terms of fourteen weeks each, beginning the first of December each year.

First Year.

Twenty-eight lectures on feeds and feeding, by Professor Henry.
Twenty-eight lectures on the breeds of live stock, with score-card practice additional in stock judging, by Professor Carlyle.
Forty-nine lectures with 70 hours' laboratory practice in agricultural physics, by Professor F. H. King.
Forty-nine lectures with 70 hours' laboratory practice in plant life, by Professor Goff.
Twenty-four lectures on veterinary science by Dr. Hopkins.
Twelve lectures on dairying, by Professor Babcock.
Seventy-two hours' practice in farm dairying and dairy laboratory, by Mr. Dewhirst.
A course in farm bookkeeping by Mr. Moore.
Fourteen lectures with drill in parliamentary practice by Mr. Moore.

Second Year.

Twenty-eight lectures or equivalent in essay writing, on animal nutrition, by Professor Henry.
Twenty-eight lectures on the breeds of live stock, with seventy-two hours' practice in stock judging, by Professor Carlyle.

---

* The figures denote the number of recitations per week.

Fifty-two lectures on agricultural physics and meteorology, with 52 hours' laboratory practice, by Professor F. H. King.

Twenty-eight lectures on horticulture, with laboratory and greenhouse practice additional, by Professor Goff.

Thirty-five lectures and recitations in elementary agricultural chemistry, by Professor Babcock.

Twenty-four lectures with demonstrations on veterinary science, by Dr. Hopkins.

One hundred and twenty hours at work-bench and forge, by Professor C. I. King.

Twelve lectures on parliamentary practice, by Mr. Moore.

Twelve lectures on agricultural economics, by Professor Scott.

Twenty lectures on bacteriology as applied to agricultural conditions, by Professor Russell.

Students completing the studies of this course in a satisfactory manner are granted a Short Course certificate.

An illustrated circular describing the Short Course in detail will be sent on application to R. A. Moore, Assistant to Dean, College of Agriculture, Madison, Wis.

COURSE IN DAIRYING.

The instruction in dairying is divided into four courses, which are as follows:

1. Lectures and class-room work.

Twenty-four lectures by Professor Babcock on the constitution of milk, the conditions which affect creaming and churning, methods of milk testing, and preservation of milk, etc.

Sixteen lectures with demonstrations by Professor Russell on the influence of bacteria in the dairy.

Eight lectures by Professor F. H. King on heating, ventilation, and other physical problems directly connected with dairy practice.

Ten lectures and demonstrations by Instructor Mors on the care and management of the boiler and engine.

Ten lectures by Dr. Hopkins on the common diseases of the dairy cow.

Eight lectures by Professor Henry on the feeding and management of dairy stock.

Eight lectures by Professor Carlyle on breeding and selection of dairy stock.

Twelve lectures by Professor Farrington on creamery management and accounts.

Twelve lectures on practical cheese making, by Mr. Baer.

2. Milk Testing. This embraces instruction in the laboratory by Professor Farrington and Mr. McCready in estimating the fat in milk, butter, and cheese by methods adapted to the factory and factory operators. Six hours per week.

3. Butter Making. Instruction in this course is given by Professor Farrington, with assistants. Butter making is carried on daily on the creamery plan. The student learns to operate the several forms of power centrifugal separators on the market. They attend to the ripening of the cream, churning and packing butter, carrying on all the operations as they would be conducted in a creamery. Twelve hours per week.

4. Cheese Making. In this course, Mr. Baer, with assistants, gives daily instruction in the manufacture of cheddar cheese, the operations being carried on as in the regular factory, the students being required to take careful notes and make reports of the process. Sixteen hours per week.

The dairy class is divided into three sections, one of which is assigned daily to the laboratory, a second to the creamery, and a third to the cheese factory. The sections alternate so that each student receives instruction twice a week in each of the three departments

ADVANCED DAIRY WORK.

Being desirous of securing pupils who have had much experience in factory work before joining us, we offer the following inducements:

Such as can pass satisfactory examinations in the practical work of the creamery or cheese factory will be advanced early in the term to the experimental dairy section, where problems connected with this branch will be studied.

Advanced dairy instruction will consist of the following courses:

1. Instruction by Professor Babcock on milk and its products.
2. Experimental investigations in butter making by Professor Farrington.
3. Investigations in cheese production by Mr. Baer.
4. Dairy bacteriology by Professor Russell. This work will include two lines:
   a. A special course in the preservation of milk and cream for commercial purposes;
   b. Students familiar with the use of the microscope will be admitted to the bacteriological laboratory for experimental work in dairy bacteriology.

EXAMINATIONS AND CERTIFICATES.

To secure a dairy certificate a student must have spent a full term in the Dairy School and successfully passed all examinations; and, further, he must have had not less than two seasons' experience in a creamery or cheese factory, one of which must follow the period spent in the Dairy School. During the second season the candidate will report the operations of his factory monthly on blanks, and have his work inspected by an authorized agent of the University.

This course opens the first of December each year and lasts twelve weeks.

Additional information concerning the Dairy Course will be sent on application to Professor E. H. Farrington, Madison, Wis.

DEPARTMENTS OF INSTRUCTION.

AGRICULTURAL CHEMISTRY.

PROFESSOR BABCOCK, ASSISTANT PROFESSOR WOLL, AND MR. VIVIAN.

1. Agricultural Chemistry. *Lectures twice a week; second semester.* Professor BABCOCK.
2. The Chemistry of the Dairy. *Lectures and laboratory practice; first semester; once a week.* Professor BABCOCK.
3. Agricultural Analysis. *Laboratory work during the year; three times a week.* Assistant Professor WOLL and Mr. VIVIAN.
4. Advanced and Original Work. *Laboratory work during the year; five times a week.* Professor BABCOCK, Assistant Professor WOLL and Mr. VIVIAN.

AGRICULTURAL PHYSICS.

PROFESSOR KING AND ASSISTANT PROFESSOR WHITSON.

1. Meteorology. The course deals chiefly with the agricultural phases of the subject. *Lectures and laboratory work; three times a week; first semester.*
2. Farm Engineering. Farm drainage and irrigation, the construction and maintenance of country roads, and the construction of farm buildings. *Twice a week; first semester.*
3. Soil Physics. *Full study; second semester.*
4. Original investigations in the physical laboratory and field. *Full study; throughout the senior year.*

ANIMAL HUSBANDRY.

PROFESSOR HENRY, PROFESSOR CARLYLE, AND MR. HOPKINS.

1. The Breeds of Live-Stock. Students taking this course are trained in selecting and judging live stock by the use of typical animals, skeletons, charts, models, and score cards. The agricultural library now embraces over 700 volumes of stud books, herd books, and flock registers. *Full study; first semester.* Professor CARLYLE.
2. Breeding. Principles and methods of breeding are taught by lectures, text-book work, and study of the practices of breeders

as shown by the various stock registries. The text-books for this course are Darwin's Animals and Plants under Domestication, and Miles' Stock Breeding. *Full study; second semester.* Professor CARLYLE.

3. Veterinary Science. Elementary anatomy and physiology of horses, cattle, sheep, swine and poultry taught by lectures, use of the skeleton, models and material afforded by post mortems; veterinary hygiene, farm medicines, animal nursing, principles of shoeing, dentition, obstetrics, diseases and methods of prevention and detection; enumeration of unsoundnesses. References: Fred Smith's Veterinary Physiology and Veterinary Hygiene; Fleming's Obstetrics; Neumann's Parasites and Parasitic Diseases; Strangeway's Anatomy.

4. Feeds and Feeding. The student will study the chemical constituents of feeding materials, and the combinations necessary to give the best results with the various kinds of live stock. He will familiarize himself with the German feeding tables, and the feeding trials conducted at our own and other Stations. Armsby's Manual of Cattle Feeding and Henry's Feeds and Feeding will be used as text-books. *Full study; first semester.* Professor HENRY.

5. Advanced work in Feeding and Breeding. Having completed the previous courses the student will assist in conducting feeding trials at our own station. *Full study; one year.* Professor HENRY and Professor CARLYLE.

HORTICULTURE.

PROFESSOR GOFF AND MR. CRANEFIELD.

1. General Principles of Horticulture. Lectures, recitations, and laboratory work. *Full study; first semester.*
2. Economic Horticulture. Instructions in the culture of the principal fruits and vegetables of our climate. Lectures, recitations, and laboratory work. *Three times a week; second semester.*
3. Aesthetic Horticulture. The principles of ornamental planting and of laying out gardens and pleasure grounds. Lectures and recitations. *Twice a week; second semester.*
4. Special investigation in subjects relating to the propagation and rearing of economic plants. Field and laboratory work. *Full study; throughout the year.*

THE ECONOMICS OF AGRICULTURE.

PROFESSOR SCOTT.

The object of this course is to furnish students of agriculture with an opportunity for acquaintance with the social aspects of their subject. The farmer is profoundly affected by general industrial conditions, and a knowledge of the forces which determine these conditions is essential to an intelligent prosecution of his business. This course will consist of one lecture each week during the short course term to second year students, and will embrace such topics as: The mutual relations of agriculture and other industries; value and prices with especial reference to land and agricultural products; money, its functions and varieties; banks and their functions; industrial and monetary crises and panics; systems of land tenure, etc. After each lecture an hour will be devoted to discussion, quiz, and questions asked by the students.

BACTERIOLOGY.

PROFESSOR RUSSELL AND MR. FROST.

1. General Bacteriology. See course 30, General Biology. *Lectures or equivalent; M., W., and F., at 11. First semester. Full study.* Professor RUSSELL and Mr. FROST.
2. Dairy Bacteriology. The relation of bacteria to dairy problems is here presented. The University herd and the practical work at the University Creamery give opportunity for the study of dairy problems under practical conditions, while such work can be closely controlled in the laboratory. The character of this work may be modified to meet the wants of the student. *Laboratory with conferences; full study; second semester.* Professor RUSSELL.
3. Agricultural Bacteriology. Bacteria as affecting agricultural problems in general, including animal diseases. *Laboratory work with conferences; full study; second semester.* Professor RUSSELL.

FARMERS' INSTITUTES.

The third division of work of the College of Agriculture is the instruction of farmers who are unable to come to the University for study. This is made possible through generous legislative provisions, by which a carefully supervised system of farmers' institutes is maintained. The institutes are in immediate charge of a Superintendent, who elaborates and controls the organization and execution of the institutes. He is aided by special conductors, who assist in perfecting the details and carrying the whole into effect. Members of the agricultural faculty render as much assistance as is consistent with their other duties. Experts in different departments are engaged to present special important themes. Lecturers are often brought from other states to treat on specific topics in which they are recognized authorities. Local talent is used to some extent and not the least of the educational benefits is the development of latent ability in writing, speaking and experimenting which has followed as a natural result of the interest awakened by this important stimulus.

During the institute season of 1899-1900 institutes lasting two days each were held at the places named below:

Adams County......Strong's Prairie, White Creek.
Barron County......Barron, Prairie Farm.
Brown County......Pine Grove, Wayside.
Buffalo County......Fountain City, Modena.
Burnett County......Trade Lake.
Calumet County......Hilbert.
Chippewa County....Stanley.
Clark County........Colby, Humbird, Neillsville.
Columbia County.....Doylestown.
Crawford County....Mt. Sterling.
Dane County.........Albion, Mazomanie, Mt. Vernon, Sun Prairie, Waunakee.
Dodge County.......Hustisford, Iron Ridge.
Dunn County........Caryville, Elk Mound, Sand Creek.
Eau Claire County...Augusta, Fall Creek.
Fond du Lac County..Brandon, Marytown.
Grant County.......Burton, Boscobel, Bagley, Cuba City, Platteville.
Green County........Albany, Monroe.
Green Lake County...Kingston.
Iowa County........Hollandale, Linden.
Jackson County......Black River Falls, York.
Jefferson County....Jefferson, Sullivan.
Juneau County......Lyndon Station.
Kenosha County.....Salem.
Kewaunee County....Bolt, Pilsen.
LaCrosse County.....Bangor.
LaFayette County....Woodford.
Langlade County.....Antigo.

Manitowoc County....Cleveland, Mishicot, School Hill.
Marathon County....Wausau.
Marinette County....Peshtigo, Pound.
Marquette County....Briggsville.
Milwaukee County...South Milwaukee.
Monroe County......Cashton, Tomah, Warrens.
Oconto County......Hickory, Sobieski.
Outagamie County...Seymour.
Pepin County.......Durand.
Pierce County......Spring Valley.
Polk County........Luck.
Portage County.....Amherst Junction.
Racine County......Franksville.
Richland County....Excelsior, Hub City.
Rock County........Beloit.
St. Croix County....Roberts.
Sauk County........North Freedom, Spring Green, Valton.
Shawano County.....Bonduel, Wittenberg.
Sheboygan County...Beechwood, Glenbeulah, Hingham, Howard.
Taylor County......Medford.
Trempealeau County.Centerville.
Vernon County......LaFarge, Ontario, Readstown.
Walworth County....Delavan.
Washington County...Kirchayn, Wayne.
Waukesha County....Brookfield, Mukwonago, Stone Bank, Wales.
Waupaca County.....Ogdensburg, New London.
Waushara County....Saxeville.
Winnebago County...Winneconne.
Wood County........Grand Rapids, Milladore.

In addition to the regular institute work cooking schools of two lectures each were held in connection with the institutes, at the following points:

Black River Falls,	Albany,	Sun Prairie,
Mukwonago,	Jefferson,	Delavan,
North Freedom,	Platteville,	Spring Green,
South Milwaukee,	Beloit.	

Institutes are placed for the most part in localities which show the greatest interest in this movement. Applications for institutes will be received by the superintendent and presented to the agricultural committee by Sept. 30th. The committee goes over the list and carefully considers the needs and interests of each locality, and places the institutes where, in its judgment, they will prove the most helpful. Generally there have been far more applications for institutes than it was possible to supply. Applications should be received before September 15, each year.

The Farmers' Institute Bulletin.

To disseminate still more widely a representative portion of the matter presented and discussed at the institutes, and to give it permanency for its own sake and for its historical value, a system of publications in the form of bulletins has been begun by the superintendent. Bulletin No. 13, the last issued, contains a stenographic report of the closing institute held at Sparta in March, 1899. Sixty thousand copies of this Bulletin have been issued. Eight thousand cloth-bound copies have been placed in the school district libraries of the state; thirty-five thousand have been given to the farmers in attendance at the institutes, and the remainder distributed through cheese factories, creameries, etc. Copies will be sent to all applicants living within the state upon receipt of 10 cts., to pay postage and mailing, for paper covers, and 25 cts. for cloth bound covers. To those outside of Wisconsin 25 cts. for paper covers and 40 cts. for cloth bound copies will be charged, to cover mailing and cost of publication.

COLLEGE OF LAW.

STAFF OF INSTRUCTION.

C. K. ADAMS, LL. D., President.
E. E. BRYANT, Dean of the Law Faculty, Professor of Elementary Law, Practice and Pleading, Equity, Railway Law, and the Law of Public Offices and Officers.
C. N. GREGORY, A. M., LL. B., Associate Dean of the Law Faculty, and Professor of Criminal Law, the Law of Contracts, of Sales, and of Probate.
J. H. CARPENTER, LL. D., Jackson Professor of Partnership.
B. W. JONES, A. M., LL. B., Professor of the Law of Evidence, Public Corporations, and Domestic Relations.
J. M. OLIN, A. M., LL. B., Professor of the Law of Real Property, Wills and Torts.
R. M. BASHFORD, A. M., LL. B., Professor of the Law of Private Corporations, and Commercial Law.
A. A. BRUCE, A. B., LL. B., Assistant Professor of the Law of Agency, Carriers, Police Powers, and Public Policy, Damages, and Illinois Pleading and Practice.
J. B. PARKINSON, A. M., Professor of Constitutional Law and International Law.
R. T. ELY, Ph. D., LL. D., Professor of Political Economy.
F. J. TURNER, Ph. D., Professor of American History.
C. H. HASKINS, Ph. D., Professor of Institutional History.
W. A. SCOTT, Ph. D., Professor of Economic History and Theory.
D. B. FRANKENBURGER, A. M., Professor of Rhetoric and Oratory.

GENERAL STATEMENT.

The superior advantages of professional schools, for the training of students in the elementary principles of law and fitting them to enter upon the practice, are now quite generally acknowledged by the members of the bar.

Among the more important of the advantages afforded to the student by the Law School over the law office or private or solitary pursuit of the study, the following are the most obvious:

1. He is taught to trace the growth, progress, and expansion of our body of law.

2. His studies are directed to give him a comprehensive, general view and analysis of the law as a system. By the inductive or case method he is taught to seek the law in its original sources and deduce principles from decided causes.

3. He is well instructed in elementary principles.

4. While studying the substantive law, he is at the same time familiarized with the principles of procedure and general rules of practice, their necessity and application.

5. Having access to large, well-selected libraries, he becomes familiar with the literature of the law, and learns where to readily find the law of any subject in the decisions and elaborate treatises.

6. Constantly examined, orally and in writing, upon his reading, he becomes more proficient in the expression of his thoughts and knowledge.

7. By constant association, study, discussion, and friendly controversy, with fellow students, he acquires self-reliance, overcomes timidity, and learns the value of thorough preparation. His mental faculties are quickened and his resources are brought under his command.

8. In the preparation and argument of cases in the moot court, under proper guidance, he has an experience of great utility in fitting him for the actual controversies of professional life.

The published statement of a member of the New York Board of Examiners for admission to the Bar shows that nearly twice as large a percentage of applicants educated in law offices fail to pass the bar examination as of applicants educated in Law Schools.

The Law Schools of the United States, as appears by the monograph on Professional Education of J. R. Parsons, Esq., of the University of the State of New York, instructed 11,883 students during the past year and have won the earnest commendation of the best English teachers and writers as: Rt. Hon. James Bryce, Q. C., M. P.; Mr. Dicey, Q. C., Vinerian Professor at Oxford, ahd Sir Frederick Pollock, Corpus Christi Professor of Jurisprudence at Oxford, as superior to the English Schools of Law.

The College of Law of the University of Wisconsin offers a course which is believed to be of merit, and to give as much valuable and practical instruction and training as can be given in a three years' course of study. The elementary instruction in substantive law usual in all law schools is here fully and carefully given. Less instruction is imparted by means of the lecture alone than in many schools; the "Case System" is in part used, and much original work

COLLEGE OF LAW.   241

carefully directed is required of the students, and examinations are rigid and conducted at frequent intervals.

The design of this College is to prepare students for practice in the several states of the Union, and to this end endeavor is made to give thorough instruction in the principles of law, including:

First. THE COMMON LAW, its history, development, and present state in the United States, with the statutory modifications generally adopted in the several states.

Second. EQUITY, its history, development, and present state in the United States.

Third. THE LAW OF PROCEDURE, including the practice and pleading in Common-law Courts, Courts of Equity, and under the Codes of Civil Procedure.

Fourth. THE PUBLIC LAW of the United States and Constitutional Law.

International Law, Roman Law, and Comparative Constitutional Law are taught in the University in classes open to students of the College of Law.

ILLINOIS PLEADING AND PRACTICE.

Owing to the presence of a large number of students who expect to practice in the State of Illinois special instruction, not required, but which a student may take at his option, has been arranged in Illinois Pleading and Practice. This is in charge of a member of the faculty late of the Chicago Bar.

Admission.

Students applying for admission to the College of Law may be admitted, as are students in other departments, by either of two methods:

1. On certificates from accredited schools or colleges.
2. On examination at the University.

The requirement for admission certificates is the same as for admission to the other departments under title "Admission." The examination required is the regular examination upon the studies of group 1 for admission to the freshman class and is conducted at the same time and by the same members of the Faculty as the examination of candidates for admission to the College of Letters and Science.

These examinations for the freshman class will be held June 14 and 15, and September 25 and 26, 1900, beginning at 9 o'clock A. M.

The examination will cover the following topics:

Group I. *Subjects required of all candidates:*
a. Geography, political and physical.
b. History of the United States: Channing, Thomas or Johnston, Montgomery (Student), or an equivalent.
c. Arithmetic.
d. Algebra: Addition, subtraction, multiplication, division, equations of the first degree with one unknown number, simultaneous equations of the first degree, factors, highest common factor, lowest common multiple, quadratic equations, simultaneous equations above the first degree, theory of indices (positive, negative, fractional, and zero), and radicals.
Geometry: Plane and solid geometry. In solid geometry special attention should be given to the geometry of the sphere.
e. English in General: No pupil will be accepted in English whose written work is notably deficient in point of *spelling, punctuation, idiom, or division into paragraphs.*
f. English Composition: 1. The candidate will be required to write two essays of not less than two hundred words each, on subjects chosen by himself from a considerable number —perhaps ten or fifteen—set before him in the examination paper, and one of the topics chosen must be taken from the books assigned for general reading under English Literature.

2. In place of the essay on the topic drawn from the books set for general reading, the candidate will be allowed to offer an exercise book containing the first draft of essays written during his preparatory course, on topics taken from the works prescribed for general reading. These essays must be written under the eye of the teacher without consulting the books from which the subjects are taken, and without other assistance, must be kept in the care of the teacher, and sent by him to the examiner at least one week before the date of the entrance examination, with his certificate that they have been written in accordance with these requirements.

g. English Literature: The following lists include (1) a series of books for general reading, which may also be used as a basis for work in English Composition; (2) a limited number of masterpieces for thorough study. In addition to the essays called for under the head of *English Composition,* there will be required such further tests as seem suited to secure a careful reading of all the books prescribed in series (1). The written statement of the teacher will be sufficient, in general, for this purpose. In the case of the books set for more thorough study, the candidate will be examined on subject-matter, form and substance, and the examination will be of such a character as to require a thorough study of each of the works named, in order to pass it successfully.

1. For General Reading and Composition work:

1900—Pope's Translation of the Iliad (Books I., VI., XXII., and XXIV.). The Sir Roger de Coverly Papers, Goldsmith's Vicar of Wakefield, Scott's Ivanhoe, De Quincey's Flight of a Tartar Tribe, Cooper's Last of the Mohicans, Tennyson's Princess, Lowell's Vision of Sir Launfal.

1901, 1902—George Eliot's Silas Marner, Pope's Translations of the Iliad (Books I., VI., XII., and XXIV.), The Sir Roger de Coverly Papers, Goldsmith's Vicar of Wakefield, Scott's Ivanhoe, Shakespeare's Merchant of Venice, Cooper's Last of the Mohicans, Tennyson's Princess, Coleridge's Rime of the Ancient Mariner.

1903, 1904, 1905—The Sir Roger de Coverly Papers, Goldsmith's Vicar of Wakefield, Scott's Ivanhoe, Shakespeare's The Merchant of Venice and Julius Cæsar, Coleridge's The Ancient Mariner, Carlyle's Essay on Burns, Tennyson's The Princess, Lowell's The Vision of Sir Launfal, George Eliot's Silas Marner.

2. For thorough study:

1900—Shakespeare's Macbeth, Milton's Paradise Lost (Books I. and II.), Burke on Conciliation with America, Macaulay's Essays on Milton and Addison.

1901—Shakespeare's Macbeth, Milton's L'Allegro, Il Penseroso, Comus, and Lycidas, Burke on Conciliation with America, Macaulay's Essays on Milton and Addison.

1902—Shakespeare's Macbeth, Milton's L'Allegro, Il Penseroso, Comus, and Lycidas, Burke on Conciliation with America, Macaulay's Essays on Milton and Addison.

1903, 1904, 1905—Shakespeare's Macbeth, Milton's Lycidas, Comus, L'Allegro and Il Penseroso, Burke's Speech on Conciliation with America, Macaulay's Essays on Milton and Addison.

ENGLISH GRAMMAR: There is included in this requirement for entrance a knowledge of the leading facts of English grammar, and tests of such knowledge will be made a part of the examination.

Those intending to apply for admission should notify the associate Dean before the commencement of the year, and apply for directions, as examinations cannot be had after the commencement of the year. No student of the junior class will be admitted to the middle class who fails to pass an examination in the principal studies of the junior year, except conditionally; and the work of the middle year must be completed before the student is entitled to full rank as a senior.

ADMISSION OF GRADUATES.

Candidates will be admitted without examination upon presenting certificates of graduation from any reputable college or university, State normal school, accredited high school or academy.

ADMISSION TO ADVANCED STANDING.

Candidates eligible for entrance, who have studied elsewhere, and can pass examinations upon the studies of the junior year or middle year, or their equivalent, can enter the middle or senior year, but such examination will be most searching and thorough, embracing all the studies of the junior and middle years. The examinations will be chiefly in writing, extending over all the topics of the first two years, except as above indicated, and occupying five days.

Students applying for admission to the middle or senior class, upon examination, must report in person for the examination, which begins on the Tuesday of the week preceding the commencement of the academic year, as the examination will occupy some five days; *and no such examinations can be held after the appointed time.* Such examinations begin September 18, 1900.

Candidates presenting duly accredited certificates from other law schools of good standing will be admitted to corresponding standing in this College, without passing examinations.

Students entering any class after the beginning of the academic year will be required to read and pass examinations in the work of the class which has been done prior to their admission. All who desire to enter the classes should begin at the opening of the year, as the disadvantage of entering a class some weeks after it is organized is one that hampers the late-coming student through his whole course.

Students who have graduated from the University of Wisconsin, and who have elected and taken six hours of the junior year's work in the College of Law, and passed examinations thereon, will be permitted to graduate upon taking a two years' course in the College of Law.

Admission of Special Students Twenty-three Years of Age and Upwards.

At a meeting of the Board of Regents held in June, 1897, a resolution was adopted by which persons twenty-three years of age will hereafter be permitted to take *special studies* in the College of Law upon giving satisfactory evidence that they are prepared to take the desired studies advantageously. If they subsequently desire to become candidates for a degree or to take a regular course, they must pass the required entrance examinations.

Under this rule students of the required age can be received without passing the entrance examination, and can prepare themselves to take and pass the entrance examinations during their law course.

The passing of the entrance examination, however, is a condition precedent to their taking a degree.

Elective Studies.

The following regulations have been authorized respecting elective studies:

1. Students of the College of Letters and Science will be permitted to elect, as part of their undergraduate course, junior studies in the College of Law to an amount not exceeding altogether six (6) hours per week for one year. The studies to be so elected are to be designated by the College of Law, and the studies for which they may be substituted, by the College of Letters and Science.

2. Students of the junior class of the College of Law may elect studies in the College of Letters and Science, and substitute them for studies in the junior year of the law course, to an amount not exceeding four hours per week for that year. The studies to be elected are to be designated by the College of Letters and Science, and those for which they may be substituted by the College of Law.

3. Graduates of the College of Letters and Science who have elected six hours of study per week for one year in the College of Law are to be admitted on graduation to the middle class of the College of Law.

4. The fees for such elective studies are prescribed by the Board of Regents at $25 per annum.

METHODS AND COURSE OF INSTRUCTION.

The methods of instruction and course of study in this College, subject to necessary modifications, are substantially as follows:

Junior Year.

First Semester. Elementary Law. *Two hours a week,* 15 *weeks.* Text-book: Bryant's Outlines of Law. Dean BRYANT.

Contracts. *Two hours a week.* Text-book: Keener's Cases on Contracts. Associate Dean GREGORY.

Domestic Relations. Text-book: Schouler on Domestic Relations. *One hour a week.* Professor JONES.

Commercial Paper. *One hour a week.* Text-book: Tiedeman on Commercial Paper. Professor BASHFORD.

The Law of Real Property. *One hour a week.* Text-book: Tiedeman on Real Property; to topic, "Trusts," in first year, accompanied by select cases on real property by Finch. Professor OLIN.

Public Officers: Text-book: Mechem on Public Officers. *One hour a week for* 18 *weeks.* Dean BRYANT.

Common-law actions and Pleading. Text-book: Andrews and Stephens on Pleading. *One hour a week, six weeks.* Dean BRYANT.

Agency. Text-books: Huffcut's Cases on Agency. Huffcut on Agency. *Two hours a week.* Assistant Professor BRUCE.

The Faculty Moot Courts meet several times weekly. These Courts give each student opportunity to prepare and argue a case on a submitted statement of facts as often as once each semester.

Written examinations at the close of topics or end of semester are required throughout the course.

Second semester. Text-book: Bryant's Notes on Taxation. *One hour a week, eight weeks.* Professor JONES.

Contracts. *Two hours a week.* Text-book: Keener's Cases on Contracts. Associate Dean GREGORY.

The Law of Public Offices and Officers. Continued. Text-book: Mechem on Public Offices and Officers. *One hour a week, four weeks.* Dean BRYANT.

Real Property. The study is pursued as indicated in the work for the first semester. *One hour a week.* Professor OLIN.

Municipal Corporations. Text-book: Elliott's Elements of Municipal Corporations. *One hour a week, nine weeks.* Professor JONES.

Common Law Pleading and Practice, continued. *Two hours a week, eighteen weeks.* Dean BRYANT.

Equity Jurisprudence. Text-book: Bryant's Outlines of Jurisprudence. *One hour a week, ten weeks.* Dean BRYANT.

Courts and Jurisdiction, Notes and Statutes. *One hour a week, ten weeks.* Dean BRYANT.

Commercial Paper, continued. *One hour a week.* Professor BASHFORD.

Agency, and Bailments. Text-books: Huffcut's Cases on Agency. Huffcut on Agency, and Lawson on Bailments. *Two hours a week.* Assistant Professor BRUCE.

Middle Year.

First semester. Real property. Text-book: Tiedeman on Real Property, commencing with the subject of Trusts, and ending with the subject of Title by Devise, accompanied by select cases on real property by Finch. *One hour each week throughout the year.* Professor OLIN.

Private Corporations. Text-book: Clark on Corporations. *One hour a week.* Professor BASHFORD.

Equity Jurisprudence, continued. Text-book: Bryant's Outlines Equity Jurisprudence. *Two hours a week, twelve weeks.* Dean BRYANT.

Equity Pleading and Practice. Text-book: Notes on Equity Pleading; Shipman and Story. *One hour a week, fourteen weeks.* Dean BRYANT.

Code Pleading. Text-book: Bryant on Code Reading. *Two hours a week, fourteen weeks.* Dean BRYANT.

Law of Sales. Text: Williston's Select Cases on Sales. *Two hours a week.* Associate Dean GREGORY.

Partnership. Text: Mechem's Elements of Partnership. *One hour a week.* Professor CARPENTER.

Municipal Corporations. Text-book: Elliott's Elements of Municipal Corporations. *One hour a week, twelve weeks.* Professor JONES.

Evidence. Text-book: Jones on Evidence. *One hour a week for six weeks.* Professor JONES.

Carriers. Text-books: McClain's Cases on Carriers and Lawson on Bailments. *One hour a week.* Assistant Professor BRUCE.

Second semester. Real Property. Text-book: Tiedeman on Real Property, accompanied by select cases on real property by Finch. The subjects of Title by Public Grant and Mining Law comes in this semester. *One hour a week.* Professor OLIN.

Equity Jurisprudence, continued. Text-book: Bryant's Outlines of Equity Jurisprudence. *One hour a week, fourteen weeks.* Dean BRYANT.

Code Pleading. *Exercises two hours a week, eight weeks.* Dean BRYANT.

Criminal Law and Procedure. *Two hours a week.* Text: Clark on Criminal Law and Clark's Criminal Procedure and Select Cases. Associate Dean GREGORY.

Private Corporations, continued. Wisconsin Statutes and Cases. *One hour a week.* Professor BASHFORD.

Equity Practice in Federal Courts. Text: Federal Court Rules. Dean BRYANT.

Eminent Domain. *One hour a week, ten weeks.* Dean BRYANT.

Evidence. *One hour a week.* Text: Jones on Evidence. Professor JONES.

Carriers. Text-books: McClain's Cases on Carriers and Lawson on Bailments. *Two hours a week.* Assistant Professor BRUCE.

Senior Year.

First semester. Constitutional Law. Notes and study of leading cases. *One hour a week.* Dean BRYANT.

Code Practice. *Two hours a week, 18 weeks.* Dean BRYANT.

The Law of Evidence. Text-book: Jones on Evidence. *One hour a week.* Professor JONES.

The Practice in Inferior Courts. *One hour a week, twelve weeks.* Text: Bryant's Justice. Dean BRYANT.

Banking, Lectures and Select Cases. *One hour a week.* Professor BASHFORD.

Probate Law. *Two hours a week.* Lectures, notes, and select cases. Associate Dean GREGORY.

The Law of Wills. *Fourteen weeks, one hour each week.* Text: Cassoday on Wills, accompanied by Mechem's Select Cases. Professor OLIN.

The Law of Torts. Bigelow on Torts as a text-book, accompanied by Bigelow's Cases on Torts, students' series. *One hour each week for three weeks.* Professor OLIN.

Actions for Foreclosure and Procedure. *One hour a week, six weeks and assigned work.* Lectures and practical instruction. Dean BRYANT.

Bankruptcy. Text-book: Bush on Bankruptcy. The statutes and leading cases in Federal Courts. *One hour a week, 12 weeks.* Dean BRYANT.

Trusts, and Procedure relating thereto. *One hour a week for ten weeks.* Text: Underhill on Trusts. Dean BRYANT.

Police Powers and Public Policy. Lectures, notes, and select cases. *One hour a week.* Assistant Professor BRUCE.

Damages. Text: Beale's Cases on Damages. Lectures and Notes. *One hour a week.* Assistant Professor BRUCE.

Elective Study for those choosing it. Illinois Pleading and Practice and Select cases. Text: Lectures, notes, and select cases. *One hour a week.* Assistant Professor BRUCE.

Second semester. Constitutional Law, continued. Notes and leading cases. *One hour a week.* Dean BRYANT.

The Law of Evidence. Text: Jones on Evidence. *One hour a week.* Professor JONES.

Insurance. Elliott on Insurance. Lectures and cases. *One hour a week.* Professor BASHFORD.

Select Cases in Equity Procedure. *One hour a week, ten weeks.* Dean BRYANT.

Voluntary Assignments. Notes. Lectures, and Statutes. *One hour a week, four weeks.* Dean BRYANT.

Forensic Oratory. Text-book: Robinson's Forensic Oratory, selections, and lectures. *One hour a week, ten weeks.* Dean BRYANT.

Select Wisconsin Cases in Law of Contracts and Personal Property. *Two hours a week.* Associate Dean GREGORY.

The Law of Torts. Continued as in the first semester. *One hour each week.* Professor OLIN.

Procedure. Methods in different systems contrasted. *One hour a week, eight weeks.* Dean BRYANT.

The Trial of Actions. *One hour a week for seventeen weeks.* Dean BRYANT.

Public Powers and Public Policy, continued as in the first semester. *One hour a week.* Assistant Professor BRUCE.

Damages. Continued as in first semester. *One hour a week.* Assistant Professor BRUCE.

Elective Study for those choosing it, Illinois Pleading and Practice and select cases continued as in first semester. Assistant Professor BRUCE.

RESOURCES OF THE COLLEGE OF LAW.

The Board of Regents annually make such an appropriation as is needed for the support of this College. The matriculation fees charged for its course constitute only a part of the resources by which it is maintained.

By the will of the late Judge Mortimer M. Jackson, funds to the amount of twenty thousand dollars were bequeathed to the University to found and maintain a Professorship of Law. In accordance with the wishes of the donor, Judge J. H. Carpenter, an instructor of long experience and well-recognized ability, has been elected to this professorship. The act of 1891, by which the legislature provided for the erection of the building for the College, provided also for its equipment; and as fast as this appropriation can be realized the library will be enlarged, and the appointments of the college kept up to maintain it in the greatest utility. One thousand dollars per year is appropriated by the legislature to the support of its library.

SPECIAL ADVANTAGES.

The advantages which the City of Madison affords to the law student, it is believed, are equal, and in many respects superior, to those to be found in any place where a law school is established in this country. Among them are the following:

Courts.

The Supreme Court of the state is in session during the most of the academic year; and students have opportunity to listen to carefully prepared arguments by the ablest lawyers of the country.

Two terms of the United States Circuit and District Courts are held here annually, and important cases are here tried, both on the law side of the court before juries and in equity causes, illustrating the procedure in the Federal Courts.

The Circuit Court for Dane County holds three terms each year, giving the student opportunity to observe the methods and practice under the code system, which is substantially like that in twenty-seven states and territories.

The Municipal Court of Dane County sits daily for the trial of criminal cases.

Facilities conveniently at hand for becoming familiar with the practice in courts and the methods pursued by able and successful practitioners are thus afforded.

The statutes of the state provide that "any resident graduate of the Law department of the University of Wisconsin shall be admitted to the bar of any court, upon the production of his diploma, and may be admitted to the Supreme Court when not in session by an order signed by one of the justices thereof and filed with the clerk" (R. S. Wis., Sec. 2586). Under this statute and a rule of the Federal court, it is customary for the graduating class, on motion of a member of the faculty, to be admitted to both courts immediately upon graduation.

The Legislature

of the state holds one or two session at Madison during each course, enabling students to observe the processes of legislation.

The University.

The University of Wisconsin has a corps of instructors selected from the best scholars in their respective specialties. On obtaining a proper certificate from the Associate Dean, students of the College of Law may pursue studies for which they are prepared in any other department without extra charge, in so far as the work of the College of Law leaves them time. Many students of law avail themselves of the privilege. The site of the University buildings is one of the most beautiful in the United States. Large sums have been and are being expended in building, libraries, and apparatus in all the departments. The attendance of students from the best youth of the country is large and steadily increasing. The student of the College of Law is surrounded by the best influences. He is not only in a "legal atmosphere," but his associations are with those who, in other lines of study, are striving for excellence.

Law College Building.

The liberality of the state has provided the means, and the Regents have erected a building, for the College of Law, which is one of the most commodious in the country. It is located on the campus or University ground, on a commanding site, built of the brown sandstone of Lake Superior, at a cost of over $86,000, and is especially designed to be convenient for the uses of the College. Its lecture rooms and library are large, capable of comfortably seating several hundred students. The most approved systems of lighting, heating, and ventilation, and the most convenient appliances for writing or taking notes, are furnished. Rooms for moot courts and class debates are, also, provided.

The School of Economics, Political Science, and History,

under the direction of Dr. Richard T. Ely, with an able corps of instructors and special lecturers, is established in other rooms of the same building. Students of the College of Law are enabled to pursue the studies of this school and attend lectures upon political economy, institutional history, constitutional and international law, civil polity and Amercan history, and special lectures on such topics as the distribution of wealth, socialism, taxation, government of cities, pauperism, criminology, public finance, economics of agriculture, and various other topics ably treated by advanced teachers and thinkers on these and similar topics. These subjects are of especial importance and value to the student of American law, and add greatly to the advantages of the College of Law, giving its students especially convenient facilities for including the economic studies in their course. To a limited extent the law students are permitted to elect studies in this School during the first year.

Libraries.

The College of Law has an excellent and rapidly increasing library of the best law books and reports. This is enlarged by an annual appropriation made by the Legislature for that purpose. It is open for the use of law students during the day and evening.

The law library of the state, the largest and most complete in the Northwest, is located in the Capitol building; and students in the College of Law are during the day permitted, under reasonable restrictions, to use its books for reference, and conveniences are afforded them for the use of the books in preparing briefs or pursuing topical investigations.

The Library of the State Historical Society, with about 103,000 volumes and 100,000 pamphlets, a collection of books of the greatest value in historical study and research, is open to all students of the University.

The General University Library, including the department libraries catalogued with it, contains about 50,000 volumes and 14,000 pamphlets, and is open every week-day and evening to students. About three hundred of the best American and foreign periodicals are taken and kept on the files for students' use.

The Bar.

The bar of Dane County is an unusually strong one, especially noted for the thoroughness of its members in preparing their cases for trial, and for their accurate and precise methods in practice. Students, who desire it, can generally obtain situations in law offices, where they have opportunities to assist in practice, in the preparation of briefs and in the conduct of legal business, at the same time attending lectures and the practical exercises of the class; and in some instances they thus have opportunity of earning something towards their support.

EXAMINATION FOR GRADUATION.

For graduation each student will be required to have passed a satisfactory examination upon all studies pursued during the three years of the course; such examinations to be made either at the end of each semester, or on completion of a particular topic; and he must have prosecuted or defended to judgment such moot court cases as shall have been assigned by the Faculty, and must also have prepared such legal papers, pleadings, etc., as have been assigned for practice; and at least one month before the close of the senior academic year, and at such time as the Dean shall appoint, must have prepared and submitted to the Faculty, a satisfactory thesis upon some legal topic, to be examined, criticised, and marked by some member of the Faculty.

As the real ground-work of legal proficiency is laid in the beginning of the course, all should strive to take the full course rather than trust to such progress as can be made in a law office or reading in private. If but one year can be spent at a law school, the first year will be the most valuable. The student can, upon the proficiency thus gained, more easily be admitted to the profession on examinations by the State Board of Examiners for admission to the bar, and, in his future studies have the benefit of elementary training.

Students, who are able to do so, should furnish their own textbooks, and books of selections of cases. They will need them in practice after graduation, and can hardly afford to be without them during their course. Arrangements have been made by which they can be ordered through the Secretary of the Board of Regents, and obtained at a considerable discount from quoted prices. It is believed that the books required for the first year can be obtained for about sixty dollars; for the second and third years, for about one hundred dollars. The law library has several copies of some of the text-books most used, for the use of students who are unable to buy their own; but it is impracticable for the public libraries to provide text-books sufficient for the use of all the students.

SOCIETIES.

The Forum and the Columbian are incorporated literary societies, composed entirely of law students. Each of them holds weekly meetings in one of the rooms of the college for debates and other literary exercises. Opportunity is afforded to each student frequently to take part in debate.

The Luther S. Dixon and Andrew A. Bruce Law Clubs are students' organizations, modeled on the Law Clubs of Harvard Law School, which afford those who attain membership, valuable added practice in the trial and argument of cases.

FEES AND EXPENSES.

The matriculation fees in the College of Law are as follows:
For the full course of three years or its equivalent..........$150.00
The fees are apportioned thus for students graduating in three years:
First year... 75.00
Second year... 50.00
Third year.. 25.00
For students graduating in two years:
First year.. 75.00
Second year... 50.00
For students admitted to the senior class and graduating
  in one year...$100.00
Students of the College of Letters and Science taking the
  elective studies in the junior class will pay for the first
  year 25.00
And such students will pay for the middle year.......... 75.00
For the senior year....................................... 50.00

All fees are payable in advance at the office of the Secretary of the Board of Regents, College of Law. Admission to membership in the classes is not permitted until the fees are paid. No deductions are made for absences nor for failure to begin at the opening of a year, nor is extension of time allowed for payment of fees. Fees must in all cases be paid in advance.

The expenses of living are moderate. Good board can be obtained at from $2.50 to $4 per week, and by forming or joining clubs the expenses can be considerably reduced. Students desiring information in regard to boarding places, or general information as to expenses, should address their inquiries to the Secretary of the Board of Regents, Madison, Wisconsin.

A careful perusal of this general statement it is believed will supply all needed information; but should further inquiries as to admission, examination, etc., be necessary, they should be addressed to the Associate Dean of the Law Faculty, Madison, Wisconsin.

SCHOOL OF PHARMACY.

STAFF OF INSTRUCTION.

C. K. ADAMS, LL. D., President of the University.
E. KREMERS, Ph. G., Ph. D., Director, and Professor of Pharmaceutical Chemistry.
E. A. BIRGE, Ph. D., Sc. D., Professor of Zoology.
L. S. CHENEY, M. S., Assistant Professor of Pharmaceutical Botany.
W. W. DANIELLS, Sc. D., M. S., Professor of Chemistry.
J. C. ELSOM, M. D., Professor of Physical Culture and Director of the Gymnasium.
C. N. GREGORY, A. M., LL. B., Professor of Law.
R. L. HARPER, Ph. D., Professor of Botany.
L. R. HEAD, A. B., M. D., Special Lecturer on "First Aid to the Injured."
H. W. HILLYER, Ph. D., Assistant Professor of Organic Chemistry.
W. H. HOBBS, Ph. D., Professor of Mineralogy and Petrology.
F. G. HUBBARD, Ph. D., Professor of the English Language.
L. KAHLENBERG, Ph. D., Assistant Professor of Physical Chemistry.
B. H. MEYER, Ph. D., Assistant Professor of Sociology.
E. T. OWEN, A. B., Professor of French Language and Literature.
W. H. ROSENSTENGEL, A. M., Professor of German Language and Literature.
H. L. RUSSELL, Ph. D., Professor of Bacteriology.
W. M. SMITH, A. B., Librarian.
B. W. SNOW, Ph. D., Professor of Physics.
C. A. VAN VELZER, Ph. D., Professor of Mathematics.
F. W. WOLL, M. S., Assistant Professor of Agricultural Chemistry.
A. N. COOK, M. A., Assistant in Chemistry.
S. R. BOYCE, Ph. C., M. D., Instructor in Pharmacognosy.
R. H. DENNISTON, B. S., Botanical Assistant in Pharmacognosy and Curator of the Drug Cabinet.
W. S. FERRIS, B. S., Chemical Assistant in Pharmacognosy.
R. E. FOWLER, B. S., Assistant in Chemistry.
W. D. FROST, M. S., Instructor in Bacteriology.
W. O. RICHTMANN, Ph. G., B. S., Instructor in Practical Pharmacy.
OSWALD SCHREINER, Ph. G., M. S., Instructor in Pharmaceutical Technique.
J. C. SHEDD, Ph. D., Instructor in Physics.
A. TINGLE, Ph. D., Assistant in Chemistry.

GENERAL STATEMENT.

The prime object of the School of Pharmacy is to furnish a thoroughly scientific foundation for the pursuit of the profession of pharmacy. The elements of the fundamental natural sciences, chemistry, botany or biology, and physics must first be studied before their application to pharmacy can rationally be considered. This is as true for pharmacy as for any other applied science or art. In pursuing these general studies the pharmacy students have the advantage of close association with students from other courses. This implies that in these studies they must be able to keep abreast with students who are graduates of accredited high schools. The best preparation for college, therefore, which the prospective pharmacy student should seek is not that of the shops, but that of a good high school or academy of like rank. The University does not demand practical experience for admission to the courses in pharmacy, but desires such preparation as will best fit for college or university work.

The general study of these fundamental sciences is followed by more or less specialized courses. General chemistry, inorganic and organic, qualitative and quantitative analysis are followed by pharmaceutical chemistry and applied chemical analysis; general botany by vegetable histology and anatomy of drugs; general physics by pharmaceutical technique. These somewhat specialized studies, in turn, not only lay the foundation for the study of the more strictly applied courses in practical pharmacy and pharmacognosy, but also prepare the student for thesis work.

The student who can spend only two years at the University is compelled to take up the more technical studies of his course before he has laid a satisfactory foundation. Such a compromise is outlined under *Courses of Study*. The three-year student, as a rule, finds time to pursue other studies besides those outlined above, *e. g.*, German, physiology, or bacteriology, etc. The four-year student has the great advantage of supplementing his high-school preparation during the freshman and sophomore years by acquiring a reading knowledge of German and French, and by the study of university mathematics, all of which studies are of the greatest importance when the more advanced work of the natural sciences is taken up during the junior and senior years.

Special attention is called to this four-years' course offered to graduates of accredited high schools. The course was created in order to accommodate those students who desire to obtain a general scientific education and to include in their course the pharmaceutical studies, and with the hope of stimulating a broader pharmaceutical education. For the more applied courses special laboratories have been equipped.

Like the sister profession, medicine, pharmacy is in need, not only of the general practitioner, but also of the specialist. To meet the demands of such, the School offers graduate courses. Graduates who desire to prepare themselves as chemists for manufacturing establishments, as analytic or sanitary chemists or as bacteriologists, will find that the graduate courses of the School of Pharmacy as well as of the various colleges of the University offer excellent opportunities for advanced and more specialized study. Special lines of research can also be pursued in various departments by those who desire to work for a higher degree. The attention of advanced students is especially called to the graduate courses outlined on pp. 50-56.

Detailed information about studies in the four years' course and in the College of Science and Letters can be found on pp. 73-80.

The School of Pharmacy is an integral part of the University and is governed by the same general policy that characterizes the institution. The methods of work differ in no essential from those adopted by the other scientific departments. This School has from the beginning demanded a large amount of laboratory instruction, believing that none of the natural sciences can be adequately taught without considerable instruction in the laboratory, and, whenever necessary, in the field.

LABORATORIES.

A description of the general physical, chemical, and biological laboratories will be found on pp. 28-31; descriptions of the mineralogical laboratory on p. 29; of the assay laboratory on p. 182; of the bacteriological laboratory on p. 30; of the electro-chemical laboratory on p. 180.

PHARMACEUTICAL CHEMICAL LABORATORY. This is located on the third floor of North Hall. It affords ample accommodation to the advanced students. Every student is assigned a desk which he alone uses. The balance room is well equipped with Becker's, Sartorius', Eimer & Amends', Nemetz's, Troemner's, and Bunge's balances, a torsion balance, etc. A Bunsen combustion furnace, a Glazer combustion furnace with the latest improvement after Anschütz and Kekulé, a Kopfer combustion furnace for compounds rich in halogen, a Kekulé gas furnace for heating substances in sealed tubes, nitrometers and much other chemical and physical apparatus can be used by the student, particularly in the experimental work for his thesis.

LABORATORY FOR PHARMACEUTICAL TECHNIQUE. This laboratory is equipped with apparatus and material for a more detailed and applied study of such chapters of mechanics and physics as are of special importance to the pharmaceutical student. It contains balance models, balances and measuring instruments of various kinds, complete apparatus for determining specific gravity according to different methods, a Laurent's polariscope, a Pulfrich's refractometer, Beckmann's apparatus for the determination of molecular weights by the freezing and boiling point methods, apparatus for the determination of vapor densities. Besides these the laboratory is liberally supplied with apparatus for conducting the processes of distillation, sublimation, comminution, extraction, filtration, crystallization, drying, etc.

LABORATORY FOR PHARMACEUTICAL BOTANY AND PHARMACOGNOSY. The large room on the fourth floor, formerly used as lecture room, has been equipped with tables, miscroscopes, and lockers, and is now used as a laboratory for botany and pharmacognosy. It accommodates a class of about thirty-five students and has a capacity when fully fitted out for about twenty more. The room is lighted in a manner favorable for microscopic work. A year ago a Naples paraffin bath and a Jung microtome were added to the equipment of this laboratory.

The students in pharmacognosy working in this laboratory have further accommodations in the adjacent room occupied by the pharmacognostical collection, in the shape of lockers to contain the drug collections made use of in this branch of work.

LABORATORY FOR PRACTICAL PHARMACY 'AND DISPENSARY. On the first floor of North Hall a laboratory has been equipped for individual rather than class instruction in practical pharmacy. It is well furnished with balances, percolation stands, extraction apparatus, a water motor, prescription case and all apparatus necessary in a complete laboratory of this kind. In the basement a room has been fitted to serve as comminution room, equipped with three drug-mills, mortars, sieves, etc.

COLLECTIONS.

The recent additions to the pharmaceutical collections have necessitated their entire rearrangement. New cabinets have been constructed, and better containers and a large number of illustrations have been purchased.

THE CHEMICAL COLLECTION contains: 1. Cabinet specimens of chemicals and minerals. The latter serve not only to supplement our knowledge of manufactured chemicals, but also to demonstrate the occurrence in nature of the chemical elements and their compounds, also to illustrate in many instances the source of many artificial chemicals. Through the liberality of the United Alkali Company of England, some fifty specimens of their products in various stages of manufacture were obtained. Dr. William Simon, of Baltimore, has contributed a series of specimens illustrating the manufacture of bichromate and ferrocyanide of potassium. Fries Bros., of New York, have donated a number of synthetics used in perfumery. Numerous smaller donations have been received within recent years. 2. Chemical apparatus for the illustration of chemical operations and processes. 3. Charts illustrating chemical processes of manufacture, curves of solubility of classes of salts, chemical apparatus, etc.

THE PHARMACOGNOSTICAL COLLECTION found on the fourth floor in a room especially devoted to it has been very largely increased by purchases made at the World's Fair, these acquisitions consisting chiefly of drugs of Asiatic origin. Notable among them are a collection of fifty Ceylon drugs and medicines and a collection of more than one hundred Malay medicines. Worthy of mention are also a collection of 122 handsome specimens of essential oils and allied synthetic products liberally donated by Messrs. Schimmel & Co., of Leipzig, Germany; a collection of choice drugs from Messrs. Lehn and Fink, a materia medica cabinet from Parke, Davis & Co., a collection of official drugs from Schieffelin & Co., another from Gilpin, Langdon & Co., etc.

Since many important new drugs from the animal kingdom have recently come into use, an effort is being put forth to make this branch of the museum as complete as possible. Already substantial contributions have been received from the laboratories of Parke, Davis & Co., and of Armour & Co.

During the past year, several hundred new entries have been made, so that at present the inventory comprises almost four thousand numbers. The collection has been relabeled during the past year.

ECONOMIC COLLECTION. This collection includes an herbarium of medicinal plants of about 4,000 sheets and many articles, derived from plants used for food, clothing, etc.; implements used in collecting or manufacturing plant products; and photographs illustrating plants of economic value. At present the economic collection is housed on the fourth floor of North Hall in part with the drug collection and in part in the herbarium room.

The biological and the mineralogical and geological museums in Science Hall are well equipped and full of interest to the student of the natural sciences.

LIBRARIES.

For a statement as to general library facilities at the University and in the city of Madison, see p. 27. The department library for ready reference is unusually well supplied with reference works and the best periodicals. The other department libraries, as well as the general library, are all on the same campus and, therefore, easy of access, the general library being open in the evening as well as the day.

TERMS OF ADMISSION.

To the Two Years' and Three Years' Courses.

I. Graduates from high schools are admitted without examination and without practical experience in a drug store.

II. Non-graduates are admitted if they comply with the following requirements:

1. They must be at least eighteen years of age.
2. They must present satisfactory certificates of *at least* one year's attendance from some standard high school, or its equivalent from a similar educational institution.
3. The time intervening between the secondary education and the college course should have been spent in a drug store, where physicians' prescriptions are regularly compounded.

To the Four Years' Course.

The terms of admission to this course are the same as those to the General Science Course, as given on page 63. No practical experience in pharmacy is required.

Students from other colleges or schools of pharmacy will be admitted on presentation of satisfactory certificates. However, no student who enters from another college will be admitted after November 1 of the year in which he intends to graduate.

DEGREES.

The degree of *Graduate in Pharmacy* (Ph. G.) is conferred upon candidates who have successfully met the requirements of either the

Two or Three Years' Courses. No practical experience is required for graduation.

The degree of *Bachelor of Science in Pharmacy* is conferred upon candidates who have successfully met the requirements of the Four Years' Course.

The degree of *Master of Pharmacy* is conferred upon graduates of the shorter courses only after a year of residence at the University. They must pursue advanced work in some science or sciences allied to pharmacy, and present a dissertation embodying the results of an original investigation, which shall be satisfactory to the committee on higher degrees.

The degree of *Master of Science in Pharmacy* can be obtained by graduates of the Four Years' Course upon fulfillment of similar requirements.

PHARMACEUTICAL FELLOWSHIPS.

The August Uihlein Fellowship.

Mr. August Uihlein, of Milwaukee, in 1895 generously established a pharmaceutical fellowship on a financial basis of $400 per annum. During the present year the income has been divided. The holders are Irvin W. Brandel, Ph. G. '99, and Frederick G. Ehlert, Ph. G. '99.

The Fred Vogel Jr. Fellowship.

Mr. Fred Vogel, Jr., of Milwaukee, generously donated $500.00 to be used in the support of graduate work. The sum was divided so as to establish a graduate scholarship of $250.00 per annum for two years. The holder of this graduate scholarship for the year 1900-1901 is Mr. Frank C. Hitchcock, Ph. C. '98 Mich.).

The United States Pharmacopoeia Research Scholarship.

The Committee on Revision of the U. S. Pharmacopoeia has for several years maintained an assistant in the School of Pharmacy for the purpose of conducting research in the line of revision of the Pharmacopoeia under the direction of the professor of pharmaceutical chemistry.

FEES AND EXPENSES.

No tuition is required from students who are residents of the State of Wisconsin; non-residents pay $20.00 each semester.

The fee for incidental expenses is $15.00 per semester.

The fees must be paid before the class cards can be issued.

The following statement applies to the laboratories of the School of Pharmacy only and does not include the charges made in the general chemical laboratories. For these see p. 40.

The laboratory fees should be paid within two weeks after the laboratory cards have been issued. For the general laboratory privileges, *i. e.*, desk-room, gas, water, general reagents, use of balances, microscopes, and other larger pieces of apparatus, a charge of one dollar per semester will be made for each fifth of a study; $2.00 for a 2-5 study; $3.00 for a 3-5 study, etc. A separate account will be kept with the accountant of the storage room for special apparatus and material. The student will purchase coupons from the Secretary ($5.00 at a time) and present them at the storage room for what he draws out. At the end of the year full credit will be given for such pieces of apparatus as are taken back by the accountant in accordance with the rules of the storage room.

Every student should make provisions to buy two coupons at the beginning of the first semester, so that he may not be delayed in taking out the necessary apparatus.

No diploma fee is required upon graduation.

The payment of all University charges is to be made to Mr. E. F. Riley, Secretary of the Board of Regents, at his office in the Law Building.

The cost of board in clubs is from $2 to $2.50 per week; in private families, from $2.50 to $4 per week; and rooms can be obtained in the city at correspondingly reasonable rates.

COURSES OF STUDY.

TWO YEARS' COURSE.

Junior Year.

Chemistry, 1*; Pharmaceutical Botany, 1; Pharmaceutical Technique, 1 and 2, and Physics, 15, all throughout the year.

Senior Year.

Chemistry, 5; Pharmaceutical Chemistry, 1, 2; Pharmaceutical Botany, 3; Pharmacognosy, 3 and 4; Practical Pharmacy, 1 and 2; Thesis.

---
*The figures refer to the numbers of the courses as given in the statements under Departments of Instruction, College of Letters and Science, and School of Pharmacy.

THREE YEARS' COURSE.

Sophomore Year.

Chemistry, 1; Pharmaceutical Botany, 1, or Biology, 1; Physics, 1S; and Pharmaceutical Tenchnique, 1; Electives.

Junior Year.

Chemistry, 5; Pharmaceutical Chemistry, 1 and 2; Pharmaceutical Botany, 2; Pharmaceutical Technique, 2; Pharmacognosy, 1; Practical Pharmacy, 3; Electives.

Senior Year.

Pharmacognosy, 1 and 2; Practical Pharmacy, 1 and 2; Thesis; Electives.

FOUR YEARS' COURSE.

Freshman Year.

Biology, 1; German, 1; Mathematics, 1, 2; English, 2; Gymnastics, Military Drill.

Sophomore Year.

French, 3; Chemistry, 1; Physics, 1; Gymnastics, Military Drill; Electives.

Junior Year.

Pharmaceutical Chemistry, 1, 2, and 3; Pharmaceutical Botany, 2; Pharmaceutical Technique; Pharmacognosy, 1; Practical Pharmacy, 3; Electives.

Senior Year.

Pharmacognosy, 1 and 2; Practical Pharmacy, 1 and 2; Thesis; Electives.

The student should decide at the beginning of the junior year whether his major study is to be of a physical, chemical, or biological character, and arrange his work accordingly. During the second semester the subject for his thesis should be chosen in one of the departments in which he is doing his major work.

DEPARTMENTS OF STUDY.

CHEMISTRY.

PROFESSOR DANIELLS, ASSISTANT PROFESSOR HILLYER, ASSISTANT PROFESSOR KAHLENBERG, AND DR. TINGLE.

The following courses are either required or frequently elected. For detailed information see pp. 122 to 124.

1. General Elementary Chemistry. Professor DANIELLS, Assistant Professor HILLYER, and assistants.
2. Advanced Inorganic Chemistry. Professor DANIELLS, and assistants.
4. Toxicology. Professor DANIELLS.
5. Quantitative Analysis for students in Pharmacy. Professor DANIELLS and Dr. TINGLE.
7. Advanced Organic Chemistry. Assistant Professor HILLYER.
9. Physical Chemistry. Assistant Professor KAHLENBERG.
12. Research Work in Physical Chemistry. Assistant Professor KAHLENBERG.

PHARMACEUTICAL CHEMISTRY.

PROFESSOR KREMERS, MR. SCHREINER, MR. HITCHCOCK.

1. Pharmaceutical and Pharmacognostical Chemistry. This course consists of a review of general chemistry, inorganic and organic, with special adaptation of the subject-matter to the interests of pharmacy. Richter's Inorganic Chemistry, Bernthsen's Organic Chemistry. Two lectures and one recitation. *M., Tu., Th.* Professor KREMERS.
2. Applied Chemical Analysis. Chemical analysis, qualitative and quantitative, gravimetric and volumetric, in its application to pharmacy. This will be chiefly a laboratory study. It will not, however, be merely a study of methods, but also of chemical principles involved. Professor KREMERS, Mr. SCHREINER.
3. Reviews with critical reading of the text of the U. S. Pharmacopoeia as far as chemicals are concerned. *W.* Mr. SCHREINER.

[4. Nitrogen derivatives of the carbon compounds preparatory to the study of alkaloids and ptomaines. For advanced students and graduates. *Lecture, W.* Professor KREMERS.]
5. The classification and study of the constituents of volatile oils. For advanced and graduate students. *Lecture, W., first semester.* Professor KREMERS.
7. Advanced laboratory work and thesis adapted to the individual. Professor KREMERS.
8. Physiological Chemistry. (a) A study of foods, body fluids, etc. Chemical analysis as applied to physiological chemistry. (b) A microscopical and chemical study of urine, blood, sputum, etc. Laboratory work supplemented by lectures and recitations. Mr. HITCHCOCK.

BIOLOGY.

PROFESSOR BIRGE, PROFESSOR HARPER, ASSISTANT PROFESSOR MARSHALL, AND ASSISTANTS.

For detailed information see pp. 127 to 131.
1. General Biology. Professor HARPER, Professor BIRGE, Dr. MARSHALL.
4. Human Physiology. Professor BIRGE.

PHARMACEUTICAL BOTANY.

ASSISTANT PROFESSOR CHENEY.

1. General Morphology of Plants. Corresponds to course 21 on p. 130. An elementary course. First semester, the morphology of fungi, algae, lichens, mosses, and ferns, illustrated by selected types. Second semester, the form and structure of the organs of seed plants, the identification of selected flowering plants and the preparation of an herbarium. The course will be supplemented by bontanical excursions. *Daily,* 8-10. Excursions on Saturdays.
2. Vegetable Histology. Corresponds to course 16, p. 129. Systematic study of the tissues of phanerogams and ferns. Use of reagents and stains, modes of embedding, section cutting and mounting. *Five times a week first semester, three times a week second semester.* Hours on consultation. The work in this course is so arranged that students electing it may take it in either semester or both. For three and four-year students.

3. Vegetable Histology. The same as course 2 for the first semester. For two-year students.
4. Trees and their Characteristics. Corresponds to course 22, p. 130. A course designed for those who desire to acquaint themselves with forest trees. It contemplates a study of the vegetative and reproductive structures; the general habit and conditions of growth; the anatomy of the wood, etc. Lectures and laboratory work with occasional excursions. Those who expect to take this course should know how to use a microscope and should have had at least the equivalent of one semester's work in general botany. *Twice a week throughout the year.* May be taken either semester or both. Hours to be arranged on consultation.
5. Advanced Work in Anatomy. Special subjects for original investigation will be assigned to such students desiring to do advanced work as are properly qualified.

Classification of Flowering Ferns and Mosses.

A course intended for those who wish to equip themselves for identifying plants in the groups named above. The work will necessarily be of an individual character. Amount of work and hours to be determined upon consultation. *Throughout the year.*

BACTERIOLOGY.

PROFESSOR RUSSELL AND MR. FROST.

For detailed information see pp. 130, 131.
30. General Bacteriology. Professor RUSSELL and Mr. FROST.
31. Medical Bacteriology. Mr. FROST.
35. Communicable Diseases. Mr. FROST.
36. Biology of Water Supplies. Mr. FROST.

PHARMACOGNOSY.

DR. BOYCE, MR. DENNISTON, AND MR. FERRIS.

1. Lectures. This course is meant to present to the student the main facts of the natural history of the plants yielding drugs, as, botanical description, habitat, history and cultivation, as well as the more strictly applied information. This course supplements the work done in the laboratory with the drugs themselves.

Two lectures per week during the second semester of the junior year and three per week during the first semester of the senior year. Required of three and four-year students.

2. Laboratory work for three-year or four-year students. Students are required to arrange systematically a collection of drugs, the material for which is in part purchased and in part collected by the students themselves. Drawings of the drug and of the preparations made by the students themselves call attention to the details of aspect and structure. Three-fifths work during the first semester of the senior year. The first half of the second semester is spent in the study of the principal groups of chemical constituents of drugs, such as alkaloids, glucosides, etc. During the second half of the second semester the time will be largely devoted to topic work. Required of seniors of the three and four-year courses.

3. This course will consist of text-book work supplemented by lectures and topics. The official and the most important non-official drugs will be studied. Text used: Sayre's Organic Materia Medica and Pharmacognosy.

Two-fifths, first semester; one-fifth, second semester.
Required of two-year seniors.

4. The laboratory work for two-year students will consist of an abridgement of course 2. Little microscopic work will be required.

Four-fifths in second semester of senior year.

5. For Pre-Medical Students. An abridgement of the work given to pharmacy students is offered for those intending to study medicine. As far as may be, the methods used are those detailed for the foregoing courses. No drug collection is required and no microscopic study is expected.

Three-fifths course during first semester. The lectures and two hours laboratory work per week.

6. Advanced laboratory work and thesis adapted to the individual.

PRACTICAL PHARMACY.

MR. RICHTMANN.

1. Theory and Practice of Pharmacy. Class work, *two hours a week during both semesters.*

History of pharmacopoeias and discussion of U. S. Pharmacopoeia. Review of subject of metrology. Pharmaceutical operations, as comminution, solution, crystallization, filtration, percolation. Galenical preparations; as solutions, tinctures, fluid extracts, spirits, pills, suppositories, ointments, plasters, etc. Apparatus used in pharmaceutical operations brought before the class and discussed. Prescription reading. Incompatabilities.

2. Operative Pharmacy. Laboratory work. *A three-fifths course throughout the year.*

Examination of commercial articles, chemicals, and vegetable drugs, including assaying of the latter. Manufacture of galenical preparations, chemicals and scale salts, and testing of same when finished. Preparations are so selected as to represent all classes official in the U. S. P.

Compounding of physicians' prescriptions with special reference to those cases in which difficulties are liable to occur.

3. Operative Pharmacy. Laboratory work. For juniors of the three and four-years' course. *Two-fifths during second semester.*

This course is continued during the senior year as course 2, being merely an extension of the latter.

5. Special work adapted to the individual, including laboratory work in preparation for thesis.

PHYSICS.

PROFESSOR SNOW, ASSISTANT PROFESSOR AUSTIN, ASSISTANT PROFESSOR WOOD, DR. SHEDD, MR. SMITH, AND MR. STANGLE.

For detailed information see pp. 119 to 121.

1. General Lectures and Introductory Laboratory Practice. Professor SNOW and assistants.
15. Introductory Physics. This will consist of a course of lectures designed exclusively for students in the two-years' and three-years' course in pharmacy. *Three times a week.* Dr. SHEDD.

PHARMACEUTICAL TECHNIQUE.

MR. SCHREINER.

1. Pharmaceutical Operations. Laboratory practice in technical processes and the use of apparatus commonly employed in pharmaceutical laboratories and in technical chemistry. Principally laboratory work, supplemented by lectures and recitations. Required of all juniors. *Three-fifths for the first semester.*
2. The Determination of Physical Constants and their Application to Pharmaceutical and Chemical Problems. Principally laboratory work, supplemented by lectures, recitations, and topic

work. Required of all juniors. *Three-fifths for the second semester.*

[3. Molecular Weight Determinations. A detailed study of the molecular theory and molecular weight determination by chemical and physical methods. This course must be preceded by course 2. Lecture and laboratory work. *Two-fifths for the first semester.* Given in 1899-1900.]

4. Optical Rotatory Power. A special study of the action of organic compounds on polarized light, and the application of the polariscope to scientific investigation and its use in the arts. This course must be preceded by course 2. Lecture and laboratory work. *Two-fifths for the second semester.* (Given in 1900-1901.)

5. Advanced work adapted to the individual, including laboratory work in preparation for thesis.

FIRST AID TO THE INJURED.

DR. HEAD.

A series of lectures upon the first care of emergency cases, embracing essential, anatomical and physiological principles; methods of preventing or combating shock after injuries; checking hemorrhage, manipulation for resuscitation of the asphyxiated; indications for the administration of some of the emergency remedies, and the practical demonstration of the application of temporary dressings.

THE ECONOMIC FUNCTIONS OF THE STATE.

DR. MEYER.

This course consists of a series of lectures, historical and critical, on the state in its relation to industry, trade, and the professions, with special reference to pharmacy. *First semester,* 1900-1901.

LAW APPLIED TO PHARMACY.

PROFESSOR GREGORY.

A course of lectures treating of the validity and construction of laws especially restraining the practice of pharmacy; of the liability of pharmacists both criminal and civil; for their own violations of laws and that of their agents; also for their own negligence and that of their agents. *Given in second semester,* 1900-1901.

All correspondence or inquiries relating to the School of Pharmacy should be addressed to Professor Edward Kremers, Madison, Wis.

SCHOOL OF MUSIC.

STAFF OF INSTRUCTION.

C. K. ADAMS, LL. D., President.
F. A. PARKER, *Director*, Musical History, Harmony, Counterpoint, and Organ.
J. S. SMITH, Piano.
ADA BIRD, Piano.
WINIFRED C. CARD, Piano.
ADELAIDE FORESMAN, Voice.
CHARLES E. ROBERTS, Voice.
CHARLES NITSCHKE, Violin, Cello, and other orchestral instruments.
HJALMAR O. ANDERSON, Mandolin.
ELIZABETH M. KEELEY, Harp.
MRS. M. E. BRAND, Guitar.
MYRON M. FOWLER, Banjo.
WILLIAM M. FOWLER, Secretary,

GENERAL ANNOUNCEMENT.

It is the purpose of the School of Music to furnish superior facilities for the study of music in any or all of its departments, theoretical or practical. The members of the faculty are teachers of acknowledged ability and large experience. Instruction is offered in organ, harp, singing, orchestral instruments, mandolin, guitar, and banjo, and in musical theory, choral practice, harmony, counterpoint and composition. In the study of piano or of singing (voice culture) instruction is given by means of private or individual lessons, or, should a sufficient number of students desire it, classes limited to three will be organized. In the study of other instruments, private lessons only are employed. In the theoretical studies students are recommended to join the University classes, but private lessons may be arranged for if preferred.

To meet the convenience of students residing either permanently or temporarily in distant parts of the city, an office and studios have been opened in the Kroncke building, in addition to those in Ladies' Hall at the University. Application for lessons may be made at either place, the lessons being given where it is found to best suit the convenience of instructor and student.

The lessons vary in length, and number per week, for the purpose of adequately meeting the wants of all classes of students, from those who take a large amount of work in other departments of the University to those who devote themselves especially to the study of music with little or no collateral work. In like manner the fees for special instruction vary according to the length and frequency of lessons. These fees, which are given on page 276, are believed to be as low as possible for competent instruction.

It should be observed that special instruction in vocal or instrumental music of any kind may be taken by students not otherwise connected with the University, and that such students are not required to pay the incidental fee.

The general classes in Musical Theory, Harmony, Counterpoint, History of Music, and Musical Composition may be taken as electives by students of the College of Letters and Science, who will receive credit for them, as for other studies. These classes are likewise open to students of the other colleges and schools of the University without extra fees.

Students of the School of Music, not otherwise connected with the University, may be admitted to these classes on the payment of the usual incidental fee charged to students of the College of Letters and Science, viz.: $10 per semester. The tuition fee for students not residents of the State is not required.

A statement of courses and classes follows. For a statement of credits, see announcements under Music, in Departments of Instruction, page 131.

COURSES.

These are two general courses, as follows:

I. The Collegiate Course,

in which the requirements for admission are the same as for the general courses in the College of Letters and Sciences, or for adult special students, together with such proficiency in some department of music, as is mentioned in the outlined courses of study. A graduate's diploma will be granted on the completion of this course. Three years of study are required, including the courses in Musical Theory, Harmony, History of Music, or their equivalents. It is, however, recommended that students extend the time to four years to enable them to take a larger proportion of general studies.

UNIVERSITY OF WISCONSIN.

II. The Academic Course,

open to persons not members of the University, and also to University students who do not desire to enter the Collegiate Course pursuant to graduation. Students of this course may, however, be admitted to the musical classes of the University on the payment of the usual incidental fees charged to students of the College of Letters, but will not be considered candidates for graduation or for a diploma. A certificate of excellence will be granted worthy students of this course on examination, after not less than three years of study.

OUTLINE OF COURSES OF STUDY.

I. COLLEGIATE COURSE.

Piano.

Applicants for admission will be expected to play music of the grade of Haydn's *Sonata No. 2*, or Mozart's *Sonata No. 1*, Cotta edition, and Heller's *Etudes, Op. 47*.

Mason's, Zwintscher's or Plaidy's Technics throughout the course.

First Year: Kuhner, *Instructive Albums*, II. and III. Loew, *Etudes, Op. 233*. Loeschhorn, *Op. 52* and *Op. 66*. Czerny, *Studies in Velocity*. Bach, *Little Preludes and Inventions*.

Second Year: Heller, *Op. 46* and *45*. Czerny, *Fingerfertigkeit*. Jensen, *Op. 32*. Cramer-Buelow, *Etudes*. Marmontel, *Mecanisme*. Bach, *Well-Tempered Clavichord*.

Third Year: Tansig, *Studies*. Kullak, *Octave School*. Moscheles, *Op. 70*. Clementi, *Gradus ad Parnassum*. Chopin, *Preludes and Etudes*.

Selections of the grade of *Perpetual Motion* by Weber; *Arabeske* by Schumann; *Impromptu, Op. 29*, by Chopin; *Variations, Op. 54*, by Mendelssohn; *Sonata Appassionata* by Beethoven.

It is not supposed that a rigid course can be given which will meet the requirements of individual students, but the foregoing outline represents, in a general way, the character of each year's work. Etudes especially are named, because they indicate grade and character of requirements more clearly than can be done otherwise. No single student is expected to take more than a portion of the studies mentioned, and equivalents are liberally used to suit individual cases. On the other hand, these studies are supplemented by ample selections from classic and modern authors for use in the parlor or concert room.

Organ.

No previous knowledge of organ playing is required. The student must be well grounded in piano playing, be possessed of a correct technique, and be able to read plain four-part music.

The course of study is continuous, beginning with Stainer's *Organ School* or Whiting's *First Six Months on the Organ* and following with the larger works of Rink and Best, supplemented by special studies by Thayer, Buck, Ritter, Schneider, Volckmar, and others. Selections from Bach's organ works, Mendelssohn's Sonatas and the compositions of modern composers are used.

Careful training is given in playing church music and voluntaries, the use of stops and the mechanism of the instrument.

Voice.

The student must be able to read plain music and must have had an amount of training equal to the first half of Concone's Fifty Lessons, and comprising the usual technical study for the same period.

First Year: Tone Placing, Breathing, and Phrasing; Ballad Singing and the Sostenuto style. Technical and other studies of the grade of Bonaldi's *Six Vocalizes*, Concone's *Fifteen Vocalizes*, Marchesi's *Exercises*, Op. 21, Book I., etc. Easy forms of Italian and German songs.

Second Year: Studies of the grade of Schubert's *Manual of Vocal Technique*, Schubert's *Special Studies*, Marchesi's *Vocalizes*, Op. 21, Book II., Bordogni's *Bravura Studies*. More difficult German and French songs, and easy oratorio and operatic arias.

Third Year: Study of Cadenzas and larger forms of execution. Recitative and the more difficult oratorio and operatic arias.

On graduation the student will be expected to sing acceptably selections (according to voice and school) from such songs and arias as: "He Was Despised," "Angels Ever Bright and Fair," "I Know That My Redeemer Liveth," and "Thou Shalt Break Them," by Handel; "With Verdure Clad," "Rolling in Foaming Billows," and "In Native Worth," by Haydn; "If With All Your Hearts," "It is Enough," and "O Rest in the Lord," by Mendelssohn; "Ah Non Giunge," by Bellini; "Infelice," by Verdi; "Roberto, tu che Adoro," by Meyerbeer; "Vedrai Carino," by Mozart; "Una Voce," and "Pro Peccatis," by Rossini.

Violin.

First Year: Hermann, *Scale Studies.* Kayser, *Violin Instructor,* I. and II. Herbert Ries, *Violin School, Part I.* Easy melodious solos.

Second Year: Kayser, *Violin Instructor,* III. Kayser, *Etudes,* Op. 29. Schubert, *Violin School,* IV. Herbert Ries, *Violin School, Part III.* Solos by *Viotti, Rode, De Beriot.*

Third Year: Schradieck, *Violin Technic.* De Beriot, *School, Part II. Etudes* by Dont, Kreutzer, and Schubert.

Solos by De Beriot, Leonard, Vieuxtemps, and Wieniawski.

THEORETICAL STUDIES.

Musical Theory and Choral Practice.

A one year course, twice a week, in the general theory of music, including notation, scale construction, intervals, distinctions of rhythm, etc., combined with a practical study of sight reading and choral singing.

This course is especially recommended to all students, whether of instrumental or vocal music, as furnishing a substantial foundation for all other work.

Harmony and Counterpoint.

The student must be able to read and play simple four-part music.

First Year: Review of scales and intervals, triads, seventh chords, augmented sixth chords, modulation, synopsis of supension and appoggiatura.

Second Year: Detailed treatment of modulation, suspension, appoggiatura, etc. Harmonizing melodies. Simple strict counterpoint.

*Third Year: Double counterpoint, canon and fugue.

History of Music.

A course of lectures, twice a week, extending through the year. In the first semester the lectures give a general survey of music before the Christian era, and down to the eighteenth century.

The second semester is devoted to the eighteenth and nineteenth centuries.

*Musical Composition.

A one year course, twice a week. One year of harmony is required as preparation.

II. ACADEMIC COURSE.

There are no requirements for entrance. Students are received and graded according to ability and amount of previous study. This course in all departments leads up to and overlaps the collegiate course. Students after reaching the proper stage of preparation may be transferred to the collegiate course, or may remain in the academic course, the work of the last three years being identical in both courses. But no certificate of excellence will be issued to any student who is not thoroughly fitted to enter the second year of the collegiate course.

Guitar, Banjo and Mandolin.

In response to the demand growing out of the popularity of these attractive instruments, the School of Music provides ample and excellent opportunities for their study. Special attention is given to expression, technique, and proper fingering. In general, correct methods leading to the highest proficiency are employed.

Text-books for Guitar: Carcassi, Sor, Ferranti, Holland, and Langey.

Text-books for Banjo: Dobson, Stewart, Henning, and others.

Text-books for Mandolin: School of Wessenberg, and Progressive Studies by Guiseppi Branzoli, supplemented by solo selections.

Orchestra.

The University Orchestra meets for rehearsal every Saturday forenoon. The purpose of the organization is the study of orchestral music, both light and serious. It is open to all students who have sufficient knowledge of any orchestral instrument to pursue the work profitably. Those who take the rehearsals regularly are entitled to credit of one hour per week.

Band.

A military band has likewise been organized, open to all students on conditions similar to those mentioned for the orchestra.

---

*The courses in counterpoint, etc., and in musical composition are inserted here under their proper headings, because they are frequently taken as electives, but they represent graduate work for the students of the School of Music.

Choral Union.

The choral Union is an organization of students of the University and citizens of Madison for the purpose of studying the oratorios and larger choral works of ancient and modern authors, interspersed with lighter part-songs and glees, and adequately presenting the same in public performance. Very successful performances of Handel's *Messiah*, and *Judas Maccabaeus*, Haydn's *Creation*, and Mendelssohn's *Elijah*, and *St. Paul*, have been given, and other works of similar magnitude will follow.

Applicants for membership are expected to be able to read plain music at sight. The rehearsals are held weekly from October until May. The annual membership fee is one dollar.

Recitals and Concerts.

Student recitals, free to all students, and open to all others by invitation, are held at intervals during the collegiate year. Recitals and concerts by eminent artists are given from time to time at a low price to students of the School of Music.

Tuition.

The school year is divided into two semesters corresponding with the divisions of the University year. The following charges for tuition are uniformly for a semester of eighteen weeks:

TWO LESSONS A WEEK.

	½-hour lessons.	¾-hour lessons.	Hour lessons.	In class of 3 hour lessons.
Piano	$27.00	$40.00	$50.00	$18.00
Voice	27.00	40.00	50.00	18.00
Organ	......	......	54.00	......
Violin, etc.	18.00	27.00	36.00	......
Mandolin, etc.	18.00	27.00	36.00	......

ONE LESSON A WEEK.

	½ hour lesson.	¾ hour lesson.	Hour lesson
Piano	$15.00	$22.00	$27.00
Voice	15.00	22.00	27.00
Organ	......	......	27.00
Violin, etc.	9.00	13.50	......
Mandolin, etc.	10.00	15.00	20.00
Diploma fee	......	......	5.00

Theoretical studies are taken in the University classes, and those who are not otherwise connected with the University are expected to pay the incidental fee of the College of Letters, which is $6.00 a semester. This fee, however, is not required of those taking only individual lessons in singing, or on some instrument.

Students are not received for less than a half semester except by permission of the Director of the School of Music. Students are expected to pay the tuition fees by the half-semester or semester in advance.

No student is entitled to lessons until tuition has been paid and a receipt secured from the Secretary of the Board of Regents.

No deduction can be made for absence from lessons, except for long continued illness, in which case the School of Music will share the loss equally with the student.

No student is expected to take part in any public entertainment without the consent of his teacher and the Director.

Students who, by reason of deficient musical ability, neglect of study, or any other valid reason, fail to make satisfactory progress, may be dropped from the classes.

The pianos in Ladies' Hall may be used for practice for a limited number of hours daily by students of the University on payment of a fee of from four dollars to ten dollars per semester. Pianos may be rented from dealers at from three to six dollars a month.

The office of the Director in Ladies' Hall at the University will be open for several days before the opening of each semester for the reception of pupils and assignment of lessons. After the opening of the University the Director may be found daily at Ladies' Hall from 10 to 11, or at the office in the Kroncke building from 9 to 10.

For further information, address

F. A. PARKER, Director, 14 W. Gilman St., or
W. M. FOWLER, Secretary, 719 State St.,
Madison, Wis.

DEGREES CONFERRED.

COMMENCEMENT, 1899.

BACHELOR OF ARTS.

Ancient Classical Course.

William Benjamin Borgers.
Lillian Effie Case.
Arthur Moore Churchill.
Lulu Blanche Fiske.
Lucretia French Hinckley.
George Allan Hopkins.
Adeline Miriam Jenney.
Alice Palmer Kasson.
Maud Elsie Miller.
Edith Nelson.
Mabel Agnes Pengra.
Eliza Harper Shaw.
Joseph Lawrence Shaw.
John Henry Stauff.
Charles Atwood Vilas.
Daniel Jenkins Williams.

BACHELOR OF LETTERS.

Modern Classical Course.

Theodore Louis Ableiter.
Nellie Martha Bush.
Grace Gage Cloes.
Orsamus Cole, Jr.
Mathilde Viola Cook,
Gertrude Elizabeth DeReamer.
Emerson Ela.
Elsie Rutherford Fargo.
Helen Ada Fowler.
Edward Tappan Fox.
Alice Relaine Friend.
Edith Van Slyke Gibson.
Jennie Elvira Goddard.
Max Wilder Griffith.
Ruth May Hanchett.
Lillian Gertrude Johnson.
William Samuel Kies.
Catherine Genevieve Kline.
Frank William Lyle.
Mary Etta McCumber,
Marcella May McKitrick.
Susan Odell.
Ernest Andrew O'Neill.
Louis Reed.
Helen Gertrude Verplanck.
Adeline Rawson White.
Allen Orvis White.

English Course.

Helen Grace Andrews.
Joseph John Aylward.
Emma Newham Bibbs.
Cathryn Maude Blodgett.
Frank Joseph Laube.
Jessamine Lee.
Olive Lipe.
Nettie Irene McCoy.

Ernest Eugene Calkins.
Daisie Campbell.
Alonzo Albert Chamberlain.
Harlem Roy Chamberlain.
Bertha Estelle Chapman.
Marion Theresa Connell.
Nathan Stephenson Curtis,
Albert Rudolph Denu.
Cora Frances Desmond.
Bert Ormond Driver.
Wanda Gladsy Ellison.
Frank Henry Gugel.
Charles Thomas Hutson.
John Percy Inglis.
Marcus A. Jacobson.
John Jonas Jeffrey.
Frank Howard Kurtz.
Peter Cornelius Langemo.

Anna Levina McCumber.
Marie Malec.
Anna L. Mashek.
Mary Elizabeth Miller.
Thomas William Mitchell.
Lydia Emma Moore.
Harry John Murrish.
Maud Grace Murrish.
Walton Hawkins Pyre.
Ferne Ryan.
Laura Alice Sceets.
Raymond H. Schumaker.
Henry Vincent Stahl.
Crystal Stair.
Alma Stock.
Jesse Raymond Stone.
Cora Marie Thompson.
James Thompson.
Fred Thomson.

Civic Historical Course.

Philip Loring Allen.
Manfred Sickle Block.
Edward Howard Hatton.
Winfred Chester Howe.
Guy Abbott Meeker.
Milton Gray Montgomery.

Anna Shaw Pinkum.
Frank Ernst Radensleben.
Nathan Green Short.
Genevieve Sylvester.
Sharp William Todd.
August William Trettien.

English Group.

Frances Mary Staver.

Hebrew Group.

Warren Gilbert Jones.
Willard Otto Nuzum.

History Group.

Jay Burdett Baldwin.
George Ives Haight.

Elizabeth Margaret Keech.
Edwin William Pahlow.

William Spence Robertson.

Mathematics Group.

Alice Louise Chubbuck.
Gladys Gale.
Eliza Estelle Medbery..
Eliza Alwilda Pollard.
Gertrude Stillman.

Philosophy Group.

George Thompson.

Political Science Group.

Lewis Albert Anderson.

BACHELOR OF SCIENCE.

General Science Course.

Anna Gertrude Anthony.
Frederick William Axley.
Adolph Frederick Beerbaum.
Gideon Benson.
Harry Nathan Carter.
Wilfrid Earl Chase.
William Sylvester Darling.
Charles George Davies.
Mary Dopp.
John Bolles Emerson.
Frederick Julius Gaenslen.
Charles Ernest Gabel.
Florence Meta Gage.
Anna Pauline Houghton.
Frank Xavier Koltes.
Hugo Francis Mehl.
Gilbert Random.
Ole S. Rice.
William Otho Rickfort.
Mabel Victoria Riley.
Louis Fred Ruschhaupt.
Martha Shopbell.
William Christian Sieker.
Thomas William Tormey.
Frank Hosford Watson.
Minnie Comstock Westover.
Luther Millard Wright.

Botany Group.

Charles Elmer Allen.
Stephen Conrad Stuntz.

Mathematics Group.

Warren Milton Persons.
Sara Guenvor Heimdal.

Physics Group.

Eldreth Gordon Allen.
Charles George Stangel.

Civil Engineering Course.

Samuel Powers Connor.
James Harry Knowles.
Richard Thomas Logemann.
Richard Arthur Nommensen.
Ralph William Stewart.

Mechanical Engineering Course.

Wilbur Azro Austin.
John Martin Barr.
Edward Freschl.
Charles Thomas Mason.
William Allan Richards.

Electrical Engineering Course.

Walter John Buckley.
Carl Hambuechen.
Henry Olaus Hanson.
John Joseph Hogan.
Carl A. Keller.
Thomas George Nee.
Louis Walter Olson.
Martin C. Olson.
William Everett Reynolds.
Arthur Valentine Scheiber.
John Wesley Shuster.

Agricultural Course.

William Dietrich.
Harry Louis Trott.

Pharmacy Course.

Rollin Henry Denniston.
Simon Christian Nolte.

BACHELOR OF PHILOSOPHY.

Annie Gorham Marston, as of the class of 1867.

BACHELOR OF PHILOSOPHY IN PEDAGOGY.

Philosophical Course.

Clara Dane Adams.
John Alfred Cederstrom.
Margaret Isabelle Deans.
Lloy Galpin.
Frederick William Gates.
John August Hagemann.
Richard Heyward.
Lewis Albert Jones.
Albert Aaron Kienholz.
William Kittle.
Rosa Lillian McBride.
Samuel E. Pearson.
Grant Ellsworth Pratt.
Mary Mitchell Rountree.
William Carl Ruediger.
Maud Sykes.
Harmon Louis Van Dusen.
Thomas Webster.
Laura Hayden Weld.

BACHELOR OF LAWS.

Earl Steede Anderson.
Charles Richard Barney.
Otto Charles Baumgarten.
Charles Melvin Baxter.
Russell Jackson.
John William Kelley.
William Augustus Klatte.
Robert Burr Lowry.

Henry Cadby Case.
Walter Scott Cate.
Frederick Harold Clausen.
Charles Alexander Cryderman.
Alfred Tennyson Curtis.
Edward James Devney.
Clarence Bushnell Edwards.
Evan Alfred Evans.
John Lincoln Fisher.
Michael Francis Foley.
Herman Sidney Frye.
Walter Scott Gannon.
John Henry Gault.
George Edward Gernon.
Frank Lynch Gilbert.
Stephen Warren Gilman.
Charles Sheen Greenwood.
John Parker Gregg.
Frederick Ford Greolle.
Frederick Hoffman Hartwell.
Bernard Goldsmith Heyn.
Heber Bishop Hoyt.
Thomas Augustus Humphrey.
Richard Gill Hutchinson.

Charles Anson Augustus McGee.
Archibald Cameron McPhail.
George Cushing Martin.
Vroman Mason.
John Oscar Miller.
Louis William Minty.
Leroy John Murat.
James Frederick Oliver.
Giles Henry Putnam.
Henry Charles Rehm.
Hamilton Roddis.
Hiram Arthur Sawyer.
Oscar John Schendel.
Harry Ozias Seymour.
James Deyo Shaw.
Cornelius Anthony Sidler.
Roy C. Smelker.
Earle Clarence Tillotson.
Thomas Anderson Tolrud.
Theodore Bernard Torkelson.
Edgar Curtis True.
Edward Voight.
Robert Wild.
John Miller Winterbotham.

John Frazier Woodmansee.

GRADUATE IN PHARMACY.

Irvin Walter Brandel.
Arthur George Criddle.
Fred Gustave Ehlert.
Elva Eighmy.
George William Funck.
Charles William Gorr.
Albert Louis Henning.

Henry Bronson Hollen.
Charles Gilbert Hubenthal.
Myra Weston Kimball.
May Inez Randall.
Henry Louis Schulz.
James Upjohn.
Albert Henry Treloar.

GRADUATE IN MUSIC.

Bessie Goodrich Brand.
Olive Amanda Dibble.
William Muzzy Fowler.
Grace Gertrude Garrison.

Zoe Lenore Gray.
Mary Eliza Pickarts.
Alice Walden.
Emma Wippert.

HIGHER DEGREES.

MASTER OF ARTS.

Herman G. A. Brauer, A. B. (Colorado College), in French and German—Thesis: *"A study in the philosophy of Renan."*

Margaret Anna Schaffner, A. B. (Emporia College), in Economics and Sociology—Thesis: *"The influence of settlement in the upper Mississippi valley on the methods of cereal culture in the United States."*

MASTER OF LETTERS.

Bertha Ida Bleedorn, B. L. (University of Wisconsin), in German and French—Thesis: *"Die nomina der Kudrun mit besonderer rucksicht auf den geschlechtswechsel."*

Zona Gale, B. L. (University of Wisconsin), in English literature and Philosophy—Thesis: *"The poetry and philosophy of Richard Wagner."*

Estelle Mary Hayden, B. L. (University of Wisconsin), in English Literature and American History—Thesis: *"Landscape Art in James Russell Lowell."*

Gensamro S. Ishikawa (Graduate Anglo-Japanese College), in Economics and Political Science—Thesis: *"The history of coinage in Japan."*

Grace Elizabeth McNair, B. L. (University of Wisconsin), in History and Political Science—Thesis: *"The relations of the students and citizens at Orleans, 1235 to 1350."*

Otto Patzer, B. L. (University of Wisconsin), in French and Italian—Thesis: *"The contradictions in the philosophy of Voltaire."*

Hjalmar Rued, B. L. (University of Wisconsin), in English Literature and Scandinavian Literature—Thesis: *Scandinavian influence on English literature."*

Joseph Schafer, B. L. (University of Wisconsin), in History and Philosophy—Thesis: *"The origin of the system of land grants in aid of education."*

MASTER OF SCIENCE.

Edwin George Hastings, B. S. (Ohio State University), in Dairy Chemistry and Bacteriology—Thesis: *"A study of the action of various types of bacteria upon the nitrogenous constituents of milk."*

Gustavus Sessinghaus, E. M. (Columbia University), in Mineralogy, Petrology, and Electrical Engineering—Thesis: *"The geology of an area in Litchfield County, Connecticut."*

Oswald Schreiner, B. S. (University of Wisconsin), in Chemistry and Mathematics—Thesis: *"On complex nitroso addition products of unsaturated hydrocarbons."*

Grant Smith, B. S. (University of Wisconsin), in Botany and Zoology—Thesis: *"The haustoria of the Erysipheae."*

Benjamin Thomas, B. S. (University of Wisconsin), in Hebrew and New Testament Greek—Thesis: *"The construction, significance, and historical reality of the Mosaic Tabernacle."*

John Weinzirl, B. S. (University of Wisconsin), in Bacteriology and Biology—Thesis: *"The bacterial flora of American cheese: its constancy and distribution."*

Henry Sherwood Youker, B. S. (University of Wisconsin), in Mathematics and Physics—Thesis: *"On the foundation of the calculus."*

ELECTRICAL ENGINEER.

William Corwin Burton, B. S. (University of Wisconsin), Electrical Installations—Thesis: *"The distribution of power electrically for the operation of the Manhattan elevated railway."*

DOCTOR OF PHILOSOPHY.

Wilmot Burkemar Lane, A. B. (University of Toronto), Psychology, Ethics, and Philosophy—Thesis: *"Some contributions to the physiology and psychology of fatigue."*

Azariah Thomas Lincoln, M. S. (University of Wisconsin), Chemistry, Geology, and Mathematics—Thesis: *"The electrical conductivity of non-aqueous solutions."*

Theodore Running, M. S. (University of Wisconsin), Mathematics, Applied Mathematics, and Astronomy—Thesis: *"On systems of circles derived from three and four base circles."*

John Bell Sanborn, B. L. (University of Wisconsin), History, Economics, and Political Science—Thesis: *"Congressional grants of land in aid of railways."*

John Cutler Shedd, M. S. (Cornell University), Physics, Mathematics, and Electricity—Thesis: *"An interferometer study of radiations in a magnetic field."*

THE SCIENCE CLUB MEDAL.

Awarded for the best baccalaureate thesis in science to Carl Hambuechen.

HONORS IN SPECIAL STUDIES.

Charles Elmer Allen, in Botany—Thesis: *"The origin and nature of the so-called middle lamella in thickened plant cell walls."*

William Benjamin Borgers, in Philosophy—Thesis: *"Moral ideas of the Hebrew prophets: Amos, Hosea, Isaiah, Micah."*

Lillian Effie Case, in Latin—Thesis: *"The indebtedness of Lucretius to Ennius."*

John Bolles Emerson, in Chemistry—Thesis: *"The toxic action of solutions on the leech and the vinegar eel."*

Carl Hambuechen, in Electrical Engineering—Thesis: *"An experimental study of the corrosion of iron under various conditions."*

*Mary Bashford Huff, in Philosophy—Thesis: *"The Philosophy of Matthew Arnold's Poetry."*

Charles Thomas Mason, in Mechanical Engineering—Thesis: *"A study of the micro-structure of iron and steel."*

Maud Elsie Miller, in Latin—Thesis: *"Concerning Cicero's representation of Epicureanism."*

Walton Hawkins Pyre, in English Literature—Thesis: *"A study in the epithets of Tennyson."*

William Spence Robertson, in American History—Thesis: *"The Pan-American policy of James G. Blaine."*

William Charles Ruediger, in Philosophy—Thesis: *"The outgrowth of the sciences from philosophy."*

Joseph Lawrence Shaw, in European History—Thesis: *"The parishes of Devonshire and Cornwall, 1301-1331, as seen in the Exeter visitations."*

Charles George Stangel, in Physics—Thesis: *"On the determination of the relative heat conductivity of poor conductors with special application to the problem of the effect on the conductivity of rocks."*

Frances Mary Staver, in English Literature—Thesis: *"The French classic conception of Shakespeare as shown by Ducis' adaptation of Romeo and Juliet, Hamlet, and Othello."*

Jesse Raymond Stone, in English Literature—Thesis: *"The influence of Scott on American literature, 1805 to 1850."*

---

*Omitted from list of 1898.

George Thompson, in Philosophy—Thesis: *"The Gothenburg method of regulating the liquor traffic, 1892 to 1898."*

Charles Atwood Vilas, in Political Science—Thesis: *"The idea of law as developed by European writers of the sixteenth and seventeenth centuries."*

Adeline Rawson White, in Psychology—Thesis: *"A study of inventiveness of school children."*

GRADUATES.

Number of University Graduates, 1854-1899	3,771	1899,	250
Ancient Classical Course, 1854-1899	379	1899,	15
Modern Classical Course, 1876-1899	431	1899,	27
English Course, 1887-1899	278	1899,	51
Civic Historical Course, 1893-1899	234	1899,	15
General Science Course, 1866-1899	584	1899,	30
Philosophical Course, 1898-1899	21	1899,	18
Normal Course, (1865-1868)	25	1899,	...
Civil Engineering Course, 1873-1899	124	1899,	5
Mechanical Engineering Course, 1876-1899	101	1899,	5
Electrical Engineering Course, 1892-1899	80	1899,	11
Metallurgical Engineering Course, 1876-1899	16	1899,	...
Law Course, 1869-1899	1,279	1899,	57
Pharmacy Courses, 1884-1899	173	1899,	14
Agricultural Course, 1878-1899	14	1899,	2

STUDENTS.

FELLOWS.

Andrews, Helen Grace, B. L., — Ladies' Hall.
  Alumni Fellow in English.
Baird, John Wallace, A. B., — 523 Lake St.
  Fellow in Philosophy.
Comstock, Elting Houghtaling, B. S., — University Hall.
  Honorary Fellow in Mathematics.
Denniston, Rollin Henry, B. S., — 435 Park St.
  Fellow in Pharmacognosy.
Henry, Alden Edson, A. M., — 631 Langdon St.
  Fellow in Economics.
Kinsman, Delos Oscar, A. M., — 213 Murray St.
  Honorary Fellow in Economics.
Magnusson, Carl Edward, M. S., — 714 State St.
  Fellow in Physics.
Mors, George Charles, B. M. E., — 141 W. Gorham St.
  Fellow in Mechanical Engineering.
Pengra, Charlotte Elvira, B. S., — 803 University Ave.
  Fellow in Mathematics.
Pitman, Annie Maria, A. B., — 414 N. Henry St.
  Fellow in Latin.
Schafer, Joseph, M. L., — 128 Charter St.
  Fellow in History.
Scribner, Annie Nyhan, A. B., — 308 N. Carroll St.
  Fellow in Greek.
Veerhusen, Elsbeth, A. B., — 120 S. Fairchild St.
  Fellow in German Philology.
*Watts, Jenny Chamberlain, A. M., — Ladies' Hall.
  Fellow in History.

SCHOLARS.

Calkins, Ernest Eugene, B. L., — 1001 University Ave.
  The John C. Freeman Graduate Scholarship (English.)
Colebeck, Edward Laughton, A. M., — 1112 W. Johnson St.
  The William F. Allen Scholarship (Greek and Latin.)
Handschin, Charles, A. B., — 212 Park St.
  The Madison Graduate Scholarship in German Philology.

*Resigned.

Odland, Martin, B. L., 511 Francis St.
The Henrik Wergeland Graduate Scholarship.
McCarthy, Charles, B. P., 712 Langdon St.
Graduate Scholarship in American History.
Willard, James Field, B. S., 224 Murray St.
Graduate Scholarship in European History.
Wicker, George Ray, 707 W. Dayton St.
Scholarship in Municipal Government.

—21

RESIDENT GRADUATES.

Allen, Charles Elmer, B. S., University of Wisconsin, *Madison*.
    Botany, Embryology.
Brandelle, David William, A. B., Augustana College, *Galva, Ill*.
    Pedagogy, Philosophy.
Brauer, Herman Gustav Adolph, A. M., University of
    Wisconsin, *Adelaide, So. Australia*.
    French, Spanish, Italian.
Brown, Sarah Edith, B. S., University of Wisconsin, *Madison*.
    Physics, Mathematics, Chemistry.
Case, Lillian Effie, A. B., University of Wisconsin, *Madison*.
    Latin, English.
Chamberlain, Harlem Roy, B. S., University of Wisconsin, *Darlington*.
    History, Political Science.
Cook, Alfred Newton, A. M., Wooster University, *Madison*.
    Chemistry, Geology.
Critchley, Bertha May, A. B., Vassar College, *Cleveland, O*.
    History.
Darrow, William, B. S., University of Wisconsin, *Madison*.
    Bacteriology, Chemistry.
Deniston, Carlton Clinton, A. B., Cornell College, *Mt. Vernon, Ia*.
    Economics, Sociology, Psychology.
Deniston, Gilbert Ward, A. B., Cornell College, *Mt. Vernon, Ia*.
    Economics, Sociology, Psychology.
Deniston, John Howard, A. B., Cornell College, *Mt. Vernon, Ia*.
    Economics, Sociology.
Eddy, Robert Jay, A. M., Beloit College, *Beloit*.
    Pedagogy.
Ela, Emerson, B. L., University of Wisconsin, *Rochester*.
    Economics, French.
Farrington, Mabel Idell, B. S., Smith College, *Mondovi*.
    Botany, German, Pedagogy.

Ferris, William Stewart, B. S., University of Wisconsin, *Whitewater.*
Pharmaceutical Chemistry, Chemistry.
Fowler, Roy Edward, B. S., University of Wisconsin, *Wauwatosa.*
Chemistry.
Franklin, Viola Price, A. M., University of Nebraska, *Madison.*
English Literature, French.
Frost, William Dodge, M. S., University of Minnesota, *Madison.*
Bacteriology, Botany, Chemistry.
Gage, Florence Meta, B. S., Univ. of Wisconsin, *Madison.*
Chemistry.
Gattiker, Emma, B. S., University of Wisconsin, *Baraboo.*
Mediaeval History.
Gilbert, Herman Armin, M. D., University of Heidelberg, *Madison.*
Bacteriology.
Griffiths, Anna Cecilia, A. B., University of Wisconsin, *Madison.*
Latin.
Hargrave, Russel W., B. S., University of Wisconsin, *Madison.*
Steam Engineering, Electrical Engineering.
Hatherell, Rosalia Amelia, B. S., University of Wisconsin, *Madison.*
Zoology, Botany.
Haver, John Arthur, A. B., Emporia College, *Emporia, Kan.*
Economics, History, Oratory.
Herfurth, Sabena Mildred, M. L., University of Wisconsin, *Madison.*
German Philology, Norse.
Heyward, Richard, Ph. B., University of Wisconsin, *Madison.*
Pedagogy, Philosophy, Biology.
Hibbard, Benjamin Horace, B. S. A., University of Iowa, *Paullina, Ia.*
Economics, History.
Hitchcock, Frank Carl, Ph. C., Univ. of Michigan, *Plainwell, Mich.*
German, Bacteriology.
Hocking, William Josephus, B. L., Univ. of Wisconsin, *Darlington.*
History, Political Science.
Howe, Winfred Chester, B. L., University of Wisconsin, *Sheboygan.*
History.
Ishikawa, Gensamro Sadakuni, M. L., Univ. of Wis., *Tokyo, Japan.*
Economics, Political Science, Sociology.
Johnson, Eugene Gustave, A. B., Luther College, *Decorah, Ia.*
Political.Science, Economics.
Johnson, Perry Spencer, A. B., Luther College, *Decorah, Ia.*
Political Science, Economics.
Jolliffe, William Morley, B. S., Lawrence University, *Berlin.*
Physics, Mathematics, Chemistry.

Kellogg, Louise Phelps, B. L., University of Wisconsin, *Milwaukee.*
History.
Langemo, Peter Cornelius, B. L., Univ. of Wisconsin, *Kenyon, Minn.*
Political Science, Economics.
Larson, Laurence Marcellus, A. B., Drake University, *Madison.*
History, English Literature.
Luetscher, George Daniel, B. L., University of Wisconsin, *Sauk City.*
History, Economics, Political Science.
Marston, Oliver Jones, Ped. B., B. S., B. A., Greer
Hoopeston College, *Hoopeston, Ill.*
Economics, History.
McCumber, Mary Etta, B. L., University of Wisconsin, *Fond du Lac.*
Latin.
Meisnest, Frederick William, B. S., University of Wisconsin, *Madison.*
German Philology, English Philology.
Munro, Alexander Allan, A. B., University of Nebraska, *Omaha, Neb.*
Economics, Sociology, Pedagogy.
Nelson, Annette, B. L., University of Wisconsin, *Madison.*
German Philology, Norse.
Norlie, Olaf Morgan, A. M., St. Olaf College, *Milwaukee.*
English, Norse, Pedagogy.
Nuzum, Willard Otto, B. L., University of Wisconsin, *Brooklyn.*
Hebrew, English Literature.
Pahlow, Edwin William, B. L., University of Wisconsin, *Milwaukee.*
History, English Literature.
Peck, Richard Gilman, Ph. B., Beloit College, *Beloit.*
Pharmaceutical Chemistry, German, Botany.
Peppel, Samuel Vernon, B. S., Ohio State University, *Madison.*
Geology, Chemistry.
Pratt, Grant Ellsworth, Ph. B., University of Wisconsin, *Madison.*
Biology, Physics, German.
Raymer, John Wesley, B. S., University of Wisconsin, *Madison.*
Physical Chemistry.
Reed, Emerson Golden, B. S. in E. E., Iowa State
College, *Knoxville, Ia.*
Electrical Engineering.
Reynolds, Everett Adelbert, B. L., University of Wisconsin, *Bassett.*
History, Philosophy.
Rice, Ernest Joseph Axtell, A. B., Gates College, *Madison.*
Economics, Sociology, Political Science.
Robertson, William Spence, B. L., University of Wisconsin, *Oxford.*
History, Economics.

Rodgers, Charles Willis, B. S., Upper Iowa University, *Fayette, Ia.*
Hebrew, Hellenistic Greek.
Sakagami, Yasuzo, M. L., Univ. of Minnesota, *Wakayamaken, Japan.*
Political Science, Economics, History.
Shapiro, Rebecca, B. L., University of Wisconsin, *Medford.*
French, Italian, Spanish.
Smith, Charles Marquis, B. S., University of Wisconsin, *Madison.*
Mathematics.
Smith, Howard Remus, B. S., Mich. Agr. College, *Addison, Mich.*
Chemistry, Animal Husbandry.
Smith, Lloyd Dean, B. L., University of Wisconsin, *Amherst.*
American History, Political Science.
Stangel, Charles George, B. S., University of Wisconsin, *Tisch Mills.*
Physics, Chemistry.
Storms, Albert Boynton, A. M., University of Michigan, *Madison.*
Ethics, American History.
Tallman, William Duane, B. S., University of Wisconsin, *Madison.*
Mathematics, Physics.
Verplanck, Helen Gertrude, B. L., University of Wisconsin, *Madison.*
Latin, German.
Walbridge, Fannie Rose, B. L., University of Wisconsin, *Beloit.*
English.
Webster, Thomas, Ph. B., University of Wisconsin, *Elk Grove.*
History, Economics.
Welty, Grace DeWitt, A. B., Rockford College, *Rockford, Ill.*
Economics, History.
Westover, Calla Phoebe, B. S., University of Wisconsin, *Madison.*
French, English, History.
Wicker, George Ray, A. M., Cornell University, *Philadelphia, Pa.*
Economics, Sociology, Political Science.
Williams, Daniel Jenkins, A. B., Univ. of Wisconsin, *Genesee Depot.*
English, Hebrew, Hellenistic Greek.
Williams, William Watkin, B. S., Lawrence University, *Ottawa.*
Pedagogy, Psychology.
Wilmarth, George Henry, B. S., University of Illinois, *Aurora, Ill.*
Electrical Engineering.
Young, Allyn Abbott, Ph. B., Hiram College, *Madison.*
Economics, History, Political Science.

—75

UNIVERSITY OF WISCONSIN.

GRADUATE STUDYING IN ABSENTIA.

Huff, Mary Bashford, Ph. B., University of Wisconsin, La Crosse.
Ethics, Sociology.

—1

UNDERGRADUATES.

COLLEGE OF LETTERS AND SCIENCE.

Senior Class.

Abbott, Lottie J.,	Westfield,	Phil.
Adams, Edna Couper,	Madison,	Eng.
Adams, Harry Wilfred,	Black Earth,	Eng. (Pol. Sci.)
Adams, William Frazier,	Mukwonago,	A. C.
Albrecht, Sebastian,	Milwaukee,	G. S.
Allen, Florence Eliza,	Madison,	C. H. (Math.)
Anderson, Andrew Runni,	Madison,	A. C.
Andresen, Oliver Sverre,	Medford,	Eng.
Arnold, Lizzie May,	Oshkosh,	Phil.
Austin, Rolland Melvin,	Monroe,	G. S.
Bachhuber, Charles Hugo,	Mayville,	Eng.
Baker, Helen Leona,	Cotton, N. Y.,	A. C.
Barber, Winchel Fay,	Waukesha,	C. H.
Bleekman, Adelbert E., Jr.,	LaCrosse,	A. C.
Bolender, Charles Barton,	Monroe,	A. C.
Bolton, Ernest LeRoy,	Tomah,	G. S.
Bowden, Josephine Horton,	West Salem,	Eng.
von Briesen, Ernst,	Columbus,	C. H.
Brigham, Bertha Blanche,	Madison,	M. C.
Brown, Hester Adeline,	Berlin,	A. C.
Brown, Luther Edward,	Rhinelander,	A. C.
Buck, Florence Trask,	Platteville,	Phil.
Burnham, Charles Lewis,	Milwaukee,	A. C.
Butt, Margaret Elizabeth,	Viroqua,	M. C.
Carney, Francis Joseph,	Eau Claire,	Eng.
Cashel, Mae,	Arcadia,	Eng.
Cassels, George Snowden,	Tomah,	G. S. (Phys.)
Castle, Mildred Alice,	Madison,	Eng. (Romance.)
Challoner, Grace Mary,	Oshkosh,	A. C.
Clark, Myrtes Estella,	Mayville,	Eng.
Cochems, Edward Bulwer,	Sturgeon Bay,	Eng.
Coen, Benjamin Franklin,	Cleveland, O.,	C. H.

Cook, Edward Albert,	Madison,	Eng.
Craig, Louise,	Viroqua,	M. C.
Crosby, Francis Hinckley,	Racine,	C. H.
Damuth, Libbie M.,	Ft. Atkinson,	C. H.
Darling, Frank Edward, Jr.,	Madison,	G. S.
Davis, Jessica Esther,	Madison,	G. S. (Phys.)
Devine, Clark Bailey,	Oregon,	G. S.
Dillingham, Grace Louise,	Baraboo,	M. C.
Dillon, Joseph Golder,	Sterling, Ill.,	G. S.
Dorset, Bernard Charles,	LaCrosse,	A. C.
Dreyer, John William,	Fitchburg,	G. S.
Eastman, Clarence Winans,	Portage,	G. S.
Egdahl, Anfin,	Menomonie,	G. S.
Elmer, Walter Edgar,	Hustler,	Eng.
Elward, Dorothy,	Madison,	C. H. (Hist.)
Farrand, Roy Felton,	Delafield,	Eng.
Fernekes, Gustave,	Milwaukee,	G. S.
Ferris, George Neb.,	Whitewater,	C. H.
Fisher, Carl Elisha,	Bayfield,	Eng.
Fletcher, Mabel Emily,	Portage,	G. S. (Zool.)
Foster, Junia Marie,	Longmont, Colo.,	Eng.
Fraser, Rebecca Smith,	Lake Beulah,	Eng.
Fries, Mary Belle,	Richland Center,	Eng.
Funck, George William,	Milwaukee,	G. S.
Goodwin, John Edward,	Madison,	Eng.
Gorr, Charles William,	Milwaukee,	G. S.
Gregory, Alice Elizabeth,	Vergennes, Vt.,	Phil.
Greverus, Ernst,	New Holstein,	C. H.
Gribble, Greta Mae,	Platteville,	Phil.
Guile, Ella May,	Madison,	G. S.
Hall, Roy Dykes,	Burnett Junction,	G. S.
Hanson, Albert,	Eau Claire,	G. S.
Hardgrove, George Patrick,	Fond du Lac,	Eng.
Herrick, William Karl,	Cherokee, Ia.,	C. H.
Hibbard, Carlisle V.,	Racine,	G. S.
Hinkley, Louise,	Green Bay,	M. C.
Hobbins, Harry Mears,	Madison,	M. C.
Hoffman, Frank,	St. Wendell,	Eng.
Holden, Roy Jay,	Sheboygan Falls,	Eng. (Bot.)
Holmes, Harvey Robson,	Geneva, Minn.,	Phil.
Hook, Edward Alfred,	So. Milwaukee,	G. S.
Howe, Winfred Chester,	Sheboygan,	A. C.

Huenkemier, Etta L.,	Freeport, Ill.,	Eng.
Jackman, Marcia Maria,	Janesville,	M. C.
Jackson, Alice Fanny,	Madison,	M. C.
Johns, Richard B.,	Madison,	Phil.
Johnson, Axel Edward,	Madison,	A. C.
Johnson, Nora Francesca,	Rockdale,	M. C.
Jones, Oliver Milton,	Georgetown,	Phil.
King, Bessie Susan,	Neillsville,	M. C.
Kittleson, Andrew Ole,	Perry,	Eng. (Phil.)
Klinkhammer, Susan Catharine,	Cassville,	Phil.
Koch, Arthur Alexander,	Beaver Dam,	G. S.
Koffend, Joseph, Jr.,	Appleton,	Eng.
Kolb, Philip Amon,	Platteville,	Phil.
Lee, Kenelm Julius,	Chippewa Falls,	G. S.
Levitt, Sadie Rosalyn,	Grand Rapids, Mich.,	C. H.
Loeb, Joseph,	Appleton,	C. H.
Lowell, Susie Eugenia,	Janesville,	M. C.
Lucas, Sarah May,	Brodhead,	M. C.
Lyle, John Thomas Stuart,	Madison,	M. C.
Macartney, Albert Joseph,	Madison,	C. H.
MacGraw, Maud Mae,	Chippewa Falls,	M. C.
Macnish, Ralph Benjamin,	Madison,	C. H.
Maercklein, Ella Dorothea,	Milwaukee,	G. S.
McClernan, Marie,	Janesville,	A. C.
McDonald, Alexander Vaughan,	Fond du Lac,	G. S.
McFadden, Mary Isabel,	Oconto,	Phil.
McGilvra, Sarah Love,	Baraboo,	M. C.
McKenna, Corey Hugh,	Platteville,	G. S.
McKenna, Francis Eugene,	Madison,	Phil.
McNeel, James Herbert,	Fond du Lac,	A. C.
Minnick, Paul Willis,	Madison,	C. H.
Moldstad, John A.,	De Forest,	A. C.
Morris, Thomas Sherman,	Madison,	C. H.
Moseley, Wayne Thornton,	Madison,	C. H.
Moser, Alma Marie,	Ashland,	A. C.
Mosher, George Warner,	Prophetstown, Ill.,	C. H.
Murphy, Daniel Hayes,	Milwaukee,	G. S.
Nelson, Norman Oscar,	Madison,	G. S.
Neuman, Julius John,	Horicon,	Phil.
Nicholson, John Frederick,	Brodhead,	G. S.
Niven, John McKean,	Sheridan,	A. C.
Nuzum, Jessie Anne,	Viroqua,	Eng.

STUDENTS IN LETTERS AND SCIENCE—SENIORS.

Ochsner, Emma Julia,	Baraboo,	G. S.
Ogilvie, Jenny,	Madison,	Eng.
Orchard, Milton,	Shullsburg,	Phil.
Osborne, John Goodrich,	Milwaukee,	M. C.
Oscar, Stephen Albert,	Washburn,	Eng.
Palmer, Bernard Morey,	Janesville,	C. H.
Parks, Edna Mary,	Crystal Falls, Mich.,	A. C.
Pearce, Charles Sumner,	Walworth,	Eng.
Pearson, William Henry,	Lancaster,	Phil.
Pease, Raymond Burnett,	Oregon,	Eng.
Peet, Katherine Olive,	Chicago, Ill.,	G. S.
Peterson, Harold Stuart,	Delafield,	A. C.
Pfisterer, Clara,	Brodhead,	Eng.
Pierce, Helen Augusta,	Madison,	Eng.
Preuss, Bertha Helen,	Belle Plaine,	Phil.
Ramsay, Sarah Isabella,	Madison,	A. C.
Randall, May Inez,	Ladoga,	G. S.
Reed, Miriam Keith,	Madison,	M. C.
Richardson, Annice True,	Eldorado, Kan.,	C. H.
Roberts, David Milton,	Madison,	A. C.
Robinson, Irving Porter,	Milwaukee,	C. H.
Roethe, Emil Leo,	Whitewater,	Phil.
Ross, Lura Llora,	Hudson,	Eng.
Rothman, Emma,	Chilton,	Eng.
Ruediger, Gustav Ferdinand,	Alma,	G. S.
Runke, Richard,	Algoma,	G. S. (Phys.)
Russell, Henry Alexander,	Ft. Scott, Kan.,	C. H.
Saby, Sever,	Baldwin,	Phil.
Scanlan, Dennis Francis,	Madison,	C. H.
Scheer, George Henry,	Sheboygan,	G. S.
Schmidt, Gertrud Charlotte,	Wauwatosa,	M. C. (Ger.)
Schultz, Alfred Reginald,	Tomah,	G. S. (Phys.)
Seiler, Livia Estelle,	Alma,	M. C.
Shelden, Mabel,	Reedsburg,	Eng.
Shephard, William Henry,	Benton,	Phil.
Sherman, Gertrude,	Milwaukee,	A. C.
Slatter, Frances,	Sun Prairie,	G. S. (Math.)
Smith, Allard Johnston,	Milwaukee,	C. H.
Smith, Harry Gray,	Madison,	M. C.
Smith, Winifred Alice,	Wheaton, Ill.,	M. C.
Snow, Edwin Augustus,	Iron River,	C. H.
Sprague, Marie Louise,	Elkhorn,	M. C.

Stanton, Florence Belle,	*Warren, Ill.,*	M. C.
Steuber, Frederick John,	*Prairie du Sac,*	Phil.
Stevens, Edith Genevieve,	*Jefferson,*	Eng.
Strong, Mary Louise,	*Dodgeville,*	Eng.
Sutherland, William Chester,	*Madison,*	G. S.
Swain, Katharine Egerton,	*Milwaukee,*	A. C.
Swartz, George Willis,	*Arkansaw,*	Phil.
Taylor, Herman Henry,	*Barron,*	Eng.
Tearse, Clarence Dudley,	*Winona, Minn.,*	Eng.
Titus, Winifred,	*Oshkosh,*	G. S.
Underwood, Enoch William,	*Baltimore, Md.,*	Eng.
Utendorfer, William Elmer,	*Madison,*	G. S.
Valentine, Anna DeRiemer,	*Janesville,*	M. C.
Vallee, Francis Arthur,	*Racine,*	C. H.
Van Horn, Frederic Milo,	*Madison,*	A. C.
Warner, Fanny,	*Windsor,*	M. C.
Warner, Florence Maurine,	*Windsor,*	G. S.
Warriner, Helen Haskell,	*Portage,*	M. C.
Washburn, Robert Glendenning,	*Milwaukee,*	G. S.
Waters, Terese Frances,	*Fond du Lac,*	Phil.
Weber, Anna Katherine,	*Monroe,*	C. H.
Welsh, Eunice Wallace,	*Madison,*	M. C.
Whelan, Dutee Allen,	*Mondovi,*	Eng.
Willett, Thomas,	*Madison,*	G. S.
Williams, Daniel Jenkins,	*Genesee Depot,*	A. C.
Williams, Wirt Clay,	*Madison,*	Phil.
Winden, Julius,	*Monroe,*	Phil.
Winter, Paul Gerhard,	*Madison,*	Eng.
Wolcott, Edson Ray,	*Sharon,*	G. S. (Phys.)
Wolf, Herman Emil,	*LaCrosse,*	G. S.
Wright, Paul Randall,	*Monroe,*	A. C.
Yankey, Charles,	*Juneau,*	Eng.
Zimmerman, Viola May,	*Milwaukee,*	Phil.
		—191

Junior Class.

Allen, Eric William,	*Milwaukee,*	A. C.
Anderson, William Ballantyne,	*Madison,*	G. S. (Phys.)
Astle, Cora Alice,	*Prairie du Sac,*	Eng.
Baer, Clarence Allen,	*Milwaukee,*	Eng.
Baldwin, Arthur Algernon,	*Madison,*	C. H.
Ball, Sydney Hobart,	*Oak Park, Ill.,*	A. C.

STUDENTS IN LETTERS AND SCIENCE—SENIORS.

Barber, William Harley,	*Black Earth,*	G. S.
Barnes, Chester David,	*Kenosha,*	C. H.
Barney, Jessie Alice,	*Mayville,*	Eng.
Barney, John McHenry,	*West Bend,*	C. H.
Bartlett, Eliza Wheelock,	*Milwaukee,*	M. C.
Beebe, Claude Spencer,	*Milwaukee,*	G. S.
Bergstrom, Willis Charles,	*Neenah,*	C. H.
Beule, Arthur Franz,	*Beaver Dam,*	G. S.
Blackburn, Arthur William,	*Madison,*	A. C.
Blackburn, Kathryne Irene,	*Madison,*	Phil.
Boehm, Paul Waldemar Leopold,	*Wausau,*	C. H.
Bostwick, Harriet M.,	*Janesville,*	Eng.
Bradley, Harry Ernest,	*Madison,*	A. C.
Brahany, Mary Eleanor,	*Madison,*	M. C.
Bredsteen, Joseph,	*Stoughton,*	Phil. (Phil.)
Bridge, Burton Hathaway,	*Monroe,*	C. H.
Bross, Agnes Marie,	*Madison,*	M. C.
Brownson, Laura,	*Sharon,*	Eng.
Buchanan, Hubert Daniel,	*Rio,*	C. H.
Buchholz, William David,	*Whitehall,*	Eng.
Buell, Kate M.,	*Sun Prairie,*	G. S.
Burke, Laurance Charles,	*Chicago, Ill.,*	C. H.
Carr, William Jarvis,	*Aurora, Ill.,*	C. H.
Carthew, Harry Edward,	*Lancaster,*	C. H.
Caulkins, Annie Knower,	*Milwaukee,*	G. S.
Cavanaugh, Abbie,	*Shullsburg,*	Eng.
Clark, William Albert,	*Lucas,*	Phil.
Clemons, William Voltaire,	*Prairie du Sac,*	Phil.
Cook, Charles Robert,	*Platteville,*	Phil.
Curtis, Dorothea Hughes,	*Madison,*	A. C.
Curtis, George Gregory,	*Madison,*	Eng.
Cutler, Horace Eaton,	*Milwaukee,*	A. C.
Davidson, Flora Neil,	*Madison,*	Eng.
Davis, Herbert Wallace,	*Camp Douglas,*	Eng.
Dickinson, William Frederick,	*Rockford, Ill.,*	Eng.
Donnell, William Kyle,	*Mattoon, Ill.,*	C. H.
Downes, Robert Hugh,	*Oshkosh,*	C. H.
Dye, Daisy Rumina,	*Madison,*	Eng.
Ellsworth, Melvina Ruth,	*Oshkosh,*	Phil.
Emery, Sydney Lawton,	*Albion,*	Eng.
Ernst, Adolfine Bianaca,	*Watertown,*	Eng.
Evans, Caroline Whettan,	*Madison,*	G. S. (Math.)

Foley, May Genevieve,	*Wauwatosa,*	A. C.
Fritsche, Gustav Armin,	*Milwaukee,*	A. C.
Gilliland, Nellie,	*Winona, Minn.,*	Phil.
Graham, James Blain,	*Roberts,*	A. C.
Grandy, Adah Georgina,	*Sioux City, Ia.,*	M. C.
Groffman, George William,	*Berlin,*	Eng.
Hackett, Carrie Fern,	*Baraboo,*	Phil.
Hall, Claudia Jeanne,	*Madison,*	M. C.
Hancock, Eugene Thomas,	*Tomah,*	G. S. (Geol.)
Hart, Henry Isaac,	*Wild Rose,*	Eng.
Harvey, Edward Joseph,	*Racine Junction,*	G. S.
Hastie, Grace Reedal,	*Hartman,*	Eng.
Hektoen, Marie,	*Westby,*	M. C.
Henning, Albert Louis,	*Madison,*	G. S. (Chem.)
Hibbard, Harry William,	*St. Cloud, Minn.,*	Phil.
Holt, Robert Bugg,	*Columbia, Tenn.,*	A. C.
Hook, Fred Luther,	*So. Milwaukee,*	G. S.
Hoy, William Pierson,	*Woodstock, Ill.,*	C. H.
Hurlbut, Stephen Augustus,	*Madison,*	A. C.
James, Ella Blanche,	*Eau Claire,*	A. C. (Math.)
Johns, Lina Mae,	*Dodgeville,*	Phil.
Jones, Nellie Bertine,	*Oshkosh,*	Phil.
Jordan, John Henry,	*Ditter, Minn.,*	Phil.
Kavanaugh, Katherine Blanche,	*Madison,*	Eng.
Kelsey, Rachel Marjorie,	*Baraboo,*	Phil.
Knoff, Robert Ernest,	*Janesville,*	Eng.
Kohler, Marie Christine,	*Sheboygan,*	Eng.
Kroehnke, Jessie Pamelia,	*Thiensville,*	Eng.
Kuechenmeister, Florence Adell,	*West Bend,*	Eng.
Lachmund, Robert,	*Sauk City,*	Eng.
Lea, Harry Richard,	*Waupaca,*	C. H.
Lea, William Francis,	*Waupaca,*	C. H.
Leatherwood, Nannie Albaugh,	*Madison,*	Phil.
Libby, Benjamin,	*Madison,*	C. H.
Luhmann, Hugo Frank,	*Manitowoc,*	C. H.
Lyman, John Quinton,	*Kenosha,*	C. H.
Maurer, Robert Adam,	*Sheboygan,*	C. H.
McCullough, Frank Michael,	*Sturgeon Bay,*	G. S. (Math.)
McGowan, Fred C.,	*Eau Claire,*	Eng.
McGregor, Jessica Kennedy,	*Platteville,*	Phil.
Meinert, Herman Timothy,	*East Green Bay,*	M. C.
Meinhardt, Leonore Agnes,	*Burlington,*	Eng.

STUDENTS IN LETTERS AND SCIENCE—JUNIORS.

Michelson, Albert G.,	*Mt. Horeb,*	Eng. (Hist.)
Morgan, James Carlos,	*Hartford,*	C. H.
Muenich, Max Michael,	*Jefferson,*	G. S.
Mumford, Eugene Bishop,	*New Harmony, Ind.,*	G. S.
Mutch, James William,	*Elroy,*	G. S.
Nash, James Bertram,	*Centralia,*	G. S.
Neilson, Allan Samuel,	*Milwaukee,*	Eng.
Nelson, Carl Emil,	*Racine,*	C. H.
Newman, Mark Humphrey,	*Madison,*	A. C.
Noelke, Augusta Elizabeth,	*La Crosse,*	Eng. (Ger.)
Olman, Charles Oscar,	*Nora,*	Phil.
Pardee, Neely Eugene,	*Wausau,*	M. C.
Parkinson, Elizabeth,	*Darlington,*	Phil.
Patten, Edith Sylvia,	*De Kalb, Ill.,*	Phil.
Pelishek, Mary Helen,	*Manitowoc,*	Phil.
Pfund, August Herman,	*Madison,*	G. S. (Phys.)
Plumb, Ralph Gordon,	*Manitowoc,*	C. H.
Pollock, Alvin Charles,	*Hebron,*	Phil.
Pray, Allan Theron,	*Stevens Point,*	Phil.
Priestly, Thomas Mortimer,	*Madison,*	M. C.
Ridlington, Daniel James,	*Dell Rapids, S. D.,*	A. C.
Roethe, Emil Leo,	*Whitewater,*	Phil.
Rogers, George Arthur,	*Rice Lake,*	Phil.
Rohde, Hugo William,	*Milwaukee,*	G. S. (Chem.)
Rounds, Charles Ralph,	*Arkansaw,*	Phil.
Ruhoff, Otto Ernst,	*La Crosse,*	G. S.
Salisbury, Winifred,	*Oregon,*	Eng.
Sargeant, Harvey Oakes,	*Omro,*	A. C.
Sawyer, Elsa Amelia,	*Hartford,*	Eng.
Sawyer, Harriet Josephine,	*Hartford,*	Eng.
Schoensigel, Frederick Christian,	*Plymouth,*	Eng.
Schubring, Edward John B.,	*Sauk City,*	Eng.
Senn, George,	*Madison,*	G. S.
Sherman, Leta,	*Milwaukee,*	A. C.
Sias, Nellie Bly,	*Sparta,*	Eng.
Sime, Diana L.,	*Castle Rock,*	Phil.
Smith, Arthur Frank,	*Madison,*	G. S.
Smith, Ashbell V.,	*Waukegan,*	Eng.
Smith, August E.,	*Berlin,*	Eng.
Smith, Janet Maud,	*Wauwatosa,*	Phil.
Smith, Julia Forster,	*Madison,*	A. C.
Spaulding, Ida Mary,	*Oshkosh,*	Eng.

Stevens, John Charles,	Milwaukee,	A. C.
Stewart, Harriet Belle,	Brodhead,	Eng.
Stillman, Clara Luemma,	Milwaukee,	G. S.
Storms, Jeanette Boynton,	Madison,	Eng.
Stover, Paul,	Milwaukee,	A. C.
Thomas, Alice Elizabeth,	Waukesha,	M. C.
Thompson, Charles Lowry,	Davenport,	A. C.
Tracy, Lynn Hickok,	Madison,	A. C.
Verberkmoes, John Martin,	Madison,	G. S.
Vroman, William Phillips,	Green Bay,	M. C.
Walker, William Arthur,	Milwaukee,	M. C.
Warning, Edith Henrietta,	Elkhorn,	M. C.
Weber, August William,	Madison,	Phil.
Wehmhoff, Eugene John,	Burlington,	A. C.
Werner, Fred William,	Milwaukee,	G. S.
Westmore, Bert Frederic,	Milwaukee,	Eng.
White, Clarence Joel,	Monroe,	A. C.
White, Edith Estella,	Milwaukee,	Phil.
White, Florence May,	Rochester,	M. C.
Wilcox, Frances May,	Rockford, Ill.	C. H.
Williams, Charles A.,	Madison,	C. H.
Wilson Mary Lang,	Burlington,	G. S.
Woollen, Herbert Milton,	Indianapolis, Ind.,	G. S.
Wyssman, Arthur Joseph,	Manitowoc,	C. H.

—156

Sophomore Class.

Abbott, Maude Elinor,	Madison,	Eng.
Acker, Ruby May,	Brandon,	M. C.
Allen, Charles Chester,	Kenosha,	Eng.
Anderson, Peter Olson,	Brodhead,	G. S.
Angell, Martin Fuller,	Delavan,	G. S.
Astle, Celia Minerva,	Prarie du Sac,	M. C.
Ballard, Bernice M.,	Warren, Ill.,	Eng.
Barkhausen, Clara Marie,	Green Bay,	C. H.
Barr, James,	Milwaukee,	A. C.
Bascom, Lelia,	Chicago, Ill.,	Eng.
Beatty, Carlotta McCutcheon,	Madison,	A. C.
Beebe, Dwight Eastman,	Racine,	C. H.
Bergstrom, Lucius Seymour,	Neenah,	C. H.
Beye, William,	Oak Park, Ill.,	C. H.

Binzel, Paul Marie,	Milwaukee,	A. C.
Blake, Chauncey Etheredge,	Rockford, Ill.,	Eng.
Bolender, Edna,	Monroe,	M. C.
Bready, James Ely,	Dubuque, Ia.,	A. C.
Brennan, John Vincent,	Tomah,	M. C.
Brindley, John Edwin,	Boscobel,	C. H.
Bryning, Pearl Grace,	Madison,	A. C.
Bucklin, Frank Winslow,	Brodhead,	Eng.
Buehler, Henry Andrew,	Monroe,	G. S.
Buell, Ella Clara,	Sun Prairie,	Eng.
Buell, Phoebe Lucinda,	Sun Prairie,	Eng.
Button, Kittie Louise,	Milton Junction,	Eng.
Cady, Elsie Clare,	Green Bay,	C. H.
Campbell, William,	Gurnee,	C. H.
Carpenter, Fred Hiltman,	Evanston, Ill.,	C. H.
Case, Agnes Embree,	North Greenfield,	G. S.
Case, Wilhelmina Georgie,	Prarie du Chien,	A. C.
Castenholz, William Burtice,	Indianapolis, Ind.,	Eng. (Pol. Sc.)
Chamberlain, Alice Emily,	Madison,	Eng.
Clawson, Harvey,	Monroe,	A. C.
Clifford, Cecil Leslie,	Madison,	A. C.
Coe, Robert Kirtland,	Whitewater,	C. H.
Conway, Mayme Agnes,	Elroy,	Eng.
Coon, John Ward,	Madison,	Eng.
Cottrell, Bessie Etta,	Spencer, Ia.,	M. C.
Cronk, Victor Doughty,	Louisville,	C. H.
Cummings, Margaret Elizabeth,	Madison,	C. H.
Curtis, Arthur Hale,	Madison,	G. S.
Dahle, Otto Bjorn,	Mt. Horeb,	M. C.
Darby, Helen Louise,	Chicago, Ill.,	A. C.
Davidson, Agnes Viola,	Sun Prairie,	Eng.
Donnelly, Esther,	Milwaukee,	C. H.
Eiche, Adela,	Marshfield,	G. S.
Elliott, Ida,	Hinsdale, Ill.,	Eng.
Esch, Ella Lydia,	Sparta,	M. C.
Fairbank, Alfred Frank,	Ladoga,	Eng. (Math.)
Fish, Herbert Clay,	Madison,	C. H.
Fisher, Charlotte Ilsley,	Milwaukee,	G. S.
Fortney, Gerhard Olaus,	Viroqua,	G. S.
Foster, Paul Clark,	Silverlake,	G. S.
Frawley, Thomas Francis,	Eau Claire,	M. C.
Fulton, Blanche,	Hudson,	M. C.

Galusha, Nellie,	Monroe,	M. C.
Gamble, Alice Janet,	Madison,	C. H.
Gamble, Lilian,	Madison,	C. H.
Gapen, Anna Mercedes,	Madison,	C. H.
Gapen, Flora,	Madison,	G. S.
Gilbert, Ivah Lulu,	Madison,	Eng.
Glasier, Emma Belle,	Bloomington,	A. C.
Grebel, Charles John,	Milwaukee,	A. C.
Grotophorst, Alfred,	Prairie du Sac,	Eng.
Grover, Dana Irving,	Milwaukee,	C. H.
Gust, George Lewis,	Baraboo,	Eng.
Haight, Robert Wilber,	Waukesha,	C. H.
Harney, Leon Lewis,	Schofield,	C. H.
Hasse, August Frederick,	Wauwatosa,	M. C.
Hawley, Ada Lovisa,	Madison,	G. S.
Hayden, Grace Mae,	Sun Prairie,	Eng.
Hayes, Genevieve Marie,	Janesville,	C. H.
Hayner, Carolyn Virginia,	Madison,	A. C.
Heaton, Ruth,	Reedsburg,	M. C.
Hecht, Grace Aguilar,	Milwaukee,	C. H.
Higby, Kenneth Edwin,	Ripon,	C. H.
Hinkley, Marie Gardner,	Milwaukee,	G. S.
Holah, Carrie Gestina,	Baraboo,	M. C.
Holland, Julia Christine,	Moscow,	Eng.
Holland, Lillian Solvei,	Moscow,	Eng.
Hooley, Edna Lydston,	Wauwatosa,	C. H.
Hopkins, Walter Sawyer,	Leeds,	Eng.
Howard, Earle Clark,	Sparta,	Eng.
Huebner, Solomon,	Manitowoc,	Eng.
Hughes, Avis Ethel,	New Lisbon,	C. H.
Hughes, Harriet Louise,	Oshkosh,	C. H.
Inbusch, Arthur Philip Henry,	Milwaukee,	C. H.
Janes, Henry Lorenzo,	Racine,	C. H.
Johnson, Myron Reed,	Sheridan,	Eng.
Jones, Theodore Thomas,	Manitowoc,	Eng.
Kennedy, Louise Mida,	Madison,	Eng.
Kennedy, Margaret Julia,	Madison,	Eng.
Kirch, Nicholas,	Mazomanie,	Eng.
Knauf, Lorine Anna,	Chilton,	M. C.
Krape, Bessie Miriam,	Freeport, Ill.,	A. C.
Kratz, Bessie Mae,	Sioux City, Ia.,	Eng.
Lamberson, Leila Maud,	Richland Center,	Eng.

STUDENTS IN LETTERS AND SCIENCE—SOPHOMORES.

Lee, William Arthur,	Madison,	C. H.
Leihy, Edna Marie,	Bayfield,	M. C.
Leiser, Fred Oscar,	Baraboo,	Eng.
Lennon, Hawley Daniel,	Decorah, Ia.,	C. H.
Lloyd, Ada Crang,	Chicago, Ill.,	Eng.
Lohr, Lewis George,	Milwaukee,	C. H.
Long, Charles Edwin,	Davenport, Ia.,	G. S.
Lounsbury, Benjamin Franklin,	Pipersville,	Eng.
Lynch, Matt John,	Madison,	G. S.
Mansfield, Flora Frances,	Johnson Creek,	G. S.
Markham, George Francis,	Milwaukee,	M. C.
McCue, Nora Bryant,	Madison,	C. H.
McFarland, James Garfield,	Dubuque, Ia.,	A. C.
McMahon, Mayme Karnes,	Baraboo,	M. C.
Menzel, Walter Reginald,	Wausau,	C. H.
Merrill, Agnes,	Ashland,	A. C.
Meyer, Ernst Christopher,	Cedarburg,	G. S.
Miller, John Calkins,	Marinette,	Eng.
Moffatt, William Francis,	Davenport, Ia.,	A. C.
Moldstad, Nelly Catherine,	De Forest,	Eng.
Moorhouse, Edward Percy,	Springfield,	Eng.
Morrison, Bessie Lorraine,	Dixon, Ill.,	Eng.
Murdock, Harry Dale,	Brodhead,	G. S.
Nash, Lawrence Eugene,	Centralia,	G. S.
Nevins, John Wilson,	Burlington, Ia.,	G. S.
Nolah, Carrie Gestina,	Baraboo,	M. C.
Olbrich, Michael Balthasar,	Lawrence, Ill.,	Eng.
O'Meara, John Albert,	West Bend,	Eng.
Palmer, Bess Gail,	Madison,	M. C.
Parsons, John Burnham,	Whitewater,	C. H.
Patrick, John Bartow,	Oak Park, Ill.,	C. H.
Peckham, Mary Gifford,	Milwaukee,	Eng.
Pesta, Rose Alice,	Milwaukee,	Eng.
Phipps, Stephen Carpenter,	Hudson,	A. C.
Pickford, Merle Sears,	Madison,	Eng.
Powers, John Francis,	Mayhew,	Eng.
Prichard, Helen McGregor,	Janesville,	M. C.
Ramsey, Florence Harriet,	Reedsburg,	M. C.
Rehberg, Fred Herman,	Brodhead,	Eng.
Renwick, Lucie Olive,	Kirkland, Ill.,	C. H.
Richardson, Berl DeWitt,	Valma, Ind.,	G. S.
Roddis, Frances Mary,	Marshfield,	G. S.

Rosenheimer, Lehman Peter,	Kewaskum,	Eng.
Ross, Josephine,	Milwaukee,	M. C.
Runner, Olive Grace,	Freeport, Ill.,	C. H.
Ryan, William,	Prairie du Sac,	Eng.
Sage, Jeannette Limbert,	Delavan,	C. H.
Sage, Laura Elisabeth,	Delavan,	C. H.
Sanborn, Katharine Wentworth,	Madison,	A. C.
Sauthoff, Harry,	Madison,	A. C.
Scholz, Richard Frederick,	Milwaukee,	A. C.
Schorer, Edwin Henry,	Plymouth,	G. S.
Schroeder, Percy Edward,	Racine,	G. S.
Schule, Frederick William, Jr.,	Chicago, Ill.,	G. S.
Schwab, Edward Charles,	Milwaukee,	G. S.
Seeber, Sarah Jennie,	Waterloo,	M. C.
Sharpe, Raymond Garfield,	Vernon,	G. S. (Math.)
Shaw, Florence Madeline,	Sioux City, Ia.,	A. C.
Sherman, Helen.	Milwaukee,	G. S.
Sherrill, Jennie Bentley,	Rockford, Ill.,	C. H.
Shimmins, Zalla Mary,	Delavan,	Eng.
Simonds, Charlotte Mayo,	Hartland,	G. S.
Smith, Warren Du Pré,	Madison,	G. S.
Smith, William Edward,	Madison,	C. H.
Spence, Florence Mitchell,	Somers,	C. H.
Spooner, Philip Loring,	Madison,	A. C.
Stark, Norma Mildred,	Davenport, Ia.,	Eng.
Stedman, Maude Frances,	Berlin,	Eng.
Steere, Glen S.,	Plymouth,	G. S.
Stephenson, Maud Martha,	Madison,	M. C.
Stockman, Ruth,	Mason City, Ia.,	A. C.
Stolte, Freda Dorothea,	Reedsburg,	M. C.
Strehlow, Max Hugo Richard,	De Forest,	C. H.
St. Sure, Frank Adolph,	Sheboygan,	G. S.
Stucki, Anna,	Milwaukee,	G. S.
Swain, Mary Brayton,	Milwaukee,	A. C.
Swoboda, Frank George,	Troy,	G. S.
Taylor, John William,	Taylorville, Ill.,	C. H.
Thompson, Edith Carrie,	Madison,	M. C.
Ticknor, Elizabeth Gaffe,	Madison,	A. C.
Tormey, Ella Frances,	Madison,	M. C.
Uihlein, Arthur Benedict,	Milwaukee,	C. H.
Van Velzer, Clara Johnson,	Madison,	M. C.
Vinson, George Bryant,	Milwaukee,	M. C.

STUDENTS IN LETTERS AND SCIENCE—FRESHMEN.   305

Vogel, Frederick August,	Milwaukee,	C. H.
Waite, Willis Willard,	Brooklyn,	G. S.
Wedge, Fred,	Rhinelander,	Eng.
Winkler, Henry Overbeck,	Milwaukee,	A. C.
Witwen, Emma Susan,	Baraboo,	M. C.
Wolfenson, Louis Bernard,	Madison,	A. C.
Wright, Mary,	Petersburg, Ill.,	C. H.

—189

Freshman Class.

Adams, William Gormly,	Cottage Grove,	A. C.
Aiken, Gertrude Emeline,	Evanston,	Eng.
Aiken, Helen Roselia,	Evanston,	M. C.
Almquist, Carl Gustave Wilhelm,	Delavan,	A. C.
Ames, John Quincy,	Brooklyn,	G. S.
Anderson, Julia Marjorie,	Racine,	M. C.
Andrews, Ruth Catherine,	Hudson,	Eng.
Ansley, Marion,	Hudson,	Eng.
Atwater, William Whittlesey,	Chicago, Ill.,	C. H.
Baker, Alonzo Clark,	Madison,	Eng.
Barnard, David Luther,	Earlville, Ill.,	M. C.
Bauer, Oscar Hugo,	Brownsville,	Eng.
Beaver, Grace May,	Baraboo,	O. H.
Beers, Leslie Weymouth,	Rhinelander,	Eng.
Bennett, Persis May,	Belleville,	G. S.
Berg, Bryngel Cornell,	Madison,	C. H.
Bevans, Alice Jean,	Decatur, Ill.,	M. C.
Bigelow, George Tyler, Jr.,	Milwaukee,	A. C.
Bird, Mabel Meigs,	Madison,	M. C.
Birge, Edward Grant,	Madison,	G. S.
Bishop, Edwin Sherwood,	Somers,	C. H.
Bissell, Elizabeth Cacendra,	Madison,	Eng.
Blair, Edwin Roberts,	Waukesha,	Eng.
Bogue, Andrew Stevenson,	Arlington,	Eng.
Bossard, Gertrude Melin,	So. Kaukauna,	M. C.
Bradley, Grace Marie,	Madison,	Eng.
Brant, Charles Edwin,	La Grange, Ind.,	Eng.
Brindley, Willis Edge,	La Crosse,	C. H.
Brown, Rufus Choate, Jr.,	Oshkosh,	Eng.
Burbank, Robert Dillon,	Cedarburg,	A. C.
Byrne, Eugene Hugh,	Baraboo,	C. H.
Cady, Charles Raymond,	Green Bay,	C. H.

Campbell, Anna Belle,	*De Forest,*	Eng.
Carpenter, Henry Fayette,	*Janesville,*	C. H.
Carter, Perry John,	*Mauston,*	C. H.
Challoner, George,	*Oshkosh,*	M. C.
Chapman, Frank Johnson,	*New Richmond,*	Eng.
Chapman, Raymond Morgan,	*Milwaukee,*	G. S.
Churchill, Myron Robert,	*Marinette,*	C. H.
Cleverdon, Vernon Burnham,	*Austin, Ill.,*	C. H.
Clough, Paul Wiswall,	*Portage,*	G. S.
Cole, Halbert Benton,	*Black River Falls,*	Eng.
Coleman, Mary Persis,	*Chippewa Falls,*	M. C.
Condit, Dudley Norman,	*Chippewa Falls,*	G. S.
Conlin, Matthew Francis,	*Madison,*	Eng.
Conway, Edward Power,	*Manitowoc,*	M. C.
Cook, Herbert Lee,	*Moline, Ill.,*	G. S.
Craigo, Cathaleen Mae,	*Monroe,*	M. C.
Crary, Charles Judson,	*Boone, Ia.,*	C. H.
Crawford, Robert Storey,	*Mineral Point,*	Eng.
Cunningham, Mary Florence,	*Chippewa Falls,*	C. H.
Currie, William Boyd,	*Milwaukee,*	A. C.
Curtis, Ernest Ezra,	*Madison,*	Eng.
Curtis, Walter Eugene,	*Wausau,*	Eng.
Davey, Luella Josephine,	*Janesville,*	G. S.
Davison, Sarah Margaret,	*Beaver Dam,*	Eng.
Dessaint, Edna,	*Davenport, Ia.,*	A. C.
Devlin, Edward Charles,	*Milwaukee,*	G. S.
Disque, Robert Conrad,	*Burlington, Ia.,*	M. C.
Dixon, Grace Shirley,	*Milwaukee,*	M. C.
Dodson, Truman Monroe,	*Berlin,*	G. S.
Dougherty, James Francis,	*Lyndon Station,*	Eng.
Eastman, Vera,	*Richland Center,*	Eng.
Eggers, Harold Everett,	*Two Rivers,*	G. S.
English, Callista Angeline,	*Kenosha,*	A. C.
Erickson, Oscar Gustav,	*Canby, Minn.,*	Eng.
Evert, Karl,	*Madison,*	G. S.
Fairchild, Herbert Bigelow,	*Green Bay,*	C. H.
Fish, Irving Andrews,	*Milwaukee,*	A. C.
Fish, Lorenzo Ezra, Jr.,	*Madison,*	G. S.
Flemming, Lucinda Elizabeth,	*Madison,*	G. S.
Flint, Joseph Turner,	*Menomonie,*	Eng.
Foelske, Henry Edward,	*National Home,*	C. H.
Foster, Wilbur Thomas,	*River Falls,*	C. H.

STUDENTS IN LETTERS AND SCIENCE—FRESHMEN.

Fox, Galen Addis,	*Durand,*	G. S.
Frambach, Carl Lewis,	*Kaukauna,*	C. H.
Friedman, Rufus Judah,	*Iron River,*	C. H.
Gibbons, Robert Oliver,	*Cottage Grove,*	Eng.
Gilbert, Newell Clark,	*Austin, Ill.,*	G. S.
Gillespie, Edwin Simpson,	*Madison,*	G. S.
Gray, Mary,	*Madison,*	M. C.
Gregory, Clarence William,	*West DePere,*	M. C.
Griesel, Julius Johannes,	*Crown Point, Ind.,*	M. C.
Griffith, Stephen Melville,	*Milwaukee,*	M. C.
Gromann, Ralph Sasse,	*Crown Point, Ind.,*	M. C.
Hagenah, William John August,	*Madison,*	Eng.
Haight, William Harrison,	*Rockdale,*	Eng.
Halbach, Norma Catherine,	*Green Bay,*	Eng.
Hale, Berndt Severin,	*Waupaca,*	M. C.
Halverson, Martin,	*Sheboygan,*	C. H.
Hamilton, William George,	*Marinette,*	C. H.
Hammersley, Charles Edward,	*Madison,*	C. H.
Hatch, Bernice Clara,	*Sturgeon Bay,*	Eng.
Heavenrich, Alvin Trounstine,	*Ashland,*	M. C.
Hebenstreit, Mary Teresa,	*Shullsburg,*	Eng.
Heller, George, Jr.,	*Sheboygan,*	C. H.
Helmholz, Henry Fred,	*Milwaukee,*	G. S.
Heuer, George Julius,	*Madison,*	G. S.
Hobbins, Mary Katherine,	*Madison,*	Eng.
Hogan, John Thomas,	*Janesville,*	Eng.
Holt, Robert,	*Alanson, Mich.,*	A. C.
Hopkins, Andrew Winkle,	*Leeds,*	Eng.
Horsfall, Lloyd Patzlaff,	*Prairie du Chien,*	C. H.
Humphrey, May Martin,	*Bloomington,*	A. C.
Hunt, Fred Ralph,	*Sioux City, Ia.,*	A. C.
Jenkins, Mary Lucretia,	*Swaledale, Ia.,*	C. H.
Johnson, Almira Catherine,	*Milwaukee,*	M. C.
Johnson, Mary Maurine,	*Centralia,*	G. S.
Jones, Chester Lloyd,	*Hillside,*	C. H.
Jorstad, Osmund Marcellus,	*LaCrosse,*	M. C.
Juneau, William Joseph,	*North Greenfield,*	Eng.
Kasberg, Alexander,	*Madison,*	Eng.
Kelling, Max John,	*Milwaukee,*	G. S.
Kellogg, Elbert Cutting,	*Centralia,*	Eng.
Kimball, Josephine Peyton,	*West Superior,*	M. C.
King, Anna Belle,	*Madison,*	Eng.

Klinkert, George Peter,	Racine,	G. S.
Knobel, Fred Henry,	Edgerton,	G. S.
Kolter, Jacob Henry,	Wausau,	G. S.
Koltes, Anna,	Madison,	Eng.
Kraus, Robert Peter,	Marshfield,	Eng.
Kuelling, Herbert John,	Shullsburg,	C. H.
Kutchin, Victor Sherwood,	Dartford,	G. S.
Laube, Herbert David,	Brodhead,	C. H.
*Lawrence, Albert William,	Lomira,	Eng.
Leighton, Leslie Sherman,	Omro,	Eng.
Lerum, Arne Christopher,	Cottage Grove,	Eng.
Libby, Lyman Arnquist,	New Richmond,	Eng.
Liljeqvist, Andrew Lawrence,	Wausau,	C. H.
Ludlow, Charles Arabut,	Monroe,	M. C.
Madsen, Carl Theophilus,	Centralia,	Eng.
Maguire, Beach Woodruff,	Rockford,	Eng.
Marlott, Frank Herbert,	Racine,	C. H.
Martin, Agnes J.,	Dubuque, Ia.,	G. S.
Mathews, Joseph Howard,	Auroraville,	G. S.
Matteson, Gertrude Sarah,	Davenport, Ia.,	A. C.
McCrossen, Jay Woodward,	Edgar,	C. H.
Merrill, Elinor,	Ashland,	M. C.
Michelson, Regina,	River Falls,	M. C.
Mihills, Guinevieve,	Fond du Lac,	M. C.
Miller, Wallace William,	Ravenswood, Ill.,	G. S.
Minahan, Eben Roger,	Green Bay,	Eng.
Minch, Rosalie Julia,	Paoli,	Eng.
Moore, Leora Lloyd,	Madison,	M. C.
Mosher, May Louise,	Sandwich, Ill.,	Eng.
Murly, Earl Warner,	Shullsburg,	Eng.
Murphy, Henry Edward,	Manitowoc,	A. C.
Murphy, John Vincent,	Hoard,	Eng.
Murphy, William Keenan,	Milwaukee,	Eng.
Nate, Bessie Rae,	Madison,	C. H.
Nelson, Tillie Eliza,	Token,	Eng.
Odell, Mabel,	Des Moines, Ia.,	M. C.
Oftelie, Ezra Thaddeus,	Madison,	Eng.
Olsen, Nora Louise,	Madison,	M. C.
Osborne, Julia Sherlock,	Madison,	M. C.
Osborne, Mary Patricia,	Madison,	M. C.
Otjen, Henry Heames,	Milwaukee,	Eng.
Parkinson, Nell Farnham,	Columbus,	M. C.

* Deceased, February 19, 1900.

Parks, Howell,	*Oconomowoc,*	A. C.
Pelton, Jessie Mary,	*Edgerton,*	M. C.
Perham, George Addison,	*Racine,*	C. H.
Perry, Jessie Ellen,	*Madison,*	M. C.
Peterson, Peter Verner,	*E. Marinette,*	Eng.
Pettigrew, Etta Salome,	*Sioux Falls, S. D.,*	A. C.
Pickard, Rawson Joseph,	*Maywood, Ill.,*	M. C.
Pinkerton, Robert Eugene,	*Mazomanie,*	G. S.
Poage, George Coleman,	*LaCrosse,*	C. H.
Pollard, Frederic Ring,	*Portage,*	C. H.
Pope, Lena Meleta,	*Mayville,*	Eng.
Post, Beulah Celecta,	*Dubuque, Ia.,*	M. C.
Primakow, Jacob,	*Milwaukee,*	C. H.
Pullen, Lloyd Winston,	*Milwaukee,*	C. H.
Putnam, Daphne Wilton,	*Waukesha,*	M. C.
Pyre, Amelia France,	*Madison,*	M. C.
Quammen, Menorah,	*Madison,*	M. C.
Rahr, Louis Frederick,	*Kenosha,*	C. H.
Reitman, Arthur,	*Milwaukee,*	G. S.
Renwick, Joe Clyde,	*Warren, Ill.,*	A. C.
Rider, Melinda Catherine,	*Dubuque, Ia.,*	C. H.
Reidy, Salena Marguerite,	*Madison,*	M. C.
Riley, William Walter,	*Erin,*	Eng.
Ross, Clara Isabel,	*Cherokee, Ia.,*	C. H.
Ross, Samuel Crawford,	*Mineral Point,*	C. H.
Roybar, Bertie M.,	*Madison,*	G. S.
Rumsey, Edith Arabel,	*Milwaukee,*	C. H.
Runo, Victor Emanuel,	*Scandinavia,*	A. C.
Rutishauser, Emil Albert,	*Aurora, Ill.,*	G. S.
Safford, Ruth Bogardus,	*Peebles,*	M. C.
Salter, Vera Belle,	*Unity,*	Eng.
Schmidt, William Frederick,	*Manitowoc,*	C. H.
Schobinger, Anna Rosalia,	*Shullsburg,*	Eng.
Schuette, Paul August,	*Manitowoc,*	C. H.
Schule, Paul Adolph,	*Chicago, Ill.,*	A. C.
Sedgwick, John Fordman,	*Whitewater,*	Eng.
Seidenglanz, Emil Tellesford,	*Kewaunee,*	Eng.
Shaw, Lulu Pearl,	*Wauwatosa,*	A. C.
Shower, Albert Edward,	*De Forest,*	Eng.
Slinde, Hans Norman,	*De Forest,*	Eng.
Slinde, Imelia Josephine,	*De Forest,*	Eng.
Smith, Phebe Maud,	*Juda,*	Eng.

Snider, Glen Rust,	Kilbourn,	Eng.
Sprecher, John Henry,	Independence,	Eng.
Stange, August John,	Merrill,	Eng.
Stemple, Carolyn,	Madison,	M. C.
Stetler, Pearlie Mae,	Richland Center,	Eng.
Stevens, Genevieve,	Boone, Ia.,	C. H.
Stevenson, Robert George,	E. Marinette,	Eng.
Stewart, Earle Bryan,	Mason City, Ia.,	G. S.
Stewart, Howard,	Delavan,	Eng.
Stewart, Mitchell Charles,	Wausau,	Eng.
Stone, Charles Harry,	Reedsburg,	Eng.
Storm, Anna,	Plainfield,	Eng.
Sweet, Belle,	Clinton, Ia.,	Eng.
Sykes, Angus Cameron,	Madison,	G. S.
Tarbox, Edna Laura,	La Crosse,	C. H.
Telford, Mae Pearl,	Mason City, Ia.,	M. C.
Thompson, Charles Scott,	Oshkosh,	G. S.
Thuerer, Edward Walter,	Baraboo,	Eng.
Toepfer, Rose Marie,	Madison,	M. C.
Tourtellotte, Augustus Monroe,	La Crosse,	Eng.
Townsend, Clyde Louis,	Shullsburg,	A. C.
Turner, Lura Jane,	Columbus,	M. C.
Updegraff, Mary,	Decorah, Ia.,	M. C.
Van Orden, Lucas Schuyler,	Baraboo,	C. H.
Van Patten, Lulu May,	Albany,	G. S.
Walter, George Adelbert,	Berlin,	G. S.
Washburn, Stuart Erdman,	Racine,	C. H.
Weber, Minna Elizabeth,	Watertown,	M. C.
Wedemeyer, Adrian August,	Sheboygan,	Eng.
Wehe, Waldemar Carl,	Milwaukee,	C. H.
Wells, Josephine Adelaide,	Portage,	C. H.
Wente, Robert Campbell,	Manistee, Mich.,	G. S.
Werder, Hudson Bernard,	Charles City, Ia.,	Eng.
White, Rhoda Mabel,	Chicago, Ill.,	C. H.
Wilkins, Robert Lee,	Viroqua,	C. H.
Williams, Stephen Ellsworth,	River Falls,	G. S.
Winch, Samuel Howard,	Marshfield,	G. S.
Winslow, Wirt,	Ft. Atkinson,	Eng.
Wood, Helen Pearl,	Monroe,	M. C.
Wood, Norma Curtis,	Madison,	M. C.
Wood, Philip Aurey, Jr.,	Baraboo,	Eng.
Wrabetz, Vojta,	Kewaunee,	Eng.

Wright, Mignon,	*Madison,*	M. C.
Zinns, Roland,	*Milwaukee,*	A. C.
		—244

Special Students.

Alden, Violet Minerva,	*Neenah,*	C. H.
Anderson, Harry Bennett,	*Memphis, Tenn.,*	C. H.
Anderson, Lela,	*Augusta,*	Eng.
Baker, Grace Lyle,	*Racine,*	Eng.
Baldwin, Bessie Russell,	*Sparta,*	Eng.
Bennett, Claudia Adele,	*Hazel Green,*	Eng.
Bent, Ruth,	*Morrison, Ill.,*	Eng.
Bishop, Jennie Frank,	*Dillon, Mont.,*	Eng.
Blake, Emmons Reed,	*Port Washington,*	Eng.
Blood, Henrietta Ada,	*Madison,*	M. C.
Bradley, Mabel Josephine,	*Madison,*	M. C.
Brugger, Harvey,	*Clyde, Ohio,*	G. S.
Butt, Jennie Hannah,	*Viroqua,*	Eng.
Butzke, Earnest John,	*Beechwood,*	G. S.
Casson, Henry, Jr.,	*Madison,*	C. H.
Chandler, Zach Anson,	*Oregon,*	Eng.
Chilcote, Warren Alexander,	*Rosendale,*	Eng.
Clark, Emily Blanche,	*Galesville,*	Eng.
Clark, William Bernard,	*Belleville,*	Eng.
Cook, Catherine Myers,	*Madison,*	M. C.
Corstvet, Alexander Oscar,	*Deerfield,*	Eng.
Cummings, Mary Irene,	*Rock Valley, Ia.,*	M. C.
Dale, William Henry,	*Iola,*	Eng.
Dopp, Homer Rodger,	*Oconomowoc,*	G. S.
Driver, Sephus Earl,	*Darlington,*	Eng.
Du Four, Clarence John,	*Milwaukee,*	G. S.
Ellis, Ard Hoyt,	*Vinton, Ia.,*	Eng.
Everett, Dorothy Jane,	*Sparta,*	Eng.
Ferguson, Bessie Caroline,	*Madison,*	Eng.
Fishburn, Donald Brady,	*Aurora, Ill.,*	Eng.
Fisher, Clarence Bennett,	*Little Rock, Ark.,*	Eng.
Fisher, Harry White,	*Belvidere, Ill.,*	C. H.
Fisher, William Edwin,	*Sheridan,*	Eng.
Foster, Junia Marie,	*Longmont, Colo.,*	Eng.
Fraser, John Francis,	*Lake Geneva,*	Eng.
Fuller, Marian Holcomb,	*Meadville, Pa.,*	C. H.
Gabel, George Herman,	*Milwaukee,*	C. H.

Gaffin, Charles Harold,	Leaf River, Ill.,	C. H.
Goddard, Jennie Mae,	Freeport, Ill.,	Eng.
Goddard, Mabel,	Freeport, Ill.,	Eng.
Godshall, Winifred Elodie,	Oshkosh,	A. C.
Grinde, Sadie Mabelle,	De Forest,	Eng.
Grindell, Arthur Bates,	Platteville,	G. S.
Gund, Torrey,	Freeport, Ill.,	Eng.
Hanson, Louis Hedden,	Eau Claire,	G. S.
Hardy, Ella Streeter,	Platteville,	M. C.
Henry, John Rex,	Fremont, Neb.,	C. H.
Higgins, Samuel George,	Rhinelander,	G. S.
Hollen, Richard Hamlin,	Eau Claire,	Eng.
Holty, Edward Olai,	Newark, Ill.,	C. H.
Horton, Angelo Burgess,	Oregon,	Eng.
Houser, Ethel Isabel,	Mondovi,	Eng.
Hunter, Charles Dana,	Merrill,	Eng.
Ireland, Cady Clifford,	Washburn, Ill.,	C. H.
Jackson, Bettina,	Madison,	Eng.
Jackson, Joseph William,	Madison,	C. H.
Jacobsen, Anna,	Stoughton,	Eng.
James, Frances Sophia Courtenay,	Eau Claire,	M. C.
John, Herbert Frank,	Milwaukee,	C. H.
Johnson, Amy Sophia,	Madison,	Eng.
Johnson, Harry C.,	Madison,	C. H.
Kahn, Rene Robert,	Milwaukee,	C. H.
Kasberg, Tinora Luthera,	Madison,	
Kemler, Clara,	Platteville,	
Kennedy, Amy Annie,	Madison,	Eng.
Knilans, Inez,	Whitewater,	C. H.
Leggett, James Wesley,	Eau Claire,	Eng.
Lewis, Carl Henry,	Sparta,	C H.
Loeb, Louise,	Apple?	M. C.
Luce, Mary Maude,	Chi!	Eng.
Main, Frances Cecelia,		M. (
Malloy, Kathryn Gertrude,	.or.	Eng.
Martin, Edith Bonar,	Ill,	
Mason, Marquis Edgar,	Ill.	
Masters, Harry John,		
Mathews, Delbert F		
McCartney, Clare		
McGrath, Mar		
McKee, Paul		

SPECIAL STUDENTS.

McKinnon, Donald James,	*Eau Claire,*	Eng.
Miller, Harry Edward,	*Grand Rapids,*	Eng.
Mowry, George Albert,	*Sturgeon Bay,*	Eng.
Muckleston, E. Milo,	*Waukesha,*	M. C.
Nalty, Josephine Agnes,	*Monroe,*	A. C.
Nelson, Florence Eugenia V.,	*Madison,*	C. H.
Nelson, Nelson Bastian,	*Eau Claire,*	Eng.
Newman, Esther Marion,	*Algoma,*	Eng.
Newton, Cordelia Lydia,	*Bangor,*	C. H.
Niles, Sidney Cleveland,	*Oak Park, Ill.,*	G. S.
Nohelty, Patrick,	*Lake Geneva,*	Eng.
North, Charles Raymond,	*Madison,*	Eng.
Oakland, Harry Gustave,	*Milwaukee,*	G. S.
O'Brien, Edwin Thomas,	*Eau Claire,*	Phil.
Owen, Dale,	*Lake Geneva,*	G. S.
Paddock, Carrie,	*Berlin,*	Eng.
Paetow, Louis John,	*Milwaukee,*	C. H.
Peck, Roy Walter,	*Milwaukee,*	M. C.
Pelton, Anna May,	*Madison,*	Eng.
Perry, Minnie Marie,	*Algoma,*	Eng.
Pickford, Theo. Beatrice,	*Madison,*	Eng.
Price, Maude Azalia,	*Wellington, Kan.,*	Eng.
Ramstad, Albert George,	*Eau Claire,*	G. S.
Ranseen, Carl Matthew,	*Chicago, Ill.,*	Eng.
Ranum, Blanche Hilma,	*La Crosse,*	G. S.
Raymer, Ethel Frances,	*Madison,*	M. C.
Regan, Katherine Patritia,	*Madison,*	Eng.
Rice, Maud Azalia,	*Wellington, Kan.,*	Eng. (Phil.)
Rich, Mabel Irene,	*Monticello, Minn.,*	Eng.
Richardson, Clarence Lemuel,	*Chippewa Falls,*	G. S.
Rhodes, Alfred John,	*Galesville,*	C. H.
Roethke, Adolph Herman,	*Chilton,*	Eng.
Rosenheimer, Marie Eliza,	*Schleisingerville,*	Eng.
Ryan, John Henry,	*Lodi,*	C. H.
Runzler, William Theodore,	*Milwaukee,*	A. C.
Savage, May Lillian,	*Madison,*	A. C.
Sawyer, John Flynn,	*Hammond, Ind.,*	Eng.
Sewards, Robert Lincoln,	*New York, N. Y.,*	Eng.
Seydel, James Albert, Jr.,	*Chippewa Falls,*	Eng.
Shadbolt, Alexander,	*Brooklyn, Ia.,*	M. C.
Shields, Joseph Ralph,	*Pewaukee,*	G. S.
Smith, Adolph Belmont,	*Brooklyn,*	G. S.

Smith, Morton Weir,	*Waupun*,	Eng.
Smith, Winifred Mary,	*Sturgeon Bay*,	Eng.
Stephens, Leila Celeste,	*Dixon, Ill.*,	C. H.
Stewart, Mabel Irene,	*Mason City, Ia.*,	Eng.
Stinehart, Charles Emerson,	*Mason City, Ia.*,	Eng.
Stone, Belva Gladys,	*Bloomington*,	Eng.
Stoner, Mary Gertrude,	*Madison*,	M. C.
Terwilliger, Walter Edward,	*Madison*,	Eng.
Thompson, Ethel Adele,	*Darlington*,	M. C.
Thompson, Helen Gladys,	*Eau Claire*,	G. S.
Throwe, Elizabeth Davies,	*Watertown*,	Eng.
Trelevan, Elizabeth Mayham,	*Fond du Lac*,	Eng.
Truax, Edyth Yates,	*Chicago, Ill.*,	C. H.
Urban, William,	*Plainfield*,	Eng.
Walker, Ellis Janet,	*So. Kaukauna*,	Eng.
Walters, William Alexander,	*Chicago, Ill.*,	Eng.
Watson, John Charles,	*Livingston*,	Eng.
Welsh, Stanley Carpenter,	*Madison*,	G. S.
Wentworth, Daisybelle,	*Milwaukee*,	Eng.
Werner, Henry William,	*Eau Claire*,	Eng.
Whare, George Bartholomew,	*Madison*,	G. S.
Whitcomb, Georgiana,	*Madison*,	G. S.
Williams, Callafern Ann,	*Grand Rapids*,	Eng.
Williams, Elias Robert,	*Genesee Depot*,	Eng.
Williams, Jason P.,	*Sparta*,	C. H.
Winkenwerder, Hugo August,	*Watertown*,	G. S.
Winn, Howard Hinsdale,	*Kansas City, Mo.*,	M. C.
Wright, Herbert Benjamin,	*Ishpeming, Mich.*,	Eng.
		—149

Adult Specials.

Allen, Elsie Caroline,	*Lake Geneva.*
Anderson, Mina Aletha,	*Argyle.*
Balsley, Edith Rachel,	*Madison.*
Bardeen, Eleanor Martha,	*Madison.*
Barnard, Elizabeth,	*Earlville, Ill.*
Barton, Ella Andria,	*Mt. Vernon.*
Bates, Walter Eugene,	*Retreat.*
Berg, Martin John,	*Madison.*
Beymer, Arthur Frank,	*Corning, Ia.*
Bishop, Sidney Harold,	*Milwaukee.*
Bold, Mabel Dixon,	*Madison.*

SPECIAL STUDENTS.

Brochhausen, Anna Mary,	*Indianapolis, Ind.*
Burke, Eva Dell,	*Houghton, S. Dak.*
Clifford, Elmer David,	*Madison.*
Cover, Ben,	*Ashland.*
Davis, Robert Moses,	*Madison.*
Ehlman, Albert Charles,	*Milwaukee.*
Erwin, Clara Louise,	*Milwaukee.*
Esterly, Heloise Gai,	*Madison.*
Esterly, Henry Minor,	*Madison.*
Ferris, Edith Agnes,	*Chicago, Ill.*
Fischer, Amelia Christina,	*Milwaukee.*
Fisher, Nellie Mathilda,	*Wauwatosa.*
Fleming, Helen Josephine,	*Madison.*
Freeborn, Lorene Oina,	*Richland Center.*
Froelich, Clara Garner,	*Milwaukee.*
Gannon, Thomas Melvin,	*Cedarburg,*
Gohlke, George Henry,	*Madison.*
Harrigan, Frank Elwood,	*Madison.*
Harris, Sally Prime,	*Madison.*
Henkes, David Albert,	*Madison.*
Herfurth, Elizabeth Marie,	*Madison.*
Holden, James Edmund,	*Mt. Horeb.*
Houser, Mortimer A.,	*Mondovi.*
Jacobs, Charlotte Mathilda,	*Madison.*
Johnson, Fred, Jr.,	*Madison.*
Johnson, Jesse Worthington,	*Sterling, Ill.*
Kelley, Helen Florence,	*Rensselaer, Ind.*
Kreutzer, Oscar William,	*Cedarburg.*
Kundert, John Emil,	*Mazomanie.*
Langenbach, Armand Gilbert,	*Mayville.*
Ludlow, May,	*Monroe.*
Marshall, Frances Belle,	*Rensselaer, Ind.*
Mathes, George,	*Elkhart.*
Meggett, Harriet,	*Madison.*
Merrill, Lillie McDonald,	*Burlington.*
Minahan, Mary Elizabeth,	*Madison.*
Montgomery, Janette Louise,	*Madison.*
Morris, Carl Edward,	*Madison.*
Nelson, Ingebor Marie,	*Sturgeon Bay.*
Nyswander, Ada May,	*Napoleon.*
Ogihara, Tokujo,	*Tokio, Japan.*
Parker, Bertha Gifford,	*Madison.*

Pelton, Jessie Myrtle, Madison.
Philips, George Chase, West Salem.
Pope, Anna Dickinson, Amherst, Mass.
Preston, Frederick Grant, Wichita, Kan.
Pyre, Mary Henrietta, Madison.
Reed, Evan Laforest, Oregon, Ill.
Roemer, Emma Marie, Madison.
Sawin, Franklin, Three Oaks, Mich.
Sherwood, Jessye Lyra, Mt. Vernon, Ia.,
Smyth, Herman Augustine, Madison.
Soucy, Pierre Emmanuel Fitte, Madison.
Steel, Bella Georgiena, Dixon, Ill.
Sutton, John James, Jr., Columbus.
Swartz, Mamie E., River Falls.
Sylvester, Fred West, Milwaukee.
Talbert, Franklin Lilburn, West Side, Cal.
Tatum, Edward Howland, Guanajuato, Mexico.
Thompson, Verne Roy, McFarland.
Vivian, William Albert, West Superior.
White, Alice Caton, New York, N. Y.
Williams, John, Sun Prairie.
Williams, Margaret Ellen, Ottawa.
Williamson, Richard, Madison.
Winegar, George Lee, Morrison, Ill.

—77

COLLEGE OF MECHANICS AND ENGINEERING.

Senior Class.

Ahara, Theodore Henry,	Evansville,	M. E.
Barnes, Charles Ballou,	Denrock, Ill.,	M. E.
Baus, Richard Edward,	Madison,	M. E.
Buttles, Ben E.,	Waterford,	E. E.
Cook, Thomas Russell,	Oshkosh,	M. E.
Dixon, John Edward,	Milwaukee,	M. E.
Emerson, Frederick Merrill,	Milwaukee,	C. E.
Farris, James Archibald,	Fennimore,	M. E.
Fowler, Myron Marshall,	Wauwatosa,	E. E.
Granke, Leo Ernest,	La Crosse,	C. E.
Harvey, John LeRoy,	Mondovi,	M. E.
Heald, Eugene Hamilton,	Oak Park, Ill.,	C. E.
Hedke, Charles Richard,	Racine,	C. E.

STUDENTS IN ENGINEERING—JUNIORS.

Hegg, John Richard,	*Cumberland,*	C. E.
Hoyt, Warren Albert,	*Madison,*	C. E.
Humphrey, Clifford Wane,	*Waterloo,*	E. E.
Hunner, Earl Emmet,	*Madison,*	C. E.
Icke, John Frederick,	*Marshfield,*	C. E.
Lindem, Olaf James,	*Marinette,*	C. E.
Marvin, Arba B., Jr.,	*Oregon,*	E. E.
McArthur, Arthur Royal,	*Johnstown Center,*	M. E.
Merrick, Eldridge Gerry,	*Danbury, Conn.,*	E. E.
Minch, Walter Bernhard,	*Madison,*	M. E.
Moore, Lewis Eugene,	*Chicago, Ill.,*	M. E.
Nelson, Clarence Lotario,	*Racine,*	C. E.
Older, Clifford,	*Portage,*	C. E.
Parsons, Walter Jay,	*Chicago, Ill.,*	C. E.
Radtke, Albert Augustus,	*Milwaukee,*	E. E.
Rhine, Charles Augustus,	*Milwaukee,*	E. E.
Sands, Edward Emmet,	*Sparta,*	C. E.
Schmitt, Frederick Emil,	*Green Bay,*	C. E.
Seaman, Harold,	*Milwaukee,*	E. E.
Smith, Sydney Thomas,	*Sturgeon Bay,*	C. E.
Stone, Melvin Bailey,	*Madison,*	C. E.
Wasmansdorf, Otto Francis,	*Madison,*	C. E.
Weed, Louis Burgess,	*Bristol,*	C. E.
Whomes, Harry Richard,	*Baraboo,*	M. E.
Williams, Lynn Alfred,	*Milwaukee,*	M. E.
Williamson, Edward Lucius,	*Janesville,*	C. E.
Wipfler, Robert Edwin,	*Detroit, Mich.,*	C. E.

—40

Junior Class.

Abbott, Clarence Eugene,	*Madison,*	M. E.
Atkins, Hubbard Chandler,	*Milwaukee,*	M. E.
Bachelder, Clare H.,	*Madison,*	M. E.
Bachelder, Frank Jerome,	*Madison,*	C. E.
Barkhausen, Louis Henry,	*Green Bay,*	M. E.
Berry, Claude,	*Madison,*	C. E.
Buerstatte, Frederick William,	*Manitowoc,*	M. E.
Bunker, George Tracy,	*Woodstock, Ill.,*	M. E.
Burdick, William Courtnay,	*Milwaukee,*	C. E.
Carter, Archy Bert,	*Humbird,*	C. E.
Colbert, Lawrence Clarence,	*Whitewater,*	M. E.

Collins, Charles Graham,	West Bend,	C. E.
Countryman, Merton Alvin,	Detroit, Mich.,	C. E.
Curtis, Norman Philip,	Madison,	C. E.
Dean, Charles Lyman,	Seymour,	M. E.
Ferris, Harold Gano,	Carthage,	M. E.
Fricke, August Charles,	Milwaukee,	M. E.
Hartman, Rudolph,	Milwaukee,	C. E.
Hawn, Russell John,	Stevens Point,	C. E.
Hirschberg, Walter Paul,	Milwaukee,	C. E.
Hurd, John Thomas,	Oregon,	C. E.
Hurd, Nathaniel Leslie,	Chippewa Falls,	M. E.
King, Arthur Charles,	Chicago, Ill.,	M. E.
Kirk, Allen Taylor,	Atlanta, Ill.,	M. E.
Leahy, John Hamilton,	Madison,	E. E.
Legg, Ernest Friend,	Wausau,	E. E.
Little, Frederick Arthur,	Fond du Lac,	M. E.
Lorch, John August,	Madison,	C. E.
Meffert, Edward Persie,	Wonewoc,	C. E.
Meyers, Alvin,	Verona,	E. E.
Morrow, Homer,	Spring Green,	M. E.
Murphy, Merritt Norton,	Twin Lakes,	E. E.
Nicolaus, Albert Adam,	Beaver Dam,	E. E.
Palmer, Ray,	Madison,	E. E.
Peele, Hereward John,	Madison,	E. E.
Plumb, Hylon Theron,	Milton,	E. E.
Rodgers, Edward Hill,	Albany, N. Y.,	C. E.
Rollmann, Alfred,	Chilton,	E. E.
Rowell, Lewis Dow,	Madison,	E. E.
Salsich, Le Roy,	Hartland,	C. E.
Sanborn, Roy Asa,	Janesville,	E. E.
Schapper, Kurt,	Chicago, Ill.,	M. E.
Severson, Harry Ashton,	Milwaukee,	C. E.
Smith, James Elmo,	Sharon,	C. E.
Street, Lester Chapin,	Madison,	C. E.
Townsend, Hubert Isaac,	Poynette,	E. E.
Vea, Fritchjof Johnson,	Stoughton,	M. E.
Washburn, Frank Edwin,	Sturgeon Bay,	C. E.
Watson, Charles Henry,	Milwaukee,	M. E.
Williams, Lester Dennison,	Fox Lake,	C. E.
Wood, Henry Harrison,	Stebbinsville,	M. E.

—51

Sophomore Class.

Adams, Bertram Francis,	*Chicago, Ill.,*	M. E.
Adams, Robert Elmore,	*Beloit,*	E. E.
Adams, Walter Kelsey,	*Oneonta, N. Y.,*	C. E.
Allen, Charles Chester,	*Kenosha,*	C. E.
Anderson, Gustave,	*West Salem,*	M. E.
Baer, Edward Sherman,	*Appleton,*	M. E.
Balding, Henry Alfred,	*Milwaukee,*	E. E.
Balsley, Eugene Albert,	*Madison,*	C. E.
Benson, Gillett Amos,	*Black River Falls,*	C. E.
Berg, William Carl,	*Ft. Atkinson,*	C. E.
Boardman, Howard Gilman,	*Milwaukee,*	C. E.
Boldenwick, Felix William,	*Chicago, Ill.,*	M. E.
Bump, Milan Ray,	*Spokane, Wash.,*	E. E.
Cole, Charles Melville, Jr.,	*Appleton,*	M. E.
Cole, Harry West,	*Milwaukee,*	M. E.
Cotton, Charles Sumner,	*Friendship, N. Y.,*	E. E.
Cummins, Frank Sherman,	*Des Moines, Ia.,*	C. E.
Davies, George Gibson,	*Racine,*	M. E.
De Lay, Frederic Abraham,	*Madison,*	E. E.
Diehl, Guy Elmon,	*Elroy,*	C. E.
Dow, Herbert William,	*Milwaukee,*	E. E.
Earle, Roy Raymond,	*Darlington,*	E. E.
Early, Arthur Numa,	*Milwaukee,*	E. E.
Ehreke, Gustave William Richard,	*Wausau,*	E. E.
Ehrnbeck, Anton Daniel,	*Appleton,*	C. E.
Fairman, Alonzo Stephen,	*Brodhead,*	C. E.
Gapen, J. Clark,	*Monroe,*	E. E.
Gardner, Stephen,	*St. Paul, Minn.,*	E. E.
Gibson, William Johnson,	*Hartland,*	M. E.
Greaves, Arthur Clayton,	*Spencer, Ia.,*	C. E.
Grey, J. Chester,	*Windsor,*	M. E.
Gund, Joseph Albert,	*Freeport, Ill.,*	C. E.
Hadfield, Ray Harrison,	*Chicago, Ill.,*	E. E.
Hammerschlag, James Garfield,	*Milwaukee,*	M. E.
Hansen, Guido, Jr.,	*Milwaukee,*	E. E.
Helmicks, Gordon Alexander,	*Deerfield,*	E. E.
Hippenmeyer, Irving Raymond,	*Madison,*	M. E.
Hughes, Edward Henry,	*Spokane, Wash.,*	M. E.
Jenson, Carl William,	*River Falls,*	C. E.
Johnson, Maurice Ingolf,	*Madison,*	M. E.

Kelley, Patrick John,	Manitowoc,	E. E.
Kimball, John Ritchie,	Kenosha,	E. E.
Kindt, Albert Frederick,	Milwaukee,	C. E.
Kohl, Oliver Bernard,	Antigo,	E. E.
Kutzke, Charles Julius,	Portage,	E. E.
Lathrop, William Frederick,	Racine,	E. E.
Mabbett, Walter Franklin,	Edgerton,	C. E.
McCollister, C. Ward,	Whitehall, Ill.,	C. E.
McDonald, Leroy Lemuel,	Rochester,	C. E.
McEvoy, George Edward,	Milwaukee,	M. E.
McNeill, Harry Thomas,	Sheboygan,	M. E.
Moore, Sherman,	Brodhead,	C. E.
Murray, Archie Rolfe,	Madison,	E. E.
Mutchler, Carl Bertolette,	Madison,	C. E.
Nichols, Raymond Eugene,	Onalaska,	E. E.
Olsen, Arthur Carl,	Madison,	C. E.
Olson, Sidney,	Racine,	C. E.
Pengra, Preston Winfield,	Madison,	E. E.
Polley, George Andrew,	Albertville,	C. E.
Reichow, Emil Frederick,	Watertown,	C. E.
Rowe, Leonard Louis,	Madison,	M. E.
Saunders, Arthur Bernard,	Milton,	E. E.
Schroeder, John Toby,	Hartford,	C. E.
Scott, George Alvin,	Oshkosh,	E. E.
Skonnord, Norman Olaf,	La Crosse,	C. E.
Spencer, Lloyd-Garrison,	Madison,	C. E.
Starks, Sanford Putnam,	Madison,	M. E.
Stevens, Chester Harris,	Mason City, Ia.,	C. E.
Stieler, Frederick Carl,	Stevens Point,	E. E.
Stillman, Carl Frederic,	Milwaukee,	M. E.
Stockman, Louis,	Milton Junction,	C. E.
Sunderland, Ira Croft,	Hartford,	C. E.
Thorkelson, William Louis,	Racine,	M. E.
Vanderloot, William John,	Chicago, Ill.,	C. E.
Ware, Julian Vivian,	Evansville, Ind.,	E. E.
White, Charles Marcus,	Delafield,	E. E.
Wilson, John,	Dodgeville,	C. E.
Yeager, Clive,	Madison,	E. E.
Young, Henry Walter,	Prairie du Sac,	E. E.
Zimmerman, Clarence Irving,	Milwaukee,	E. E.

—80

STUDENTS IN ENGINEERING—FRESHMEN.

Freshman Class.

Adams, Benjamin Cullen,	*Madison,*	E. E.
Alexander, Archie Ferguson,	*Madison,*	M. E.
Anderson, Arthur Edward,	*Janesville,*	M. E.
Armstrong, James Arthur,	*Ashland,*	E. E.
Belanger, John Charles,	*Grand Rapids,*	C. E.
Belling, John William,	*Mondovi,*	E. E.
Bennett, William Bryant,	*Mineral Point,*	E. E.
Bertke, William John,	*Milwaukee,*	E. E.
Bingham, Joseph Inhoff,	*Lockwood, N. Y.,*	C. E.
Bishop, Warren Joseph,	*Milwaukee,*	C. E.
Borden, Fred Guy,	*Plainfield,*	E. E.
Brewer, Roscoe Varnum,	*Hurley,*	E. E.
Brown, Lewis Raymond,	*Oshkosh,*	E. E.
Cadby, John Nelson,	*Waukesha,*	E. E.
Chamberlain, Fred Arthur,	*Madison,*	E. E.
Coon, Ira Lyman, Jr.,	*Plainfield,*	C. E.
Corlie, Glenn Cooper,	*Madison,*	M. E.
Cowley, Arthur William,	*Spokane, Wash.,*	E. E.
Crandel, Willis Earl,	*Plainfield,*	E. E.
Crowe, Edward Lawrence,	*Chicago, Ill.,*	E. E.
Dean, Garrison Culy,	*Eau Claire,*	M. E.
Dean, John Seabury,	*Madison,*	M. E.
Dessert, Howard Louis,	*Mosinee,*	C. E.
Dodge, Charles Warren, Jr.,	*Milwaukee,*	M. E.
Douglass, Courtney Carlos,	*Fontana,*	M. E.
Driscoll, Daniel Mathew,	*Antigo,*	C. E.
Ehrnbeck, Arthur Rudolph,	*Appleton,*	C. E.
Ekern, Emil Alfred,	*West Superior,*	E. E.
Elliott, Howard Stickney,	*Dell Rapids, S. D.,*	E. E.
Evans, Evan Samuel,	*Sparta,*	E. E.
Foster, Rollins Nelson,	*Reedsburg,*	C. E.
Frendberg, August Fred,	*Ashland,*	C. E.
Friend, John Henry,	*Antigo,*	E. E.
Fuller, Fay Noyes,	*Elkhorn,*	M. E.
Fulmer, Joseph Wellington,	*Florence,*	E. E.
Garvens, Gustav Walter,	*Wauwatosa,*	C. E.
Geerlings, Henry John, Jr.,	*Milwaukee,*	E. E.
Gilman, James Moseley,	*Madison,*	C. E.
Goodenough, Charles Frederick,	*West de Pere,*	M. E.
Goudie, James,	*Ironwood, Mich.,*	E. E.

Griffin, Edward,	*Eagle,*
Haase, Alvin,	*Milwaukee,*
Hahn, John Francis,	*Tyndall, S. D.,*
Hall, Edwin Morgan,	*Chicago, Ill.,*
Haman, Morris Emile,	*Milwaukee,*
Hamilton, Elmer William,	*Hyde,*
Hansen, Frederick William,	*Madison,*
Hatleberg, Christian C.,	*Keyeser,*
Hawley, Edward James,	*Green Bay,*
Hejda, Charles Joseph,	*Manitowoc,*
Hejda, Charles William,	*Manitowoc,*
Hill, Minot James,	*Almond,*
Holloway, Don Clement,	*Janesville,*
Hotchkiss, William Otis,	*Eau Claire,*
Huels, Frederick William,	*Madison,*
Hughes, Frank Japheth,	*Omaha, Neb.,*
Hulberg, Oscar Harvey,	*La Crosse,*
Johnson, Arthur Lewis,	*Chicago, Ill.,*
Keachie, George Robertson,	*Dubuque, Ia.,*
Krumrey, Robert Garfield,	*Plymouth,*
Lachmund, Bruno,	*Sauk City, Ia.,*
Lathrop, Leigh Hunt,	*Delavan,*
Laurgaard, Olaf,	*La Crosse,*
Lea, Harry Leslie,	*Iron River,*
Levisee, Lester Halford,	*Clintonville,*
Lynch, Daniel Webster,	*West Bend,*
Lyons, Benjamin Franklin,	*Appleton,*
Manington, Joseph Alfred,	*Chicago, Ill.,*
Marvin, Frank Conway,	*Zumbrota, Minn*
*McGuire, John Richard,	*Aurora, Ill.,*
McNitt, Gilbert Fayette, Jr.,	*Racine,*
McNown, William Coleman,	*Houston,*
Moorehouse, Louis Benjamin,	
Morrison, Rowland Hill,	
Mott, William Roy,	
Mueller, Edgar Bruno,	
Noyes, Clifford Henry,	
Olson, Herman Edw	
Page, Harry Willa	
Parfrey, Charles	
Patton, Howard	

STUDENTS IN ENGINEERING—FRESHMEN.

Peirce, Andrew Elmer,	*Madison,*	C. E.
Peotter, Reuben Sylvester,	*Appleton,*	C. E.
Peters, Charles Sumner,	*Dodgeville,*	E. E.
Perritt, Fred Robert,	*Fargo, N. D.,*	C. E.
Pugh, John, Jr.,	*Racine,*	E. E.
Quigley, Arthur Joseph,	*Fontana,*	E. E.
Ripley, George William,	*Iron River,*	E. E.
Rowe, William Jonathan,	*Warren, Ill.,*	E. E.
Rueping, Louis Henry,	*Fond du Lac,*	M. E.
Saridakis, Frank John,	*Milwaukee,*	M. E.
Saunders, Henry Jenness,	*Council Bluffs, Ia.,*	C. E.
Savage, John Lucian,	*Madison,*	C. E.
Saxton, Willard Roy,	*Berlin,*	C. E.
Schniglau, Charles Herbert,	*Chicago, Ill.,*	E. E.
Seaman, Irving,	*Milwaukee,*	E. E.
Sickels, William Wheelock,	*Evanston, Ill.,*	M. E.
Sheldon, Frank De Salle,	*Milwaukee,*	C. E.
Slater, Charles James,	*Escanaba, Mich.,*	M. E.
Southworth, Ray Lloyde,	*Mondovi,*	M. E.
Spalding, William,	*Oshkosh,*	E. E.
Toogood, James Earle,	*Manchester, Ia.,*	E. E.
Torkelson, Martin Wilhelm,	*Black River Falls,*	C. E.
Treber, Albert Philip,	*Deadwood, S. D.,*	E. E.
Trevarthen, Dwight Clyde,	*Madison,*	M. E.
Trowbridge, Paul,	*Columbus,*	M. E.
Urquhart, Norman Anthony,	*Medford,*	C. E.
Vanderhoof, Ernest Rockwell,	*Black River Falls,*	C. E.
Walker, James Alexander,	*Rockford, Ill.,*	M. E.
Watson, Charles Thomas,	*Baraboo,*	C. E.
Weber, Frederic Carl,	*Fond du Lac,*	E. E.
Wehe, August George,	*Milwaukee,*	C. E.
Weigen, Anders Elia,	*Sun Prairie,*	E. E.
Whitney, Charles Ray,	*Waukegan, Ill.,*	M. E.
Wilde, Frank August,	*Milwaukee,*	M. E.
Wollaeger, Edwin Fred,	*Milwaukee,*	E. E.
Woodruff, Leslie Bateman,	*Milwaukee,*	C. E.
Woy, Frank Palmer,	*Sparta,*	E. E.
Zimmerman, James Garfield,	*Milwaukee,*	E. E.

Special Students.

Anderson, Bertie Samuel,	Hartford,	M. E.
Atkinson, Oliver Curtis,	Chicago, Ill.,	E. E.
Bailey, Hiram Edwin,	Madison,	E. E.
Brenning, William Hobart,	Columbus,	E. E.
Campbell, Willard Van Brunt,	Horicon,	E. E.
Chamberlain, Paul Fairfield,	Madison,	C. E.
Cowie, Harry James,	West Superior,	C. E.
Cutcheon, Lewis Dana,	Grand Rapids, Mich.,	C. E.
Dean, Earle Stewart,	Hinsdale, Ill.,	C. E.
Dorschel, Oscar Lucas,	Chilton,	E. E.
Eaton, William Dunseith,	Kenosha,	C. E.
Frick, Orlando H.,	Antigo,	C. E.
Goodsell, Charles Glenn,	La Crosse,	E. E.
Grant, John Forrest,	Whitewater,	M. E.
Haskins, Edwin Easter,	Milwaukee,	M. E.
Haun, Franklin Elijah,	Syracuse, N. Y.,	M. E.
Jones, Frank William,	Milwaukee,	E. E.
Lacey, Frank Herbert,	Chamberlin, S. D.,	E. E.
Lewis, Arthur Warner,	Madison,	C. E.
Long, James Cozby,	Tiskilwa, Ill.,	C. E.
McKay, Clyde Marshall,	Chippewa Falls,	M. E.
McKee, Louis Alvan,	Madison,	M. E.
Perry, Claude Halpine,	La Crosse,	C. E.
Pesta, Martin Henry,	Milwaukee,	M. E.
Sawyer, George Kingsley,	Carpentersville, Ill.,	M. E.
Simmons, George Matthews,	Viola,	E. E.
Smith, Robert Tynes, Jr.,	Baltimore, Md.,	M. E.
Smyth, Edwin Willis,	Stuart, Ia.,	E. E.
Tait, John Martin,	Chicago, Ill.,	M. E.
Taylor, John Clarence,	Barron,	E. E.
Trine, Virgil Christian,	Madison,	M. E.
Westergaard, Christian,	Buffalo, N. D.,	M. E.
Whittemore, Herbert Lucien,	Milwaukee,	M. E.

—33

COLLEGE OF AGRICULTURE.

Long Course.

Davies, Llewellyn Rhys,	Madison,	Freshman.
Funk, Robert Stephen,	La Crosse,	Junior.
Gaffin, Benjamin Hiestand,	Leaf River, Ill.,	Sophomore.

STUDENTS IN AGRICULTURE—SHORT COURSE.   325

Michels, John,	*Calumet Harbor,*	Senior.
Olson, George Alfred,	*Madison,*	Sophomore.
Richards, William Bonner,	*Racine,*	Freshman.
Ross, John Agard,	*Hinsdale, Ill.,*	Sophomore.
Starke, Conrad Godlieb,	*Milwaukee,*	Freshman.
Taylor, Frederick Dan,	*Bates, Ill.,*	Junior.

—9

Short Course (Second Year.)

Abbott, Orlo,	*Appleton.*
Abbott, Willard,	*Appleton.*
Anderson, George Ankerberg,	*Whitehall.*
Anderson, Leroy,	*Ithaca, N. Y.*
Anderson, Abraham,	*Wilder, Minn.*
Arneson, Clarence Martin,	*Mt. Horeb.*
Atwood, John Roy,	*Roscoe, Ill.*
Bailey, Homer Edwin,	*Cobb.*
Bass, John Edward,	*Beloit,*
Bell, Herbert Charles,	*Leitersburg, Md.*
Bennett, Charles Shattuck,	*Belvidere, Ill.*
Bibby, William Arroll,	*Glasgow.*
Boardman, Francis Hamilton, Jr.,	*Boardman.*
Bokma, Bokke Alberts,	*Lake Geneva.*
Cannon, Elbert Amos,	*Marcellon.*
Carlyle, Adam,	*Lynd, Minn.*
Clark, Lafayette Franklin,	*West Brattleboro, Vt.*
Convey, Frank,	*Ridgeway.*
Cummins, William Mitchell,	*New York, N. Y.*
Danielson, Alfred,	*Irving.*
Davis, L. Howard,	*Sparta.*
Drissen, Peter John,	*Alaska.*
Erickson, Conrad,	*West Salem.*
Fay, Albert William,	*New Richmond.*
Foll, Otto,	*Deerfield.*
Freeman, George Albert,	*Madison.*
Fried, Gandenz,	*Fountain City.*
Froggatt, George,	*Ashton.*
Gillespie, Earl Lawrence,	*Kilbourn.*
Gordon, Jesse Roy,	*Mineral Point.*
Graffien, Amil Otto,	*Deerfield.*
Grubb, Max,	*Carbondale, Colo.*
Hackett, Charles Henry,	*Baraboo.*

Hackett, Granville Prescott, — Baraboo.
Hammond, Fred Lawrence, — Eau Claire.
Hanchett, George Edwin, Jr., — Sparta.
Hardie, Laverd Ernest, — Glasgow.
Hitchcock, Homer Ross, — Pecatonica, Ill.
Hobbs, Ross Melvin, — Madison.
Holtz, John Christ, — Columbus.
Huebbe, Edgar Ernst, — Watertown.
Jeffery, William James, — Shullsburg.
Jennings, Warren Price, — Chippewa Falls.
Jensen, James, — Lind.
Jensen, William Christian, — Waupaca.
Jones, Eben Ezra, — Rockland.
Klein, Emil R., — Fountain City.
Kosso, Charles, — Algoma.
Kukowinski, John, — Sharon.
Larson, Casper, — Bloomer.
Lawson, Wilfred Irving, — Browning.
Little, George Dixon, — Janesville.
Lobre, Andrew, — Madison.
Mattison, Thomas, — Blair.
McClure, Ara Morgan, — Manhattan, Ill.
McClure, Mark Sydney, — Manhattan, Ill.
McRae, Frank Wallace, — West Salem.
Nelson, Louis, — Argyle.
Nicolaus, David Christopher, — Troy Center.
Niven, William Irving, — Sheridan.
Nix, Herman Joseph, — Nix Corners.
Oleson, James Peter, — Ripon.
Pachernigg, Anthony, — Taylor.
Paden, Harry B., — Kasbeer, Ill.
Phelps, Frank Fletcher, — Granton.
Price, Albert Charles, — South Byron.
Reineking, Lorenz Fred, — Franklin.
Roesch, Clyde Earl, — Potosi.
Russell, Arthur Clark, — Augusta.
Rust, Shirley Horatio, — Mukwonago.
Sarver, Wesley M., — Pecatonica, Ill.
Sattler, James Henry, — W. Rosendale.
Sauers, Abe, — Bluff Siding.
Schmidt, John Joseph, — Wayne.
Schwartz, John Joseph, — Troy Center.

Sherman, William,	*Reedsburg.*
Storer, Willis Andrew,	*Swaledale, Ia.*
Swartzlow, John Julius,	*Sparta.*
Tate, George Harvey,	*La Farge.*
Taylor, John Martin,	*La Grange.*
Thomas, Charles William,	*Baraboo.*
Tomkins, William Clark,	*Ashland.*
Tratt, Ralph,	*Whitewater.*
Underwood, Laurence Charles,	*Avoca.*
Van Slyke, Melvin David,	*Centreville.*
Welles, Merritt Lyman,	*Pike, N.Y.*
Wilkinson, Ralph Negley,	*Alto, Ia.*

—87

Short Course (First Year.)

Alton, Elmer,	*Mifflin.*
Andrus, Robert,	*Reedsburg.*
Armour, Robert Mittchell,	*Mondovi.*
Atwood, George Gleasman,	*Roscoe, Ill.*
Baker, Ralph,	*Blandinsville, Ill.*
Baker, Roscoe Ernest,	*Britt, Ia.*
Bauer, John Wilson,	*Naperville, Ill.*
Borgen, Martin Ingwald,	*Dallas.*
Brinkman, Albert,	*Lancaster.*
Bumgarner, William Leslie,	*Magnolia, Ill.*
Burrows, Harry,	*Boardman.*
Burton, Roy,	*Palmyra.*
Carncross, George Irving,	*Lodi.*
Carter, Ralph Wesley,	*Osseo.*
Castle, Fred S.,	*Buffalo Prairie, Ill.*
Cheney, Charles Walter,	*Washington, O.*
Clark, Charles Francis,	*Babcock.*
Clark, David Bert,	*Rock Prairie.*
Clark, John Daniel,	*Johnstown.*
Clausing, Adolph,	*Bartel.*
Comer, Elmer,	*St. Croix Falls.*
Cooper, Charles James,	*Ladoga.*
Cornelius, Brigman,	*Oneida.*
Craig, Henry Alonzo,	*Elida, Ill.*
Cramer, John Jacob,	*Marshfield.*
Cronkhite, Nettie L.,	*Hastings, Neb.*
Curran, George D.,	*Madison.*

Curtiss, William Rudolph,	*Trevor.*
Cutler, Louis Hezekiah,	*East Dubuque, Ill.*
Cutting, Walter Livingston,	*Pittsfield, Mass.*
Dana, Ralph Elsworth,	*Sparta.*
Danks, Arthur Garfield,	*Allamuchy, N. J.*
Davis, Porter H.,	*St. Johns, Mich.*
DeLong, Ralph Webster,	*Leon.*
Dietrich, John,	*Black River Falls.*
Dittinger, William Fred,	*Northfield.*
Doelle, William Andrew,	*Doelle.*
Downer Arthur George,	*Appleton.*
Duecker, Herman John,	*Kiel.*
Dutton, Carroll Arthur,	*Centerville.*
Ellis, Frank Henry,	*Mt. Hope.*
Ellis, James Archer,	*Woodman.*
Eno, John L.,	*Luana, Ia.*
Eno, William H.,	*Sheffield, Ia.*
Evans, David William,	*Columbus.*
Fleishauer, Charles Kendall,	*Tarrant.*
Ford, James Allison,	*De Soto.*
Fox, Almeron Horace,	*Menominee.*
Fruth, Loy Miles,	*Fostoria.*
Fuiten, Benjamin Henry,	*Ripon.*
Ganschow, Henry F.,	*Bonduel.*
Geller, Henry,	*Chicago, Ill.*
Gillett, Rufus Atwood,	*Fitchburg.*
Glasgow, Warren Carlish,	*Waterloo, Ia.*
Gordon, Clifford Dale,	*Mineral Point.*
Graffien, William Herman,	*Deerfield.*
Haddleton, Walter John,	*Hinsdale, Ill.*
Hanson, Martin Nodaasen,	*Hollandale.*
Hanson, Tellef,	*Elcho.*
Haseltine, William Erwin,	*Baraboo.*
Hatch, Watson Irvin,	*Richland Center.*
Hockney, Chester Lionel,	*Antioch, Ill.*
Holman, Clair Roderick,	*Waupaca.*
Holt, Emil Eber,	*Ono.*
Howard, Alonzo,	*Melrose.*
Hubbard, Sherman,	*Evansville.*
Imholt, Benjamin Andrew,	*Houlton.*
Instenes, Lars,	*Melrose.*
Jackson, Perry,	*Argyle.*

STUDENTS IN AGRICULTURE—SHORT COURSE.

Jennings, Frank,	*Chippewa Falls.*
Jensen, Walter Peter,	*Waupaca.*
Johnson, William Oscar,	*South Wayne.*
Keyes, William,	*Grand Rapids.*
Korf, Jesse,	*Forreston, Ill.*
Lampland, Gilbert M.,	*Hayfield, Minn.*
Larson, James Martin,	*Mt. Morris.*
Larson, Ole Even,	*Emerald Grove.*
Larson, Samuel,	*Dallas.*
Lassen, Christian Wildfang,	*Winnetke, Ill.*
Lehmann, William,	*Neosho.*
Liebe, John Herman, Jr.,	*Grand Rapids.*
Lien, Alfred,	*Blanchardville.*
Linton, Forrest,	*Ft. Atkinson.*
Lord, James Wesley,	*Neenah.*
Lytle, John Leroy,	*Luana, Ia.*
Macauley, Robert Henry,	*Dunnville,*
Mann, Bruno Max,	*San Francisco, Cal.*
Malec, Louis,	*Madison.*
Martin, Harley A.,	*Richland City.*
Mason, Claude Miren,	*Albion.*
May, John,	*West Bend.*
McGeachie, Edward Peter,	*Rockford, Ill.*
Mildenhauer, Gustav Carl,	*Rube.*
Miles, John,	*Stone Bank.*
Miritz, Alfred,	*Kewaskum.*
Moore, Charles Kellogg,	*Wauwatosa.*
Moyle, Milton Cecil,	*Yorkville.*
Murphy, Robert Gamble,	*Woodbine, Penn.*
Neeley, William Charles,	*Pecatonica, Ill.*
Nickel, Charles D.,	*Waupaca.*
Nicols, Charles Levi, Jr.,	*Hebron, Ill.*
Nustad, Tenney,	*Westby.*
Ode, William Herman,	*Portage.*
Pardee, Donald Waite,	*Eagle.*
Patterson, James Victor,	*Bloomington.*
Paulson, Peter Antonius,	*Hudson.*
Pickhardt, Paul,	*Milwaukee.*
Poellman, Michael John,	*Granville.*
Poss, Louis Carl,	*Galesville.*
Poston, Richard,	*Knapp.*
Powell, Dwight Ephriam,	*Shirland, Ill.*

Powless, Alfred,	Oneida.
Prather, John William,	Springfield, Ill.
Pride, Walter Garfield,	Osseo.
Pyan, Edward,	Marathon.
Radcliffe, William,	Eagle River.
Roberts, David Ira,	Portage.
Roberts, Henry Brown,	Elida Ill.
Runke, Walter,	Algoma.
Sanborn, Wade Hampton,	Spring Grove, Ill.
Schaffner, Samuel,	Kinley.
Schroeder, Frank Charles,	Kewaunee.
Schultz, Henry Michael,	Nora, Ill.
Sexton, Stephen,	Quincy, Mich.
Shultis, Averill Davis,	Waukesha.
Smiley, Arnold Bennett,	Albany.
Smith, David Albert.	Prion.
Smith, Theodore Jesse,	Mt. Palatine, Ill.
Snow, Charles Brooks,	Chicago, Ill.
Snyder, Henry Albert,	Brooklyn.
Starritt, Bruce Wheelock,	Nunda, Ill.
Stauffacher, Anton Jacob,	Stearns.
Stokes, Lorenzo,	Newark.
Stone, Alden Lescombe,	Burnett Jct.
Strommen, Martin Emandus,	Cambridge.
Stuart, Alexander,	Walnut, Ia.
Tanner, Ren Childs,	Capron, Ill.
Teurnell, Emil,	Hillside.
Thom, James Alexander,	Millburn, Ill.
Thompson, Oscar Oswald,	Argyle.
Thompson, Thomas,	Blair.
Thompson, Thomas Paul,	Blair.
Tobler, Alfred,	Knoxville, Tenn.
Treat, Perley Seymour,	Franks, Ill.
Tschudy, Andrew Rudolph,	Monroe.
Uehling, Louis Edwin,	Afton.
Vance, Claude,	Decatur, Ill.
Vance, Guy Pugh,	Decatur, Ill.
Varnum, George F.,	Melrose.
Walter, Andrew,	Waukesha.
Watkins, James Edwin,	Baraboo.
Watson, Stanley Edward,	Sommerville.
Weidig, Heinrich Robert,	Hinsdale, Ill.

STUDENTS IN AGRICULTURE—DAIRY CLASS.

Weller, Paul Richard,	*Ashland.*
Welborn, Ernest Paul,	*Cynthiana, Ind.*
Wendt, George,	*Belle Fountain.*
Wesenberg, Theodore,	*Oshkosh.*
Williams, John Raymon,	*Hurricane.*
Williamson, Andrew Baird,	*Millville.*
Wochos, Jacob,	*Stangelville.*
Wolcott, Walter Alonzo,	*Appleton.*
Wolf, Edward H.,	*St. Kilian.*
Works, Arthur Garfield,	*Augusta.*
Wright, William James,	*Waukesha.*
Young, John H.,	*Madison.*

—165

DAIRY CLASS.
Second Year.

Klotz, John Louis,	*East Farmington.*
Zeitler, Albert Henry,	*Johnson's Creek.*

—2

First Year.

Aieken, Fred,	*Waukesha.*
Bang, Andrew James,	*Klevenville.*
Barker, Frank Ellsworth,	*Janesville.*
Bartholomew, Walter Ebert,	*Galesville.*
Beebe, Clinton Claudeus,	*Boardman.*
Bemowski, Paul,	*Stevens Point.*
Bielke, Robert Julous Ferdinand,	*Stettin.*
Bowar, Frank Peter,	*Cazenovia.*
Bowen, John Edwin,	*Burns.*
Bowers, William Frank,	*Lima.*
Button, Curtis Eugene,	*Melrose.*
Campbell, Archibald William,	*Beaver Dam.*
Carroll, Charles Chester,	*Fredericksburg, Ia.*
Carswell, Ralph Vivian,	*Lone Rock.*
Chapin, John Chester,	*Waupaca.*
Clough, George Russell,	*Black Earth.*
Clover, Murray Clark,	*Rockton, Ill.*
Collins, Frank Myron,	*Albion.*
Coppins, Gavin,	*Ft. Atkinson.*
Coulson, Leonard Howard,	*Grafton.*

Crogen, John,	Boscobel.
Crowell, Leo Calvin,	Hanford, Cal.
Davidson, Manly Amandus,	Trade Lake.
Dressler, Valentine,	Kieler.
Drova, Alick,	Berlin.
Eichorst, Otto Gustav,	Milwaukee.
Ellis, Burr James,	Oregon.
Faast, Albert Edmond,	Durand.
Fassbender, Hubert,	Bungert.
Fingerhuth, Lewis Henry,	Spring Green.
Finstad, Anthon N.,	Lawton.
Fisher, John Adams,	Alaska.
Fitzgerald, Charles Gerald,	Richland Center.
Fochs, Anton Albert,	Chilton.
Frazer, Darwin Alfonso,	Frazer.
Frederick, Herman August,	Reedsville.
French, Arthur Neeves,	Lebanon.
Gallup, Charles Lyman,	North Adams, Mass.
Gillett, Randal Mills,	Plainfield.
Golden, Thomas Arthur,	Whitehall.
Grady, John Henry,	Cook Valley.
Griffin, Herbert Eugene,	Pardeeville.
Guillitte, Herbert,	Duvall.
Haack, Frank John,	Rankin.
Halpin, William Clarson,	Cedarburg.
Handy, Selah Addison,	North Andover.
Hanrath, Frank Lee,	Bristol.
Hardison, Warren Francis,	Alma Center.
Hartung, Henry,	Arkansaw.
Haven, Davis,	Hartford, Mich.
Higday, John Sherman,	Evansville.
Hoh, Charles Samuel,	Appleton.
Holzholter, William Henry,	London.
Hoppe, Leonard Ferdinand,	Rio Creek.
Horton, George Fred,	Austin, Texas.
Howe, Jesse Helfer,	Highland.
Jaques, Arthur Lewis,	Ladoga.
Jaquith, Fred,	Burlington.
Jeffries, Jesse Alexander,	Hiawatha, Kan.
Kaley, Michael Ambrose,	Loyd.
Kieler, William,	Louisburg.
Kirkham, Wallace Everett,	Augusta.

Koepping, Joseph,	*West Point, Ia.*
Kratz, William Phillip,	*Fontenoy.*
Kraus, Henry Andrew,	*Grellton.*
Kruger, Fred Albert,	*Sandusky.*
Lawson, Sydney Wilson,	*Rosendale.*
Ludvigson, Ludvig,	*Elk Mound.*
Manning, Rudolph,	*Neenah.*
Martin, Martin,	*Edmund.*
McComb, Justin Alvard,	*Lima.*
McDougall, Cyrus William,	*Guelph, Ontario, Can.*
McFerren, Jacob,	*Abilene, Kan.*
Meier, George,	*Arcada.*
Moore, Joseph Sterling,	*Agricultural College, Miss.*
Moore, Jay Wheeler,	*Richland City.*
Moats, Harry Henry,	*Modena.*
Mozeley, William James,	*Marquette.*
Newland, Wales William,	*Leon.*
Newman, Balch William,	*Elgin, Ill.*
Nisbet, Hugh,	*Woodstock.*
Ortscheid, Lewis Henry,	*North Andover.*
Peterson, Charles E.,	*Sandy Bay.*
Peterson, Cornelius,	*Byrds Creek.*
Purves, John Thomas,	*Big Bend.*
Reeve, William Eugene,	*Ironton.*
Reid, Fred Hugh,	*Oxford.*
Ristow, William Henry,	*North Bend.*
Rockman, Edward William,	*Barron.*
Roemer, Charles Joseph,	*Appleton.*
Rohn, Frank Joseph,	*Arcadia.*
Roys, Herbert Myron,	*Ironton.*
Safford, Orton Palmer,	*Peebles.*
Schamberger, Jasper,	*Pleasant Valley, Ill.*
Schubert, Ernest John,	*Hellenville.*
Schulz, Reinhold Rudolph,	*Clifton.*
Schwingel, Phillip Christian,	*Avoca.*
Scott, John Edmund,	*Scales Mound, Ill.*
Searls, Howard Charles,	*Plainfield.*
Seefeld, Benjamin Otto,	*Milwaukee.*
Short, William Henry,	*Neillsville.*
Sorge, Albert Owen,	*Reedsburgh.*
Stadel, Paul Robert,	*Sharpville, Ill.*
Thompson, John,	*Waldwick.*

Thore, Frank, Kieler.
Tyler, Guy, Patch Grove.
Unger, Frank, Parkston, S. D.
Van Dresser, Merton Lemual, Elk Mound.
Wagner, Paul Whitcomb, Green Bay.
Waterman, William Ira, Neillsville.
Weuthrich, Fred, Iron Ridge.
Wheeler, Ralph, New Richmond.
Whitney, David Curtis, Ft. Atkinson.
Wilkening, William C., Schaumburg, Ill.
Winter, Theodore, Wonewoc.
Winters, James Franklin, Belleville, Kans.
Woldt, Henry, Kirchhayn.
Zilisch, Carl August, Mayville.

—118

COLLEGE OF LAW.
Senior Class.

Alexander, Albert Fred, Grand Rapids.
Alexander, George Arnold, Manitowoc.
Andrews, Ross Everett, Muckwanago.
Backus, August Charles, Kewaskum.
Bartman, John Henry, Appleton,
Bartlett, Charles Lackey, Clayton, Ill.
Berg, Theodore, Appleton.
Biersach, William Mann, Milwaukee.
Bowler, James J., Sparta.
Brazeau, Theodore Walter, Grand Rapids.
Bowers, Ray, Delavan.
Comstock, Nathan, Philadelphia, Pa.
Coyle, John Joseph, Freeport, Ill.
Crego, Irving, Aurora, Ill.
Crawford, George, Oconto.
Dietz, Robert Earl, Mayville.
Gilmore, Eugene Leffler, Monticello, Ia.
Glasier, Gilson Gardner, Wauwatosa.
Gold, Walter Louis, Milwaukee.
Gurnee, Paul Dennison, Madison.
Hanks, David Arthur, Jr., Madison.
Hensel, Earl Franklin, Arcadia.
Hillesheim, John Adolphus, Dwight, Ill.

Husting, Berthold Juneau,	*Mayville.*
Jeffers, Stephen Rowan,	*Hanover, Ill.*
Johnson, Buchanan,	*Sheridan.*
Johnson, Olie Lawrence,	*Black River Falls.*
Jones, William Thomas,	*Spring Water.*
Kopp, Arthur William,	*Platteville.*
Main, John Smith,	*Madison.*
McGrath, William Howard,	*Argyle.*
McManamy, Francis Vincent,	*Cashton.*
McMillan, Donald J.,	*Neillsville.*
McNamara, Frank Landis,	*Janesville.*
Metzler, Charles Henry,	*Portage.*
Montgomery, Charles Carroll,	*Omaha, Neb.*
Moran, John,	*De Forest.*
Morrow, William Ambrose,	*Omro.*
Norton, William Clarence,	*Elkhorn.*
O'Dea, Patrick John,	*Melborne, Australia.*
Oestreich, Otto Albert,	*Kewaunee.*
Okoneski, John Joseph,	*Wausau.*
Pattee, Frank Bent,	*Lowell, Ind.*
Peterson, Charles Nelson,	*Union Grove.*
Peterson, Frederick Burns,	*Madison.*
Pierrelee, Victor Theodore,	*Granton.*
Pritzlaff, Adolph Herman,	*Milwaukee.*
Radcliffe, Jonas,	*Eagle River.*
Robbins, Samuel Brownlee,	*Carthage, Ill.*
Rush, Walter James,	*Waterford.*
Sarau, George Adolphus,	*Oshkosh.*
Saucerman, Willard,	*Winslow, Ill.*
Siggelko, Herbert Scott,	*Madison.*
Silber, Harry Mamlock,	*Milwaukee.*
Smith, Lloyd D.,	*Amherst.*
Smith, Ralph Elbert,	*Waupun.*
Smith, Richard Edwin,	*Stanley.*
Smith, Sidney William,	*Victoria, B. C.*
Smith, William Noble,	*Madison.*
Tallman, George Kemp,	*Janesville.*
Thomas, Herbert Henry,	*Darlington.*
Tilden, George Huntington,	*Ames, Ia.*
Tirrill, Edward Drew,	*Madison.*
Werve, Charles Benjamin,	*Kenosha.*

Williams, Glenn Herbert, Grand Rapids.
Wolfe, Albert Christian, Greenville.

—66.

Middle Class.

Bender, Walter Henry Colyer,	Milwaukee.
Beymer, Ralph Waldo,	Corning, Ia.
Bigham, Roy Elson,	Arcadia.
Bowman, Robert Oscar,	Lodi.
Boynton, William Parker,	Jerseyville, Ill.
Christensen, Nels Peter,	Neenah.
Classon, Allan Vain,	Oconto.
Cody, Harry Arthur,	Ripon.
Crabtree, John Birch,	Dixon, Ill.
Curtis, Nathan Stephenson,	Madison.
Davies, Joseph Edward Paynter,	Watertown.
Detling, Henry Arthur,	Sheboygan,
Doolan, Francis Lawrence,	Milwaukee.
Ela, Emerson,	Rochester.
Elver, Elmer Theodore,	Madison.
Fairchild, Arthur Wilson,	Green Bay.
Fox, Edward Tappan,	Milwaukee.
Geilfuss, Carl Frederick,	Milwaukee.
Gugel, Frank Henry,	Madison.
Hicks, Jay William,	Oshkosh.
Hines, Martin Stephen,	Highland.
Holte, Nels Elias,	Newark, Ill.
Hutson, Charles Thomas,	Edgerton.
Jenner, Edward David,	Milwaukee.
Kroesing, Oscar,	Chilton.
Kroncke, Jacob,	Kenosha.
Landeck, Fred August,	Milwaukee.
Leahy, Thomas William,	Marion, Ia.
McArdle, Michael William,	Bailey's Harbor.
McCarthy, Loyal Henry,	Albion.
Morrissey, Edward Marcus,	Fontana.
Nelson, Robert Nicholie,	Lodi.
Owen, Asa Kenton,	Arcadia.
Pollard, Amos Weber,	Portage.
Potts, Ira David,	Fox Lake.
Price, Clinton Guilford,	Madison.
Regner, Frank Patrick,	West Bend.

STUDENTS IN LAW—MIDDLE CLASS.

Schneider, Charles Alfred,	Oshkosh.
Schoengarth, Oscar William,	Neillsville.
Smith, Delbert K.,	Big Bend.
Smith, Elroy Wallace,	Milwaukee.
Stebbins, Byron Houghton,	Little Falls, N. Y.
Stellwagen, Stephen Augustus,	Colorado Springs, Colo.
Tratt, Paul,	Whitewater.
Treweck, Joseph Nicholas,	Mineral Point.
Tscharner, Peter,	Alma.
Tomlinson, Roy Everett,	Oak Park, Ill.
Wheeler, Albert Kimball,	Janesville.
Wilcox, Nelson James,	Eau Claire.
Whipperman, Richard Olin,	Grand Rapids.

50

Junior Class.

Abel, Thorwald Peter,	Kenosha.
Alexander, Lake Cohen,	Manitowoc.
Andrews, John Burton,	Birnamwood.
Austin, Chauncey Goodrich, Jr.,	St. Albans, Vt.
Bardwell, Worth Sherman,	Plainfield.
Bays, Lee Fenton,	Sullivan, Ind.
Berg, William Carl,	Madison.
Blethen, Ralph Van,	Rochester, Minn.
Braun, August Ernest,	Milwaukee.
Brunchorst, Louis Arthur,	Kewaunee.
Campman, Will Arthur,	Neillsville.
Carow, Jorge Wilmer,	Elroy.
Cashin, Charles Henry,	Stevens Point.
Chamberlain, Alonzo Albert,	Darlington.
Cleary, Michael Joseph,	Blanchardsville.
Cockerill, Edward James,	Berlin.
Davelaar, Gilbert John,	Wauwatosa.
Davidson, Morton Stanley,	Madison.
Davlin, Thomas Francis,	Berlin.
Edwards, Harry,	Dixon, Ill.
Fellenz, Henry Mathias,	Campbell's Point.
Fritz, Oscar Marion,	Milwaukee.
Gordon, Clement Aloysius,	Freeport, Ill.
Greenthal, Alexander Philip,	Milwaukee.
Griesel, Edward Charles,	Crown Point, Ind.
Gross, Edwin Jacob,	Milwaukee.

Gunderson, Ole Severin,	*Colfax.*
Hardgrove, John Gilbert,	*Eden.*
Harkin, Earl Bertram,	*Marshfield.*
Hewett, Harry Roland,	*Madison.*
Hirleman, Forrest Clyde,	*Spencer, Ia.*
Hyman, Frank Sylvester,	*Chicago, Ill.*
Jacobson, Marcus A.,	*Waukesha.*
Joannes, Eugene Charles,	*Green Bay.*
Johntry, John Henry,	*Chicago, Ill.*
Jolliffe, Arthur,	*Berlin.*
Kaftan, Robert Albert,	*Tyndall, S. D.*
Kelley, Harry F.,	*Manitowoc.*
Kemp, Harry Gladstone,	*Rhinelander.*
Kemp, John Earle	*Sparta.*
Kies, Samuel William,	*Oshkosh.*
Kirwan, Charles,	*Manitowoc.*
Knowles, Edwin Coryden French,	*West Superior.*
Kopplin, Philip Cornelius,	*Lowell.*
Larson, Albert Frederick,	*Sioux Falls, S. D.*
Larson, George Eddie,	*Sioux Falls, S. D.*
Leatherwood, Elmer O.,	*Madison.*
Lucas, Frank Warren,	*Brodhead.*
Lundahl, Herbert Alvin,	*Chicago, Ill.*
Manson, Lester Columbus,	*Beaver Dam.*
McCormick, William Laird,	*Hayward.*
McKesson, James Cooper,	*Genoa Junction.*
McMillan, John Walter,	*Milwaukee.*
Meyers, Daniel Paul,	*Forreston, Ill.*
Michaelson, James Andrew,	*Darlington.*
Minahan, Victor Ivan,	*Chilton.*
Monahan, Barney Andrew,	*East Troy.*
Nohl, Leo Fred,	*Milwaukee.*
Oberne, William Jones,	*Chicago, Ill.*
O'Keliher, Victor Joseph,	*Oconto.*
O'Neill, Ernest Andrew,	*Neillsville.*
Raphael, Nathan,	*Madison.*
Reedel, George Banks,	*DeKorra.*
Reevs, Harry Lee,	*New York City, N. Y.*
Reynolds, Edward John,	*Madison.*
Rogers, Victor Eugene,	*Plankinton, S. D.*
Ryan, Thomas Hartley,	*Wausau.*
Salisbury, Charles Edward,	*Marietta, Cal.*

STUDENTS IN LAW—MIDDLE CLASS.

Schwittay, Albert Edward,	*Pound.*
Scow, Emil,	*Arcadia.*
Shepard, Franklin Richard,	*Janesville.*
Smieding, Herman,	*Racine.*
Smith, Wallace Stanley,	*Onalaska.*
Thompson, George,	*Moscow.*
Turner, Alexander,	*Roberts.*
Vilas, Charles Atwood,	*Milwaukee.*
Voigt, Ferdinand George Charles,	*Milwaukee.*
Walters, Martin Fred,	*Appleton.*
Wilson, Bunn Thatcher,	*Rochester, Minn.*
Yankey, Charles,	*Juneau.*

—80

Special Students.

Clancy, Henry Patrick,	*Racine.*
Coombs, Albert Nathan,	*Honey Creek.*
Drybread, Ivory J.,	*Franklin, Ind.*
Hirschberg, Gustave Joseph,	*Milwaukee.*
Huntington, Paul,	*Green Bay.*
Jackowska, Antoinette Victoria,	*Milwaukee.*
Phoenix, Charles Edward,	*Baraboo.*
Ringle, Oscar Lewis,	*Wausau.*
Roberts, David Milton,	*Leeds Center.*
Sweet, William,	*Kilbourn.*
Truesdell, Ernest Page,	*Belvidere, Ill.*
Walsh, James Alexander,	*Eagle River.*

—12

Adult Special Students.

Boyce, Albert Henry,	*Sturgeon Bay.*
Clark, Perry Eugene,	*Evansville.*
Fairbank, Raymond Clarence,	*Ladoga.*
Helfrich, George Victor,	*Carthage, Ill.*
Husting, Bondnel Albert,	*Mayville.*
Kelley, John Martin,	*Portage.*
Kittleson, Isaac Milo,	*Mt. Horeb.*
Lavoy, Michael Joseph,	*St. Julienne, Can.*
Maxey, John,	*Antigo.*
Nedderson, John Louis,	*Milwaukee.*
Parkinson, Walter Knox,	*Appleton.*
Rickmire, Ara Patton,	*Cylon.*

—12

Students in College of Letters and Science Electing Six-Fifths Law Studies.

von Briesen, Ernest,	*Columbus.*
Crosby, Francis Hinckley,	*Racine.*
Esterly, Henry Minor,	*Hillside.*
Fisher, Carl Elisha,	*Bayfield.*
Hobbins, Harry Mears,	*Madison.*
Koffend, Joseph,	*Appleton.*
Loeb, Joseph,	*Appleton.*
Murphy, Daniel Hays,	*Milwaukee.*
Pearce, Charles Sumner,	*Walworth.*
Scanlan, Dennis Francis,	*Fulton, Kan.*
Whelan, Dutee Robert,	*Genessee Depot.*

—11

SCHOOL OF PHARMACY.
Four Years' Course.

Alden, Frederick William,	*Madison,*	Senior.
Brandel, Irvin Walter,	*Oshkosh,*	Junior.
Ehlert, Frederick Gustave,	*Madison,*	Junior.
Hitchcock, Frank Carl,	*Plainwell, Mich.,*	Special.
Major, Thomas Ambrose,	*Manistee, Mich.,*	Junior.
Swarthout, Susie,	*La Crosse,*	Sophomore.
Wigdale, Enos Samuel,	*Fort Atkinson,*	Junior.

—7

Three Years' Course.

Check, Charles William,	*Madison,*	Junior.
Copp, Ben Linsey,	*Madison,*	Sophomore.
Dieffenbach, Ernst William,	*Milwaukee,*	Junior.
Eastman, Cora Belle,	*Montfort,*	Junior.
Eighmy, Frank Wilbur,	*McFarland,*	Senior.
Forsyth, John Leonard, Jr.,	*Stevens Point,*	Sophomore.
Hatton, Fred Hammond,	*Madison,*	Senior.
Horne, Robert William,	*Brodhead,*	Sophomore.
Klueter, Harry,	*Madison,*	Senior.
Kopp, George Hermann,	*Chippewa Falls,*	Senior.
Krembs, Alexander, Jr.,	*Stevens Point,*	Junior.
Lehmann, Conrad Charles,	*Cedarburg,*	Sophomore.
Shields, George Alvin,	*Mazomanie,*	Senior.
Showalter, Edwin Andrew,	*Milwaukee,*	Senior.
Soell, Otto Arthur,	*La Crosse,*	Sophomore.

Strauss, Richard Jacques,	*Appleton,*	Senior.
Swanton, Bert John,	*Brodhead,*	Sophomore.
Tandvig, Albert Nicholas,	*Madison,*	Senior.
Treber, John Alfred,	*Deadwood, S. D.,*	Junior.
Treber, William Lawrence,	*Deadwood, S. D.,*	Junior.
Williams, John Herman,	*Merrillan,*	Sophomore.
Windes, Thomas Guy,	*Winnetka, Ill.,*	Junior.

—22

Two Years' Course.

Brook, Harley McSpadden,	*Milwaukee,*	Junior.
Chamberlain, Fred Henry,	*Sparta,*	Junior.
Dexheimer, Frederick Rudolph,	*Fort Atkinson,*	Senior.
Downer, William Ralph,	*Appleton,*	Junior.
Eberle, Arthur Ralph,	*Watertown,*	Junior.
Kundert, Alfred Emil,	*Monroe,*	Junior.
McIntosh, James Allen,	*Macomb, Ill.,*	Junior.
Nelson, John Caleb,	*Beloit,*	Junior.
Newmann, Edmund Christian,	*Milwaukee,*	Junior.
Newton, Carl A.,	*Sparta,*	Junior.
Patterson, John Leon,	*Evansville,*	Junior.
Proulx, Emile,	*Chippewa Falls,*	Junior.
Rose, Emmason Charles,	*Scranton, Pa.,*	Junior.
Ross, Emile,	*Lake Geneva,*	Junior.
Slightam, Ida Elizabeth,	*Prairie du Chien,*	Junior.
Thomas, Carolyn Cornelia,	*Prairie du Chien,*	Senior.
Thomas, John Alexander,	*Prairie du Chien,*	Senior.
Walker, William Henry,	*Madison,*	Junior.
Woltersdorf, Albert Henry,	*Columbus,*	Senior.

—19

SCHOOL OF MUSIC.

Graduate.

Bliss, Eleanor Beattie,	*Madison.*
Brand, Bessie Goodrich,	*Madison.*
Dibble, Olive Amanda,	*South Madison.*
Fowler, Wm. Muzzy,	*Madison.*
Pickarts, Mary Eliza,	*Madison.*
Walden, Alice,	*Argyle.*

—6

Collegiate.

Third Year.

Baer, Clarence Allen,	Milwaukee.
Bolender, Charles Barton,	Monroe.
Brigham, Bertha Blanche,	Madison.
Buhlman, Grace L.,	Waunakee.
Clement, Grace Beatrice,	Sun Prairie.
Lueders, Minnie Magdalen,	Madison.
Pease, Raymond Burnett,	Oregon.
Pound, Martha,	Madison.
Thompson, Martha,	Mt. Horeb.
Young, Allyn Abbott,	Madison.

—10

Second Year.

Ackerman, Anna Elizabeth,	Coleta, Ill.
Bird, Louise Marie,	Madison.
Brodrick, Gertrude Adelaide,	Madison.
Brown, Bertha Louise,	Madison.
Brownson, Laura,	Sharon.
Butt, Margaret Elizabeth,	Viroqua.
Coleman, Mary Persis,	Chippewa Falls.
Comstock, Leila,	Oregon.
Cummings, Mary Irene,	Rock Valley, Ia.
Dixon, Grace Shirley,	Milwaukee.
Fuller, Shirly,	Madison.
Gibbons, Frank Clark,	Sun Prairie.
Gilbertson, Martha,	Mount Horeb.
Glen, Mary Alice,	Chicago, Ill.
Hansen, Daisy Etta,	Madison.
Harrington, Florence,	Madison.
Hubbell, Charles Herbert,	Madison.
Kanouse, Robert Beecham,	Sun Prairie.
Koltes, Mary,	Madison.
Lucas, Sarah May,	Brodhead,
Martin, Emily Davidson	Madison.
McKenna, Lucy,	Blanchardville.
Montgomery, Janette Louise,	Madison.
Newton, Cordelia Lydia,	Bangor.
Pickford, Theo. Beatrice,	Madison.
Renk, Katherine,	Sun Prairie.

Riley, Caroline Mae, Madison.
Russell, Harry Alexander, Madison.
Smith, Winifred Mary, Sturgeon Bay.
Wagner, Meta, Madison.
Winterbotham, Ada Eliza, Madison.

—31

First Year.

Allen, Elsie Caroline, Lake Geneva.
Allyn, Abigail Mary, Tomah.
Anderson, Anna Louise, Madison.
Anderson, Lela, Augusta.
Arnold, Bertha Vie, Fennimore.
Astle, Celia Minerva, Prairie du Sac.
Banting, Lilian, Montreal, Canada.
Bonniwell, Riva Rice, Whitewood, S. D.
Burmester, Nellie Mildred, Verona.
Button, Kittie Louise, Milton Junction.
Byrne, Agnes Kate, Madison.
Clifford, Elmer David, Madison.
Crary, Charles Judson, Boone, Ia.
Davison, Sarah Margaret, Beaver Dam.
Dye, Rose Aileen, Madison.
Everett, Dorothy Jane, Sparta.
Fairchild, Arthur Wilson, Green Bay.
Fay, Helen Armine, Madison.
Fay, Martha Marion, Madison.
Fox, Anna Kathleen, Madison.
Freeborn, Lorena Oina, Richland Center.
Glenz, Johanna Frances, Madison.
Goodwin, Myrtle, Mazomanie.
Green, Adah Carmellita, Madison.
Groves, Regina Eunice, Madison.
Haner, Cordelia, Sun Prairie.
Hart, Henry Isaac, Wild Rose.
Hawley, Mae, Madison.
Hayden, Willard Ware, Sun Prairie.
Hoepner, Nora, Two Rivers.
Hull, Bessie Ella, Madison.
Kasberg, Petra Elvine, Bratsberg, Minn.
Martin, Edith Bonar, Morrison, Ill.
Mosel, Clara Belle, Sun Prairie.

Murray, Josephine Mary,   Madison.
Nalty, Josephine Agnes,   Monroe.
Nash, James Bertram,   Centralia.
Nyswander, Ada May,   Napoleon, Ohio.
Pettigrew, Bessie,   Sioux Falls, S. D.
Pettigrew, Etta Salome,   Sioux Falls, S. D.
Pierce, Helen Murroe,   Madison.
Pray, Allan Theron,   Stevens Point.
Rinder, Elinore Anna,   Madison.
Robinson, Ida May,   Mazomanie.
Sanders, Otilda,   Perry.
Savage, May Lilian,   Madison.
Schott, Lucca Clara,   Madison.
Sheldon, Frank DeSalle,   Milwaukee.
Stone, Belva,   Bloomington.
Tarbox, Edna Laura,   La Crosse.
Taylor, Frederick Dan,   Bates, Ill.
Thompson, Charles Fredrick,   Whitewood, S. D.
Thompson, Ethel Adele,   Darlington.
Thompson, George,   Moscow.
Toepfer, Mathilda Louise,   Madison.
Williams, Callafern Ann,   Milwaukee.

—56

Academic.

Alford, Alice Irene,   Madison.
Alford, Hazel Viola,   Madison.
Allen, Charles Chester,   Kenosha.
Arnold, Cora Pearl,   Fennimore.
Austin, Joseph Raymond,   Madison.
Austin, Mary,   Madison.
Bagley, Lorna Doone,   Madison.
Balsley, Edith Rachel,   Madison.
Barnes, Chester David,   Kenosha.
Barnes, Ella,   Madison.
Bemis, Lotta Cora,   Lodi.
Blake, Chauncey Etheredge,   Rockford, Ill.
Blood, Henrietta Ada,   Madison.
Bull, Eyvind,   Madison.
Button, Kittie Louise,   Milton Junction.
Chamberlain, Harlem Roy,   Darlington.
Charleton, Fanny,   Madison.

Chatterton, Alta Endora, *Basco.*
Chatterton, Rose Genevieve, *Basco.*
Chynoweth, Emily Ellen, *Madison.*
Cobb, Olive E., *Sun Prairie.*
Copeland, Gertrude Louise, *Vulcan, Mich.*
Cosgrove, Laura Louise, *Kenosha.*
Cottrell, Bessie Etta, *Spencer, Ia.*
Cox, Charlotte Myra, *Milwaukee.*
Dawson, Clarence Orlo, *Mason City, Ia.*
Dodge, Charles Warren, *Milwaukee.*
Elliott, Frank Gilliland, *Madison.*
Erwin, Clara Louise, *Milwaukee.*
Fredrickson, Marion Emma, *Madison.*
Gamm, Benjamin Julius, *Madison.*
Geerlings, Henry John, Jr., *Milwaukee.*
Gibbons, Vera, *Sun Prairie.*
Harrison, Edna Lucretia, *Madison.*
Hart, Henry Isaac, *Wild Rose.*
Hatch, Grace, *Madison.*
Hayden, Willard Ware, *Sun Prairie.*
Heavenrich, Alvin Trounstine, *Ashland.*
Heim, Frederick Carl, *Madison.*
Herfurth, Sabena Mildred, *Madison.*
Hobbins, James R., *Madison.*
Kahn, Renne Robert, *Milwaukee.*
Keachie, George Robertson, *Cedar Rapids, Ia.*
Kelley, Minnie Ellen, *Madison.*
Kellogg, Elbert Cutting, *Centralia.*
Klein, Mathilda, *Black River Falls.*
Kleinpell, Irma Meta, *Madison.*
Kney, Ena Elsbeth, *Madison.*
Liedtke, Hulda Lydia Agnes, *Leland.*
Ludlow, May, *Monroe.*
Lyon, Janette Sherman, *Madison.*
Marshall, Mary Elizabeth, *Madison.*
Michelson, Albert G., *Mount Horeb.*
Minahan, Mary Elizabeth, *Calumetville.*
Miritz, Alfred, *Kewaskum.*
Monahan, Alice, *Madison.*
Morgan, Alexander William, *Madison.*
Morris, Julia Sophia, *Madison.*
Murray, Josephine Mary, *Madison.*

Naffz, Ina Gertrude,	Madison.
Naffz, Louis Edwin,	Madison.
Naffz, Otto,	Madison.
Nate, Bessie Rae,	Chicago, Ill.
Nelson, Grace Coleta,	Madison.
Nelson, Susie,	Madison.
Ottum, Thomas Engebret,	McFarland.
Parker, Bertha Gifford,	Madison.
Powless, Alfred,	Oneida.
Proctor, Ermina,	Madison.
Purdy, Myrtle,	Oconomowoc.
Pyre, Walton Hawkins,	Madison.
Quan, Clara Eugenie,	Madison.
Quigley, Arthur Joseph,	Lake Geneva.
Rhodes, Alfred John,	Galesville.
Ruediger, Gustave Ferdinand,	Alma.
Sanders, Harma Bell,	Marshall.
Saunders, Arthur Bernard,	Milton.
Sheldon, Frank De Salle,	Milwaukee.
Shepard, Frank Richard,	Janesville.
Smith, Jesse Clemons,	Madison.
Smith, Mary Campbell,	Madison.
Smyth, Jesse Blanche,	Stuart, Ia.
Squires, Lizzie Melissa,	Madison.
Stephens, Leila Celeste,	Dixon, Ill.
Stevens, Helen Elizabeth,	Madison.
Swarthout, Susie,	La Crosse.
Taylor, Jennie May,	Madison.
Treleven, Elizabeth Mayhem,	Fond du Lac.
Twitchell, Hannah,	Madison.
Van Etta, Jacob King,	Madison.
Van Hise, Janet,	Madison.
Vilas, Katherine Porter,	Madison.
Wallace, Leila Harriet,	Madison.
White, Florence Mary,	Rochester.
Winterbotham, Emma Rose,	Madison.
Winterroth, Grace,	Madison.

SUMMER SESSION OF 1899.

GRADUATES.

Alderson, Persis Hurd, Ph. M., Northwestern Univ.,   *Fayette, Ia.*
   History.
Barrett, Richard Warren, Ph. B., Earlham College,   *Richmond, Ind.*
   Latin.
Beddall, Marcus Melvin, B. L., University of Wisconsin,   *Madison.*
   Economics, History.
Beeman, Edward Monroe, B. L., University of Wisconsin, *Fairchild.*
   History, Economics, Physics.
Benner, Henry, Ph. D., University of Berlin,   *Albion, Mich.*
   Astronomy.
Brown, Sarah Edith, B. S., University of Wisconsin,   *Madison.*
   Physics, Mathematics.
Campbell, Mary Randolph, A. B., Univ. of Nebraska,   *Lincoln, Neb.*
   Greek.
Cederstrom, John Alfred, Ph. B., Univ. of Wis., *Elbow Lake, Minn.*
   Mathematics, Pedagogy.
Chynoweth, Edna Ruth, M. L., University of Wisconsin,   *Madison.*
   English Literature, History.
Cook, Alfred Newton, A. M., University of Wisconsin,   *Madison.*
   Chemistry, French.
Crull, Adam Ulysses, A. M., Indiana University,   *Osceola, Ind.*
   German.
Dobie, Ellen, B. S., University of Minnesota, *Minneapolis, Minn.*
   Physics.
Dubois, Nellie, M. S., Lawrence University,   *Appleton.*
   French, Drawing.
Fisher, Charles Edward, A. B., Iowa College,   *Grinnell, Ia.*
   Latin.
Flom, George Tobias, Ph. D., Columbia University,   *Utica.*
   French.
Gates, Frederick William, Ph. B., Univ. of Wis., *Pickwick, Minn.*
   Mathematics.
Gattiker, Emma, B. S., University of Wisconsin,   *Baraboo.*
   French, German, Economics.

Geer, Bennette Eugene, A. M., Furman University, *Greenville, S. C.*
English, English Literature.
Gile, Durant Carlyle, A. B., University of Wisconsin, *Marshfield.*
Botany, Zoology.
Guthormsen, Gunluf, Ph. B., Lawrence University, *Neenah.*
History, Philosophy.
Hady, Edward Schrock, Ph. M., Northwestern University,*Lanark, Ill.*
English, German, Pedagogy.
Hager, Albert Ralph, B. S., University of Wisconsin, *Madison.*
Physics.
Haines, Arthur Lee, B. S., Upper Iowa University, *Charles City, Ia.*
Chemistry.
Hancock, Edward Lee, B. S., University of Wisconsin, *Shullsburg.*
Mathematics, Astronomy.
Hanna, Belle, M. S., Cornell College, *Vinton, Ia.*
English, English Literature, Latin.
Hardy, Clarence Foster, B. L., University of Wisconsin, *Waukesha.*
French, Anatomy.
Harrison, Frederick Arthur, Ph. B., Univ. of Wisconsin, *Ashland.*
History, Political Science.
Heimdal, Sara Guenvor, B. S., University of Wisconsin, *Madison.*
Physics.
Henderson, Martha Bertina, B. L., Univ. of Wisconsin, *Cambridge.*
English, Philosophy, History.
Herron, Belva Mary, B. L., University of Chicago, *Lincoln, Neb.*
Economics, Political Science.
Higbee, Florence Johnson, Ph. D., Wooster University, *Clinton, N. Y.*
Chemistry.
Higbee, Howard Haines, Ph. D., Johns Hopkins Univ., *Clinton, N. Y.*
Chemistry.
Hoag, Ernest Bryant, A. B., Stanford University, *Evanston, Ill.*
Bacteriology.
Hooper, Cyrus Lauren, A. M., Indiana University, *Chicago, Ill.*
Latin.
Howes, Myra Jane, A. B., Oberlin College, *Mendota, Ill.*
English, English Literature.
Inglis, John Percy, B. L., University of Wisconsin, *Bayfield.*
Botany.
Jeffery, Joseph Alexander, B. S. in Agr., Univ. of Wis.; *Madison.*
Chemistry.
Jolliffe, William Morley, B. S., Lawrence University, *Berlin.*
Chemistry.

Jones, Gorman, A. M., Denison University,   *Williamsburg, Ky.*
    History, Political Science.
Jones, Lewis Albert, Ph. B., University of Wisconsin,   *Georgetown.*
    Botany, History, Physics.
Jones, Thomas John, B. L., Univ. of Wisconsin,   *Port Washington.*
    History.
Keppel, James Tobias, B. S., Upper Iowa University,   *Fayette, Ia.*
    Chemistry.
Kinsman, Delos Oscar, A. M., University of Chicago,   *Platteville.*
    Economics, History, Political Science.
Kluge, Paul Gideon, A. B., Mission House College,   *Franklin.*
    English, History.
Koltes, Frank Xavier, B. S., University of Wisconsin,   *Madison.*
    Astronomy, Botany.
Langemo, Peter Cornelius, B. L., Univ. of Wis.,   *Kenyon, Minn.*
    Political Science.
Leonard, Heman Burr, B. S., University of Michigan, *Detroit, Mich.*
    Chemistry, Physics.
Lewis, Nettie Claire, Ph. B., Upper Iowa Univ.,   *Charles City, Ia.*
    English Literature.
Lindley, Harlow, A. M., Earlham College,   *Bloomingdale, Ind.*
    Mathematics.
Lowell, Franklin Adams, B. S., University of Wisconsin,   *Berlin.*
    History, English.
Magnusson, Carl Edward, M. S., Univ. of Minnesota,   *Stark, Minn.*
    Physics.
Marsh, Ellen Fowler, B. L., Northwestern University,   *Bristol.*
    Botany, German, Pedagogy.
Marting, George Henry, A. B., German Wallace College,   *Green Bay.*
    German.
Mason, Max, B. S., University of Wisconsin,   *Madison.*
    Mathematics.
McCumber, Anna Levina, B. L., Univ. of Wisconsin,   *Fond du Lac.*
    Botany, Anatomy.
McGlachlin, Lucy Kate, B. L., University of Wisconsin, *Stevens Point.*
    English, English Literature, Pedagogy.
McGregor, Margaret Elizabeth, B. L., Univ. of Wis.,   *Stevens Point.*
    English Literature, German, Latin.
McVicar, Katharine, B. L., University of Wisconsin,   *Waukesha.*
    English, English Literature.
McVicar, Mary Christiana, B. L., Univ. of Wisconsin,   *Waukesha.*
    Latin.

Meany, Edmond Stephen, M. S., Univ. of Washington, *Seattle, Wash.*
Botany, Economics, History.
Meland, Edward Christopher, B. L., Univ. of Wis., *De Forest.*
Philosophy, Physics.
Mendenhall, Ida May, Ph. B., Earlham College, *Bloomingdale, Ind.*
English, Latin.
Merrill, Harriet Bell, M. S., University of Wisconsin, *Milwaukee.*
Chemistry, Geology.
Meyer, Arthur William, B. S., University of Wisconsin, *Delafield.*
Chemistry.
Miller, Frank Hayden, A. M., University of Wisconsin, *Edgerton.*
History, Political Science.
Miller, Maud Elsie, A. B., University of Wisconsin, *Edgerton.*
German.
Moessner, Lillie Elda, B. S., University of Wisconsin, *Madison.*
Geology, German.
Morey, Julia Louise, Ph. B., University of Michigan, *LaGrange, Ill.*
Economics, Greek, Latin.
Morris, Robert, A. B., Ripon College, *Baraboo.*
Physics.
Moseley, Anna Burr, A. M., University of Wisconsin, *Madison.*
Latin.
Moseley, Flora Carolina, B. L., University of Wisconsin, *Madison.*
English Literature.
Mott, Florence Beatrice, A. B., Lawrence University, *Neenah.*
Botany, History.
Nicholson, George Montague, A. B., Yale Univ. *Kansas City, Mo.*
Chemistry.
Olney, Frank Hart, A. B., Kansas University *Lawrence, Kan.*
Mathematics, Pedagogy, Political Science.
Parker, Adella May, A. B., University of Washington, *Seattle, Wash.*
Economics.
Patten, Alice Cary, Ph. B., University of Michigan, *De Kalb, Ill.*
German, Greek, Latin.
Pooley, William Vifund, A. B., University of Illinois, *Galena, Ill.*
Chemistry.
Pratt, Grant Ellsworth, Ph. B., University of Wisconsin, *Madison.*
Mathematics, Philosophy.
Ralph, Agnes Clarissa, B. L., University of Wisconsin, *Columbus.*
Botany, Physics.
Rice, Ole S., B. S., University of Wisconsin, *Madison.*
German, Philosophy.

Rindlaub, Martin Phillip, Jr., B. L., Univ. of Wisconsin, *Platteville.*
  English Literature, French, Latin.
Ring, David Carl, A. B., Milton College. *Milton.*
  Botany, Pedagogy, Physics.
Ruebhausen, Ella Elisabeth, B. S., Univ. of Wisconsin, *Watertown.*
  Botany, Zoology.
Schlundt, Herman, M. S., University of Wisconsin, *Milwaukee.*
  Chemistry.
Shong, Albert Clifton, B. L., University of Wisconsin, *West Superior.*
  Economics, History, Political Science.
Shott, John Abraham, Ph. M., Ohio University, *Carthage, Ill.*
  Physics.
Sim, Keturah Elizabeth, M. L., University of Illinois, *Urbana, Ill.*
  English, English Literature.
Smith, Mary Allegra, B. L., University of Wisconsin, *Madison.*
  Astronomy, Latin.
Squire, Charles Albert, B. S., University of Wisconsin, *Sheboygan.*
  Bacteriology, Geology.
Stahl, Henry Vincent, B. L., University of Wisconsin, *Bayfield.*
  Chemistry.
Stangel, Charles George, B. S., University of Wisconsin, *Tisch Mills.*
  Mathematics, Physics.
Stauff, John Henry, A. B., University of Wisconsin, *Milwaukee.*
  French, Greek.
Stavrum, Ernst Arthur, B. L., University of Wisconsin, *La Crosse.*
  English Literature, Greek,
Thomas, Caroline Eames, B. L., Univ. of Wisconsin, *Green Bay.*
  Latin.
Thomas, Sarah Jennie, A. B., University of Wisconsin, *Waukesha.*
  Greek, Latin.
Towne, Ezra Thayer, B. L., University of Wisconsin, *Waupun.*
  Mathematics.
Tullis, Sue, A. B., University of Wisconsin, *Madison.*
  Latin.
Urdahl, Thomas K., Ph. D., Univ. of Wisconsin, *Madison.*
  Economics.
White, Harry K., M. L., Northwestern University, *Sheboygan.*
  Economics, History.
Wolff, Henry Charles, M. S., University of Wisconsin, *West Superior.*
  English.
Young, Allyn Abbott, Ph. B., Hiram College, *Rapid City, S. D.*
  Economics, History. —101

UNDERGRADUATES AND TEACHERS.

Abbott, Clarence Eugene,	Madison.
Acker, Ruby May,	Brandon.
Adams, Cynthia Emroy,	Minneapolis, Minn.
Agnew, Matilda Buhl,	Stevens Point.
Avery, Melville Daudridge,	St. Cloud, Minn.
Axley, Frederick William,	Madison.
Axley, Sophie Marie,	Meeme.
Baldwin, Arthur Algernon,	Madison.
Baird, Joel Gordon,	Wessington Springs, S. D.
Barbee, Louise Springer,	St. Louis, Mo.
Barkhausen, Louis Henry,	Green Bay.
Barnes, Laura Belle,	Waukesha.
Barton, Ella Andria,	Mt. Vernon.
Baus, Richard Edward,	Madison.
Beatty, Carlotta McCutcheon,	Madison.
Beck, Joseph David,	Henrietta.
Berg, Martin John,	Madison.
Bergstrom, Willis Charles,	Neenah.
Blackburn, Arthur William,	Madison.
Blake, Chauncey Etheredge,	Rockford, Ill.
Block, Lilly Dora,	Chicago, Ill.
Bold, Mabel Dixon,	Madison.
Borsh, Elizabeth Converse,	Kenosha.
Bosworth, Ellen Mary,	Merrill.
Bross, Agnes Marie,	Chicago, Ill.
von Briesen, Ernst,	Columbus.
Brindley, John Edwin,	Madison.
Buehler, Henry Andrew,	Monroe.
Bull, Eyvind,	Madison.
Buchholz, William David,	Whitehall.
Bunker, George Tracy,	Woodstock, Ill.
Burnham, Charles Lewis,	Milwaukee.
Byrnes, Rose Ella,	Grand Rapids.
Canty, Margaret,	Oshkosh.
Casson, Henry, Jr.,	Viroqua.
Church, Grace Adeline,	Walworth.
Clark, Myrtes Estella,	Mayville.
Clark, Vinnie Belle,	Mayville.
Clark, William Bernard,	Belleville.
Coen, Benjamin Franklin,	Madison.

Colbert, Laurence Clarence,	*Whitewater.*
Collins, William Benjamin,	*Sheboygan.*
Conaway, Hortense Grace,	*Urbana, Ill.*
Corson, Cora Maybelle,	*Monroe.*
Connell, Marion Theresa,	*Fond du Lac.*
Cotton, Charles Sumner,	*Friendship, N. Y.*
Darling, Walter Gregory,	*Crystal Falls, Mich.*
Devlin, Alice Elizabeth,	*Woodworth.*
Devlin, Sarah Roselle,	*Whitewater.*
Dighton, Martha Olive,	*West Superior.*
Dippel, John Robert,	*Chippewa Falls.*
Dodge, Bernard Ogilvie,	*Greenwood.*
Dodson, Truman Monroe,	*Berlin.*
Downes, Robert Hugh,	*Oshkosh.*
Drissen, William Henry,	*Kewaunee.*
Du Four, Clarence John,	*Milwaukee.*
Dye, Daisy Rumina,	*Madison.*
Earle, Marshall Delph,	*Greenville, S. C.*
Edgar, Thomas Oscar,	*Athens.*
Edwards, John Thomas,	*Marinette.*
Ellis, Ard Hoyt,	*Vinton, Ia.*
Elmer, Walter Edgar,	*Hustler.*
England, Mary Delia,	*Wessington Springs, S. D.*
Enright, John Joseph,	*Glencoe.*
Esterley, Henry Minor,	*Madison.*
Everett, Edward,	*Madison.*
Everett, Marie Louise,	*Boston, Mass.*
Evert, Lewis Magnus,	*Pewaukee.*
Farrand, Roy Felton,	*Galesville.*
Ferguson, Bessie Carolinn,	*Madison.*
Fernekes, Gustave,	*Milwaukee.*
Fowler, Myron Marshall,	*Wauwatosa.*
Fuller, William David,	*Hancock.*
Funck, George William,	*Milwaukee.*
Gabel, Charles Ernst,	*Milwaukee.*
Gantz, Mary Louise,	*Oregon, Ill.*
Gapen, Anna Mercedes,	*Madison.*
Gapen, Flora,	*Madison.*
Gapen, J. Clark,	*Madison.*
Gayton, Gertrude Alice,	*Beloit.*
Gehrand, Gustav William,	*Boscobel.*
Gilmore, Dora Emma,	*Beaver Dam.*

Goodwin, John Edward, Madison.
Gorr, Charles William, Milwaukee.
Grosshuesch, John William, Franklin.
Guile, Ella May, Madison.
Gunderson, Henry Adolph, Rio.
Gunderson, Oscar, Iola.
Halligan, Annie, Madison.
Hambrecht, George Philip, Grand Rapids.
Hanson, Charles, Monroe.
Hardwick, Anastasia, Milwaukee.
Harris, Edward William, Ardoch, N. D.
Hatton, Fred Hammond, Madison.
Hawley, Ada Lovisa, Madison.
Heyward, Richard, Madison.
Hilts, Effie, Towanda, Ill.
Holty, Edward Olaf, Madison.
Hoyt, Warren Albert, Madison.
Huebner, Solomon, Manitowoc.
Hubbard, George Colvin, St. Cloud, Minn.
Hubbard, Margaret Elizabeth, Carlinville, Ill.
Inbusch, Arthur Philip Henry, Milwaukee.
Ingersoll, Alice Louise, Cherokee, Ia.
Jamieson, William Henry, Shullsburg.
Joerns, Alma, Winooski.
Johns, Richard B., Madison.
Johnson, Arthur Lewis, Chicago, Ill.
Johnson, Axel Edward, Madison.
Johnson, Fred, Jr., Madison.
Johnson, John Kendall, Viroqua.
Jones, Oliver Milton, Georgetown.
Kaapke, Minnie, Maywood, Ill.
Karlen, Louis Robert, Monroe.
Kellogg, John Richard, Woodstock, Ill.
Kelly, William Hartt, Marshall.
Ketchum, Florence Josephine, Madison.
King, Arthur Charles, Chicago, Ill.
Kittleson, Ole Andrew, Perry.
Knoff, Robert Ernest, Janesville.
Krape, Will Gorman, Freeport, Ill.
Lamb, Charles Emery, Bangor.
Lea, William Francis, Waupaca.
Leahy, John Hamilton, Madison.

Leatherwood, Elmer O.,	*Hiawatha, Kan.*
Leidenberg, Julius,	*Lodi.*
Lennon, Hawley Daniel,	*Decorah, Ia.*
Lowell, Mary Manchester,	*Berlin.*
Lyle, Frank William,	*Ripon.*
Lyle, J. F. Stuart,	*Madison.*
Macartney, Albert Joseph,	*Madison.*
Macartney, Clarence Edward,	*Madison.*
Macnish, Ralph Benjamin,	*Madison.*
Marquart, Bertha,	*Watertown.*
McArthur, Arthur R.,	*Johnstown.*
McDonald, Alexander Vaughan,	*Fond du Lac.*
McGrath, Edward,	*Argyle.*
McGovern, Mary,	*Madison.*
McIntyre, Eugene LaVerne,	*Waldo.*
McMahon, Alma Louise,	*Ripon.*
McNown, Clara Isabel,	*Mauston.*
Mead, Ruth Nettie,	*Waterloo.*
Miles, Esther Kate,	*Oshkosh.*
Miller, Minnie Joan,	*Minneapolis, Minn.*
Minch, Walter Bernhard,	*Madison.*
Montgomery, Ida Margaretta,	*Rosendale.*
Moon, Rollin Otis,	*Richland Center.*
Moore, Ransom Asa,	*Madison.*
Morris, Minnie Ellen,	*Champaign, Ill.*
Mumford, Eugene Bishop,	*Madison.*
Murdock, John Wenzel,	*Tisch Mills.*
Murley, Hal,	*Shullsburg.*
Murphy, Daniel Hayes,	*Milwaukee.*
Nevins, Charles Veranus,	*Oshkosh.*
Newman, Mark Humphrey,	*Madison.*
Nickell, Rose Ellen,	*Omaha, Neb.*
Niles, Sidney Cleveland,	*Oak Park, Ill.*
Numan, Howard Clermont,	*Dakota, Ill.*
O'Brien, Edwin Thomas,	*Eau Claire.*
O'Hara, William Henry,	*Manitowoc.*
Oldrey, Eva Jane,	*Erie, Pa.*
Orchard, Milton,	*Shullsburg.*
Palmer, Ray,	*Madison.*
Parish, Louise Abey,	*Randolph.*
Parks, Edna Mary,	*Crystal Falls, Mich.*
Patten, Edith Sylvia,	*DeKalb, Ill.*

Patten, Mary Leone,	*DeKalb, Ill.*
Patton, Thurlow Jay,	*Brooklyn.*
Peele, Hereward John,	*Madison.*
Perham, George Addison,	*Racine.*
Peterson, Harold Stuart,	*Delafield.*
Phipps, Stephen Carpenter,	*Hudson.*
Plumb, Hylon Theron,	*Milton.*
Preuss, Bertha Helen,	*Belle Plaine.*
Radtke, Albert Augustus,	*Madison.*
Ray, Samuel Beatty,	*Waukesha.*
Reber, James Watt,	*Wheaton, Ill.*
Reed, Evan Laforrest,	*Oregon, Ill.*
Reed, Louis,	*Ripon.*
Rhinesmith, Grace Edith,	*Bement.*
Rhoads, George Benson,	*Hartland.*
Rhoads, Hattie Cornelia,	*Hartland.*
Rhodes, Arthur Lee,	*Madison.*
Rice, Hildor Petrehn,	*Madison.*
Richardson, Jessie Elizabeth,	*Newport, Ky.*
Roemer, Emma Marie,	*Madison.*
Roethe, Emil Leo,	*Whitewater.*
Rohde, Hugo William,	*Milwaukee.*
Rollman, Alfred,	*Chilton.*
Runke, Richard,	*Algoma.*
Ruschhaupt, Louis Fred,	*Milwaukee.*
Schmidt, Gertrud Charlotte,	*Wauwatosa.*
Schule, Frederick William, Jr.,	*Chicago, Ill.*
Schule, Paul Alolph,	*Chicago, Ill.*
Seeley, Sadie,	*Maiden Rock.*
Shephard, William Henry,	*Benton.*
Shinnick, Nellie Marie,	*Watertown.*
Sias, Nellie Bly,	*Sparta.*
Sieker, William Christian,	*Manitowoc.*
Simpson, Edward Bert,	*Chippewa Falls.*
Smith, Warren DuPré,	*Madison.*
Stager, John Mickle,	*Sterling, Ill.*
Stair, Henry C.,	*Brodhead.*
Steinmann, Leona,	*Watertown.*
Steuber, Frederick John,	*Prairie du Sac.*
Steve, William Frederick,	*Verona.*
Stevens, John Charles,	*Milwaukee.*
Stickney, Frank Mills,	*Baraboo.*

Sweeney, Kate G.,	*Virginia, Minn.*
Swett, Minnie Elvira,	*Fond du Lac.*
Swett, Nettie,	*Fond du Lac.*
Townsend, Hubert Isaac,	*Poynette.*
Treakle, Maud Talbot,	*Cortland.*
Tulley, Mattie,	*Denver, Colo.*
Uihlein, Arthur Benedict,	*Milwaukee.*
Underwood, Enoch William,	*Baltimore, Md.*
Utendorfer, William Elmer,	*Madison.*
Vea, Fritchjof Johnson,	*Stoughton.*
Vivian, William Albert,	*West Superior.*
Waite, Willis Willard,	*Brooklyn.*
Wakefield, Arthur Milan,	*Baldwin.*
Wells, Bessie Elsa,	*Kenosha.*
Wells, Earl Harold,	*Manawa.*
Welty, Harry,	*Roodhouse, Ill.*
White, Alice Caton,	*New York, N. Y.*
White, Charles Marcus,	*Delafield.*
White, Merritt Horace,	*Wonewoc.*
Whitham, Clara Estelle,	*Platteville.*
Whitfield, Charles John,	*Chicago, Ill.*
Williams, John,	*Sun Prairie.*
Williamsen, Edward Lucien,	*Janesville.*
Wing, Elizabeth,	*La Crosse.*
Winston, Verne Earnest,	*Evansville.*
Wolcott, Edson Ray,	*Sharon.*
Wolf, Herman Emil,	*La Crosse.*
Wolfenson, Louis Bernard,	*Madison.*
Woodbury, William Walden,	*Sandwich, Ill.*
Woodward, Florence,	*Madison.*
Woodward, John Lester,	*Madison.*
Zeininger, Caroline Frederica,	*Janesville.*

—240

SUMMARY OF STUDENTS.

GRADUATES—97.

    Fellows and Scholars.................................... 21
    Graduates in Residence................................. 75
    Graduates Studying *in absentia*....................... 1

COLLEGE OF LETTERS AND SCIENCE—1,096.

    Fellows and Graduates................................. 90

    Senior Class—191.

        Ancient Classical Course............................ 26
        Modern Classical Course............................ 27
        English Course.................................... 42
        Civic Course.. 27
        General Science Course............................. 44
        Philosophical Course............................... 25

    Junior Class—156.

        Ancient Classical Course............................ 23
        Modern Classical Course............................ 14
        English Course.................................... 40
        Civic Historical Course............................ 25
        General Science Course............................. 26
        Philosophical Course............................... 28

    Sophomore Class—189.

        Ancient Classical Course............................ 27
        Modern Classical Course............................ 30
        English Course.................................... 52
        Civic Historical Course............................ 46
        General Science Course............................. 34

    Freshman Class—244.

        Ancient Classical Course............................ 21
        Modern Classical Course............................ 50

SUMMARY OF STUDENTS.

COLLEGE OF LETTERS AND SCIENCE—Continued.

English Course	82
Civic Historical Course	51
General Science Course	40
Special Students	149
Adult Special Students	77—226

COLLEGE OF MECHANICS AND ENGINEERING—327.

Fellows and Graduates 4

Senior Class—40.
- Civil Engineering Course 20
- Mechanical Engineering Course 12
- Electrical Engineering Course 8

Junior Class—51.
- Civil Engineering Course 20
- Mechanical Engineering Course 19
- Electrical Engineering Course 12

Sophomore Class—80.
- Civil Engineering Course 31
- Mechanical Engineering Course 19
- Electrical Engineering Course 30

Freshman Class—119.
- Civil Engineering Course 39
- Mechanical Engineering Course 25
- Electrical Engineering Course 55

Special Students 33

COLLEGE OF AGRICULTURE—381.

Long Course 9

Short Course { Second Year 87
              { First Year 165

Dairy Course { Second Year 2
             { First Year 118

COLLEGE OF LAW—231.

    Senior Class... 66
    Middle Class.. 50
    Junior Class.. 80
    Special Students.. 12
    Adult Specials.. 12
    Students electing six-fifths law studies................. 11

SCHOOL OF PHARMACY—51.

    Fellows and Graduates................................... 3
        Four Years' Course................................. 7
        Three Years' Course................................ 22
        Two Years' Course.................................. 19

SCHOOL OF MUSIC—199.

                Graduate 6
                Third Year..................................... 10
    Collegiate   Second Year................................... 31
                First Year..................................... 56
    Academic 96

SUMMER SESSION OF 1899.

    Graduate Students...............................101
    Undergraduates and Teachers....................240—341
    Students also included in above courses........120—221

    TOTAL NUMBER OF STUDENTS...........................2,506
    Twice enumerated 84, leaving as actual number......2,422

In the enumeration of special students above, the classification by courses is as follows: A. C., 5; M. C., 15; C. H., 26; G. S., 22; Eng., 80; Phil., 1; C. E., 9; M. E. 13; E. E., 11.

INDEX.

Academic year, 5, 44.
Accredited Schools, 66.
Adaptive work for admission, 63.
Admission, 59-72.
    in Adaptive Work, 63.
    in Algebra, 60.
    in Botany, 63.
    on Certificate, 65.
    to College of Agriculture, 228.
    to College of Engineering, 174.
    to College of Law, 241.
    to College of Letters and Science, 59-72.
    in English, 60.
    in English Literature, 61.
    in French, 63.
    in Geometry, 60.
    in German, 63.
    in Greek, 62.
    of Graduate Students, 72.
    in History, 60, 62.
    in Latin, 62.
    of Normal School Graduates, 71.
    in Physiology, 63.
    in Physics, 63.
    to School of Pharmacy, 260.
    of Special Students, 64.
    of Students from other Colleges, 72.
Adult Special Students, 314.
Aesthetics, Course in, 83.
Agricultural Chemistry, Courses in, 233.
Agricultural Experiment Station, 226.
Agricultural Physics, Courses in, 233.
Agriculture, Courses in, 233.
Algebra for entrance, 60.
    Courses in, 115.
    Summer Course in, 160.
Analytic Geometry, 116.
Anatomy, Invertebrate, Courses in, 128.
    Vertebrate, Courses in, 128.

Ancient Classical Course, Admission, 62.
    Graduation in, 77.
Anglo-Saxon, Courses in, 114.
Animal Husbandry, Courses in, 233.
Applied Mechanics, Courses in, 199.
Arabic, Courses in, 102.
Armory and Gymnasium, 135.
Astronomy, Courses in, 118.
Athletic Field, 34.
Bachelor of Arts, Requirements for, 77.
    Letters, Requirements for, 78.
    Philosophy, Requirements for, 80.
    Science, Requirements for, 79.
    Science in Engineering, 192.
    Science in Pharmacy, 262.
Bachelor's Degrees, conferred, 278.
Bacteriology, Courses in, 130.
    Summer Courses in, 164.
Battalion, University, Roster of, 134.
Biology, Courses in, 127.
    Laboratories, 28.
    Museum, 31.
    Summer Courses in, 164.
Board, Cost of, 41.
Botany for Admission, 63.
    Courses in, 129.
    Summer Courses in, 165.
    Herbarium, 33.
    see Biology.
Buildings of the University, 24.
Bulletins, University, 34.
    College Agriculture, 227.
Calendar, 5.
Certificate, Dairy, 232.
Charges and Fees, 38.
    College of Agriculture, 226.
    College of Law, 254.
    Library School, 168.
    College of Engineering, 184
    School of Pharmacy, 255.
    Summer Session, 145.

INDEX.

Chemistry, Agricultural, Courses in, 233.
    Courses in, 122.
    Laboratories, 28.
    Pharmaceutical, Courses in, 264.
    Summer Courses in, 163.
Child Study, Courses in, 84.
Civic Historical Course, Admission, 63.
    Requirements for Graduation, 73.
Civil Engineering Course, 186.
Civil Engineer, see Degrees.
Class Officers, 26.
College of Agriculture, 222-238.
    Admission to, 228.
    Buildings, 225.
    Certificates, 232.
    Corps of Instruction, 222.
    Course in Dairying, 230.
    Degrees, 228.
    Departments of Instruction, 233-235.
    Expenses and Fees, 226.
    Experiment Station, 226.
    Farmers' Institutes, 235.
    Graduate Courses, 227.
    Laboratories, 225.
    Libraries, 225.
    Long Course, 229.
    Short Course, 229.
    Students, 324.
College of Law, 239-254.
    Admission to, 241.
    Corps of Instruction, 239.
    Courses of Study, 246.
    Degrees, 47.
    Expenses and Fees, 254.
    Graduates, 1899, 281.
    Library, 252.
    Methods of Instruction, 239.
    Mortimer Jackson Professorship, 250.
    Societies, 253.
    Students, 334.

College of Letters and Science, 57-146.
    Admission to, 59-72.
    Corps of Instruction, 57.
    Departments of Instruction, 81-146.
    Degrees, 47.
    Expenses and Fees, 38.
    Graduate Department, 50.
    Graduates, 1899, 278.
    Graduation from, 73.
    Group System, 76.
    School of Economics, 138.
    School of Education, 141.
    Students, 287.
    Summer Session, 148.
    Undergraduate Department, 73.
Coll. of Mech. and Eng., 171-221.
    Admission to, 174.
    Civil Engineering Course, 186.
    Corps of Instruction, 171.
    Degrees, 177.
    Departments of Instruction, 195-221.
    Electrical Engineering Course, 190.
    Electro-Chemistry Course, 191.
    Expenses and Fees, 184.
    Graduate Courses, 188.
    Graduates, 1899, 280.
    Laboratories, 178.
    Mechanical Engineering Course, 189.
    Sanitary Engineering Course, 188.
    Students, 316.
Comparative Philology, Courses in, 99.
Constitutional History, Courses in, 94.
Constitutional Law, Courses in, 90.
Convocations, 26.
Counterpoint, Courses in, 132.
Course, Ancient Classical, etc., see Ancient Classical Course, etc.

Dairy Class, List of Students, 331.
    Certificate, 232.
    Course, 230.
Dairying, Instructors in, 222.
Danish, Courses in, 106.
Degrees, Baccalaureate, 47.
    College of Agriculture, 228.
    College of Law, 47.
    College of Letters and Science, 47.
    College of Mechanics and Engineering, 177.
    Committee on higher, 50.
    Conferred, 1899, 278.
    Doctor of Philosophy, Conditions, 55.
    Masters', Conditions of, 54.
    School of Pharmacy, 260.
Doctor of Philosophy, 55.
Doctors' Degrees Conferred, 1899, 284.
Doyon Scholarships, 49.
Drawing, Summer Courses in, 166.
Economics, Courses in, 85.
    Agricultural, 86.
Economics, School of, 138.
Electrical Engineering Course, 190.
Electricity, Courses in, 211, see Physics.
Electro-Chemistry, Courses in, 213.
Elementary Law, Course in, 89.
Elocution, Courses in, 112.
Embryology, Courses in, 128.
Engineering Courses, see College of Mechanics and Engineering.
English for Admission, 60.
    Courses in, 112.
    Summer Courses in, 159.
English Course, Admission to, 61.
    Graduation in, 78.
English Literature for Admission, 60.
    Courses in, 114.
    Summer Courses in, 159.
Entrance to University, see Admission.
Ethics, Courses in, 82.

Examinations for Admission, 59.
    For Accrediting Schools, 65.
Expenses, see Charges, 38.
Experiment Station, 226.
Extension, University, see University Extension.
Faculty, 9-19.
Farmers' Institutes, 235.
Fellows, 287.
Fellowships, 51.
    Pharmaceutical, 261.
French for Admission, 63.
    Courses in, 108.
    Summer Courses in, 157.
Freshman Class, Coll. Lett., 305.
    Coll. Engineering, 321.
General Science Course, Admission to, 63.
    Requirements for Graduation, 79.
Geodesy, Courses in, 200.
Geography, Summer Courses in, 164.
Geology, Courses in, 124.
    Museum, 82.
    Summer Courses in, 164.
Geometry for Admission, 60.
    Summer Course in, 160.
German for Admission, 63.
    Courses in, 107.
    Summer Courses in, 157.
Gothic, Course in, 111.
Government of University, 25.
Grad. in Phar., Conditions for, 260.
Graduate Study, Dept. of, 50-56.
    Degrees, 47.
    Fellowships, 50.
    Scholarships, 48.
Graduates of Colleges, Admission, 72.
    Normal Schools, 71.
Graduates, Number of, 286.
Graduates, Resident 288.
Greek for Admission, 62.
    Courses in, 96.
    Hellenistic, Courses in, 102.

Summer Courses in, 156.
Group System, Graduation under, 76.
Gymnasium, 135.
    Fees, 88.
Harmony, Courses in, 132.
Hebrew, Courses in, 101.
Herbarium, 33.
Histology, Animal Courses in, 128.
    Vegetable, Course in, 129.
    Summer Courses in, 164.
Historical Society Library, 28.
History for Entrance, 60, 62.
    Courses in, 92.
    Summer Courses in, 154.
Honors in Special Studies, 48.
    Conferred, 1899, 285.
Horticulture, Courses in, 284.
Hydraulic Engineering, Courses in, 205.
Icelandic, Course in, 106.
Institutes, Farmers', 235.
Italian, Courses in, 105.
Jackson Professorship of Law, 250.
Johnson, John A., Scholarships, 48.
Junior Class, Coll. of Law, 337.
    Coll. of Letters, 296.
    Coll. of Engineering, 317.
Laboratory, Assay, 182.
    Bacteriology, 30.
    Biological, 30.
    Cement, 178.
    Chemical, 28.
    Electrical, 180.
    Fees, 39.
    Hydraulic, 178.
    Mineralogical, 29.
    Petrographical, 29.
    Pharmaceutical, 257.
    Physical, 29.
    Psychological, 31.
    Steam Engineering, 179.
    Surveying, 182.
    Testing, 178.
Ladies' Hall, 41.
Latin for Admission, 62.

Courses in, 99.
Summer Courses in, 156.
Law School, see College of Law.
Lecturers, University Extension, 144.
Library, Agricultural, 225.
    City of Madison, 27.
    College of Law, 27.
    Historical Society, 28.
    State Law, 27.
    University, 27.
    Washburn Observatory, 170.
Library Science, Courses in, 167.
Logic, Courses in, 82.
Machine Construction, Courses in, 221.
    Design, Courses in, 209.
Machine Shop, 183.
Master's Degree, Requirements for, 54.
Master's Degrees conferred, 1899, 283.
Master of Arts, see Degrees.
Mathematics for Admission, 60.
    Courses in, 115.
    Summer Courses in, 160.
Mechanical Engineering Course, 189.
Mechanics, Courses in, 198.
Metallurgy, Museum, 32.
Military Science, Course in, 132.
Mineralogy, Laboratory, 29.
    Courses in, 127.
    Museum, 32.
Modern Classical Course, Admission, 68.
    Requirements for Graduation, 78.
Museum, Botanical, 32.
    Engineering, 183.
    of Geology and Mineralogy, 32.
    of Pharmacy, 258.
    Zoological, 32.
Music, Courses in, 131.
    see School of Music.
Normal Graduates, Admission of, 71.
    Course for, 80.
Norse, Courses in, 106.
Observatory, 169.

Oratory, Courses in, 112.
Paleontology, Course in, 125.
  Museum, 32.
Pedagogy, Courses in, 88.
  Summer Courses in, 151.
Petrography, Laboratory, 29.
Petrology, Course in, 125.
Pharmaceutical Technique, 268.
Pharmacognosy, Course in, 266.
Pharmacy, Courses in, 267.
  see School of Pharmacy.
Philosophy, Courses in, 81.
  Summer Courses in, 151.
Physical Chemistry, 123.
Physical Geography, Summer Courses in, 164.
Physical Training, 34.
  Courses in, 135.
  Military Department, 132.
Physics, Agricultural, Courses in, 233.
Physics for Admission, 63.
  Laboratories, 29.
  Courses in, 119.
  Summer Courses in, 161.
Physiology for Admission, 63.
  Animal, Course in, 128.
  Vegetable, Courses in, 129.
Political Science, Courses in, 89.
Pre-Medical Course, 79.
Psychology, Courses in, 81.
  Laboratory, 31.
  Summer Courses in, 151.
Publications, Student, 45; University, 34.
Railway Engineering, Courses in, 203.
Regents, Board of, 7.
Rhetoric, Courses in, 112.
  Summer Courses in, 160.
Rivers and Canals, Courses in, 205.
Rooms, Cost of, 41.
Sanskrit, Course in, 99.
Sanitary Engineering, Course in, 218.
Scandinavian Languages, Courses in, 106.

Scholars, University, 287.
Scholarships, Doyon, 49.
  John A. Johnson, 48.
  University, 53.
School of Economics, Political Science, and History, 138-140.
  Admission to, 63.
  Corps of Instruction, 138.
  Courses of Study, 139.
School of Music, 270-277.
  Academic Course, 275.
  Collegiate Course, 272.
  Corps of Instruction, 270.
  Expenses and Fees, 276.
  Students, 341.
School of Pharmacy, 255-269.
  Admission to, 260.
  Corps of Instruction, 255.
  Courses of Study, 262.
  Degrees, 260.
  Departments of Instruction, 264.
  Expenses, 261.
  Fellowships, 261.
  Four Years' Course, 263.
  Graduates, 1899, 281, 282.
  Laboratories, 257.
  Museum, 258.
  Students, 340.
  Three Years' Course, 263.
  Two Years' Course, 262.
Schools, Accredited, 65.
Semesters, 44.
Senior Class, Coll. of Law, 334.
  College of Letters, 292.
  College of Engineering, 316.
Shop work, 219.
Short Course in Agriculture, 229.
Societies, 45.
Sociology, Courses in, 88.
Sophomore Class, Coll. of Lett., 300.
  College of Engineering, 319.
Spanish, Courses in, 105.
Special Students, Admission, 64.
  List of, 311.
Station, Agricultural Experiment, 226.

INDEX.

Statistics, Courses in, 86.
Steam Engineering, Courses in, 206.
Structural Engineering, Courses in, 216.
Students, List of, 287.
    College of Agriculture, 324.
    College of Law, 334.
    College of Letters, 292.
    College of Engineering, 316.
    Graduate, 288.
    School of Music, 341.
    School of Pharmacy, 340.
    Summer Session, 347.
Summary of Students, 358.
Summer School, 147.
Summer Session, 148.
    Admission, 150.
    Corps of Instruction, 148.
    General Statement, 149.
    Departments of Study, 151.
    Expenses, 150.
    Library Science, 167.
    Students, 1899, 347.
Surveying, Courses in, 201.
Tactics, Course in, 132.
Thermodynamics, Courses in, 206.
Topographical Engineering, 201.
Tuition, 38.
University, Admission to, 59.
    Armory and Gymnasium, 135.
    Calendar, 5.
    College of Agriculture, 222.
    College of Law, 239.
    College of Letters and Science, 57.
    College of Mech. and Eng., 171.
    Degrees, 47, 54.
    Faculty, 9.

Fellows, 287.
Fellowships, 51.
Government, 25.
Graduate Department, 50.
Graduate Students, 288.
History of, 23.
Honors in Special Studies, 48.
Laboratories, 28, 178, 257.
Library, 27.
Museum, 31, 183, 258.
Organization, 20.
Publications, 34, 45.
Regents, Board of, 7.
Scholars, 287.
Scholarships, 48, 53.
School of Economics, 138.
School of Music, 270.
School of Pharmacy, 255.
Students, 287.
Summer School, 147.
Summer Session, 148.
Undergraduates, 292.
Vacations, 45.
Visitors, Board of, 6.
Washburn Observatory, 169.
University Extension, 144.
Vacations, 45.
Veterinary Science, Course in, 234.
Visitors, Board of, 6.
Washburn Observatory, 34, 169.
Woodman Library, 170.
Wisconsin Summer Session, 148.
Year, College, 44.
Zoology, Courses in, 128.
    Museum, 32.
    Summer Courses in, 164.
    see Biology.

Lightning Source UK Ltd.
Milton Keynes UK
UKHW010003160119
335608UK00009B/488/P